The People of Sonora and Yankee Capitalists

Capitalism, the economic system of Western Europe and the United States at the turn of the century, had a major impact on every country of the Third World. In the Western Hemisphere, no country escaped its influence, particularly the North American version, increasingly omnipotent. Mexico, next door to the powerful colossus, often felt the brunt of that impact. *The People of Sonora and Yankee Capitalists* examines how the advent of North American dollars between 1882 and 1910 helped reshape the economic, social, and political contours of a Mexican province on the border of Arizona. The activity of Yankee promoters, particularly miners, land speculators, and cattle barons, altered dramatically the colonial structure left behind by its former Spanish masters. Even the psychology of the inhabitants of Sonora underwent a kind of metamorphosis. This book, in short, explains what happened to Mexico's traditional society when Yankee capitalists made their appearance.

Ramón Eduardo Ruiz

The People of Sonora and Yankee Capitalists

The University of Arizona Press
Tucson

THE UNIVERSITY OF ARIZONA PRESS
Copyright © 1988
The Arizona Board of Regents
All Rights Reserved

This book was set in 10/12 Baskerville.
Manufactured in the U.S.A.

Library of Congress Cataloging-in-Publication Data

Ruiz, Ramón Eduardo
The people of Sonora and Yankee capitalists / Ramón Eduardo Ruiz.
    p.   cm.—(Profmex monograph series)
Bibliography: p.
Includes index.
ISBN 0-8165-1012-1 (alk. paper)
1. Sonora (Mexico : State)—Economic conditions. 2. Sonora
(Mexico : State)—Social conditions. 3. Investments, American—
Mexico—Sonora (State)—History. I. Title. II. Series.
HC137.S75R85 1988
330.972'17081—dc19   87-30133
CIP

British Library Cataloguing in Publicatation data are available.

A la memoria de mi madre, Dolores Urueta,
hija de Chihuahua y ejemplar mujer del norte.

CONTENTS

PROLOGUE

A fluke of fate led to this book. Our eldest daughter, Olivia, an anthropology student, chose to write her doctoral dissertation on the middle class in Hermosillo, capital of the Mexican state of Sonora. In the course of driving her down from our home in California, and returning scores of times for visits during her nearly year and a half there, I began to know the people of Sonora. Gradually, my wife and I made a host of friends. I learned that the Mexicans of this desert province have a rich history and, unlike many of their neighbors, they have written about it. Further, I discovered, again thanks to my daughter, that Hermosillo has excellent historical archives, a rarity in much of Mexico. The more I learned about this arid kingdom, the greater my fascination. Thoroughly smitten, I decided to write a book about my friends, the people of Sonora.

Partly because of what I found in the archives, and partly because of work I had done previously on the Porfiriato, I decided to concentrate on the years from 1880 to 1910. My father and his father before him, moreover, had served in the military of don Porfirio: papá in its navy and grandfather as a foot soldier, part of the time fighting Yaquis in Sonora. Initially, I had in mind a social history that would explore the ideas, customs, and traditions of this border world. Then, one day, after a month or two of archival research, I stumbled upon a letter from the mayor of La Aduana, a key mining town of the nineteenth century, to Ramón Corral, a master *politico* in Hermosillo. His Honor wanted money for a bigger jail—with three rooms—two for male drunks and criminals, and a third for prostitutes and female miscreants. If it were not built, he swore, he would take no responsibility for the horrendous immorality polluting the town and the jail. Every weekend, he complained, miners with money to spend, whores, gamblers, and criminals of various hues fell upon La Aduana, to get drunk, fight with each other, fleece the unwary, and generally raise hell.

This letter turned my research around, giving it an entirely different perspective. As I puzzled over this cryptic cry for help, I began to understand that, on a deeper level, it voiced the mayor's keen discomfort with the changes that were taking place all around him. The revival of mining on a grand scale in the late nineteenth century unleashed disruptive forces that were turning traditional society upside down. The mining boom, of course, was triggered by the arrival of the railroad in Sonora in 1882, and by a steady flow of foreign capital, by and large North American. The mayor of La Aduana, in his own way, was responding to the breakup of a former mode of life. Once I understood this I knew what my principal theme would be; and so, the title of this book.

In the bargain, I also saw the connection between what occurred in Sonora and dependency theories or approaches. That hypothesis, in a general way, helped to explain the transformation taking shape. I must confess, however, that I wrote the book without reference to the dependency argument. Only at its conclusion did I see its relevance to fact. So, as the introduction reveals, I added theory to the study by way of the back door. But from start to finish, the emphasis is on the people of Sonora, not theory or Yankee capitalists.

I owe this book to many people. To Olivia and to Maura, her younger sister, who, while a student at the Universidad de Sonora, gave me insights into northern Mexicans. Many Sonorenses helped, especially Armando Quijada, to whom I turned for guidance time and time again, and Juan Antonio Ruibal Corella, who opened many doors for me. Armando Hopkins Durazo, who grew up in a small hamlet, never let me forget the significance of Sonora's regional diversity. I thank Leobardo Espejel of the Archivo Histórico de Sonora and the staff of the Archivo Histórico del Gobierno del Estado de Sonora. Michael C. Meyer, Cynthia Radding de Murrieta, and Stuart F. Voss read the entire manuscript and corrected errors; I am grateful for their sagacious wisdom. Mario García and Marvin Bernstein helped with the chapters on railroads and labor.

The book would not now appear, however, if it were not for the Center for Advanced Study in the Behavioral Sciences of Stanford, California, where I spent a profitable year. I am thankful also for financial support to The Andrew Mellon Foundation, benefactors of scholars.

I claim responsibility for all errors of fact, and for the interpretation. The errors, I wish I had caught in time; the interpretation, I stand by.

                                              Ramón Eduardo Ruiz

BY WAY OF INTRODUCTION

I

The Mexicans of Sonora, a desert province of skeletal saguaro cactus and hardy mesquite trees on the border of Arizona, jubilantly celebrated their independence on September 16, 1910. On that day a century earlier, Father Miguel Hidalgo, curate of the parish of Dolores, a village in Guanajuato, had initiated a struggle destined to liberate Mexico from Spanish rule. Yet, incongruously, Mexico, and with it the elated people of Sonora, were probably less "free" in 1910 than when the last of the King's troops boarded ship in the harbor of Veracruz. Less than a century after becoming a sovereign nation, Mexico had fallen under the control of a foreign master more formidable than the hated Spaniard. He was the Yankee, the neighbor to the north, and the "unfree" status of Mexico came to be known as "dependency." After a brief interlude of English supremacy in mid-nineteenth century, the Yankee made his conquest between 1880 and 1910, which history recalls as the age of the New Imperialism.

For Sonora, pulled into the Yankee vortex by its proximity and fabulous deposits of ores, particularly copper, bondage brought a metamorphosis. From ranking among the poorest states, Sonora came to have one of the biggest investments of dollars in Mexico. Virtually by that fact alone, it became one of the wealthiest of the states. Progress, gloated the merchant oligarchy that was running things, had taken hold. With the blessings of Mexico City, then under the steady hand of Porfirio Díaz, the merchants had courted the giant next door. To their way of thinking, those connections had paid spectacular dividends. The merchant elite was enjoying banner sales; an agriculture and a cattle industry for export to the United States had a foothold; and the mining boom, thanks to American capital and a railroad built by it, had created well-paying jobs for thousands of Mexicans, to cite

1

the glowing statistics of that time. In the centennial year of 1910, at least from the oligarchy's perspective, there was ample justification to celebrate.

As the child of Spanish parents, Sonora had from the beginning been a colonial society. Its modern trappings dated from the early 1880s when American capitalists built a railroad joining Guaymas, the chief port of the province, to Arizona. From that time on, the invasion of Sonora by Yankee capitalists went full steam ahead as miners, farmers, and cattlemen from the north traveled south on the iron horse.

II

Dependency, as those who have examined it know, embodies complex phenomena; it defies a simple explanation. Its outlines are both native and foreign: no matter how powerful the outside forces, they never completely determine the contours of local society. To say that the economy of Sonora was simply a product of capitalism as it ripened on a global scale distorts history. True, turnabouts in its economy reflected milestones in the international economy. Mercantilism and free competition left their mark, and the monopoly capitalism fueling the New Imperialism had a salient impact on Sonora. The complex and diverse societies of Mexico, including those in Sonora, evolved partly in response to the expansion of European and American capitalism. Be that as it may, a careful historical study requires an analysis of the special features of each dependent society, lest the overall interpretation mislead and take empty generalities for fact. Economic, political, and, obviously, cultural singularities shape the character and history of every dominated people. Mechanistic conceptions that overlook these peculiarities, to cite the distinguished scholars Fernando Henrique Cardoso and Enzo Faletto, "oversimplify . . . and lead to error" because they fail to "grasp the dynamic aspects of history" given life "by social struggles in dependent countries."[1]

Viewed from this perspective, domination becomes an internal force, that is subject, clearly, to manipulations from the outside. Native classes walk hand in glove with foreigners because values and interests coincide.[2] Dependency rests on international foundations, with both foreigners and natives often joining hands to uphold the system. Among the natives who do are members of the middle class and, when times are good, the "aristocracy of labor," which, in Sonora, was made up of miners, who partly shared the profits of the mining boom of the turn of the century. In regions where there is an oligarchy of sorts, partly traditional because of its ties to the past, foreign capital quickly turns it into a hereditary satrapy. That is largely what happened in Sonora.[3]

The New Imperialism, the backdrop for the drama in Sonora, opened up an era of pivotal importance for the entire world. Only then "did a worldwide civilization begin to take shape."[4] The world became one huge international network, divided into core and peripheral countries, the handiwork of industrial capitalism's conquest of Latin America, Asia, and Africa. It was the birth of a new civilization; Sonora would find it very different from the Spanish colonial one. Sonora's rich silver veins, bedrock of the Spanish mining economy, had petered out, hampered by primitive technology. The old system fell into bankruptcy. As Eric Hobsbaum put it in his study of an earlier era, "old colonialism did not grow into new colonialism; it collapsed and was replaced by it."[5] That description fits Sonora, where a rudimentary mining structure barely survived the turmoil of the first years of independence, to be supplanted at the end of the nineteenth century by a dynamic mining economy financed and controlled mainly by Yankee capitalists.

III

The debate over Mexico's future, however, antedated the appearance of the Americans by decades. Centering around the issues of free trade and tariffs, the arguments dealt in the terminology of the day with what is now known as dependency. Under Liberalism, the flag of the emerging bourgeoisie in Europe, Mexican mine owners, merchants, and, at times, *hacendados*, the producers of foodstuffs, hoisted aloft the doctrine of free trade. José María Luís Mora, oracle of the Liberals, and Lucas Alamán, the fountain of wisdom for the Conservatives, debated the relative merits of the Spanish past and the European system as guides for Mexico's future. Keen students of Mexican reality, they both gave mining a key role to play. Mora, however, looked to the European model of capitalism for inspiration and believed national industry based on tariffs was nonsense. Alamán, less inclined to worship outsiders, thought in terms of native factories and protectionism. As a minister of government in the 1830s, Alamán went so far as to establish a Banco de Avío, a development bank, to encourage Mexican capitalists to build industries. Mexico's textile mills date from his effort.

National debate during the chaotic years between 1810, when Father Hidalgo upset the Spanish apple cart, and 1867, when the puppet French empire fell to Benito Juárez and his Liberals, often focused on free trade and related issues. In a general way, the drama featured an

"American" party, advocates of national industry, against a "European"
party, believers in free trade. The victory of the free traders, led by
Juárez and his successor, Díaz, dashed hopes for a native industrial
edifice and meaningful political sovereignty. As this scene was played
out in Mexico, the capitalist powers of Europe and the United States
divided up the world among themselves. In this age of the New Imperialism, Díaz ruled the nation and the Triumvirate ruled Sonora.
Both became symbols of toadying to the foreigner.

                                    IV

The Industrial Revolution and the New Imperialism distorted the old
colonial picture. The building of steam railways in the peripheral countries led to a shift in the economy of the industrial nations from imports
to exports, with England paving the way. From now on, England and
the other capitalist powers would both buy raw materials and flood
local markets with cheap manufactured goods. The change brought
ruin to native crafts, and the flow of capital abroad caused international banking to flower. During this phase, speculators opened lands
in the dependent countries to export agriculture and laid out railway
grids and built infrastructures to handle the export of raw materials
and the import of factory goods. At the turn of the century, the ripen-
ing of monopoly capital and the new technology worked together to
increase the manufacture of steel and the use of electricity and the internal combustion engine.[6] With the hunt on for raw materials and new
markets, the investment of capital in such places as Sonora grew
rapidly.[7] By 1908, over 40 percent of direct United States investment
abroad, much of it in Mexico, was in mining and, to a lesser extent, in
petroleum.[8] Between 1897 and 1914, the export of dollars had climbed
from $1.7 billion to $3.5 billion.[9]

Distant regions, often self-contained before, became hubs of a world
economy. Before long, an international division of labor developed:
the industrial West made and sold goods, while the rest of the world,
the periphery, worked to supply it with raw materials and minerals, the
fruits of cheap labor. Much of the earth and its people came to depend,
to a greater or lesser degree, on the West. After 1880, the terms of
trade grew worse for the "colonial" peoples.[10] By 1910, it cost the
peripheral countries far more to buy factory goods than it had half a
century earlier. At mid-nineteenth century, prices were 50 percent
higher in the West than in Latin America, Asia, and Africa. But as the
century wore on, the price gap reversed itself and widened quickly
after that.[11] With this decline in buying power, living standards in the

peripheral countries dropped precipitously in comparison with those in the West. Worse still, little of the money exported to the dependent countries went into industry, partly because European and American capitalists did not want these countries competing with them for markets.[12]

Huge numbers of the native populations increasingly discovered themselves on the margins. Oddly, despite the capital flowing into their countries, the poor in the periphery went from want to want. Dirt farmers and artisans joined the ranks of the job seekers, while peasants who held onto their lands had little money to spend. In Mexico, the Liberal rulers divided up the *ejidos* ("communal lands"), believing that the institution blocked capitalist development. Such was the fate of the communal lands of the hill and river hamlets of Sonora. In the mining camps of Sonora, the ups and downs of the world economy dictated whether workers had jobs or not, and whether they had food on the table. To add insult to injury, international depressions blighted about half of the years from the 1870s to the turn of the century.[13]

The local economy, distorted to supply the needs of the industrial nations, left at home a ruling class that purchased its power at the cost of its independence. Having risen by being submissive to outsiders, the oligarchy in power had no room to maneuver on its own. By 1910, dollars from north of the border had created in Sonora an economy, a class system, and a political, social, and psychological milieu subservient to the United States.

To march in step with the outsider, upon whom they depended, Mexicans had to change. They conceded the power of the foreigner over their economic and political affairs and adopted much of his culture and values. A healthy economy required political stability, so law and order took top priority. A cheap and docile labor force was also crucial. Out of these needs emerged a strong and centralized state. The government sought to ease restrictions on trade, eliminate *alcabalas*—customs duties and taxes of a local nature—and institute a standard system of weights and measures.

V

Sonora, of course, never enjoyed the status of a "sovereign" nation. From the beginning, it was merely a state in the Republic of Mexico. Until nearly 1910, however, it lived in relative isolation from the rest of the Republic. On the east, the Sierra Madre Occidental, a range of mountains rising to 10,000 feet, limited ties with Chihuahua, its sister state. To the west, the Gulf of Baja California washed up on a coastline

900 miles long. On the north, above a 400-mile border, lay the North American colossus. With Arizona, Sonora shared the Primería Alta, a series of flat deserts and mountains stretching northward from Hermosillo all the way to Tucson.

Next to Chihuahua, Sonora was the biggest state in Mexico—and one of the most underpopulated. When Luis Emeterio Torres and his camarilla ("clique") took over politics, roads to the south from Sonora defied the most daring of travelers. The best way north from central Mexico was by ship through the gulf to the Sonoran port of Guaymas, sixty miles south of Hermosillo. Not until almost 1910 did a railroad join Hermosillo and Guaymas, Sonora's principal urban enclaves, with Mazatlán, the port of Sinaloa, the state immediately to the south. But already in 1882, that same railroad, eventually uncovered as a Trojan Horse, had opened a way north to the United States. It helped establish the commerical town of Nogales, gateway to the capital and markets on the other side of the border. Sonora's growth between 1882 and 1910, can be studied with only passing reference to the rest of Mexico.

This account of three decades in the life of Sonorenses is not a study of dependency theories. It makes no claim either to expand or refine what their oracles ages ago concluded. To the contrary, their verification came about by accident. This book took shape as an attempt to chronicle the daily life of a province during the Porfiriato, to take the historical spotlight off Mexico City and to shine it on the periphery instead. Dependency theories, plus a bit of orthodox Marxist wisdom, became a logical hypothesis because it helped to explain what transpired in this border community between 1882 and 1910. To put it a little differently, local events bore out the validity of the formula.

CHAPTER 1

A Trojan Horse

I

An old, rusty steam locomotive, pulling boxcars and dated passenger coaches that had all earlier been used north of the border, unlocked the door to American speculation in Sonora. In doing so, the old train, the property of the Santa Fe Railway, altered dramatically the contours of Sonoran society. Ever since the ancient Greeks employed a wooden horse to gain entrance to the city in their legendary battle with the people of Troy, the Trojan Horse has come to refer to subversion from the outside. For Sonora, the iron horse, like its mythical ancestor, opened the gates to an invasion of ominous portent.

From colonial days until 1882, when the iron horse joined the entrepôts of Guaymas and Hermosillo to Yankee markets and manufacturers, Sonora's inhabitants, rich and poor alike, had experienced only a modicum of change. A cluster of towns and hamlets cradled by mountains or set amidst the wide expanses of desert flatlands, Sonora was decidedly rural, though the land was rich in mineral ores. To Yankee entrepreneurs accustomed to exploiting nature's gifts for profit, the Mexicans of this arid kingdom resembled beggars atop a pot of gold. With the coming of the iron horse, the province, once an antiquarian's delight, was forever transformed.

On a November day in 1881, a large and enthusiastic crowd gathered at the newly built railroad depot in the capital city of Hermosillo. In a holiday mood, the men and women had dressed in their Sunday best. In black derbies and broad-brimmed straw hats, they laughed, talked,

7

and, at intervals, listened to three orchestras playing popular melodies. They had come to await the arrival of the first train from Guaymas, the port city to the south, a memorable event in local affairs. Among the dignitaries awaiting the train were General Luis E. Torres, a kingpin of local politics, and his two allies, Rafael Izábal, an *hacendado* of note, and Ramón Corral, a *politico* destined for higher office. These three figures, referred to as the Triumvirate, were to rule Sonora off and on until 1910. Also at the station that day were the leading merchants of Hermosillo. Looking to the example of Western Europe and the United States, these entrepreneurs were convinced that the opening of the railroad would also bring their homeland into the industrial age.

Viewed from the perspective of hindsight, the crowd that day was in fact watching a momentous episode. The railroad indeed transformed the local economy, and with it the outlines of the whole society. Most important, the iron horse injected new life into a languid, backward mining sector. It opened the formerly isolated province to foreign speculators who in a matter of two decades reshaped the mining scene. By 1910, Sonora became one of the world's richest mining enclaves, ranking second among Mexican provinces in the amount of foreign investment. Additionally, when the railroad threaded its way through southern Sonora, traversing the fertile Yaqui and Mayo valleys, it linked a commercial agriculture, then in its infancy, to markets in California. That development eventually transformed Sonora into a rich farm belt.

Until the advent of the iron horse, Sonora had lived in isolation. What roads existed, even when passable, hardly encouraged trade between distant points. Only euphemistically could the route between Hermosillo and Guaymas, the salient urban settlements, be called a road. It was so bad, according to a contemporary account, that at certain junctures it virtually vanished from the map.[1] Only daring, not to say foolhardy, travelers ventured forth with horse and buggy to journey from port city to state capital. It took days by horse-drawn wagon to make the sixty-mile trip. The first regular passenger stage between Guaymas and Hermosillo did not appear until 1856, becoming a scheduled run only in 1876. The stage departed from Guaymas on Monday at four in the morning, with cock crows still in the air, and arrived in Hermosillo on late Thursday afternoon, its exhausted and dusty passengers having traveled all three nights.[2] Occasionally, other stagecoaches, *diligencias* as they were called, ran between Ures, the ancient capital on the Río Sonora, and Hermosillo.[3] Roads, loosely defined, were inaugurated in 1879 from Hermosillo to Altar (a former Spanish *presidio* and commercial depot in the western desert) and Magdalena (the northern burial grounds of Father Eusebio Kino, the peripatetic friar). The roads were then extended to Tucson, constituting a pioneer international highway. By 1880, stagecoaches built and run by Mexicans ran between Tucson, Hermosillo, and Guaymas.[4]

The business of running stagecoaches—really just heavy wagons pulled by pesky mules—between Guaymas and Tucson, with stops at Hermosillo, Santa Ana, and Magdalena along the way, proved lucrative. Even by mule wagon or horse, trade with the northern neighbors, the inhabitants of the sparsely populated Territory of Arizona, had its pecuniary rewards. By 1880, the year the building of the railroad began, the route north had become the most important in Sonora.[5] Still, travel was risky at best. Bandits infested the countryside, frequently waylaying stages and robbing passengers. No one was exempt from these forays by *bandoleros* ("highwaymen"), the scourge of the frontier in the 1880s. One account told of masked bandits who robbed a stage carrying two American dignitaries and the tax collector of Guaymas, a worthy gentleman.[6] Travel throughout Sonora called for daring and a willingness to endure not merely the heat and dust, formidable afflictions in themselves, but also crooks who might easily make off with whatever the traveler carried. To journey south of Guaymas, gossip had it, was an even greater "nightmare."[7]

More to the point, the absence of roads passable by heavy wagons in fair and foul weather had stunted mining. To cite the report of the prefect of Arizpe, mining had failed to take off because heavy ores could not be transported cheaply from the mines to potential buyers. Even after the railroad was running between Hermosillo and the border, the lack of feeder roads blocked the speedy development of mining in Arizpe. It took twenty days to go by wagon from Magdalena, on the rail line, to the town of Arizpe, the district capital.[8]

Torres and Corral and their predecessor, Governor Carlos R. Ortiz, saw that Sonora was a potentially prosperous province held back by inadequate means of transporting goods and people. They began to repair existing roads and to construct others. In their opinion, however, the railroad remained the key to the future. Mining of ores, the chief treasure of the state, would profit immediately; metals once too costly to exploit could be sold at a profit.[9] Moreover, by opening markets north of the border, the railroad would spur agriculture, giving dirt farmers money to spend on manufactured goods.

All the same, Corral had the welfare of merchants uppermost in his mind. From the start, the merchants, particularly the storekeepers of Guaymas, backed the idea of a railway. What they wanted, obviously, was access to foreign goods, specifically American manufactures, for local resale, as well as markets *al otro lado*, "on the other side," where they could sell raw materials, ores, and grains from Sonora. Since the

mid-nineteenth century, more and more of the local economy, particularly the merchant sector, had begun to thrive through links with Yankee markets and goods. To the merchants and their spokesmen in Hermosillo, an iron highway joining Sonora to the United States would give
a tremendous shot in the arm to an economy that had been ailing ever
since the French attempted, with bayonet and cannon, to impose a puppet emperor on a Mexican throne.[10]

Still, fears in Mexico City, shared by some merchants and *politicos* in
Sonora—fears amply justified by later events—halted construction for
years. The holdouts worried that building a railroad north to the border before building one to the south would mean that Sonora was lost
to Mexico. Ties to the United States would come at the expense of
domestic merchants who, unable to compete with their powerful neighbors, would simply disappear or, equally distressing, become lackeys of
the North Americans.[11] Proponents of the railroad believed that the
critics were holding back "progress." Sonora, with its skeletal population, they argued, lacked a market for its goods and hence the capital
and customers for a native industry.[12]

Ultimately, of course, the advocates of the northern railroad won
out. The federal government in Mexico City authorized the project
and, following the time-honored custom in the United States, paid a
subsidy of 7,000 pesos per kilometer to its architects.[13] The first rail was
put down at Punta Arena, on the outskirts of Guaymas, on May 6,
1880. The line reached Hermosillo soon afterward, and in 1882 arrived in Nogales, until then a customs house sheltered in a tent.

II

By 1910, the Sonora Railway, as it was called, had fulfilled the dreams
of its Mexican supporters.[14] It had joined, more firmly than ever, the
domestic economy to markets and industries in the United States. By
the same token, the iron rail had unlocked local mineral ores for exploitation by American speculators, giving birth to an economic boom that
benefited thousands of Mexicans. Of no less significance, after the turn
of the century, the railroad paved the way for a halcyon period for cash-
crop planters in the Yaqui and Mayo valleys, and laid the cornerstone
for cattle ranching tied to markets on the other side.

This was partly what Americans eager to extend their railroad system south into Mexico had in mind. A railroad from the north down
to Guaymas, according to one idea popular in New York and Boston,
would shorten the distance and cut costs between the United States and
ports in Asia and Australia; that plan never bore fruit. But dreams of

a different sort did. A rail line "running through the heart of Sonora," rhapsodized the Yankee vice-consul in 1872, "will speedily" develop "her vast mineral resources," while bringing to "market her immense tracts of fertile lands, hitherto out of reach of rapid and cheap communication." It would, he predicted, bring "capital into the country and stimulate industry and enterprise and extend civilization."[15] More to the point, added Alexander Willard, American consul in Guaymas in 1880 and a man with an eye for turning a fast buck, "the completion of the Railway with a reduced tariff would virtually exclude European goods" from local stores, and, by implication, give Americans a monopoly.[16] Both Willard and his diplomatic colleague turned out to be prophets in their own time.

To begin with, Americans built the railroad.[17] Capital for it came from the United States, as did the locomotives, rolling stock, and many of the rails, which were made of American steel and iron. The giant mills in Pittsburgh and the sellers of steel and iron profited from this export of American capital. The railway opened new markets and, as the consul prophesized, protected them from foreign competition. The architects and engineers who planned it, the construction companies who built it, the surveyors who plotted the routes, and the labor bosses who watched over the grading of the railbeds and the laying of the track all were Americans, as were some of the workers. Even the railroad ties had Yankee origins. They were of pine imported from Oregon by way of Guaymas.

From the beginning, the project, the brainchild of American speculators, was meant to make money for its backers. Occasionally they lent money to the state to further a worthy cause: 1,000 pesos, for example, to fight an outbreak of yellow fever in 1884. When the danger was gone, however, the Sonora Railway wanted its money back. The Mexicans in Hermosillo, not illogically, given their own capitalist values, thought the demand fair.[18] The railroad, in short, had made its way into Sonora because Americans, with profits in mind, wanted it there; the dreams of Mexican merchants and *politicos*, avid for dollars, helped bring it about but did not put it there. Further, given the population increase in the Territory of Arizona, it became virtually inevitable that a railroad would be constructed connecting the southwestern United States with northwestern Mexico.[19]

So in 1879, in the distant state of Massachusetts, under the leadership of Thomas Nickerson, president of the Santa Fe Railroad, American speculators voted to build the Sonora Railway. It would run from Guaymas to Nogales, and with two spur lines, join the American rail system at Benson, Arizona.[20] "The people and authorities of the state favor the enterprise," reported Consul Willard, who anticipated no

difficulties in securing a "right of way" through private land to the
"American frontier."[21] The Santa Fe group later turned over the Sonora
Railway to the Southern Pacific, first leasing it and then selling it outright in 1905, along with authority to extend the line south to Guadala-
jara. In 1909, like the original Sonora Railway, the new company was
registered in Massachusetts, this time with a capital of $75 million.[22]
For the American speculators, the railroad proved anything but a gold
mine; until 1890, it operated at a loss, showing an occasional profit
after that.[23] By 1900, however, the Southern Pacific had become the
leviathan of railroads in the American West, ultimately controlling
southern California and much of the Territory of Arizona.[24]

Despite the speculative loss, Americans who kept up with Sonora
judged the railroad a smashing success. "It is doubtful," emphasized
officials in the Department of Commerce in Washington, "whether any
equal amount has produced greater results in civilization and modern
progress than the 40 to 50 million dollars spent by the southern Pacific
in the construction of its Mexican West Coast line." From their perspective, the railroad had reshaped the Mexican countryside. "Isolated
communities, in which the results of intermarriage, want of spirit, disease and the lack of outside contacts were only too apparent," they said,
"were awakened and began to get into step with modern progress."[25]

Whether the consequences were either "modern" or a sign of "progress" is a matter of debate, but there is no question that the iron horse
brought Sonora into the capitalist vortex. The isolation of the past had
ended; from now on, the fate of Mexicans in Sonora would be irrevo-
cably linked to that of their northern neighbors. The Sonora Railway
was in reality a spur line in the vast intercontinental rail systems joining
New York and Boston with the West Coast of the United States. By making the export of Mexican ores profitable, the railway kindled the
flames of economic growth.[26] Of course, it also opened up Sonora to
Yankee speculators bent on making fast profits. The railway put Sonora
within six days of New York, the financial center of the United States.
"The effect of this daily and speedy transportation of merchandise,
mail and passengers from one country to another," Willard enthused,
"is . . . an increase of communications and friendly relations between
the people of the two nations."[27] More succinctly, as a writer for *Sunset
Magazine* put it, the rail line laid bare "a lot of country for the exploitation of promoters."[28] As predicted by Willard, the rail line gave American "investors" huge advantages over both Mexican and European
rivals.[29] From then on, Americans would exploit the natural resources
of Sonora. By 1910, Sonora had become part of the "area with the
highest growth of foreign [i.e., North American] commerce in all of
Mexico." Similarly, Mexico's Pacific northwest, of which Sonora

formed an integral part, controlled one-third the commerce of the Republic.[30] To no one's surprise, the railway brought a flood of Americans into Sonora and, conversely, further isolated Sonora from the rest of Mexico.

From the beginning, the railroad, lock, stock, and barrel, was an American venture. "Men with blue eyes," as Mexicans were wont to say, owned and ran it. Until 1906, the year of the heralded "nationalization" of the Mexican railway system, Americans held every job of any importance. Only the track gangs, barring the labor boss, of course, were entirely Mexican. The "Yankee conductor, with black suit and black cap with visor," became the symbol of the passenger trains that ran south from Nogales.[31] Hardly any of the Americans bothered to learn Spanish. Claiming superiority in training and experience, Americans held the best jobs. Thus young men barely beyond puberty, often juveniles in thought and deed, told Mexicans what to do. One such American, just twenty years old in 1883, was chief of Estación Pesqueira; another, barely twenty-three, was a telegraph operator, a "dandy job." George Lesser, a year out of his teens, had the job of clerk in the accounting department.[32]

No Mexicans, apparently, could be found to fill these jobs or to be trained to do them—not even the low-ranking job of clerk. When one Mexican judge dared jail an American locomotive engineer in 1906, the year Mexicans supposedly purchased a majority interest in their railways, his companions went on strike, announcing that they would not run the trains until authorities set him free. The American manager of the Southern Pacific, a railroad not included in the nationalization deal, asked Hermosillo to set aside the judge's ruling.[33] The engineer got off, and the trains ran again.[34] When a rail line was inaugurated in 1910 from Tucson to the south, it was called the Tucson and West Coast of Mexico Railroad.

Above all, the railroad was shaped by mining speculators. To both Americans and Mexicans who predicted that a modern mining industry would bring prosperity, the antiquated transportation system could be wholly blamed for the industry's present backwardness.[35] When the steam locomotive arrived, many believed that a rosy future had arrived. At that juncture, recalled a delighted Ramón Corral, a Mexican who thought mining a panacea, "foreign businessmen began to invest in our mines."[36] Just demographically, the results of that influx of capital, no matter how limited, were amazing. Between 1900 and 1910, for example, both Hermosillo and Ures lost population, while Arizpe and Moctezuma, the copper bastions of the state, once plagued by frequent Apache raids, added 28,000 new residents.[37]

That the success of mining ventures should await the appearance of the iron horse was both logical and perhaps inevitable. Railroads, it seems, had been designed with mining specifically in mind. Heavy, large, and bulky loads could be handled easily and at low cost. It became lucrative to mine in remote regions, because the trains could haul out ore at good rates and the use of heavy machinery was possible. Low-grade ore could be mined at a profit, with cheap coal imported from the United States, while ores from Sonora could be sold north of the border. Also, railroads made feasible the use of giant smelters, such as the one at Douglas, Arizona, just across the border from Agua Prieta, where ores from Bisbee and Nacozari were carried.[38] Timber by the car-load for the mines, fuel to run the engines, explosives, tools, and other equipment could be brought in cheaply. Similarly, clothing, furniture of every style, kitchenware, and household articles of diverse types could be shipped to nostalgic American employees and their wives. Railroads, in short, overcame the transportation problem, the "most difficult and costly a mining company" had to meet.[39]

News of the construction of the railroad quickly attracted the attention of mining promoters. Visions of immediate, easy pickings beckoned men willing to risk money and, in many cases, limbs. No sooner had the locomotive joined Guaymas and Hermosillo to Nogales than speculators from as far away as New York and Chicago began to buy mines in Sonora. In a few months in 1881, Americans, anticipating the advantages of the railroad, purchased six mines, none for less than $20,000.[40] Earlier, the American consul in Guaymas had reported the sale of the fabulous Quintero mines near Alamos, reportedly for $200,000, to the San Felipe Mining Company of New York. Other foreigners, mostly Americans, had undertaken to work the neighboring mines of Barranca, Bronces, Trinidad, Libertad, and Promontorio.[41] North of the border in Arizona, meanwhile, the railroads opened the door to the rich ore deposits around Bisbee, site of the celebrated Copper Queen Mine. News of the completion of the Southern Pacific Railroad line from Los Angeles to El Paso further accelerated the value of mining claims, multiplying manyfold the number of Yankee prospectors and promoters in Sonora.[42] For Mexico as a whole, the number of mining claims, many of them in Sonora, nearly doubled by 1906.[43]

Additionally, the big mining companies took it upon themselves to build more railroads. By 1910, four spur lines ran between Sonora and Arizona. With 95 percent of railroad mileage in northern Sonora, these companies had a powerful hand in the shaping of the region's economy. The first of these lines, a Phelps Dodge enterprise, joined the smelter at Douglas with the copper mines at Nacozari, second in

size only to those at Cananea. Completed in 1904, it ran for eighty-two
miles. The Ferrocarril de Cananea was finished in 1908. It originally
linked Cananea with Naco, a place name on the map on the way to Bisbee, and later with Nogales. Neither line did more than join Mexican
mine towns, owned and operated by American entrepreneurs, with
points in the United States.[44] Except for Agua Prieta, a border hamlet
across from Douglas, none of these spur lines served a Mexican city or
town. For all practical purposes, they were extensions of the American
economy; what commercial interests they served had their headquarters north of the border. Once the lines were completed, merchants in
Arizona supplied stores in Cananea and Nacozari with clothing,
hardware, and other articles of American manufacture.[45] Apart from
the ores, no goods came out of Mexico by way of these railroads. Agua
Prieta, for its part, grew out of the spur line to Douglas, home to the
smelter for the ores from Nacozari. As one writer noted, the railway
between Nacozari and Douglas went unnoticed by Mexicans, who, un-
derstandably, viewed it as a private line.[46]

Somewhat dissimilar was the spur line completed in 1897 between
the mining complex at Minas Prietas and the Sonora Railway at Estación Torres, about forty miles east of Hermosillo. It added no mileage
to the railroad grid because the track, locomotive, and cars had formerly connected Cerro Blanco, site of the Imuris Mines Limited, to
the Sonora Railway at a point south of Nogales. When news of the line's
construction became public, it gave fresh "impetus to mining," embold-
ening scores of speculators to look into the "silver and gold" deposits
of Minas Prietas.[47] One group, the Minas Prietas Mining Company of
New York, purchased Las Prietas for $200,000.[48] A narrow-gauge rail-
way, the line transported passengers and freight to the mining camps.
The train, an ancient relic, ran at what one eyewitness described as a
"snail's pace, taking hours to travel the length of 3 city blocks."[49] Slow
or not, the spur line transformed La Colorada, the mining camp adjoining Minas Prietas, into a boom town, so that together the two
turned into the chief mining enclave in the state.[50]

Unlike the Sonora Railway, which apparently never proved lucrative,
these spur lines of scant public utility made money for their owners.
The Nacozari line, for instance, in 1906 declared a profit for the Moctezuma Copper Company, a Phelps Dodge subsidiary, of nearly half a
million dollars, while profits on the Naco and Cananea line, the property of the Cananea Consolidated Copper Company, totaled $362,291
that same year.[51]

In September 1905, the Southern Pacific began to grade land for
track south of Guaymas.[52] Its labor gangs reached Cajeme (Ciudad

Obregón) two years later, Navojoa in 1907, and, with a branch line, Alamos, the charming colonial Ciudad de los Portales. By 1910, Mazatlán, the port city of Sinaloa, had been joined by railroad to Guaymas and points north.[53] The line south, like its counterpart to the north, revamped the contours of the Mayo and Yaqui valleys. By an accident of fate, the southward advance of the rail builders coincided with the economic crisis of 1907, which left mining, particularly in the silver camps of Alamos, in shambles. By 1909, La Dura, Palmarejo, and La Quintera, the only mines still operating, had either shut down or reduced their activities. As the railroad entered the valleys, a flood of inhabitants, both miners and storekeepers, departed the mining hamlets for the towns on the path of the iron horse.[54]

With ready access to markets north of the border, the Mayo and Yaqui valleys bloomed as the heartland of an export agriculture. Almost overnight, Navojoa, a sleepy hamlet, was tranformed into a bustling entrepôt.[55] By 1909, Navojoa, along with nearby Huatabampo and Etchojoa, had nearly 9,000 inhabitants, a huge increase over just a few years before.[56] Correspondingly, towns bypassed by the Southern Pacific, Tórin for example, lost population.[57] Lamentably, the coming of the iron horse into the fertile valleys helped spell the end of the Yaqui Indian's heroic resistance to white immigrants, both Mexicans and Americans.[58] No matter what the cost in blood and money, the whites, with dreams of becoming rich by planting crops for export, were more determined than ever to make these lands their own.

The Southern Pacific revamped the face of the Mayo and Yaqui valleys. Now enterprising planters could cultivate garbanzos, tomatoes, oranges, melons, onions, and cucumbers for export.[59] Produce could be shipped by way of Nogales to buyers from Los Angeles to San Francisco. The railroad meant, furthermore, giving a lower priority to traditional crops, such as wheat and corn, grown by dirt farmers who tilled their own plots of land. Large estates where wage laborers did the work began to take shape, and they needed more and more land. Export agriculture hurt the small farms, especially the "individual plots" given the Yaquis and Mayos after 1886. The railroad stimulated federal and local authorities, often racist at heart, to think of "colonizing" the valleys, as the elite of the time was apt to say, with industrious and enterprising European types.[60] And the advent of the Southern Pacific of course meant an opportunity for Americans to buy up the land for which the Yaqui had paid in blood.

But to the later regret of the ruling cliques, the metamorphosis of the valleys, which they applauded at the time, began to distort the political structure. Having lost its monopoly on transportation, the Hermosillo group increasingly confronted ever-powerful and hungry rivals, the planters and merchants of the valleys with ties to the business houses of Guaymas. In the course of events, the Hermosillo cabal began to lose some of its commercial advantage and fought back with political chicanery.[61] During his final stint as governor, Rafael Izábal even employed strong-arm tactics, importing armed *gringos* to quash the labor strike at Cananea in 1906 and deporting Yaquis out of Sonora despite howls of complaints from *hacendados* in the Mayo valley. By helping to build a southern economic bloc, the Southern Pacific made virtually inescapable the confrontation in 1910 between the old clique and its ambitious rivals.

Even before the completion of the railroad, the price of land along its projected route began to soar.[62] News of its approach awakened the speculative instincts of both Mexicans and foreigners with money to gamble. Prices rose from 1.50 pesos (2 pesos = 1 dollar) for an acre of land to ten to fifteen dollars, especially in the rich valleys, after Mexican soldiers had beaten their Yaqui defenders. By 1909, the Richardson brothers, speculators from Los Angeles, had sold 100,000 acres, nearly all to farmers from California, and dug fifty miles of irrigation canals.[63] Among a multitude of notorious land hawkers, the Richardsons stand out. Yet one rival, at the other end of the state, ended up with 4.5 million acres. By 1883, just a year after the locomotive had joined Guaymas and Hermosillo to the border at Nogales, Sonora had signed away more of its public lands to private individuals than any other state in the Republic. Land companies, as they were called, operated even in the desert of Altar.[64]

All things considered, the railroad strongly accelerated the concentration of land in the hands of a few.[65] In Sonora, as in the neighboring border states of Chihuahua and Coahuila, the laws of *terrenos baldíos* ("idle lands") of the 1880s held sway largely because of the coming of the iron horse and, of course, a sparse population. Statistics for the era reveal an astonishing relationship between the pace of railroad construction and claims for idle lands. As the railroad labor gangs pushed ahead, an army of land speculators, anticipating a rise in land values, rushed to claim lands on both sides of the right of way. The land rush began before a single mile of track had been laid. In 1880, the year the Santa Fe started to build its line north from Guaymas, speculators filed claims on nearly 100,000 hectares of idle lands. That was but a first step; in two years alone, 1886 and 1888, nearly 500,000 hectares fell into the laps of speculators.[66]

Economic growth had dire repercussions for the domestic social structure. The steel highway, along with the mining boom it ignited, made the already unbalanced distribution of wealth and income even more uneven. By putting still more money into the pockets of the better off, it hardened class distinctions. By hauling the latest machinery into the state at affordable prices, it updated the production of raw materials and farm goods—but not the social structure or its political institutions.[67] To the contrary, the iron horse gave impetus to the growth of the large estate, making it master in the Yaqui and Mayo valleys, where it formerly had just a foothold. The railroad paved the way for the large planter, particularly in the south, to make himself king of the export agriculture that rapidly replaced subsistence farming. The worker in the field and the dirt farmer, less numerous now, both saw their income decline while that of the planter climbed. The division between rich and poor, the gap between classes, thus grew wider and more onerous.

On the heels of the railroad came a flood of Americans, companions to the mine promoter, in search of cheap, fertile lands, not infrequently speculators themselves. Not surprisingly, they flocked to the rich lands of the Yaqui and Mayo. The Richardson brothers purchased, or more likely acquired by concession, large tracts of land, which they immediately put on the market for resale to American farmers, after making cursory "improvements." To sell their lands, these promoters put ads in American newspapers and journals. An ad in the *Overland Monthly* of June 1910 proclaimed the availability of "five million acres of the best land on earth—with the best climate on earth." It went on to talk about "new railroads, new ports and a small army of new people" on a "coastal plain between the mountains and the sea, watered by a dozen rivers. . . . Land at California prices of forty years ago." Having opened up the American West, and fomented a revolution in land prices in California, the railroad, these promoters believed, would do the same for southern Sonora.[68] The ads paid off. By the scores, Americans came to Sonora, attracted by cheap land and promises of vast irrigation systems. By 1910, about 1,000 Americans had settled along the West Coast of Mexico from Sonora to Nayarit, the majority in the Yaqui valley.[69]

In distinctive ways, the port of Guaymas as well as Hermosillo felt the impact of the railroad. Guaymas, paradoxically, both gained and lost. With the arrival of the railroad, its commerce grew. The merchants of the city, with American goods to sell, strengthened their trade ties to towns as far away as Ures, Moctezuma, Altar, and Alamos. Overnight, Guaymas became a major entrepôt for goods from the United States. From Guaymas, merchants shipped goods by steamers or sailing ships up and down the coast, and across the Sea of Cortez to the French

Boleo Mining Company in Baja California. Similarly, ores, hides, dyewoods, sugar, and other articles arrived in Guaymas by sea for shipment by rail to the American Southwest.[70] Lumber from Oregon, for example, destined for the Copper Queen Mine in Arizona, landed on the docks at Guaymas and was sent north by rail.[71] The port became the doorway to the Yaqui and Mayo valleys. Likewise, the railroad made it profitable to build an iron foundry in Guaymas to service the mines in its hinterland. By 1910, because of the growth of trade, and here and there a nascent "industry," the population of Guaymas had grown to 10,000, while sales experts estimated the number of potential buyers of foreign goods, largely American, at 56,000 people.[72] Perhaps more significantly, amidst the prosperity of Guaymas, a middle class, minuscule earlier, began to grow and thrive.

On the negative side, the port never emerged as a rival to San Francisco in the trade with Australia and Central and South America, the dream of certain American promoters of the railroad.[73] Further, when the steel highway reached Mazatlán, a port to the south, Guaymas lost much of its former importance, although it remained the entrepôt for trade with the Yaqui and Mayo valleys.[74] To add to its woes, the rail links between the United States and Hermosillo and other towns to the north—a boon for them—undercut Guaymas's preeminence as a port. With the appearance of the "magnificent locomotive," Guaymas ceased to be the top customs house in the state; that honor passed to Nogales, with Agua Prieta and La Morita not far behind. Before 1882, when the Santa Fe turned Nogales into a city, Sonora's foreign trade had been decidedly maritime. After that, the bulk of its trade was conducted overland, with goods entering and departing by way of Nogales.[75] Nor did the Santa Fe promoters deal gently with the merchants of Guaymas, their fervent if shortsighted backers. Despite the merchant's pleas that the railroad enter Guaymas, its builders bypassed the city. A short trunk line had to be constructed to connect Guaymas to the main route. Empalme, where the two lines met, became home to the railroad yards of the Southern Pacific.[76] A worse fate befell Agiabampo, a small port to the south. An entrepôt for the mining industry of Alamos, Agiabampo lost population and began its descent into obscurity partly because the railroad passed it by.[77]

Hermosillo, rather than Guaymas, reaped the golden bounty of the railroad. Its chief merchants grew rich with sales of imported articles, largely from the United States, to nearby towns, and its bankers prospered when Hermosillo emerged as the financial capital of the state. As in Guaymas, a middle class, in an embryonic state in 1880, began to make its presence felt. Even agriculture got a shot in the arm. The

hinterland of Hermosillo had long grown fine oranges, a gift of the
Spaniards who planted the first trees. Only with the advent of the railroad, however, did the oranges find a lucrative market. Unlocking markets in the United States and Canada, the railroad turned Hermosillo
into the Ciudad de las Naranjas, the City of Oranges, and its inhabitants into *los naranjeros* ("the orange-sellers").[78] Oranges from Hermosillo, and from Guaymas too, went north by rail, "quickly and cheaply,"
well "in advance of the same class of fruit from California and Florida."
At the New Orleans Exposition, oranges from Hermosillo won a gold
medal for excellence. Before the coming of the railroad, these oranges
had been sent by ship to be sold in San Francisco, often arriving there
"almost ruined by the sea voyage . . . and sold at greatly reduced
prices." Now they found "a ready sale and better prices."[79]

   For better or for worse, the railroad also helped solidify American
values in Hermosillo, and in other towns along its route. To other Mexicans, the *Hermosillenses*, the natives of the city, had become the "Yankees of Mexico," to judge by their habits of "thrift, advancement and
close relations with Americans."[80] On the positive side, the railroad
opened up travel to the poor, widening the labor market. With cheap
fares, dirt farmers and laborers could find jobs in the cities. Natives
of rural hamlets began to flock to the towns along the right of way, the
larger towns ultimately becoming "crowded" with recent arrivals.[81] As
Corral reported in 1889, the population grew along the border and on
the margins of the railroad tracks; new towns sprang up, including the
thriving centers of Nogales, Santa Ana, and Carbó to the south, and,
beyond Hermosillo, Estaciones Torres and Ortiz.[82] Naco, south of the
border from Bisbee, emerged when railroad workers and customs
officers built homes there.[83]

   But the iron horse played favorites. Not every corner of Sonora prospered. To the contrary: while districts on its route took on new life,
those that were bypassed stagnated and even declined. Both Sahuaripa
and Alamos, the colonial heartland, found themselves on the outside
looking in.[84] As late as 1906, neither the telegraph nor the telephone
had bequeathed its blessings on Sahuaripa. The nearest railway stations, Nacozari to the north and La Colorada to the west, were over 100
miles distant.[85] The decline of Alamos, obvious to many by the turn of
the century, had started with the fall in silver prices but worsened when
the rail line heading south from Guaymas bypassed it. A trunk line
built to Alamos in 1908, an afterthought, failed to rescue the city. Instead, its merchants were reduced to go-betweens, retailers of goods
shipped in from Guaymas, Hermosillo, and Nogales. From 1900 to
1910, the population of Alamos fell from 6,180 to 5,736 mainly because of the flight of its residents to Navojoa, Huatabampo, and Etcho-

joa, towns turned prosperous by the railroad. To make matters worse, the trunk line failed to show a profit and was abandoned in 1912.[86] At this juncture, Alamos, like the town of Sahuaripa, had no outlet to the coast.

Grading the roadbed and laying the track for the locomotive required a pool of cheap labor. From the beginning, this was a major hurdle because Sonora, as *hacendados* and mine owners knew, suffered from a scarcity of laborers of any kind. Construction of the railbed, reported the American consul, went ahead "steadily but not rapidly," in part because of the shortage of workers.[87] Recruiting labor therefore meant hiring anyone available, in particular Yaqui Indians. Of the first labor gang of 300, "Mexicans and Yaqui Indians," to quote the consul, made up two-thirds. The others were Americans.[88] The Yaquis, recruited in Huatabampo, were transported north, first to lay track and then, in section gangs along the right of way, to maintain it. So important did Governor Izábal judge the railroads that even after he began to deport Yaquis to Yucatán, the railroads were allowed to keep their Yaqui workers.[89]

When promoters of the railroad exhausted the pool of cheap Yaqui labor, they took a leaf from their experience north of the border, importing Chinese coolies and a scattering of Japanese.[90] There had been plans to employ them at the start, but a racially motivated public outcry had set them back. Use of the Chinese seemed inevitable; the engineers in charge of construction were of the opinion that native labor could not be counted on for "steady and uninterrupted employment."[91] Eventually, despite local sentiment, the Chinese came, initially to build the spur line from Nacozari.[92] They first appeared in large numbers at the construction of the railbed south of Guaymas, wearing "brightly colored pants and opaque jackets." The labor gangs of Chinese, Yaquis, and Mexicans reminded one Mexican observer of armies of ants. As many as 300 Chinese wielded ax, pick, and shovel to clear land for the railroad bed through the Yaqui and Mayo valleys.[93]

Mexican authorities believed that, by helping to provide jobs, the iron horse would not merely bring about good times, but render the popular pastime of rebellion improbable.[94] Yet, to their dismay, jobs on the railroad or in the mines did not always guarantee tranquillity. Constructing and maintaining the railroad required multiple labor gangs, who added to an incipient but growing army of wage workers. The mining industry that flourished in the railroads' wake multiplied the workers' number manyfold. Together, railroad and mine stimulated the rise of a rootless, hard-drinking, and not always docile proletariat dependent on the whims of Yankee bosses.[95]

Trouble started early. In time-honored fashion, the "docile" Yaquis sheltered their brethren who were fighting to protect their lands or spent their paychecks on weapons and ammunition to use against the hated *yori*, the white man. Some, their employers suspected, labored on the railroad and, when the opportunity arose, left their jobs to take up arms against the authorities. Though Chinese workers were thought at first to be docile, they proved restless and, according to their critics, prone to troublemaking.[96] When their jobs ended, unemployed Chinese were a particular problem. In 1907, a railroad boss noted that at Cumuripa there were 100 jobless Chinese, whom he wanted settled elsewhere. To him, they were nothing but a "headache."[97]

Another problem was that by employing Yaquis or Mayos, the railroad builders antagonized the southern planters. The planters, the traditional employers in the valleys, had always relied on the Indians to cultivate and harvest their crops. The railroad gangs, which paid better, upset local wage scales and left *hacendados* without field hands. After all, why should a Yaqui or Mayo work an entire month for five pesos when he could earn more in a week on the railroad?[98]

Moreover, railroad building, particularly from Guaymas south, upset the balance between supply and demand and caused inflation. The higher wages paid by the Sonora Railway to its construction crews added to the money in circulation. That, along with the ensuing influx of Yankee prospectors with dollars to spend, upped the demand for articles of all types, particularly imports. The price of goods, including food, grew by leaps and bounds in Guaymas.[99] Thus workers with more money to spend found themselves spending a larger slice of their paycheck on fewer goods.

More lamentable, in the opinion of employers at least, were the labor troubles that followed in the railroad's wake. By 1906, the strike, only dimly recalled in Sonora, had made its dramatic entrance onto the railroad scene. At Empalme, the railroad yards of the Southern Pacific just outside Guaymas, the workers went on strike on the first of June, the same day Mexican miners at Cananea defied their American bosses. Like Mr. Greene, the copper mogul at Cananea, Mr. J. A. Naugle, the American patriarch for the Southern Pacific, wired local authorities for help.[100] The workers had struck to protest a company decision to cut wages from 1.75 to 1.50 pesos a day. When the strikers met with the railroad bosses to discuss their differences, shouts of "death to the *gringos*" could be heard. If their demands were not met, the strikers declared, they would burn down the storehouses. Only the timely arrival of Mexican police stopped the strike from getting out of hand. Over 100 men abandoned their jobs rather than work for less money.[101] With another pay cut in 1909, a new strike flared, and again workers left their jobs.[102] On both occasions Mexican officials, consistently sympathetic to management, put down the "disorders," permitting the Southern Pacific to fire 250 workers, either out of economic need or willful spite.[103]

No sooner had the trains started their runs than a host of undesirables suddenly appeared. Petty crooks, men shorn of "honorable skills or professions," plagued the route from Hermosillo to Nogales. Gamblers exploited the gullibility of passengers by engaging them in poker and dice games prohibited by law. At the station stops, with the connivance of unscrupulous police, they set up their games in full public view.[104] Along with the crooks and gamblers, petty thieves turned up, stealing from passengers whatever they could get their hands on. The pilfering occurred particularly at the station stops, when gangs of sneak thieves and pickpockets climbed aboard to rob unwary travelers.[105]

A train robbery with all the melodrama of a Wild West movie took place in 1888. At Agua Zarca, a stop on the run south of Nogales, a band of masked robbers ambushed the train, killed the conductor and fireman, wounded the brakeman and a Wells Fargo agent, and escaped with the safe from the express car. To the thieves' undoubted sorrow, the safe contained a measly 130 pesos—65 dollars. The dead and wounded, the men with the best jobs on the train, were Americans. The crooks, who fled over the border, proved to be an international gang: two American kingpins and four Mexicans. A reward of 2,000 pesos, offered jointly by state authorities and the Sonora Railway, eventually led to their capture, but only after a seriocomic pageant of blunders and goofs by marshals on both sides of the border.[106]

To the discomfort of the promoters of progress, debauchery and immorality, at least as defined by the Victorian Age, beset one particular stretch of the run. Disorders, brawls of every type, and public drunkenness plagued the towns near labor camps from Hermosillo north to Magdalena, and women of "loose morals" infested the towns as well. Mexican and American laborers, heavy drinkers by night and by day, mocked law and morals. Authorities banned the sale of hard liquor, but could not ban drunkenness.[107] At Santa Cruz, a town not far from Magdalena, police shut down the bordellos and saloons, hoping to keep both Mexican and American railroad workers from brawling and even killing one another.[108] At one camp between Nogales and Cananea, workers who had had too much to drink beat up the constable and left him for dead.[109] The prefect of Magdalena district, meanwhile, fearing more trouble as the transient workers' camps moved closer and closer to the saloons of Nogales, pleaded for contingents of rural police.[110]

Most of the railroad stops, *estaciones* in the mold of Carbó and Torres, early required police to keep order.[111]

Mexican farmers in the path of the railroad also had their grievances. They accused its promoters of trampling their property rights. Construction crews, they charged, invaded their lands, cut down fences, and destroyed crops. Even their homes were endangered by the advancing railroad. Later, when sparks from locomotive engines set fire to their fields, farmers deluged Hermosillo with complaints. Mexican nationalists felt that authorities in Hermosillo, by encouraging the iron horse, had permitted foreigners to occupy their land.[112] To their further distress, American workers, with the connivance of Mexican *politicos*, enjoyed special privileges, such as the right to import duty-free cigarettes, beer, and household items. Mexicans had none of these rights.[113]

Resentful Mexicans retaliated by placing rocks, boulders, and heavy tree trunks in the paths of the locomotives. It was a secret war, usually waged at night, by anonymous Mexican enemies of the iron horse and its Yankee owners. Some mischief-makers did even more. In one episode in Guaymas district, the engineer of a run from Nogales discovered in time that someone had broken the lock on a switch in order to derail his train. At the same spot, another engineer who failed to note that someone had tampered with the switch drove his locomotive off the tracks. At Estación Pesqueira, north of Hermosillo, unknown persons dismantled the plates joining the rails together.[114]

III

The iron horse, along with the telegraph and telephone, which were introduced subsequently, contributed mightily to the integration of the political and social elite of Sonora. Old regional groupings tended to disappear, replaced by new groups bound by economic ties. Family names, as before, continued to play significant roles, but now on a state level. Old Alamos surnames, for example, could now be found from Guaymas to Nogales. At the start, a new consensus supplanted the regional differences of the past. In time, the iron horse would undermine the early unity it had helped create, setting south against northwest, but that conflict would not erupt until the first decade of the twentieth century.

After the railroad's coming, Sonora was never the same again. As an ecstatic Consul Willard noted, the energies of the people turned more and more to business.[115] No longer did political turmoil offer the only path to economic reward or social mobility. Business and commerce, strengthened by the mining boom, had flung open wider doors. By creating new jobs in mining, agriculture, and commerce, the railroad brought prosperity to Sonora and, likewise, solidified the regime in Hermosillo.[116]

Of no less significance, the iron horse put a disproportionate share of the benefits of "progress" into the hands of a tiny retail sector. This class had all the traits of a dependent bourgeoisie, intimately linked to American capital and markets. Industry, the dream of Corral and his cohorts, did not flourish. In this age of the New Imperialism, the industrial West put its export capital into the search for raw materials—which in Sonora meant mineral ores—not into new industry. The factory had been the cornerstone of the North American speculators' own climb to preeminence, but it had no part in their plans for Mexico. By joining Sonora's fate to that of its neighbor north of the border, the new Trojan Horse would ultimately make Sonora a victim of the dependent capitalism of underdevelopment.[117]

CHAPTER 2

The Importance of Mining

I

For the generation of the Triumvirate, no feature of the economy struck a happier chord than mining. The bountiful days of copper mining at the turn of the century dismantled traditional society while cementing in place a new capitalist edifice. Formerly among the poorest states in the Republic, by 1910 Sonora ranked with the richest, thanks to its copper ores. Mining and the export agriculture of the Mayo and Yaqui valleys, both stimulated by the railroad, had led Sonora into a modern world managed by capitalist ideologues.

By altering the contours of society, mining paradoxically exacerbated old class divisions while helping to give birth to a middle class, a creation of modern industrial society. Outside of the realm of mining, however, Sonora hardly had any industry. By 1910 there was only a factory here and there, none of any major consequence. Nevertheless, because of its mining industry, Sonora had the makings of both an industrial proletariat and a dependent bourgeoisie.

II

For mining to become king, a petulant mother nature had paved the way. To begin with, she had made much of Sonora a desert. Outside of the Yaqui and Mayo, and perhaps the Sonora, no rivers of any note watered the arid landscape, thus preventing the colonizer from turning dirt farmer. By contrast, fickle nature had hidden ores of every type in the bosoms of the mountains, converting Sonora, in the opinion of an admirer, into "one of the richest in natural resources of any on the American continent."[1] Such an exalted view, he insisted, was "within the bounds of truth." That "truth," an early discovery, quickly drew the Spaniards to Sonora. The Yankee speculators who converted the long-known hidden wealth into a bonanza for themselves and their Mexican allies were merely the last arrivals.

Spaniards, the conquerors of Moctezuma and his ancient Tenochtit-lán, made their first forays into Sonora between 1533 and 1564. During the first two decades of the next century, Jesuit missionaries, companions-in-conquest of the explorers, erected missions in the Mayo and Yaqui valleys. Permanent settlements, the work of lay Spaniards who ventured north, had to await the discovery of the mines. The unlocking of the earth's riches opened the way for the building of towns and the establishment of *ranchos* and—in the local vocabulary—*haciendas* on the edges of sparse rivers and streams. Their owners cultivated corn, wheat, and diverse other grains and, on occasion, cattle for beef, a good part of it destined for the dinner tables of miners.

Mining first got a toehold in the northeast, around Tepache and Bacanuche, and then moved south to Trinidad and Alamos, on the edges of Sinaloa. From there, the Spaniards, hoping to strike it rich, spread out in different directions. They were lured by rich ore finds, of silver primarily but also of gold and occasionally of mercury, which was used to separate the precious metals from the chaff. In nearby valleys fed by tiny rivers or streams, enterprising Spaniards found land suitable for crops and for cattle.[2]

Slowly, two regions of Spanish settlement emerged. To the south stood the town of Alamos and its hinterland, which included tiny enclaves of intrepid Spaniards living among the missions of the Mayo and Yaqui valleys. In the north, Spaniards gained a foothold in the upland valleys where the Sonora and Yaqui rivers began their descent to the sea. Western Sonora, an arid land stretching north from the Yaqui valley to the Gila River of Arizona, had only a handful of Spaniards, mostly hardy miners in Altar. Hermosillo, capital of Sonora during the days of Ramón Corral, in the early days had but "a few score white inhabitants." The scarcity of water and the presence of hostile nomadic Indian tribes, the Seris especially, kept the Spaniards out of the desert, the heartland of nineteenth-century Sonora.[3]

This pattern of settlement, consisting more often than not of Spaniards in quest of mines, survived into the eighteenth century. One major center became Magdalena, a district lying between Hermosillo and today's border with Arizona. At a site appropriately titled Planchas de Plata, bold Spanish prospectors stumbled upon a fabulous treasure, veins of silver ore that yielded chunks weighing as much as a quarter of a ton. News of the mine spread from the New World to Europe, drawing more settlers to Magdalena.[4] Next followed the discovery, again in Magdalena district, of the mines of Cocóspera, Higuera, and Cerro Prieto. The town of Magdalena emerged out of the rush to convert "heathens" to the true faith, as well as from the mining fervor. Founded in 1690 by Father Eusebio Kino, the peripatetic missionary, the town sat nestled in a fertile agricultural valley on the banks of a river of the same name. It became headquarters for a lucrative trade with the surrounding mining camps.[5]

Earlier, other towns had taken shape in the Oposura Valley, nearly all close to mines. The oldest were Moctezuma, later to become Catholic, conservative, and home to several powerful families, and Cumpas, ultimately a town of diametrically opposed inclinations: liberal and anticlerical.[6] A year later, in 1645, the Spaniards founded the towns of Oputo, Guásabas, and Bavispe, and, in 1678, Tepache. In adjoining Arizpe, also a mining zone, other towns sprang up: Baviácora (1639), Fronteras (1645), and Bacoachi (1650). Arizpe, the heart of this mineral domain, became the capital of the western Provincias Internas late in the eighteenth century. Some of the mineral wealth carried to Spain at that time by the galleons came from Arizpe.[7] Its ties, like those of Ures, which was capital of the state between 1855 and 1879, were with the port city of Guaymas, which lay at the end of a sea route from Mazatlán and San Blas.[8]

III

Of the colonial towns, none surpassed Alamos, either in size or in importance for the history of Sonora. Alamos gave form to the values and character of local society, becoming the womb of nineteenth century Sonoran culture. It epitomized not just the particularities of the society, but also the predominance of town over country. Its powerful merchant sector implanted its values, many bordering on a nascent capitalism, on the popular mind. It was in Alamos that the network of families destined to control the fate of Sonora for much of the nineteenth century emerged.

In Sonora, as in much of Mexico, family clans with an unchallenged role in the economy largely decided the nature of municipal politics.[9] The powerful Sonoran families often had roots in Alamos. Calling themselves *notables*, they wed one another and gradually formed clan networks the length and breadth of the province. In the towns, they had the upper hand.[10] Others emulated their example, so much so, an exasperated Yankee remarked to the governor in 1890, that in the small towns "nearly everyone belonged to the same family or . . . were partners, relatives, friends or brothers by the dictates of Jesus Christ of the partners." This outburst was in response to an attempt by three Americans to get the Compaña Industrial de Moctezuma to pay their wages. The judges responsible apparently had refused to hear their complaints: the district judicial chief because he was a stockholder in the company; the local magistrate because he had "certain religious obligations with another stockholder;" and so on. Such a family monopoly system had first partly appeared in Alamos.[11]

Among the patriarchs were the Salidos. The first of them, don Bartolomé Salido y Exoder, arrived in Alamos late in the eighteenth century, as clerk and later head of the royal treasury. With his marriage to Bárbara Elías González, herself daughter of another patriarch, don Bartolomé founded the Salido dynasty. Included in its list of luminaries were Rafael Izábal Salido, son of Ramón Salido—himself a son of a Bartolomé—with Eufemia Ortiz; and Benjamin G. Hill and Alvaro Obregón, both Salidos who helped topple the later kingdom of Izábal and Ramón Corral.[12] When he married doña Bárbara, don Bartolomé took as his wife the daughter of a clan established by Francisco Elías de González y Zayas, who settled in Alamos in the 1720s. Before moving on to Arizpe, where its members became kingpins, the Elías González family joined itself not only to the Salidos but also to the Almada and Santiago Palomares clans. The family tree embraced not just Obregón, Hill, and Izábal, but also Plutarco Elías Calles, Ignacio Pesqueira, Jesús García Morales, and José María Almada, all celebrated figures.[13]

The Almadas, another illustrious family of Alamos, owed their origins to don Antonio Almada y Reyes, a native of the city of León in Spain. In company with Antonio de los Reyes, the first bishop of Sonora, he settled in Alamos in 1783, marrying doña Luz Alvarado y Elías González. Don Antonio, a speculator, struck it rich with his famous Quintera mine.[14] Don Francisco Monteverde, sire of another line of *notables*, linked his family with the Alamos clans though he was a native of Hermosillo. The most distinguished of his offspring, Manuel Monteverde, a mine owner, died a rich man.[15] These families, along with Goycolea, Corbalá, Urrea, and Palomares, were the *notables* of Alamos.

A majority of these *notables*, despite their later pretensions, had merchant backgrounds. With a few exceptions, don Bartolomé Salido y Exoder, for instance, they had made the climb into the lap of luxury as storekeepers, selling clothing, shoes, and tools to miners in nearby camps. Ignacio N. Alameda, a son of don Antonio, for example, owned La Aurora del Comercio, a leading merchant house. While these merchants were citizens of a Spain still categorized as "feudal" by audacious Englishmen, they had a keen instinct for turning a profit and held aloft the values of hard work, thrift, and ambition, cornerstones of capitalist doctrine. Later, Yankee entrepreneurs helped shape nineteenth century Sonora, a land dedicated to transforming itself by practicing what Adam Smith and David Ricardo had taught, according to Corral and his cohorts. Yet upon closer examination, it seems the Yankee capitalist did not impose his doctrines on a dissimilar society. More likely, given the spirit and values of the Alamos clans, he had stepped onto a familiar stage.

Sitting at the foot of the Sierra de los Frailes, the tallest mountain in Sonora, Alamos basked in a "benign climate." Founded in 1682, like many of its sister towns in Arizpe and Moctezuma districts, Alamos owed its existence to the surrounding mines, the source of its wealth. It dated from the discovery of the rich silver mine of Promontorios. Out of this mine, baptized Europa by its Spanish owners, emerged Alamos, settled by people attracted by the mining boom. As early as 1687, when Father Kino visited Alamos on his journey north to establish missions, he noted that there were forty-three silver mines in the town's vicinity.[16] Although not declared a city until 1826, actually after independence, colonial Alamos ranked among the most important in western New Spain. At the close of the colonial years, Alamos had 5,000 inhabitants.

Next door to Alamos, the Real de San Ildefonso de Ostimuri embraced other important *reales* or mining centers, Río Chico, San Javier, Baroyeca, and Antonio de la Huerta among them.[17] Mines made colonial Alamos rich and kept its good fortune alive for over 200 years. That prosperity laid the basis for a thriving commerce. In 1826 alone, Alamos imported articles worth 160,000 pesos, impressive for those chaotic times.[18]

A decline set in after the independence of Mexico, particularly in the late 1860s.[19] Some authors place the blame on Maximilian, the ambitious Austrian prince who tried to rule Mexico with the aid of French bayonets and the backing of conservatives. Part of the ruling clan in Alamos, captained by José María Almada, say these writers, mistakenly supported Maximilian. With his defeat at the hands of the Liberals, in Sonora led by Ignacio Pesqueira, Alamos and some of the Almadas found themselves outcasts in the game of politics. When Toribio Almada, the stubborn son of don José, was shot on Pesqueira's orders, the break between Pesqueira and Alamos was complete.[20]

Other writers, less inclined to interpret history as the story of the whims of men, point out that by 1876 Alamos stood alone, isolated by the Yaqui and Mayo wars. These battles resulted from the ambitions of the Salidos, Almadas, and their brethren to own the rich lands of the valleys. Mexican independence, moreover, with its attendant political turmoil and economic disarray, set back mining everywhere in Mexico, not excluding Alamos. Not until the late years of the nineteenth century did mining recover. The growing isolation of Alamos, exploited by the Pesqueira clique in Ures, cut into its economy. Its commerce, especially, took a turn for the worse. Overall, however, Alamos fared better than its sister mining towns.[21]

The collapse of mining, whatever the responsibility of the Mexican Republic, nonetheless had deeper roots. The kings of Spain and their lackeys had fattened their purses with gold and silver plundered from Sonora but had reinvested scarcely a penny. Little had been done to modernize mining. Roads, neglected from the day Spaniards set foot in the New World, barely existed; the burro or mule in the rugged sierras served as the beast of burden. In the north, marauding Apaches nearly always kept mining at a standstill. Mines lay abandoned, or were worked sporadically when Apache raids subsided. To aggravate the problems, flooding closed many mines, La Quintera from 1806 to 1835, for example, and San Francisco Javier, La Clarina, San Antonio de la Huerta, Las Animas, and Nuestra Señora de Jalpa, to name just a few. Unable to find jobs because of the turmoil of the times, countless inhabitants of Sonora pulled up stakes and went off to California, depopulating entire mining districts. The civil strife, exacerbated by the French Intervention of the 1860s, took a heavy toll on mining. Until mid-century, the sale of silver and gold totaled two-fifths of the value of local exports.[22] Because of the drop in ore exports, the economy faltered and fell upon evil days. By 1880, Sonora had turned into "an enormous region of . . . rich but unworked mines."[23]

In hindsight, the ups and downs of mining—despite a "bull's-eye" hit here and there—and its demise after independence may have been a blessing in disguise. Distortions in the social structure, so common to primary-export economies, were never too pronounced. True, a small flock in Alamos, with a family network in Guaymas and Hermosillo, had feathered its nest. Compared to the poverty of their neighbors, the family mafia at Alamos was quite rich. The tiny but important merchant class in Guaymas and Hermosillo had also lined its pockets. Still, compared to the social ladder in central Mexico, the gap was less between rich and poor in Sonora.

By the same token, *hacendados* were like poor relations of their opulent brothers to the south, though they had an important part to play in the desert kingdom. Most inhabitants of rural Sonora had land of their own to till, whether *ejidos*, where Spaniards had built missions among Indians, or in the form of private plots. A class of wage workers, men without roots to the soil, was still in its infancy. Most of them were Yaquis or Mayos who, in the dead seasons of agriculture, left their fields or mission lands to labor in the mines. In the towns, artisans plied their trades, selling their goods to their neighbors, or to *hacendados, rancheros*, and dirt farmers. Town and countryside interchanged goods and services and were indispensable to each other's survival. Mine owners were generally Mexicans, as were storekeepers, wholesale merchants, and exporters. No wealthy or powerful outsider told Mexicans what to do.

IV

That relatively simple world began to turn upside down in the late 1800s. Both political and economic phenomena, the inevitable twins of societal change, were responsible. In Mexico City, Porfirio Díaz, a crafty and masterful *politico*, had put himself in the national palace. By manipulation—not excluding the use of soldiers to muzzle discordant voices—and, astutely, by courting provincial oligarchies, don Porfirio hammered out three miraculous decades of law, order, and, boasted sycophants, "progress." The revival on a grand scale of the mining industry opened a Pandora's box that boded ill for the future. Foreigners, mostly North Americans, made the revival possible, with don Porfirio luring speculators to the banquet table with fat guarantees.

Events north of the border enjoyed heady roles in this drama. The American Civil War was a victory for the industrial Northeast. Its robber barons—or, as their followers knew them, "industrial statesmen"— were eager to expand their empire in the manner of their English cousins and looked beyond their confines for new raw materials and markets. Having conquered the planters of the South, the barons annexed the American West to their growing dominion. They did this by building huge transcontinental railroads linking East with West, laying an iron grid that reached such out-of-the-way spots as Benson, Arizona, and, ultimately, Mexican cities.

Sonora as well as Arizona basked in prosperity, as eastern speculators rushed to find copper, the elixir of the electrical age, at Bisbee, Nacozari, and Cananea. Often risking life and limb, Americans reopened old mines shut since the Spaniards had departed Mexico, and dug new ones. Between 1900 and 1909, the number of mining claims, for the most part filed by Yankees, jumped from 1,400 to 5,335[24]. The shift from silver to copper gave fresh life to the mining industry. Rising demands for copper in the industrial world, a response to the tremendous jump in the use of electricity, spurred on the boom. "Smelters, copper concentrators, leaching plants, the flotation process, steam shovels, and larger concentrators, and larger steam shovels," the latest technological innovations, rendered copper less costly to mine and thus more profitable.[25] By 1910, no state in the Republic of Mexico yielded more copper than Sonora. But it was not only copper that gave the economy a burst of energy; gold and silver helped. Mines at Minas Prietas, for example, produced gold and silver valued at $3 million.[26] Governor Rafael Izábal boasted in 1907 that the mines of Sonora had yielded over 1,297 kilograms of gold, silver, and copper, worth nearly 25 million pesos. Just in 1906, a year of fine profits, he noted, the exports of ores had topped 13 million pesos.[27] The peso at that time stood at a half-dollar.

Mining, to quote Izábal, had been the pillar of the economy since at least 1890 when Ramón Corral, in his two-volume report of his accomplishments as governor, had accentuated what Izábal acknowledged two decades later.[28] By 1910, Sonora, with its 5,391 mines, had become a major mining state and the chief copper bastion of Mexico.[29] In that twenty-year era mining indisputably held sway. Its significance rested by and large on its dependence on industrial markets in the United States. Nearly the entire payload, moreover, went north as raw ore to smelters on the other side of the border.[30]

Not unlike the sugar industry in Cuba, or coffee and banana cultivation in El Salvador and Honduras in the late nineteenth century, mining put money in the pocketbooks of a majority in Sonora, at least for the moment.[31] With the mines operating, workers had jobs and money to spend on food and clothing, and, once in a while, on imported articles. Nearly everyone benefited: the miners, the storekeepers who sold them goods, and the dirt farmers, *hacendados*, and cattle ranchers who fed them. As mining fared, so did the people of Sonora. Everyone thought mining a doorway to a better future. According to a report on Arizpe district in 1884, mining signified "rapid growth . . . to a region destined to thrive because of its ores and link with markets in the United States." When developed fully, Arizpe's mines would confer on it a wealth to rival that of Alamos, whose own riches were drawn from the mines.[32] Time proved the authors of the report prophets: the subsoil at Cananea in Arizpa concealed untold tons of copper ore.

Ultimately, almost every corner of Sonora had operating mines. In Hermosillo district, the gold and silver mines of the Creston Colorado

Company rewarded their stockholders with a rich booty, as did the mines of La Barranca, San Javier, and Los Bronces. To the south, the mines of La Concentración and La Dura, rejuvenated with injections of dollars, won fresh international acclaim. The mines of La Trinidad and Mulatos again put Sahuaripa district on the map. In Moctezuma district, Nacozari, El Tigre, Lampazos, Dos Cabezas, and La Verde, to name just a few, showered rewards on their owners, in the pattern of Cananea in adjoining Arizpe. Both Magdalena and Ures districts had their own mines.[33]

Mining detonated an explosive charge up and down the economy. It brought miners and, at times, entire families to set up housekeeping in mining camps. Their needs stimulated others, as the prefect of Arizpe explained. With the coming of mining to his district demand for goods grew. Food particularly was needed, so dirt farmers planted more crops. The extra plantings required additional laborers, and so on. Cattle ranching responded in similar ways.[34] Economic growth lured new people to Arizpe, which almost tripled its population in a decade and a half. The inhabitants of Moctezuma district had more than doubled by 1910, with Cumpas and Moctezuma, its urban "metropolis," each having populations of 2,500.[35] By 1910, Agua Prieta, established in 1899, had 3,000 people, many natives of nearby Fronteras, Cuquiárachi, and towns to the south. A dusty hamlet of perhaps fifty mud huts in 1903, Agua Prieta had taken off with the coming of the trunk line from the mines at Nacozari to the smelter at Douglas "on the other side." Naco, a few miles to the west, took root because of the mines at both Cananea and Nacozari.[36]

Yet no matter how many mines a region had, if the railroad failed to make its bow, the place languished. That was the fate of Sahuaripa. Ures, bypassed by the railroad builders, shared a similar destiny, its population dropping by 2,500 between 1895 and 1910. The same tragedy befell Alamos. Sahuaripa had been praised by a noted geologist "as one of the most heavily and richly mineralized regions in the world."[37] Unfortunately for Sahuaripa, however, it lacked rich deposits of copper ore. Thus the *gambusino*, the lone prospector working abandoned diggings, instead of the large commercial operation, was typical of mining in Sahuaripa.

The hordes of job seekers built mining camps, some of which blossomed into towns. Until the mining boom, Fronteras, for example, a settlement several miles from Nacozari, was just a sleepy old hamlet. With the discovery of gold in the Sierra de Navabi, at a spot called Cañada de Las Aguilas, Fronteras was transformed. Further enriched by the boom at Nacozari, Fronteras had suddenly outlived its era of obscurity.[38] At other diggings, the mining renaissance kept old towns alive; such was the destiny of towns in Alamos, that had been on the edge of oblivion. The revival of mining rescued scores of colonial towns from extinction.

Still, as the people of Sonora learned, mining had its good and bad moments. Its blessings lingered only fleetingly. Once ore deposits petered out, its hunters moved on, leaving behind crumbling adobe walls, rusty machinery, and rubble. People abandoned their homes. The merchants, whose businesses depended on the sale of goods to miners, also left. The mining town was just that, a mining town, and nothing more. What remained was a ghost town. With the collapse of the mining economy, Sonora became known for towns bereft of people.

Such was the destiny of Los Bronces, the famous mining center in Hermosillo district. Its age of prosperity, as well as its decline and demise, antedated the turn of the century. By 1890, to quote the prefect of the district, Los Bronces, "once a model for other towns, as much for its exemplary way of life as for its support of good government, had only a few inhabitants left." The blame, he charged, rested on the shoulders of English speculators who had formed the Silver Queen United Limited to exploit the silver ore deposits. Their tinhorn venture, turning mining into a sweepstakes, went bankrupt. It was merely a matter of time, he predicted, before a revival occurred, especially since another mining group wanted to purchase the property.[39] There was no reason for his optimism. By 1892, Los Bronces existed in name only, a ghost town. Its old patrons, having taken the silver ore out of the bowels of the earth, pulled up stakes.[40] Like a broken record, the story of Los Bronces played over and over again: at Pitiquito, whose mines lay bare by 1910;[41] at Minas Prietas, La Aduana, Promontorios, and La Quintera; and eventually everywhere in the state. The mining prosperity of these towns, like that of much of Sonora, had proved ephemeral.

But that had always been the history of mining in Sonora. Silver, the white metal that drew the Spanish speculator to the New World, had provided an initial era of prosperity. Between 1683 and 1684, adventurous Spanish prospectors discovered silver in the Cerro de los Frailes not far from the Mayo river in southern Sonora.[42] The *real* became Alamos, the heartland of colonial mining. From the Real de los Frailes, Spaniards discovered more silver at Baroyeca, Promontorios, La Quintera, and Minas Nuevas, one of the few mines to survive the silver debacle of the turn of the twentieth century. Because of its silver wealth, the Spaniards established a mint in Alamos.[43] At the close of the colonial era, after 130 years of exploitation, the mines of Alamos were still producing monthly between 80 and 100 million dollars' worth of ore, mostly silver.[44] Despite the multiple plagues of independence—civil strife, Indian wars, and hard times—in 1879 the mines of Alamos exported silver ore worth over 700 million pesos.[45] In its heyday La Quintera, the legendary mine acquired by Ignacio Almada in 1830, alone produced silver ore valued at 25 million pesos every year.[46]

But Alamos had rivals. At Minas Prietas, about a day's ride from Hermosillo, the Spaniards discovered gold as well as silver. In 1893, Minas Prietas ranked among the principal enterprises of Sonora.[47] Its five mines (La Prieta, La Verde, San Juan, Amparo, and Florencia), the property of the Minas Prietas Mining Company, had reduction works ranking with "the most modern," the American consul in Guaymas declared.[48] Its ores were shipped to San Francisco. Although a fire temporarily closed the mines in 1892, they continued to function into the twentieth century.[49] As the mines thrived, the local population grew. By 1892, the mines employed 250 workers, while 1,750 people lived in the town of Minas Prietas. So important was the town that the state legislature ruled it the headquarters of a *municipio* (municipality).[50] In time, however, the gold petered out, Minas Prietas declined, and its people went elsewhere. In 1907, a saddened legislature, despite cries of anguish from local residents, reduced Minas Prietas to the status of a *comisaría*, a hamlet worthy only of a constable, and placed it under the jurisdiction of neighboring La Colorada, now a *municipio* with 5,000 inhabitants.[51] At this juncture in history, La Colorada, not Minas Prietas, won the accolades of mining experts.[52] Its silver ore was "exceedingly rich," the American consul enthused.[53]

The mines in Alamos district, Minas Prietas, and La Colorada were but a fraction of the diggings. The Spaniards also unearthed silver deposits in Magdalena, Arizpe, Moctezuma, Sahuaripa, and Guaymas districts. The mines of Sahuaripa (La Trinidad, Río Chico, San Javier, and Baroyeca) were among the earliest. At Santa Rosalía, Spanish miners found gold. After independence, Apache raids compelled its owners to close the mine. So well did they conceal its shaft that not until years later was it discovered again, revealing "an ore vein . . . 12 feet wide" and another "2 feet wide." When it was reopened, its owners netted "$24,000 for the first carload shipped to San Francisco, $18,000 for the second, and $22,000 for the third."[54] Opodepe in the district of Ures yielded more gold mines. In Moctezuma, the mines at Lampazos and Nacozari rewarded their owners for over a century, a feat virtually matched by El Tigre.[55]

Until late in the nineteenth century, mining in Sonora meant primarily digging for silver.[56] Of the 519 mines operating in 1893, reported the American consulate, 353 were of silver, 62 of both silver and gold, and 43 of gold.[57] A good many of these mines had Mexican owners. As late as 1872, to cite the figures of the consulate, only two big foreign mining companies, one American and one British, operated in Sonora, plus two or three "tolerably sized German companies." The other foreign concerns were smaller or were simply individual adventurers of many nationalities: American, English, German, French, and Italian. Alongside these were "innumerable small Mexican companies, some three or four of considerable extent, all mostly engaged in silver mining."[58] Statistics for 1888 placed the value of the silver and gold bullion exported at $2.5 million, probably a fair indication of the average annual yield at the time.[59] While not a huge dollar figure, it was a substantial amount. More significantly, judged by the number of native mine owners, Mexicans enjoyed a healthy share of that return.

Yet most inhabitants of Sonora had not tasted the fruits of mining. They were poor or merely moderately well-off.[60] Then, a catastrophe befell Sonora. In 1892, the bottom fell out of the silver market, and by 1905 "the Mexican peso had largely lost its ancient and honorable place in the daily commerce of hundreds of millions of human beings." Even China and India, traditional customers, stopped buying silver.[61] In 1905, Mexico went on the gold standard. The silver formula, obviously, was no longer working. On the heels of the silver debacle appeared an economic crisis in Sonora. Government revenues petered out as commerce and agriculture, both tied to mining, fell into the doldrums. To hurl insult upon injury, an international depression that brought business to its knees in the United States accompanied the drop in silver prices.[62] Its effects reverberated in Sonora wherever there were links with Yankee capital and markets.

Those links, increasingly, were strongest in the vital arteries, the heralded "modern" sectors. One such place was Nogales, the pathway for trade with the colossus to the north. The mayor of Nogales lamented that the depression, which he identified with the silver crisis, had brought untold harm. Unable to find jobs, most of its workers abandoned the city, leaving merchants without customers. Shorn of sales and profits, the merchants could not import goods for local resale. When the merchants fell upon hard times, so did the city's tax base.[63] The decline of Alamos, once home of the "400" of Sonora, partly had its origins in the misfortunes of silver.[64] Pouring salt on the wound, the United States adopted the McKinley Tariff, which curtailed exports from Sonora to markets across the border. The silver debacle, the collapse of the international economy, and the McKinley bill, formidable hurdles separately, together played havoc with the economy of Sonora. To give just one example, before 1893, the ancient mine at Tobacachi, the property of a Yankee entrepreneur, had exported over 100 tons of silver annually. "Now," the American consul stressed, "it introduces nothing at all into the United States."[65] The disaster of Tobacachi also turned the commerce of nearby Cumpas into a shambles. The misfortunes of Nogales, Tobacachi, and other silver centers brought the state treasury to the brink of bankruptcy.[66]

V

The transformation of the mining industry, and with it local society, had to await the age of copper. Its story is a twentieth-century epic. Until then, the low selling price of copper discouraged efforts to extract it.[67] The demand for copper, like other industrial metals, arose out of the needs of the manufacturing world beyond Mexico. Copper's heyday began with the electrical revolution of the 1880s and lasted well into the second decade of the twentieth century. It was electricity that made copper so desirable. To begin with, the electrification of the railways required a lavish use of copper for cables and fittings. In the 1880s, hard-drawn copper wire began to substitute for the galvanized iron or soft-copper wire Bell Telephone had used earlier. The multiplication of telephone, telegraph, and cable systems provided a constantly expanding market for copper. Additionally, it had other uses: in the forging of brass or bronze, and in cooking vessels, boilers, nails, water pipes, lightning rods, and a host of other articles. Meeting these needs led to a veritable upheaval in the mining industry and, obviously, to more and more copper.[68] On the latter point, statistics speak eloquently. In 1800, the copper mines of the world produced less than 2,000 metric tons, twice that figure in 1830, 240,000 metric tons a year in the 1880s, and over 1 million metric tons by 1913.[69] With rising demand, profits soared. By 1900, profits per pound of copper were nearly double the cost of producing that amount.[70]

The copper explosion had a major impact on Sonora. Nature had richly endowed the Pimería Alta with copper. The copper belt stretched through the old, colonial mission frontier from Globe, Clifton, Morenci, and Bisbee on the Arizona side southward into Sonora, especially in the districts of Moctezuma and Arizpe. Cananea and Nacozari held the bulk of Mexico's copper resources.[71] These two giant copper camps, one eventually a small city, put the mining industry of Sonora on the map.[72]

Nacozari appeared on the scene first. Sitting between canyons and deep ravines, the town had been carved from the majestic mountains that sheltered it, allowing only partial access, from the north and south.

Nacozari hung from a series of ledges, giving its streets the shape of a pretzel. It required a sharp climb from its southern tip, site of the mines, to its northern edge, on the route to the border. Resembling colonial Taxco, Nacozari was a northern version of that fabulous silver town in the mountain hinterland of Mexico City. The town, in the district of Moctezuma—or Oposura as the Spaniards had called it—had begun as Nuestra Señora del Rosario de Nacozari, and later was baptized Pilares de Nacozari. After the heroic feat of Jesús García, the locomotive engineer who saved the town from destruction, the Mexicans changed its name to Nacozari de García. Its principal mines were La Esperanza, El Porvenir, and, especially, Pilares, from which the town borrowed one of its names.[73]

Nacozari went through a golden age in the first decade of the twentieth century. The Moctezuma Copper Company purchased the mines in 1895, but their rise to fame dated from their sale to the Phelps Dodge Corporation in 1900. Copper radically altered the outlines of Nacozari, changing it from a sleepy hamlet into a bustling town linked by rail to the smelter at Douglas. The copper production of the Phelps Dodge empire, with mines at Nacozari, Bisbee, and Morenci, jumped from 45 million pounds in 1900 to 157.5 million by 1913.[74] With about 5,000 inhabitants, Nacozari was the biggest town in Arizpe district.[75] They had come from other parts of Sonora; from Chihuahua, Durango, and Coahuila; and from north of the border.[76] Luis Cabrera, a luminary of the Mexico that was born after the Revolution of 1910, would later say that "Sonora is to the Republic what Nacozari is to Sonora," in reference to the key role played by both in the rise of new epochs.[77]

Yet Cananea, not Nacozari, stamped Mexico with its exalted reputation in the copper world. When William C. Greene, an American adventurer and speculator, purchased its mining properties late in the nineteenth century, Cananea had merely local fame. Its American owner gave it a new look when he opened La Demócrata, the initial mine, built housing for his employees, put up a mill and an ore oven, and laid track for the ore carts.[78] Eventually, Cananea became the biggest "city" in the state, whereas earlier it had been merely a *comisaría*, a police station administratively attached to Fronteras. By 1901, Cananea, the miracle camp, had ninety-six city blocks, each with twenty-four lots for homes or other buildings, lying between two major parallel streets. Its architects had laid out nine avenues running from east to west and three streets going north and south. Prime lots sold for fifteen cents a square meter; for ten cents for lots of less quality; and the rest, cliffhanging sites on the sides of *barrancas* ("ravines") and gullies, for "free" to the "notoriously poor." On the eve of the strike that shook the entire Republic in 1906, Cananea had 22,000 inhabitants.[79] Its political clout, meanwhile, had grown by leaps and bounds, so much so that Governor Rafael Izábal had even urged the legislature to designate Cananea the headquarters for Arizpe district.[80] For its part, the town of Arizpe, with less than a tenth of the population of Cananea, could only stand on its birthright as the ancient colonial capital.[81]

The properties of the Cananea Consolidated Copper Company embraced ten square miles of territory. Its empire included six mines: Veta Grande, Oversight, and Capote, the largest, as well as Esperanza, Elenita, and Puertecito.[82] The market value of the ores from these mines stood at nearly 14.5 million pesos (7.2 million dollars).[83] In addition to copper, the mines of Cananea yielded zinc, lead, and silver. The power of this vast empire, an admiring Mexican journalist wrote, could be felt the moment "one stepped across the border at Naco, where the spur line tying Cananea to the outside world began."[84]

CHAPTER 3

A Fickle Partner

I

From the outset, mining proved fickle and untrustworthy, a double-edged sword. In good times, mining heaped lofty returns on its clients, amply rewarding the mining baron and, to a far lesser degree, the miner with a good-paying job. Merchant, farmer, and rancher also turned an honest penny. But the other side of the sword cut sharply. Mining had an ephemeral and volatile nature, and its adulators, of whom Sonora had legions, could not control its path.

That some mining regions in certain epochs flourished and grew goes without saying. Alamos district, and the city of Alamos itself, birth-place of the mining society originated by the Spaniards, offered abundant proof of that. Its colonial golden age and its brief renaissance in the 1800s rested on mining. Colonial Sonora, essentially a land of *ejidos* and small *ranchos*, and here and there an *hacienda*, had, paradoxically, given life to towns. The vigorous towns—Sonora's salient peculiarity—developed largely because mining, more than any other activity, had spurred commerce ever since the early days of Alamos.

II

The revival of mining in the late nineteenth century, centering on the export of industrial ores, had a phenomenal impact. The appearance of foreigners, whether speculators, promoters, or miners, set a drab economy aglow. A prefect of Arizpe enthused that the coming of the mining companies had conferred untold benefits. With the establishment of mining camps, nearby farmers filled their pocketbooks because miners, their wives, and their bountiful array of children, had to eat. With additional customers, the farmers planted more lands and, with more work to do, hired more field hands, while ranchers, who made money selling their beef to hungry miners, multiplied their herds. All goods of the district had a better market.[1]

Varied groups profited from the growing economy: artisans, who made the articles purchased by customers with money to spend; farmers and ranchers, who produced the foodstuffs consumed; and storekeepers, who resold imported goods. Trade between buyers and producers grew apace, breaking down barriers of yesteryear peculiar to the tiny, "self-sufficient" local unit. What transpired resembled, to some extent, the breakdown of the isolated medieval town, as localities and then regions began to channel their energies into a specialty, whether the weaving of cloth, the tanning of leather for saddles and bridles, or the planting of wheat to bake bread. The late nineteenth-century mining renaissance, in short, cemented in place the fledgling capitalism that had risen out of the early mining industry of colonial Alamos.

The boom engineered by the export of copper, in particular, had a boomerang effect. From 1900 to 1910, the production of metals nearly doubled.[2] The value of copper exports, the staff of life, went from 564,201 pesos in 1895 to almost 8.4 million in 1910.[3] The happy beneficiaries were largely the northeastern districts. Both Arizpe, home of the 4C's, as Mexicans called the Cananea Consolidated Copper Company, and Moctezuma, headquarters of the Moctezuma Copper Company, were bursting at the seams with people. In just one decade, Moctezuma added 11,000 inhabitants while Arizpe just missed doubling its population. Agua Prieta and Naco, only place names before, came to have approximately 15,000 people apiece.[4] The ore trains from Nacozari and Cananea injected them with life, just as they did adjoining Douglas, where Phelps Dodge built a smelter to handle the ores from its mines. Because of their mining enclaves, Arizpe and Moctezuma, formerly underpopulated, jumped to the forefront as the fastest-growing districts in the state.[5]

King copper transformed Nacozari from a sleepy village resting on its exhausted gold and silver laurels into a hustling boom town. Since the town was a rail stop on the way to Douglas across the border, from where American manufactured goods could be shipped easily to its *tiendas de raya* ("company stores"), Nacozari supplanted both Guaymas and Hermosillo as the supplier of local needs. Farmers of the hinterland, for their part, sold their harvests in Nacozari and purchased articles at the *tiendas de raya* with their profits. Moctezuma and Cumpas, neighboring citadels, flourished as markets for dirt farmers and ranchers of the region.[6] A tall, black metal chimney, a signpost of the recently installed foundry, trumpeted the good times of Cumpas.[7] With the arrival of the Transvaal Copper Company, boasted its American boss, Cumpas and its hinterland waxed fat.[8] Everything was a matter of superlatives. The town had almost doubled its population; real estate values had shot up; wages had multiplied twofold, as had the prices of local harvests such as corn, wheat, and hay. Whereas Cumpas formerly had only five general stores, now "30 or 40" had opened for business. The *tienda de raya*, the American went on to explain, handled merchandise of every description at "reasonable prices." Before its advent, the monopolist merchants of Cumpas had charged exorbitant prices for their goods. The competition of the company store had cut them "almost in half."[9]

To the delight of public functionaries, mining brought added revenues to state and local coffers. Mine operators, to begin with, paid a federal tax of no small importance to the finances of the Republic. For their part, state authorities, in the contracts signed with miners, imposed their own tax, originally 3 percent of the value of the raw ore but cut to 2 percent in 1887.[10] Beginning in 1887, however, *haciendas de beneficio* ("reduction works") had to pay a tax.[11] More often than not, mining operators had to pay a municipal tax on articles imported for use at the mine. Nevertheless, exemptions from the tax were not infrequently granted. Such companies as the 4C's or the Creston Colorado Company, for example, won exemptions in return for a promise to support a school or, ironically, to pay the salary of the police.[12] However, when it was collected, the tax helped keep municipal governments solvent.

III

Mining, to the sorrow of its devotees, had an ephemeral makeup. No ore deposit, after all, was inexhaustible; a stingy mother nature had set limits on its gifts. Of the hundreds of mines, just a few enjoyed any longevity. In his *Informe* of 1889, Governor Ramón Corral reported more abandoned mines than operating ones. Of Sonora's 937 silver mines, the key industry at that time, only 353 were still open.[13]

Mining also gyrated according to the ups and downs of the international economy. Ores from Sonora found their markets in the industrialized world, more often than not in the United States. For Sonora to bask in prosperity, outsiders, specifically Yankees, had to buy its ores. Its economy went up and down like a yo-yo in response to the needs of foreign buyers. More than ever before, the inhabitants of Sonora had tied their fate to an economy dependent on forces beyond their control. Every cyclical downturn of the industrial world reverberated locally. Sonorenses vividly remembered 1893, 1901, and 1907 as hard times, bust years in the international cycle.[14]

Nothing better illustrated the cost of relying on the fickle fortunes of copper than the crisis of 1907. So widespread were its devastating effects that it set in motion the collapse of the Old Regime in Sonora as well as the outbreak of the Great Rebellion of 1910. By halting industrial activity, the Financial Panic of 1907—so named in the United States—undercut the consumption of copper and, consequently, the well-being of Sonora. By putting a stop to work at both Cananea and Nacozari, the depression sowed despair and discontent in its wake.[15] Authorities in Hermosillo acknowledged that for Sonora the debacle of 1907 "constituted a disaster." Not only had it created an army of unemployed men who could be found in every corner of the state in search of jobs, but it had also woefully hurt commerce and banking. The damage, bad as bad can be, was "irreparable."[16]

The catastrophe also exacerbated the ills of silver mining, already a sick industry. The devaluation of silver almost worldwide, combined with the adoption of the gold standard, a stance endorsed by Mexico, and the world economic doldrums dealt hammer blows to the "white metal."[17] The demise of silver helped sound a death knell for Alamos. By 1905, all but five of its mines, almost all silver, had shut down; by 1909, even Promontorios and La Quintera, the venerable silver queens, no longer called their men to work.[18] At Promontorios, wrote the prefect of Alamos, the people "walk about in despair."[19]

News of mine closings filled the pages of newspapers until 1910. Statistics outline the dimensions of the crawling cancer. To cite the report of Governor Rafael Izábal, 1,413 mines, mostly silver, had been shut by 1907.[20] The disaster was felt by the entire state, including the copper north. Based on approximate figures, with additional bad news still to come after 1907, the scope of the disaster had the following contours. In Arizpe, sixty-three of its sixty-nine mines had shut down; sixty-two of eighty-one in Magdalena; eighty of 110 in Moctezuma; fifty-six of eighty in Ures; and 112 of 118 in Sahuaripa. In Hermosillo, twelve of the sixteen mines at Minas Prietas, the golden nugget of yesteryear, had shut down and, worse yet, so had nearby La Colorada, its fabled rival.[21] Both ultimately disappeared from the mining map of Sonora.

The mine owners who were Mexican felt the sting of bad times even more than the foreign operators. None of the Mexicans, first and foremost, owned a major mine; nearly all ranked among the smaller operators, speculators who lived from day to day. They worked mines of silver or, once in a while, a combination of silver and gold; silver, of course, had the least value. Only a tiny handful had copper mines, none of major consequence. By 1906, of the approximately 1,413 mines, about a third of the mines had Mexican owners; only ten with Spanish-surname owners, not necessarily Mexicans, still operated.[22] One story graphically depicts their plight. Miguel A. López, a member of the Mexican elite, had struggled for some time to turn his mine in Lampazos into a moneymaker. At one point, James Douglas, the American boss at Nacozari, thinking that López sat on a pot of gold, had offered him the "fantastic" price of 1 million pesos for the mine. Enamored of his mine and not ready to call it quits, López, to his later regret, rejected the offer. A short while later, finding himself in dire straits, López tried to sell his mine to Douglas. "Mr. López," replied Douglas on this occasion, "your mine is not worth a penny to me."[23] The debacle, as the López story bears out, hit Mexican mine owners hard.

The mine shutdowns left an army of unemployed in their wake. With each additional closing, more names joined the jobless rolls. The specter of unemployment haunted every corner of Sonora. When La Sultana in Alamos shut down, reported its owner, he kept only caretakers on the job.[24] At El Alacrán, Las Cabezas, and Las Chispas, thriving enterprises earlier, just twenty workers of the old labor force survived, including six men left to care for the plant at El Alacrán. The prefect of Altar lamented that a mere fraction of the men formerly employed in local mines had jobs. News of mine closings in Moctezuma district, a common item, conveyed identical stories of men without work. Such stories appeared with increasing frequency until 1909.[25] Worse yet, over 3,000 men, formerly employed in the mines of Bisbee and the smelter in Douglas, suddenly appeared in Fronteras in the spring of 1907, adding to local jobless woes.[26]

Not only were men out of work, the bosses not infrequently let them go without paying them the back wages they were owed. Naturally, the miners did not take kindly either to being fired or to getting cheated of their pay. Trouble flared when fly-by-night promoters, all too common on the local scene, skipped out, leaving their workers holding the proverbial bag. This happened at the Dawson Mining Company operations in Moctezuma.[27] That company eventually paid its workers but others did not. When the Roy Consolidated Mining Company went bankrupt, it left unpaid wages totaling 5,500 pesos but assets of just 1,500 pesos. Even the cupboards of its *tienda de raya* were bare.[28]

As mines closed, the miners and their families, individually at first and then in wholesale lots, abandoned the mining camps and towns. When the 4C's stopped operating, the jobless by the thousands packed their bags and went elsewhere in search of work.[29] It happened on a lesser scale at Nacozari.[30] At Cananea, the mayor boasted, the jobless left without "prodding on our part."[31] At Caborca, the mayor talked of the "flight of large numbers who had left to look for work."[32] When the mines at La Trinidad closed, the town lost its only industry, and the better part of its inhabitants went off, abandoning their houses. "Even before this," lamented the prefect of the district, "there were already houses in ruins, some no more than foundations or parts of walls."[33]

The lawyer of the 4C's reported that Cananea also suffered a decrease of money in circulation, money that had kept its merchants in business.[34] Without miners and their wages, the merchants of the towns and camps lost their customers. Thus most business houses in Sonora, a Mexican journalist underlined, felt the shock of the economic crisis with devastating effect.[35] In all but the largest mining towns, the stores were small. In La Trinidad, for example, all but three of its ten merchants had yearly sales under 800 pesos.[36] Hardly impressive by the standards of Cananea, these sales, nonetheless, had made their owners the kingpins of the town. Their stores survived and prospered on sales to miners. The larger the number of miners at work, the greater the sales. Unemployment hurt small business. "Everyday," complained a shoe merchant in Alamos, "we sell fewer shoes because miners, our best customers, are jobless."[37] Or, as the mayor of Caborca put it, when mines shut down, "everyone paid the penalty, storekeepers as well as the municipal treasury."[38]

But mine closings, as the people of Sahuaripa had learned by 1909, damaged not just the camps and towns but every sector in a district's economy. Business came to a halt; agriculture and cattle ranching declined. Jobless men and their families, after all, ate sparingly, only what kept body and soul together. As one band of disgruntled cattle ranchers in Sahuaripa wrote, beef sales had dropped drastically in the mining towns, their principal markets. Authorities in Dolores, a town in neighboring Chihuahua, also added to their woes. Overwhelmed by similar problems, the officials banned sales of beef from Sahuaripa in order to protect their own stockmen. Unable to sell their beef at home or in Dolores, local ranchers stopped trying to keep up their herds. Unless the government took action, the writers warned, "the economy of Sahuaripa would be a total wreck."[39]

The economic crisis of 1907 spared no mining center. All felt its blows, the big along with the puny: mighty Cananea along with tiny La Trinidad. As Cananea's merchants told the governor, the closing of the 4C's had left them "in the wrong pew in the wrong church." From the start, authorities had given them false assurances. Instead of being temporary, as public officials had predicted, the crisis lasted an eternity. Hermosillo granted the merchants a reduction in the sales tax they paid, but that concession did not keep sales alive. The layoff of virtually the entire labor force of the 4C's left them with goods on their shelves and no buyers. The only people left in Cananea were those who could not afford to leave or could not abandon what they owned. Whatever the case, the remaining inhabitants bought only what was absolutely essential. The merchants now asked for the cancellation of the entire tax on sales.[40]

But the crisis, to the despair of the merchants, lingered on and became worse. By the fall of 1908, the year-old depression had hurt business so much that even the partial reopening of the 4C's failed to revive it. Cananea's ills, meanwhile, spread like a plague, inflicting pain on everyone linked to it. As the owners of shoe and clothing shops in Guaymas pointed out, their sales, largely in Cananea, had "dropped off alarmingly." With miners no longer buying cheap shoes, pants, and shirts, sales had spiraled downward during the latter half of 1907, from approximately 5,500 pesos in July to 3,500 pesos in December, as the accompanying chart shows.[41]

Sales in Guaymas, 1907

Month	Value in Pesos*
July	5,535.54
August	5,065.75
September	3,590.63
October	4,725.38
November	3,216.68
December	3,527.75

*The peso was equivalent to half a dollar.

As business declined, so did municipal revenues. Unbalanced municipal budgets were the result, and town after town went into the red. Cananea was among the first. By the fall of 1906, its mayor had begun to complain that expenditures exceeded income, a situation he blamed partly on the cost of quelling a labor strike in June. When the mines shut down, the town went bankrupt.[42] In every northern mining town,

similar stories were played out. With the closing of the mines at Caborca, in Altar—at Lista Blanca, La Calera, and Gran Provedora de
Cobre—its officials declared that Caborca had fallen on "hard times."
Revenues for 1908, they warned, would be but 66 percent of those of
1907, a most difficult year in itself. Subsequent events confirmed the
accuracy of their prediction; 1908 indeed was a bad year for the municipal treasury.[43] To the south, at Promontorios, revenues fell off to
such an extent that each year town officials had only enough funds to
cover the costs of the first six months.[44] At La Trinidad and adjoining
mining towns such as La Bufa, revenues failed to cover "the most ur-
gent needs."[45]

Inevitably, the new middle class felt the crunch. To meet budget
deficits, town officials began to pare expenditures to the bare bone.
Schools and jails, the twin bulwarks of middle-class society, got less
money; street maintenance fell off; electric lights were turned off earlier than usual; and so on. Once it became clear that even these cuts
would not balance the budget, there were but one thing to do: expunge
the public payroll of teachers, clerks, and other white-collar employees.
When the ax fell, the screams of anguish could be heard the length
and breadth of the state.

By 1908, every town linked to mining had wielded the same ax.
Cananea, the biggest employer among the mining towns, let go school-
teachers, judges, clerks, jailers, and other municipal employees.[46] At
Agua Prieta, child of the rail link with Nacozari, huge deficits still
plagued the budget even after public employees had been dismissed
and salaries cut. Municipal revenues, Agua Prieta's police chief lamented in 1908, were less than half of what they had been in the past.[47]
At La Aduana, where the closing of the Quintera mine left the treasury
bare, its council voted to shut down the school, dismiss its teacher, and
stop paying the salaries of treasurer, secretary, and judge. Only the
policeman survived the budget cuts.[48] At El Alacrán, designated a *comisaría*, even the constable lost his job when the mine closed.[49] Since many
mining camps fell into the category of *comisaría*, the plaint of the constable at El Alacrán had a familiar ring. Further, as events at La
Trinidad illustrated, this was not the first time costs were cut at the expense of public employees. They suffered at each mining debacle. During downswings, public servants were paid months late, paid only par-
tially, or not paid at all. If financial affairs did not improve, a *juez local*
("local judge") declared, public servants would have to serve without
pay. When that happened, he added, he would resign.[50] But whatever
the ill effects of earlier ups and downs, the nascent middle class in the
mining camps and towns met its Waterloo in the crisis of 1907.

A recovery of sorts, at least in copper, set in by 1908. In July of that year the mines at Cananea reopened.[51] Nacozari was back in business by 1910. Not all of the mines, however, opened their doors again. For the most part, the silver mines stayed shut. Even the recovery of copper was incomplete. Cananea had jobs for only 3,500 miners, and as late as 1910 some of its mines still were not operating. Ore produced that year totaled 45 million pounds, as against 60 million in 1905, a good year.[52] Not until 1911 did the 4C's again return a profit to its stock-holders. Up until then, as a company lawyer said, the mines at Cananea had experienced only a partial recovery. The American consul, in perhaps the understatement of the year, reported that mining had not been "very active."[53]

IV

The mining boom of the turn of the century came to resemble a game of billiards played in an American parlor. The principal players, almost always with Anglo or European surnames, spoke English and claimed United States citizenship. Mexican mine owners had a marginal role to enjoy. Yet this had not always been so. Ironically, at the start, in the 1860s or even a decade later, early North American investments may have helped to revive Mexican interest in mining. The flow of American capital into the mines had encouraged a few wealthy Mexicans to risk money of their own. Most of them, often scions of distinguished families, had made their money in commerce or in agriculture. The list included men such as Matías Alsúa and Fernando Cubillas, of the business circles of Guaymas; the Camou brothers, José de Aguilar, and Celedonio Ortiz of Hermosillo; and, of course, the Almadas from Alamos.[54]

Some of these early speculators eventually gave up on mining but those who stayed were joined by other Mexicans. Unlike the earlier in-vestors, the newcomers were mostly speculators on a shoestring. Among them were men destined to rebel against the Old Regime in Hermosillo. A few were jacks-of-all-trades. Ignacio Serrano, for in-stance, not only owned the mine at Villa de Rayón in the district of Ures, but its reduction works and its *tienda de raya* as well.[55] In Arizpe, Ylario Gabilondo, a majority stockholder, served as manager of the Cananea Mining Company, a property worth $300,000 in 1893.[56] In Alamos, Antonio Goycolea and Quirino Corbalá, stalwarts of old clans, owned mines. Goycolea's Zambona mine each year produced 2,000 tons of silver ore, all exported north of the border.[57] The gold mines at Mulatos, sold at a healthy price, made their owners, the Aguayo brothers, rich.[58] Until the end, the names of the old family clans dotted the list of mine owners. In addition to Goycolea and Corbalá, the names of mining promoters included Salido, Robinson Bours, Elías, Marcor, Esquer, Monteverde, Palomares, and, no less important, Ramón Corral, Rafael Izábal, and Colonel Lorenzo Torres, political heavyweights. Almost every prefect or former prefect dabbled in mining, from Balvanero Robles, Leonardo Gámez, and Ignacio Elías to the Encinas, Alfredo and Francisco, and Colonel Emilio Kosterlitsky, chief of the mounted police in Sonora. Near Nogales, Sandoval y Cía., a leading business house, owned the mines at Las Planchas.[59]

Despite the significance of these family names and, at first glance, their numerical importance, the list merely testified to the minority status of Mexican mine owners. Of the 1,535 mines in 1906, perhaps a third belonged to Mexicans.[60] Even these figures do not tell the full story. That the big social names or that leading political figures should own mines merely underscored the elite base of economic and political life. A tiny fraternity, joined to foreign speculators by ties of wealth or politics, indeed profited. Outside that charmed circle, few enjoyed similar opportunities. Miguel A. López, the Lampazos speculator who failed to sell his mine to James Douglas, was one of a "tiny band of Mexicans, perhaps the only one in his region, who had met the challenge of the Yankee." López purchased his mine with a loan from the Banco de Sonora, a testimony to his place on the social ladder, and employed Arthur Hendy and James Lord, names scarcely Mexican, as key subordinates.[61]

Mexican mine owners had an even less important part to play in 1910 than before. As Ramón Corral pointed out, Mexican mining legislation of the late nineteenth century favored foreigners. Mining concessions to foreigners had been generous. The favors had stimulated mining, according to Corral, but at the expense of small Mexican mine operators, who were relegated to a secondary status.[62] Ultimately, to cite Antonio Rivera, one of Sonora's venerated historians, "with few exceptions, and these among the least important, mining enterprises belonged to foreigners."[63] To make matters worse, the mining calamity of 1907 and the collapse of silver prices hit the small mine owner like a hurricane.[64] He simply could not weather the storm, "going under," as did Clemente Ibarra, owner of La Valencia mine at Promontorios.[65] In Alamos, nearly every mine owned by Mexicans had shut down by 1906. In Sahuaripa, the mines of the influencial Encinas clan, Antonio Moreno, and Antonio F. Porchas at La Trinidad had closed. Of the approximately sixty reduction works, just six had Mexican owners, one of them Corral. His enterprise, too, had stopped working.

CHAPTER 4

The Foreigner

I

The Chinese had a word for him, the man who was not of their own kind. They called him the "foreign devil." Devil or not, it was the foreigner who transformed mining in Sonora. With his capital and his willingness to risk his money as well as life and limb, he had a powerful hand in bringing about the metamorphosis in mining.

The foreigner, usually a Yankee, would not have come without inducements. When he arrived, he came to strike it rich; that was the nature of the mining speculator. Whether called a speculator, promoter, or "investor"—the description chosen was determined by one's nationality and politics—he began to arrive after the promulgation of the mining code of 1884. That legislation set aside old restrictions on the role permitted foreigners in the mining industry. Until then, the gist of the colonial *Ordenanzas* of 1783 had been kept on the statute books. While amended in 1842 to allow foreigners to acquire mines on nearly equal terms with Mexicans, the *Código Minero* left the ownership of the subsoil in the nation's hands.

Believing that only foreign capital could spur economic growth, the Mexican Congress altered the *Código Minero* in 1884, and included revisions specifically intended to encourage foreigners to invest in mining. Under the legislation, the states lost their old jurisdiction over mining. From now on, Mexico City would call the tune. In theory, the revised *Código* kept alive the proviso requiring "regular workings to retain title," stipulated "close government inspection," and barred

foreigners from owning land within twenty leagues of the border unless they obtained a special concession. Significantly, the legislation had
nothing to say about ownership of the subsoil. With the *Código* of 1884,
Mexico City gave its blessings to a laissez faire mining policy, a reflec-
tion of a shift in attitudes in ruling circles.[1]

II

The new mining code, helped along by the appearance of the iron
horse, begot the desired results. Foreigners, mostly North Americans,
began to cross the border in larger and larger numbers. They took over
abandoned mines or others only marginally exploited, buying them
from their Mexican owners. Spaniards and Mexicans had not exploited them for lack of capital, machinery, at times know-how and
public security, and, clearly, the means to transport the ores to market.
Foreigners also began to stake claims to new mines, often on public
lands. This meant obtaining concessions from Mexico City.

Mexican law always had banned the sale of lands near the border,
but Mexico City, naturally, could grant exemptions to "worthy and honorable" outlanders. Requests for exemptions came quick and fast because the northern lands often proved rich in ores or lush with green
pastures that were perfect for cattle. They were also just a hop, skip,
and a jump to markets on the other side. Since officials in Hermosillo
were usually asked for their opinion of the foreigner requesting the
exemption, they had much to say about who acquired mining properties or pasture lands. Interestingly, an early applicant was Alexander
Willard who, the governor of Sonora assured Mexico City, "had been
the consul of the United States in Guaymas for years." As his private
and public behavior demonstrated, he was "a good friend of Mexico,
a hard-working man of unblemished reputation, admired and respected by Mexicans."[2] When important Mexicans sold their border
properties, Hermosillo even helped them and their buyers to circumvent federal red tape.[3]

From the governor on down, officials in Hermosillo took pride in
the growing number of foreigners acquiring mining properties in their
state. To quote Governor Rafael Izábal—pleased as a child with a new
toy—so dramatic was their increase that Sonora "ranked at the top of
the list" of states with mining properties held by foreigners.[4] If that
was not enough, it stood next to the top in the number of land titles
granted. To Izábal, who often seemed to worship the ground Americans walked on, this was splendid news. Judging from the jump in ap-

plications in 1908, as the chart shows, not even the specter of harsh economic times had frightened foreign speculators who dreamed of rolling in money.

Mining Titles Registered[5]

Year	Number	Hectares
1900	1,400	12,994
1903	2,290	40,529
1906	3,341	60,870
1908	5,311	125,593
1909	5,335	120,904
1910	5,254	119,135

Getting title, however, proved to be the easiest of the hurdles the foreign speculator had to cross. Much more difficult were digging the ore out of the subsoil and transporting it to market at a profit. Nor was it a simple undertaking, as one American noted, to put up with corrupt officials, workers who knew nothing of mining techniques, unreliable subordinates, and, on top of everything else, bandits.[6] Or, to quote another American, his mine "was not the sort where one had merely to walk out with a pick and chop large pieces of silver off a convenient mountainside." To extract "a single speck of mineral" required transporting "a hundred thousand dollars [worth] of machinery across a barren desert."[7] Instead of the easy surface diggings celebrated in the folklore of adventurers, these testimonials indicate that Mexican mines generally required "large and extensive underground workings and beneficiation plants." This kind of operation called for wealthy speculators, men willing to risk large amounts of capital.[8]

Foreigners arrived in ever bigger numbers. Not just in Sonora, but in the entire Republic more Americans took up residence. Between 1895 and 1910, their numbers doubled from 10,222 to 20,693 for the country as a whole. Nearly three-fourths of them (72 percent) settled in the six border states and in Mexico City. The biggest upsurge occurred in Sonora, where, according to a Mexican historian, American residents went from 570 in 1895 to 3,164 in 1910.[9] The first substantial increase came in 1880 with the building of the Sonora Railway. Nearly half of the United States colony in Sonora, according to Consul Willard, arrived with the railroad. Willard, for his part, estimated the number of Americans "at about 700, not including the men in the employ of the Railway" and, as early as 1882 at approximately 1,500, one-half of the foreigners in Sonora. By his calculations, Americans held "half of the foreign capital invested."[10] The census of 1900, probably more accurate than the consul, listed 2,933 foreigners. Of that figure, 1,453 were Americans who, along with the Chinese (855), Governor Izábal pointed out, had proliferated considerably. By 1910, only Chihuahua had more Americans.[11]

In no other state was American control over the economy more visible. In 1910, as one author notes, Americans held a virtual monopoly on mining; owned vast tracts of land, including, in the Yaqui valley, tracts amply watered by the Yaqui River; had a foot in the door in commerce and "industry"; and had even invaded the fields of medicine and engineering.[12] If mining camps had a physician, he was, as a rule, an American—even in such isolated sites as Santa Elena, a dot on the mining map of Arizpe.[13] R. S. Vickers, an American in Moctezuma, illustrates his countrymen's impact on commerce and banking. Not only did Vickers own the largest general store in the district, he also held the Casa de Banco, the sole source of loans.[14]

As their accomplishments testify, the Americans fared well, although failures were not uncommon. They reopened colonial diggings abandoned long ago because of high water tables. They exploited copper deposits that had been earlier ignored because the price of copper was too low. With modern methods and machinery even deposits of low-grade ore could be worked at a profit.[15] The Yankee mining speculator belonged to a hardy breed of men, bold and willing to rough it. At times, their adventures drew the admiration of Mexicans. "Being next door to the United States," wrote a prefect of Arizpe, "we have in our midst . . . that endless tide of men who come with money to exploit our mines." They "invade our countryside, explore our mountains, and, when their wanderings yield results, they look for others who will finance their ventures and then set about extracting the ore." Encouraged by their success, "others joined them, elevating the mining industry in Arizpe to an importance unmatched by agriculture, cattle ranching, or lumbering."[16]

The Yankees, however, were not the pioneers on the mining scene. That distinction belonged to the British. One English group, La Sonora Silver Mining Company, claimed to have invested 100,000 pounds as early as 1867.[17] Until the 1880s, only a trickle of Americans went south. In 1872, the American consul reported just one large American mining company, at San Marcial, and "many others in a limited way."[18] Capitalists, he explained, refused to invest under what he called a "system of oppressive taxation . . . without . . . protection or security for life or property . . . and a general lack of confidence in . . . the government."[19]

The English enjoyed only a fleeting supremacy. The picture began to change in the 1880s, undoubtedly animated by the revisions in the Código Minero. Of the 1,200 or so foreigners in 1885, by one calculation, half were Americans "engaged almost exclusively in mining" in one way or another. Their capital made up one-half of the entire foreign investment in Sonora.[20] At that time, fifteen major groups, all incorporated north of the border, owned mining properties in Sonora; the English had but four.[21] Among the new companies were Minas Prietas, North Mexico Mining, and Santa María, with home offices in New York. La Prieta and La Quintera, both in Alamos, had been sold for 200,000 pesos each to American mining promoters.[22]

By 1892, 30 percent of the American capital invested in Mexican mining was in Sonora.[23] On the eve of the Great Rebellion of 1910, Sonora, outranked only by Coahuila, had $37.5 million invested by Americans, $27 million in mining alone.[24] Much of the capital in Coahuila, furthermore, was claimed by the Mexican International Railroad, a foreign enterprise not confined to the limits of the state. Mining, with most of its capital American, had become the principal industry of Sonora.[25] With just an occasional exception, the American mining companies, naturally with American boards of directors, had their home offices in cities such as New York, Chicago, Los Angeles, Denver, and San Francisco. Nearly all had ties with the giant American corporations: American Smelting and Refining (ASARCO), a Guggenheim venture; Phelps Dodge; and Greene Consolidated Copper Company.[26]

III

For all intents and purposes, mining operations at Cananea and Nacozari might just as well have been located in the United States. Both had spur lines to the border, but none with Mexican cities; Nacozari had its smelter in Douglas; and the two mining towns lived in splendid isolation from the rest of Mexico. The two companies, Phelps Dodge and the 4C's, as well as sister companies to the south, "enjoyed a degree of extraterritoriality which made a mockery of the international boundary." Authorities in Hermosillo had a marginal say in the affairs of these enterprises and, to make matters worse for Mexican nationalists, local public officials willingly did the bidding of the Yankee company bosses.[27] Cananea, Nacozari, and La Colorada, the leading mining centers of their time, epitomized these bastions of Yankee ambition.

The father of the Cananea copper kingdom, William C. Greene, a man of independent bent and bold deeds, had spent years in northern Sonora. He had dabbled in cattle ranching in company with H. Canfield, running horses and cattle at a ranch called Ojo de Agua. Mexican authorities suspected Greene and Canfield of keeping stolen horses.[28] In the 1890s, Greene learned of the copper deposits at a place known as Rancho Cananea, hardly news since colonial Spaniards had known of them. In the middle of the nineteenth century, Ignacio Pesqueira, the political boss of Sonora, had purchased the Rancho, attempted to work its mines, and built a small ore concentrator. Unable to turn a profit, Pesqueira gave up the venture. Upon his death, Pesqueira's widow (now married to an American) sold Greene the property for $47,000, a deal that ranks with the notorious bargains of history.[29] Greene came along at just the right time, when electricity had given copper mining new vigor. Without sufficient funds of his own, Greene had to find backers to get his venture started. Ultimately, he organized the Greene Consolidated Copper Company, incorporated in West Virginia, to raise the capital for his Cananea Consolidated Copper Company.

Greene, to cite the mumbo jumbo current at the time, was the most prominent "nonresident capitalist in Sonora." These men, usually East Coast potentates, invested capital in faraway lands but stayed home. Greene only sporadically visited his costly Cananea home, which was designed to resemble a mansion of the American midwest. To quote one description of his role as "an absentee emperor," Greene lived in New York City, with "an office near Wall Street, and devoted his time to the complementary tasks of raising money and placating worried stockholders."[30] His copper ores gave Greene world renown but he had other irons in the fire. In Arizona, Greene had acquired thousands of acres of land, specifically the San Rafael del Valle grant, from the Camou family of Hermosillo. To feed his burgeoning population at Cananea, he established the Cananea Cattle Company and the Turkey Track Cattle Company, while his Sierra Madre Land and Lumber Company acquired timber concessions in Sonora and Chihuahua. To carry his ores to the border, he put together the Cananea, Yaqui River, and Pacific Railroad, a trunk line that would eventually run south into the Yaqui Valley and east to join the Mexican Central between Ciudad Juárez and Chihuahua City. He installed the telephones in Cananea and ran the system at a profit, as he did the power plant that furnished electricity to the town.[31] In one case, to keep out Mexican competitors—merchants with meat of their own to sell—he erected a barbed-wire fence around his property and stationed guards at its gates.

Greene, in essence, ran a small empire. In 1902, he prevailed upon Hermosillo to declare Cananea a *municipio*, then kept for himself ninety of the best of the 150 lots included in the city plan. The land turned over to the town was sliced up by gullies and ravines. Municipal authorities, whom Greene and his entourage picked, had no jurisdiction over his mining properties, although they lay within their official territory. He appointed the police chief, the infamous Pablo Rubio, and told him what to do. To the 3,000 hectares of mining lands, Greene added 150,000 hectares of cattle and timber lands.[32]

Greene managed his fiefdom as though it were an enclave of the United States. One could easily travel from Cananea to towns across the border but not to those in Sonora. An arrogant man, he paid scant heed to Mexican law or to Mexican officials, whom he belittled in private. At the time of the labor strike of 1906, he put pressure upon Governor Izábal to use armed Americans to break it up.[33] Long before that, testified a former cook of his, Greene had slipped rifles and ammunition into Cananea clandestinely on his private Pullman car.[34]

Mr. Greene, as he was known, had written a Yankee scenario for Mexico. He never appointed Mexicans to key jobs in his company. Without exception, its superintendent, general manager, engineers, and labor bosses were Yankees. In 1905, for example, the list of top employees read: Kirk, superintendent; Young, secretary; Campbell, treasurer; Lloyd, manager; Butzon, hospital chief; Carpenter, assistant hospital chief; MacManus, president of Greene's Banco de Cananea; Hallihan, railway head; and Cole, chief of the ore concentrators. The man in charge of the Club Cananea, where Yankee bosses and an occasional visiting Mexican dignitary ate and drank, was a Mr. Brown; earlier, Frank L. Proctor, Greene's father-in-law, had been its manager.[35] George Young, a New York native who was typical of Greene's subordinates, organized the accounting system for the mining operation. Able and politically astute, Young won Greene's confidence, eventually becoming his right-hand man. He rose through the ranks to become secretary and later treasurer. Six months after coming to Cananea, he brought his wife and daughters to join him. He sent his daughters to the local American school and hired a Chinese cook whose name his family never bothered to learn, while his wife, not one to offend anybody, spent her days with the other American wives in town.[36] Other Americans ultimately cast their lot with Mr. Greene: merchants, hotel owners, bartenders and saloonkeepers, bankers, boarding house entrepreneurs, and their kin.[37] Cananea, certainly the colony on La Mesa, had a distinctly made-in-the-U.S.A. aura. Over this enclave, Mr. Greene, whether in New York or Cananea, presided.

The bosses of Nacozari were cast in a similar mold. Not one of them, however, towered over the town's history as Mr. Greene did at Cananea. As they had nearly everywhere in Sonora, Spaniards originally discovered the local mineral deposits. As at Cananea, exploitation of the ores awaited the electrical age and the locomotive. In 1867, U. B. Treaner, an American, purchased the Nacozari properties. In the mid-eighties, the Moctezuma Concentrating Company, a small New Jersey outfit, bought them from Treaner and with varying success tried for the better part of a decade to exploit them. John Wein, another American, bought the properties from the New Jersey group, and sold them to Meyer Guggenheim and his sons who, for their part, turned them over to the Phelps Dodge Corporation. Louis D. Ricketts, a mining engineer, earlier identified with the Copper Queen Mine in Bisbee, had urged Phelps Dodge to purchase the property.[38]

Having accepted his advice, Phelps Dodge named Ricketts general manager of the Moctezuma Copper Company, its affiliate. In less than a decade, Ricketts and his New York backers transformed "a semi-wilderness into one of the largest and most active mining centers" in Mexico. Its profitable ventures at Nacozari and Bisbee encouraged Phelps Dodge to commit itself "lock, stock, and barrel to its western" copper operations.[39] By 1910, with an initial investment of 450,000 pesos (about $225,000) at Nacozari, Phelps Dodge controlled mines, an ore concentrator, and a railroad, valued at $2.2 million.[40]

Unlike Greene, who was neither a mining engineer nor a college graduate, Ricketts carried impressive credentials. At Princeton, he had earned a bachelor of science degree and a doctorate in chemistry. A tall, thin man, he had spent years wandering about the desert in search of mineral ores. Ricketts cared not a jot for the way he looked. In his worn khaki pants and tattered, blue-cotton shirt, people who did not know him often mistook him for just another "desert rat" down on his luck. Until 1901, when he resigned to supervise the rebuilding of the mill at Cananea, Ricketts piloted the copper ship of Nacozari.[41] James Douglas, another founder of the thriving enterprise, was a mining engineer and metallurgist born in Canada. He was named for his father, a member of the Royal College of Surgeons in London with a degree in medicine from Edinburgh University. This medical man had once joined a filibustering expedition to Nicaragua. James, his son, studied chemistry, geology, and mineralogy at Quebec, and then spent nine months in Chile installing a copper-treating works. Journeying to Arizona, he joined the Copper Queen staff in the late 1880s and became an American. By the time of his death in 1918, he had contributed more "to the metallurgical success of more big copper companies than any other mining engineer of his generation."[42]

Ricketts and Douglas, like Greene at Cananea, were Americans of their time. This was the age of the New Imperialism, of Rudyard Kipling and his famous remark justifying imperialism as "the white man's burden." In Washington, Theodore Roosevelt barely hid his disdain for Spanish-Americans. Douglas and Ricketts, like their parent company, Phelps Dodge, had no stomach for labor unions, a disposition that dictated policy at the Copper Queen Mine. The Queen, not unimportantly, had a large body of miners from Sonora. Douglas, who was associated with Nacozari longer than Ricketts, handled his miners in the manner of an oriental potentate. They had only to work and to follow orders. When Governor Izábal permitted Arizona Rangers to help squelch the strike at Cananea, Douglas wired his approval. "Americans and Mexicans," he congratulated the governor, "should be eternally grateful because you took on the responsibility . . . of accepting the offer of Americans at Naco to go to Cananea . . . to conserve order."[43] That armed foreigners had invaded the territory of a supposedly sovereign nation bothered him not a bit. Douglas watched expenditures at Nacozari with wary eyes, never spending a dime unless the purchase had a "practical application."[44]

Like the Cananea of Mr. Greene, the Nacozari of Ricketts and Douglas sported American trademarks. An American colony, its railroad joined it to Douglas, where Phelps Dodge had its smelter. Only horse and wagon trails went south from Nacozari. As at Cananea, from Douglas on down, Yankees held the key jobs at Nacozari. The list of 1905 included Williams, assistant superintendent; Strachen, ore concentrator; Kelly, railroad; Kingdom, labor boss; Conway, power plant; Manville, electrical system; McLaughlin, company store; and Ayer, physician. When Douglas retired in 1909, he left his son in charge.[45]

The complex of mines at La Colorada and Minas Prietas, ranking next in importance to the copper towns of the north, had American ownership, too. Less than a mile apart, the mines had a history dating back to colonial days. Richard Johnson sold them at a profit for $200,000, having recently purchased them for less. The annual report for 1893 of the American consul in Guaymas called the mines at La Colorada the "most valuable . . . in Sonora."[46] Its eventual owners were from Cleveland, Ohio, capitalists who also controlled Minas Prietas.[47] An English adventurer, Federico H. Seymour, helped get things under way at Minas Prietas, first by buying and selling mining property and then, to promote his own mining claims, by building a spur line to Estación Torres on the route of the Sonora Railway.[48] The spur line helped transform La Colorada into a tiny metropolis, attracting so many Americans that "the principal thoroughfare was named Main Street."[49] Wells Fargo, in a decision that confirmed the importance of the spur line, installed an office at Estación Torres, named after one of the political bigwigs of Sonora.

Something of an international promoter, Seymour arrived in Sonora in 1890 from Spain, where he had worked in mining.[50] At a small hamlet south of Nogales, Seymour became superintendent of the Imuris Mines Limited, briefly the largest mining venture in Magdalena. Its mines enjoyed such exotic names as Sheba, Erin, and Ophir, appellations anything but Mexican. As boss of Imuris, Seymour acquired a dubious reputation for making pious declarations of good intentions and then racking up a sordid record of labor practices.[51] He stopped at nothing when he wanted to fatten his purse. When the Imuris business turned unprofitable, Seymour hauled its railway and mill south to Minas Prietas.

The Grand Central Mining Company, where Seymour took his railroad, had been put together by The Exploration Company, an American outfit. Some time later, the Mines Company of America absorbed the Grand Central Mine and the Creston Colorado Company. A host of other American enterprises, some absorbed by the Mines Company of America, operated in the vicinity of Minas Prietas: Charles Butters, Prietas Development, Victoria Gold Mining, Gold Bullion Mining and Development, U.S. Graphite, Santa Rosa Mining, and Don Ygnacio. Like their sister companies in Nacozari and Cananea, their officials, from superintendent to labor boss, had American names: E. A. Price, Howell Hinds, Gerald E. Ward, H. Webster, and E. F. Harris, to name but a few. No Mexican held a key post.

But Americans did not own and manage just the big operations at Cananea, Nacozari, and La Colorada; they were everywhere, "from Indus to the pole." In the hinterland of Río Chico, the Dura Concentrating Company owned every one of the silver mines: La Prieta, Cobrizo, Cosmopólito, Dura, Ramona, San Felipe, Agua Salta, and California.[52] In Alamos, they controlled virtually every mine of significance. Both of the old colonial mines of Alamos had foreign masters: the Quintera Mining Company and Promontorio Consolidated Mining Company.[53] Other Americans owned The Erbe Exploration Company and Los Alamos Milling Company.[54] By 1910, similarly, hordes of Yankee mining prospectors, the consul at Guaymas reported, had "scattered throughout the Yaqui country."[55]

North and east of Alamos, Americans had staked out mines in Sahuaripa, the powerful Anaconda Copper Company, for example, at Bacanora.[56] At La Trinidad, the principal mining center of the district, the diplomas and degrees of the employees in the mine companies read like a *Who's Who* of universities and colleges in the United States.[57]

As early as 1890, so many Yankees lived in Tierra de Bermudes, a mining hamlet under the political jurisdiction of La Trinidad, that its mayor, when appointing the police chief, his subordinate, and a local judge, picked "Santiago" Clark, "Reyes" Clark, and "Alejandro" Moore.[58] Upon learning of these appointments, Ramón Corral, the *secretario de estado*, admonished the mayor that if these men were not Mexican citizens they could not hold public office.[59] Even so, when a Mexican proved ineligible to be the local judge in Tierra de Bermudes, the mayor replaced him with "Emeterio" Clark.[60] That same year, "Gabriel" O. Robinson was elected mayor of La Trinidad.[61] In the mining region of La Trinidad, Yankee entrepreneurs either controlled the political machinery directly, or indirectly by telling Mexican officials what to do.

Farther north, the Richfield Mining Company exploited what was believed at the time to be "one of the richest" copper deposits in Sonora.[62] Americans worked El Bajío and Las Amarillas, mines in La Alameda, as well as La Sultana, Santa Rosalía, El Oro, El Negocio, and San Rafael. In Arizpe, the gold and silver mines of Santa Helena, enriched by steam power and a mill, were American property. Among other significant American mining ventures in Arizpe were Hoffman y Claud, Indiana Copper Company, and La Paloma. One Yankee promoter, R. C. Clancy, operated a gold and silver mine at El Basaítegui, a mining town that in 1905 had 503 inhabitants, more than a third of the population of Arizpe, the largest town in the district.[63] In Moctezuma, two Yankee adventurers stumbled upon rich veins of silver between Nacozari and Agua Prieta; they formed El Tigre Mining Company, a subsidiary of The Lucky Tiger Combination Gold Mining Company. Wealthy speculators from Missouri controlled the venture, which yielded profits of $167,644 in 1907. Notwithstanding the economic crisis of that year, three years later the capacity of its concentrating mill, just built in 1908, had to be doubled.[64] Southwest of the town of Cumpas, the Transvaal Copper Mining Company, organized in 1902 in Cincinnati, Ohio, controlled the Piedra Verde group; the copper, silver, and gold mines of Juanita; Cobre Rico; La Roma; La Grande; Ultima Chanza; and Buckeye. The company built a mill in 1906.[65] Meanwhile, George F. Woodward, a leading mining entrepreneur in Moctezuma, built and managed the principal hotel in town and its best restaurant, and ran stagecoaches between Moctezuma and Nacozari.[66]

To the west, diverse American mining promoters established themselves in Magdalena district. Their holdings included the Mineral de Cerro Prieto of the Banco de Oro Mining Company, La Higuera Mining Company, and the Pembrake Mining Company, among many others. A few miles south of Nogales, the Hays Mining, Milling, and Lumber Company, an outfit from Washington, D.C., owned 5,000 acres of "fine timberland" with "numerous large and well-defined ledges of copper, carrying gold and silver" in the subsoil.[67] The Yerkes Gold Mining Company, perhaps the biggest in Altar, the desert district to the west of Magdalena, had American owners, as did El Rosario and Las Palomas on the outskirts of Caborca, among others.[68]

Not only did Americans own the mines, but also the *haciendas de beneficio*, the reduction works. Of the sixty or so in Sonora, all but seven had foreign owners, fifty-one of them American.[69] The northern districts, not surprisingly, had the largest number. Altar, with 11, headed the list, followed by Hermosillo with 8, and Magdalena, Moctezuma, and Ures with 7.[70] Ironically, although Sonora ranked among the states with the most reduction works, most mining promoters still had to pay exorbitant fees to transport raw ore from the mines to the closest railroad station.[71] Only smelters, plants melting raw ore down to metal, would have overcome that problem. With the exception of the plant at Cananea, Americans did not build smelters in Sonora. The American mining companies, in short, dug the ore out of the subsoil and shipped it raw to plants across the border, a system unchanged since its inception in 1886.[72]

CHAPTER 5

Legacy of the Yankee

I

Until after the turn of the century, Mexicans welcomed foreigners, usually Yankees, with open arms. Gradually, as more and more of them arrived, nearly always hellbent on striking it rich, Mexican attitudes underwent a change. As a rule, the more North Americans in a place, the more dramatic the shift in opinion. Mexican nationalism, dormant since the war against the French in the 1860s, began to revive.[1]

From the start, the appearance of the Yankee in Sonora had awakened misgivings. Already, in 1881, just as the tide of Americans was beginning to rise, General Bernardo Reyes, military commander in Sonora, warned of its consequences. The flood of Yankees, as he phrased it, "threatened to engulf the Mexican element."[2] Archival records leave no room for doubt: Mexicans in Sonora, whatever the benefits the outsider conferred, mistrusted him. That distrust flourished despite the official welcome bestowed on him.

II

The relationship of Sonorans and Americans had always been a curious mixture of admiration, fear, and envy. With the passage of time, fear and envy got the upper hand. By 1906, when describing the confrontation at Cananea between the Yankee bosses and the Mexican

workers, a dumbfounded American vice consul talked of "a con-
strained state of mind . . . noticeable on every hand" and of "a feeling
bordering on race hatred." He knew of what he spoke: he had watched
and heard the strikers at Cananea.[3] The strike was a failure, history
tells us, but not every American at Cananea thought so at the time. A
number of them, fearing reprisals by angry Mexicans, fled the mining
town for the safer pastures of Arizona.[4] What had happened to make
the Yankees, the rich and daring who had spurred Sonora to economic
growth, unwelcome in their adopted home?

Sheer numbers, undoubtedly, partly explain the turnabout. Too
many Americans had come to Sonora. Even if every one of them had
behaved properly, inevitably they would have antagonized their hosts.
They were simply just too visible a minority. Worse still, the Americans
kept their success—the good jobs in the mines and railroads that they
built—to themselves.[5] At Cananea, where they were highly visible, they
enjoyed a monopoly of the best posts in the 4C's and its subsidiaries,
controlled the most profitable stores and the most elegant saloons, and,
to quote blunt-spoken Governor Rafael Izábal, enjoyed the delights of
the most expensive whores.

They also snubbed the locals. The "*gringos* did not mix with the Mexican," certainly not with the working class. The Yankee, though a
foreigner, arrived in Sonora as if he were coming home, wrote a distinguished Mexican scholar.[6] Even when he was not the boss, he worked
for men who spoke his language and worshiped his gods, men who
shared his background and prejudices, including a belief in his own
racial superiority. The Yankee thought of himself as a *conquistador* and
demanded the privileges of a conqueror. Sonorans who were ambitious and opportunistic, or who believed the salvation of their state was
in the hands of the outsider, readily gave up the tribute demanded.
Scions of the elite families not infrequently jumped at the chance to
rub elbows with the wealthy *gringo*. It mattered not that he might be a
country hick who had suddenly struck it rich. In Cananea, in the times
of a William C. Greene, Americans and Mexican *politicos* alike turned
out to celebrate the Fourth of July, a major event in the town.[7]

The revival of mining also undermined the old social structure.
Economic growth weakened the fabric of society, and ultimately
frightened Mexicans. Not only did mining bring Yankees, it opened the
doors to other outsiders, Mexicans not native to the community. "Outsiders of disrepute," complained the local citizens of Río Chico in 1890,
a town "blessed" by the mining boom, "have taken over our town. Who
are these men who now run the government of Río Chico? We do not
know them." They were "*forasteros*, outlanders who marched to the tune

of the mining companies in our midst." They had but one goal in mind: "by hook or crook to make money, no matter what the fate of the town."[8] In Río Chico, a new day had dawned, overcast and gloomy; it was a harbinger of darker days to come.

Yankees of diverse types came to Sonora, from wealthy graduates of Ivy League colleges to Texas rednecks. Whether rich or poor, some adapted to their new world, played by its rules, and made Mexican friends. A handful married Mexican women and fathered Mexicans with English surnames, as the Robinson, Johnson, and Randall families, stalwarts of Guaymas by 1910, testify. But another type also made its bow, the kind who abjured "ideas . . . concerning the equality of men and let their prejudices run free."[9] They adhered, in the manner of Kipling, to the doctrine of white infallibility and Mexican inferiority.

At Nacozari, these types had the final say, backed by their gospel of "racial" supremacy, to quote Ralph M. Ingersoll, an engineering graduate of Yale who wrote a book about his life in the mining town. Prestige at the mine stood on an American pyramid, with the white superintendent at the pinnacle and the Mexican laborers at the bottom. The mine "was divided into sections, three or four levels underground to a section," with "an American foreman and an engineer" over each. Upon arriving at Nacozari, Ingersoll learned "that all Mexicans are children and have to be treated accordingly."[10] This attitude, "as American as apple pie" in the Southwest, had staunch advocates. In 1883, to cite one instance, the *Arizona Daily Star* quoted a Sam Lewis, a man with years of experience in Sonora. Lewis spoke "of American miners . . . often in the habit of behaving as if the fact of their being Americans served to require servility from the Mexicans." After having gotten "drunk on *mezcal*," they would "start to take the town in, insulting men and women alike."[11]

Time and again, such racial arrogance led to the humiliation of Mexicans, especially the poor. In mining, one of its manifestations was the strip search. Thinking of Mexicans as potential thieves, mine bosses compelled their workers to strip naked after a day's work in the bowels of the earth. In this manner, Americans thought, the workers could take away no gold or silver ore. This practice was as old as the attitudes that justified it, so deeply ingrained that its implications went by unnoticed. From the perspective of the whites, it was logical to strip brown men naked, as if these Mexicans were not men at all, but mere beasts who would feel no shame at their nakedness. "The ore at the Creston Colorada mine is so exceedingly rich," the American consul waxed eloquently in 1893, "that the mines are closed during the night, and when opened during the day all laborers are searched as they come out."[12] Mexican miners, however, did not take kindly to the practice of publicly disrobing in order to be certified honest by Yankees. Miners at Las Chispas, a camp in Arizpe, made that abundantly clear. In 1906, they went on strike rather than take off their clothes.[13] They lost their case but two years later they refused again to enter the mine, saying they would not "walk naked from one room to another in order to be searched."[14] This custom, "immoral and indecent" according to the prefect of Arizpe, survived—with the compliance of the Mexican constable who claimed the practice was "voluntary." Which was to say, the prefect interposed, that poor miners had no choice but "to work under degrading, humiliating, and even immoral conditions."[15] Until the end, however, nothing was done to put an end to the practice.

Many Americans who entered Sonora held Mexican labor in low esteem. To their way of thinking, as one of them said, it was a "particularly unsatisfactory . . . commodity."[16] The litany of complaints went on and on. Mexicans could not be counted on to work a full day; they were unreliable; they drank too much; they followed orders poorly, or they simply looked for ways to "loaf." Mexicans had but one right: "to work or move on."[17] The strike at Cananea shocked Americans. After all, if the Mexicans were unhappy they should have "looked for another job." Yet the Mexicans at Cananea should have known what was in store for them. The men who ran Cananea and other mining camps, like their brethren across the border, were not inclined to amend their ideas. To them, labor was just another commodity to be bought and sold. That attitude had ruled in 1902 when a strike of American construction laborers halted work on the plant at Cananea. To break the strike, company officials imported scabs from Colorado.[18]

To make matters worse, most of the Americans could not talk to their Mexican neighbors. They knew no Spanish and seldom bothered to learn it. To their way of thinking, the Lord had made English the cosmic language. At best, they spoke a "pidgin Spanish."[19] As one Yankee adventurer applying for a special concession from Hermosillo bluntly stated, "I do not speak or read Spanish."[20] When dealing with these Americans, Mexicans spoke to them in English if they could; if unable to speak English they found a Mexican who did or communicated with a mixture of sign language and pidgin English. American wives were no different from their husbands. At Nacozari, remembered Ingersoll, "with one or two exceptions, none of the women spoke even tolerable Spanish, or cared to." Like their husbands, brothers, and fathers, "they were strongly convinced of the inferiority of the Mexicans, their chief criticism . . . being that they were clumsy waiting on tables and did not know how to make beds."[21]

The typical Yankee labor boss, manager, or superintendent of a mining camp seldom captured the respect of his workers. Quite the opposite. Wary Mexicans kept their distance and left behind unflattering descriptions for the record. Recalled Pedro M. Almada, a future rebel soldier who kept a journal of his adventures, the superintendent of La Colorada "was a *gringo* with the traits of a bulldog." When "I gave him my papers, he read them carefully, not once stopping from chewing the wad of tobacco in his mouth." He asked if "I could do the job, at 3 pesos a day, from sunrise to sundown, that is, eleven hours of work."[22]

The behavior of Americans went beyond mere haughtiness, callousness, or scorn. To many Mexicans, the Yankee proved an unkind, indeed often cruel, boss. In the town of Promontorios, so poorly did one boss treat his workers that the mayor, as he told the prefect of Alamos, had to "read the riot act to him." If he continued to abuse his workers, the mayor had admonished the labor boss, "they could easily tire of his injustices and, to his later regret, turn on him."[23] One of the demands of the strikers at Cananea was the dismissal of American foremen who were particularly obnoxious.[24] Less than a year afterward, forty-seven Mexicans were again saying that they would not work for two Americans they found arrogant.[25] Authorities in Hermosillo, not wishing a repetition of the labor troubles, told the mayor of Cananea to see to it that the company fired the two tyrants. On this occasion, unlike the earlier one, the company honored the demands of Hermosillo.[26] At El Alacrán, a mining camp in Arizpe, even its constable, who was at least partly in cahoots with management, testified in 1908 to the "despotic and tyrannical character" of the general manager, who "dealt harshly with his workers while ignoring Mexican laws and local authority." Unless he changed his ways, the constable feared, the workers "might easily decide to punish his insolence."[27] Before Phelps Dodge took over, an American labor boss at Nacozari hit a man with the butt of his rifle, calling him a "drunken Mexican." The American superintendent maintained that this incident—which he characterized as Mexican defiance of the labor boss—demonstrated that "the lives and property of Americans in this place were unsafe." He wanted the Mexican military to come and defend them.[28] In a memoir, a Mexican who worked in a mine near Bacanora, a town in Sahuaripa, recalled an altercation with a boss. "While we were hard at work, the foreman, a *gringo* of ill repute, appeared suddenly," he wrote. The American was angry, the writer remembered, and shouting profanities. "I don't speak English but I understood perfectly well his *gademes* and *sanabichis*," he wrote. The two quarreled and on the following morning they "summoned me to the office of the superintendent, a *gringo* of course, who fired me."[29]

The Mexican who looked for work in a mine, obviously, needed a job. Mining labor, no matter what apologists might say in its defense, had little to recommend it. Although it paid well, it was hard and dangerous work, hardly conducive to living to a ripe old age. Lung diseases, especially the dreaded twins silicosis and tuberculosis, ran rampant, while the dampness of the mines invited arthritis and other ills of the bones. Mine accidents occurred frequently. That miners earned more than they could get for tilling the fields only partly compensated for the arduous physical toil demanded of them. Mexican miners not only had to risk their lives, they had to do the most backbreaking jobs. Foreign workers, if asked to undertake these jobs, often refused.[30]

For doing the same work, foreigners got better pay, to the anger of Mexicans. Not all Americans in the mining industry, after all, had jobs as labor bosses, technicians, or managers. The majority, in reality, were just miners, skilled at their work but nonetheless laborers—mechanics, drillers, and ditchers.[31] Americans earned fatter paychecks than Mexicans for doing these jobs. At the time of the labor troubles at Cananea, when William C. Greene offered to pay Mexican miners more, Porfirio Díaz, the president of Mexico, said no. "Don't stir up my stud of horses" was his famous reply.[32]

The disparity in wages, the often heavy-handed treatment by American bosses, and the harshness of the work itself created deep resentment that festered like a sore. From time to time, the bitterness turned into anger and exploded into deeds. Mexicans retaliated the best they could, by staying home on work days, neglecting company property, abusing machinery and equipment, or on occasion, by hiding gold and silver ore on their persons when they left the mines. Sometimes Mexican anger led to more flagrant acts, such as a 1908 incident at the Santa Rosa Mining Company, not far from Agua Prieta. Disgruntled Mexicans planted dynamite under the company buildings, including the house where the superintendent, foreman, head carpenter, and engineer, all Americans, ate. The explosion rocked the camp at mealtime, and barely missed killing them. Local officials customarily sided with management, but this time they put the blame for the bombing on company hiring practices.[33] Such violent incidents were probably isolated, but their causes were not. A letter from the Partido Liberal Mexicano, critical of labor policy at Nacozari, put the matter this way: abuses "underlay the exploitation and humiliation of the Mexican people."[34]

At Cananea in 1906 Greene, Dwight, Lindly, and the Brown brothers, kingpins of the 4C's, had Mexican strikers beat up.[35] Others shot and killed them.[36] When miners and their neighbors tried to buy land for *ejidos* at Minas Prietas, management refused to part with any, even though authorities in Hermosillo favored the sale.[37] When the

Compañía Minera de Cerro Blanco shut down, the American boss had the houses of the workers torn down because they were on company property, conveniently forgetting that he had made their construction a condition for employment.[38] The constable at Las Cabezas said in a telegram that the manager "wants me to help move the homes of thirty miners on land the company plans to use to build a foundry." The miners, who had built their homes with the well wishes of the previous manager, were willing to move on—if the company covered their losses or helped them move. The manager refused any help and threatened to fire the men if they disobeyed him. "Today I learned," the constable added, "that the day before yesterday, while one of the homeowners was away, the foreman had his men tear it down." The land where the manager wanted the homeowners to move, in the opinion of the constable, was "the least usable of company property."[39]

One hot spot was Cerro Prieto in Magdalena, site of the American Banco de Oro Mining Company, which acquired a one-square league of land by right of public domain. Its manager wanted to evict anyone who was caught selling liquor without notifying the manager in advance. This official planned to give the violators just four days to pack up and leave. According to the local constable, the American told him to use whatever force was necessary to get the Mexicans "out of their houses and out of the mining camp, family and furniture included." But the Mexicans threatened to defend themselves with guns. Were the constable to attempt to evict them, the Mexicans in the vicinity would consider it "an outrage, tempers would flare, and armed clashes break out, the constable reported."[40] Authorities in Hermosillo, in the meantime, told the company to appeal to the courts for a settlement.[41] The manager, however, took matters into his own hands, getting the constable, according to one bitter homeowner, "to tear down his house, in company with four policemen and six men with picks and shovels." Though the owner was sick in bed, his furniture and household goods were tossed out into the street. "This type of behavior, carried out by a Mexican official blind to his obligations," the angry victim wrote the governor, "[and] in compliance with the wishes of the representative of a foreign business seeking to strike it rich in Mexico, which neither respected its laws nor its citizens, must be stopped."[42] Despite the angry outburst, a month later the company demolished another dwelling, the property of a merchant, "a large one built of adobe and worth over a thousand pesos." It was destroyed, the owner explained, by "forty Mexican workers and a Chinese boss."[43]

At Nacozari, the superintendent of the Moctezuma Copper Company, when preparing to grade a railroad bed, had his men "tear down sixty homes in just forty-eight hours, giving their owners only two hours' notice." The constable, who reported this act to Hermosillo, added that the company lawyer, a Mexican who carried out the orders of the company, claimed to have the backing of Rafael Izábal, the governor of Sonora. Apparently he did, because the constable never received orders to halt the evictions.[44]

Company arrogance, however, went beyond merely wrecking homes, as the story of San Francisco de los Llanos testifies. It was a mining camp, owned lock, stock, and barrel by the Llanos Consolidated Mining Company, a United States enterprise. Sitting amidst the hot, dusty desert of Altar, Llanos had rectangular streets, a *zocalo* or plaza, and, most importantly, a faucet, the sole source of water in town, jutting up squarely in its center. The company added to its income by selling the water to its workers. In 1909, four years after installing the faucet, the company decided to move it from its place in the plaza to the outskirts of town. The workers, most of whom lived near the faucet, would now have to buy their water, at a higher price of course, from vendors who would haul it into town. When the company refused to keep the faucet in its rightful place, the miners asked the town constable to intervene.

In reply, the company manager told the constable that it had become simply too costly to maintain the faucet in its old location and, at the same time, keep a man there to sell its water. Mining operations, he explained, had moved to the far side of town. Attempting to placate both sides, the constable offered to contribute twenty-five pesos a month from the town's treasury to pay for the keeper of the water faucet. The manager, "a haughty individual," according to the workers, refused, saying "it was not in the best interest of the company to do so." Not until the prefect of Altar prevailed upon the governor to speak to the manager did he restore the faucet to its "rightful" site. This occurred in May.[45] One month later, the company, perhaps in retaliation, cut the wages of certain workers, many of whom walked off their jobs rather than work for less money.[46] One explanation for the troubles that befell mining after 1910, insists a Mexican historian, was that miners by droves went off to join the rebel armies.[47] They voiced their disenchantment with strip searches and peripatetic water faucets with their rifles.

But foreign arrogance did not stop at the mines. It pervaded every sphere the outlander touched. On the railway not far from Imuris, for example, an American train conductor, who spoke not a word of Spanish, stuffed a ten-year-old boy into a gunnysack, tied it shut, and wrote C.O.D. on its tag. What crime had the Mexican child committed?

He had smuggled himself aboard without buying a ticket![48] On another occasion, an American conductor, again in the vicinity of Imuris, beat a Mexican and threw him off the moving train. Like the boy, he had had no ticket. Farmers discovered his body a few days later.[49]

III

The mining revival, to the chagrin of its Mexican disciples, brought with it untold scores of half-baked schemes, ill-planned ventures, and, the record shows, fraudulent deals. As Tomás Robinson Bours, a scion of Alamos and Guaymas, once pontificated, La Zambona, the Mexican company he represented, "could not be compared to the wildcat ventures so commonly organized by foreigners."[50] Much of the initial foreign mining activity, admitted Ramón Corral, one of its proponents, had been speculative and poorly planned. For every successful venture, there were more than a few failures. There were so many failures, Corral thought, that it was not unreasonable to believe that the goal was to enrich a coterie of speculators while appearing to deal with important business so as to gamble with the stock market.[51] According to a special state committee, by 1886 so numerous were the failures of foreign mining ventures that outside capitalists no longer wanted to invest. Poor management and faulty organization were largely responsible.[52] By 1890, Corral said, a virtual state of "panic" reigned in mining because of the "bankruptcy of companies due to imprudence and sheer stupidity."[53]

From the start, it was commonplace for promoters and speculators to exaggerate the money they had invested in their mining ventures. Mexicans alleged that this was particularly true of foreigners. As Ignacio Bonillas, for years the sole Mexican mining engineer in Sonora, put it, "their word had to be taken with a grain of salt."[54] At this moment, Bonillas did not have in mind a fly-by-night venture, but the infant 4C's of 1900. The governor had asked Bonillas to visit Cananea and report on whether Greene and his group had lived up to the terms of their contract with state authorities, which called for an initial investment of $300,000. Bonillas found the company's claims "grossly exaggerated." At best, it had invested no more than $235,000, while the foundry, which the company insisted had a capacity of 200 tons a day, had never processed more than 135 tons in twenty-four hours. He believed the sum of $181,263, which the company claimed to have spent on the digging of tunnels, wells, and other surface works, was enormously inflated. That type of work, he pointed out, could be done at

$10 a meter, for a total of $16,810, a far cry from the figure given by
the company.[55] Greene and his associates had not lived up to their end
of the bargain.

That frauds occurred cannot be disputed. Obviously, as the biggest
group of speculators, Americans were largely responsible for schemes
to bilk the unwary. In the laconic words of the United States Department of Commerce, "mining in Sonora brought in its wake the usual
number of irresponsible promoters."[56] Commerce put the matter
kindly; in reality, an army of con men came south, men whose one ambition was to make money, no matter how. They cheated Mexicans and,
along the way, their own countrymen, selling stock in mines that were
rich only in the false descriptions of the promoters. Some of these
crooks went so far as to build reduction works where no ores existed
in order to sell stock to gullible investors back home. Companies were
formed not to dig ores out of the subsoil but to "steal money" from
naive investors.[57]

The stench of fraud, while more common to wildcat operations,
wafted over even as successful an operation as Nacozari. In the late
1880s, the Moctezuma Company Mill, a forerunner of what eventually
became the copper giant at Nacozari, employed Willard Richards as its
superintendent. Earlier, he had been identified with the New Jersey
and Sonora Reduction Company in Granados, a town in Moctezuma.
The venture had gone bankrupt, and its fall left scores of "ruined and
duped creditors," among them José María Torres, former prefect of
the district and brother of Lorenzo Torres.[58] According to his American
creditors, Richards's business in Granados was a wildcat venture, run
on credit and cheap labor. They accused him of often paying his miners
in worthless drafts. Among the duped creditors was Edward Foster, an
American who called Richards "a curse to the poor working people of
the district," a man who had "defrauded hundreds out of their hard-
earned wages," paying them with "checks of doubtful value." Foster
and his band of angry co-creditors came to Nacozari to collect their
debts. Richards accused them of invading company property "pistol in
hand."[59]

Without doubt, Foster and his friends felt themselves the victims of
fraud. According to a letter to Corral from an American friend of
Lorenzo Torres, Richards and his associates had "wronged the dead
and the living," refusing to "pay up their honest and just debts."
Richards and his group, the letter went on, "if they have money in the
United States . . . have not credit here for I have had to endorse many
of their drafts given to poor workmen before they could obtain one
dollar upon the same." By the failure of the Sonora Reduction Company, "of which they were the manipulators," Richards and the others

had brought "ruin and distress to the poor people of the district," until now not paying "one dollar . . . [for] their hard-earned labor." Of the foreign mining companies in Sonora, said the author of the letter, "I challenge any person to tell me of one that failed so fraudulently . . . and from which many of its creditors have not recovered their credit standing since the failure." To the people of Granados alone, he alleged, "they owe . . . over $7,000."[60]

By 1910, fraud and deceit acquired an international flavor. Mexicans, having learned the art from Spaniards—no strangers to the seamy side of mining—and Americans, also practiced duplicity on each other and on unwary foreigners. One such scheme involved the mines at Mulatos, which the owners, the Aguayos, wanted to sell at an inflated price. Advertisements placed by the Aguayos in journals in the United States exaggerated the value of the ores in their mines. A group of American and English capitalists, believing what they read, paid $1.5 million for the mines. To their astonishment, they purchased a mine "shot with ore." The Aguayos had "seeded" the mine to make it appear richer than it actually was. Luckily for the buyers, they convinced President Porfirio Díaz to compel the Aguayos to return their ill-gotten gains.[61] Honor for the Aguayos, members of the Alamos social elite, had a price tag.

The art of hypocrisy, likewise, won adepts. Foreigners' claims that they had worked a miracle in Sonora barely trailed their inflated estimates of the money they had invested. Mining, they proclaimed, meant economic growth, more income for everyone, and jobs for the poor. In the *municipio* of Imuris, boasted the English adventurer, Federico H. Seymour, "I have given jobs to Mexicans in the building of the railroad and the reduction works." He employed, he claimed, nearly 400 men "for the month of February alone," spending 6,640 pesos just on wages. To make life better for his workers and their families, he had established "stores selling goods at fair prices, charging only what is needed to keep them open." Once a week, he added, he had a physician visit the mining camp, while his wife took care of the sick: "We do everything to make them comfortable." Everything the company needed, he purchased in Mexico, always attempting to employ natives, "to teach them mining techniques, so as to replace my American employees with them." All of this, said the manager of the Imuris mine, "in order to repay the people of Sonora for what they had done for me."[62]

Deeds did not match the rhetoric, however. Work on the reduction works and on the railroad had gone slowly, he admitted, but only because of an insufficient number of "qualified workers." Most Mexicans tilled the land for a livelihood, and were unaccustomed to doing the kind of labor he wanted, he said, although upon his arrival he had raised wages from 1 to 1.25 pesos a day.[63] But Seymour's Mexicans had another version. According to them, as a condition for hiring them, the Englishman had demanded that they build their houses on company land. Seymour sold the lots to the workers and, in some cases, houses that were already built.[64]

With the completion of the railroad, Seymour dismissed 250 workers, telling them to vacate company property immediately. Single men obeyed promptly but some workers with families, to Seymour's dismay, lingered on. The mayor of Imuris, H. S. Gabilondo, then just starting his ascent up the economic ladder, on Seymour's orders gave the recalcitrant homeowners forty-eight hours to leave. True to his threat, Gabilondo brought men to evict the "squatters" and to tear down their houses. Not surprisingly, the Mexicans complained to Governor Corral, asking with some justification that the Imuris Company pay for the cost of the houses which, they said, represented their life savings. Without funds, they could not move on.[65]

Often, it seemed, the obligations taken on by foreign mining promoters in agreements with the government of Sonora were not worth the paper they were printed on. Once established, many moguls behaved as if they were sovereigns of the land. The story of the smelter promised but abandoned by Phelps Dodge at Nacozari supports this jaundiced view of contractual honor. One key stipulation in the concession granted in 1898 called for the building of a smelter by the Moctezuma Copper Company. The company, later acquired by Phelps Dodge, built the smelter. In 1904, however, to the dismay of Mexican officials, Phelps Dodge erected a smelter in Douglas, across the border from Agua Prieta, and closed down its plant in Nacozari. Expanding copper production at both its mining operations—Bisbee and Nacozari—had convinced Phelps Dodge that it would be more profitable to build one big plant in Douglas.[66]

Phelps Dodge made this decision without regard to contract stipulations or to the opinion of Mexicans. Nor did the corporation care one whit about the consequences of its action on Nacozari or on mining in Sonora in general. When the company abandoned its plant, the state was left with only one smelter, at Cananea. The shutdown also caused the layoffs of 150 Mexican workers. One reason Hermosillo had wanted the smelter was the expectation that it would create more jobs on the Mexican side; now that hope was dashed. Another, of course, was that the Mexicans wanted the raw ore processed in Mexico and not simply shipped to smelters in the United States.[67] Governor Rafael Izábal, perhaps sincerely so, complained to Phelps Dodge, calling its action illegal. When the company ignored him, he cancelled its tax exemption and, closing the barn door after the horse had fled, revoked its right to build a smelter in Nacozari.[68] The company only had its hands slapped. Across the border, meanwhile, as the smelter flourished, so did Douglas. The former hamlet of "tents, shacks, streets ankle deep in dust," with "saloons, gamblers, and prostitutes," by the fall of 1904 had turned into "a very thriving town" of 5,000 inhabitants.[69]

IV

In the course of their invasion, Yankees converted Sonora, it seemed, into a private arena for their own skirmishes. Rival factions fought pitched battles over the spoils of mining and killed one another. Mexicans, at times, watched a Wild West show put on by Yankee actors. When it suited them, Americans forgot Mexican law and took matters into their own hands. At Agua Prieta, in 1906, a gang of ten Americans crossed the border on a special train and headed for the Tigre Mining Company on the outskirts of Fronteras.[70] They came armed to the teeth, reported the *Daily Dispatch* of Nogales, having purchased a day or so before "a perfect arsenal," including the "forty-five revolvers" in stock in the Copper Queen store in Bisbee "and nine Winchester rifles."[71] Upon arriving at the mining camp, they captured it, and drove off the Mexicans, its American manager reported. The invaders, shareholders in a rival company, had a stock disput with the Tigre group.[72]

Mining promoters wanted to profit not just from the ore extracted but from all related business. They established sales monopolies, either through their *tienda de raya* or through permits they sold to a select group of merchants or vendors. Meat, especially, was restricted; only certain butchers could sell it. This practice had old roots. Already by 1890, at La Colorada, just the "official butcher" had the right to sell meat—always, of course, at a higher price. The police, meanwhile, had orders to ban the sale of meat from neighboring Minas Prietas.[73]

The 4C's erected an elaborate system to keep the sale of meat a monopoly of its subsidiary, the Cananea Cattle Company. It put up a fence around its property, with signs at its gates "telling independent butchers to stay out." Because the company had built the roads into Cananea, so went its argument, it had a right to ban travel on them. The constable at El Ronquillo, the Mexican barrio of Cananea, did not permit the sale of meat by outsiders, even keeping police on duty to ban its clandestine introduction by residents of Cananea. If they were caught, they had the option of returning it to the butcher who had sold it to them or of dumping it. If they refused, they were not permitted to return home.

The meat monopoly functioned in other ways. The company slaughterhouse, for example, had permission to kill "40, 50, or more animals" daily, but "only four or five" could be slaughtered in the municipal plant. Butchers who brought their animals to the municipal slaughterhouse had to pay up to four pesos a head to have them killed. Residents of Campana, Chivatina, and Pueblo Nuevo, barrios controlled by the 4C's, complained that they could buy food and meat only at inflated prices, and it nearly always was of poor quality. Because of poor wages, they said, they were forced to buy from merchants who sold for less outside the jurisdiction of the 4C's. On their return, they confronted armed police, at times Americans, who told them to dump their purchases or stay out of company property. Aside from meat, goods barred included sugar, coffee, and liquor.[74]

A similar situation prevailed in Magdalena with the Compañía Minera de Cerro Prieto. The constable barred independent vendors from entering its mining camp.[75] According to a letter sent to the governor in 1908, farmers and merchants could dispose of their goods in only two ways. First, however, they had to pay a sales tax at the gate to the mining camp. Once their goods had been counted, they could sell their merchandise at a fixed price to the *tienda de raya* or at the *mercado*. If they chose to sell in the *mercado*, they had to rent a stall in "a shack built of old boxes." Its rent, a fee of ten pesos a month, gave the seller use of a stall "a meter wide and 1.5 meters long"; additionally, the user had to pay the cost of the electric lighting and a municipal tax of 7.50 pesos. However, no article could be sold in the *mercado* if the *tienda de raya* handled it.[76] To uphold its monopolistic practices, the company stationed "customs officers" at the gates to its property. On duty twenty-four hours, the guards, to the surprise of no one, exacted a toll in bribes. In the eyes of the Mexican critics, the Americans had separated Cerro Prieto from the *municipio* of Cucurpe, declared it independent of the district of Magdalena, and established a law of their own.[77]

The *tienda de raya*, as events in Cerro Prieto document, stood as the cornerstone of company dominance. With it, management could adjust wages, add to its profits, and make neighboring farmers and merchants toe the line. As late as 1899, when a new law banned the practice, companies not uncommonly paid their workers in chits redeemable only at the *tienda de raya*. The law, which had the Moctezuma Copper Company in mind, specifically demanded the payment of wages in cash.[78] It did not, however, entirely rid the worker of this custom, a bastardized version of debt peonage.

The monopoly of the *tienda de raya* hurt Mexican business. Sales at the *tienda* thrived but those of its competitors did not. In Cananea, the company store enjoyed yearly sales of 145,000 pesos, as against 20,000 for its closest rival, Hoffman y Claud. The *tienda de raya* of El Rey Mining Company in Shauaripa sold 40,000 pesos of goods, but no competitor had annual sales above 1,500 pesos. In Nacozari, the company store brought in 30,000 pesos a year, compared with 8,000 for its nearest competitor. Francisco H. Langston, the leading merchant of Oputo, a town in Arizpe, had sales of 21,000 pesos per year, but the *tienda de raya* of the Lucky Tiger Mining Company, the major store in town, sold 25,000 pesos. Langston later took up arms against the old regime.[79]

The companies broadly interpreted property rights. They considered roads private property, even while state legislation designated them as in the public domain. A clash over the ownership of roads may have helped bring about the strike in Cananea in 1906. In April of that year, on the eve of the labor troubles, Lázaro Gutiérrez de Lara, a lawyer and instigator of the strike, was denied access to a road in Cananea by an American. Gutiérrez de Lara, the co-owner of a mining venture in the vicinity, El Picacho Gold Mines, learned abruptly that he could not transport supplies to his own mine. Property controlled by R. C. Clancy, an American, stood in the way.

Gutiérrez de Lara had sent supplies by horse and wagon. At El Basáitegui, where the road ended, they were unloaded for transport by donkey to the mine, about two miles away. In El Basáitegui, an American mining camp, Clancy held sway. Having made a number of trips, the donkey or mule skinner (*arriero*) returned for the last one—only to find Clancy standing over what was left of the supplies, muttering "through an interpreter" that he meant to keep them because the *arriero* had crossed his property "without his permission." In light of that, the donkey skinner went home.[80] Days later, Clancy sent a letter to the Picacho Gold Mines Company, in which he categorically declared that no one from it, "you, or your employees, servants, dependents, or representatives," could cross "the properties of the mining company I represent" or use "its roads."[81] The embittered Gutiérrez de Lara filed a complaint, but the prefect of Arizpe, referring to "Mr. Clancy" as "civilized and honorable," rejected it, as did authorities in Hermosillo. Gutiérrez de Lara had "erred" when he took the word of a "donkey skinner" over that of Mr. Clancy. The exchange of letters, dated May 1906, antedated the labor flare-up by just days.[82]

The mining companies also behaved irresponsibly in matters of the environment. As countless laments testify, they destroyed what blocked their way, and disposed of wastes in whatever manner suited them best regardless of the consequences. When they were through with a place, they left behind the rubble of their diggings. Rarely did they exhibit concern for the well-being of their Mexican neighbors. The Banco de Oro Mining Company on the outskirts of Cucurpe, for instance, emptied its toxic wastes into water that flowed onto the fields of downstream farmers. In a complaint, the victims alleged that the company had polluted their water, rendering it unfit either for irrigation or for drinking—by humans or cattle.[83] The company paid no attention; two years later, it was still dumping waste into the stream, hurting, the farmers declared, four of their harvests. They wanted the culprit to pay for their losses, as it had earlier compensated one farmer, at the insistence of Hermosillo.[84] This time, Mexican authorities levied a fine on the company, but one so small that it hardly paid for the damage done. It was a slap on the wrist. When the farmers objected, Hermosillo told them "to take it or leave it."[85] In Moctezuma, the Purdy Gold & Silver Company emptied waste into the local creek, killing burros who drank its water, a rancher told the prefect. And, he warned, the contaminated water could kill cattle and people unless authorities put an end to this abuse.[86]

V

Respect for Mexican law hardly distinguished the speculators who descended upon Sonora. Many of them, whether in isolated mining camps or in towns, simply turned their backs on local laws or bribed officials entrusted with its enforcement. Occasionally, they shot the lawmen. Behavior of this type began early. Eventually, circumventing Mexican laws became a popular Yankee pastime. One incident occurred in 1884 at the Copper King Mining Company in Cuitaca, a hamlet in Magdalena with just a handful of inhabitants, located on the road to the border. On a Sunday, as the prefect of Magdalena related the story, two drunken American miners fell to fighting. When they pulled out pistols and threatened to shoot each other, the constable of the town asked them for their weapons. One obeyed, but the other shot and wounded the constable who, despite his pain, managed to shoot and kill his assailant.[87]

At this point, bedlam broke loose. Other drunken Americans at the scene attacked the wounded constable, who called for help. Before the uproar subsided, nine Americans, "high as a kite on drink" went on a rampage with rifles taken from the *tienda de raya*, shooting at everything in sight. After an hour, the toll stood at one American dead, and one American and two Mexicans wounded. The local judge jailed nine

Americans and held for questioning the mine superintendents and three Mexicans.[88] The American consul in Guaymas, making light of the affair, asked the governor to release the Americans, telling him that they were "key men" and that, owing to their absence, construction of the reduction works had been "suspended."[89] The consul got his way; the courts acquitted the Americans "of any intentional violation of the law."[90]

In 1908, the same Mr. Clancy who had barred the way of Gutiérrez de Lara's supplies found himself in the middle of another controversy. This time, however, he brought the anger of public officials down upon himself. The Oro Maximo Mining Company, over which Clancy presided, had gone bankrupt and, on demand of its American creditors, Mexican authorities had imposed an embargo on its property. When a Mexican judge, joined by the American lawyer who represented the creditors, sought to take an inventory of the company's holdings, Clancy blocked their way. Backed by a band of armed thugs, he ordered the Mexican judge to get out and threatened to kill the lawyer. The prefect of the district had to send armed men to El Basáitegui to compel Clancy, earlier described as a model of "honor," to obey the law.[91]

Big and little fish defied Mexican authority. In 1900, William C. Greene figured prominently in a classic confrontation. According to the American embassy, which convinced Mexico City to send a telegram to the governor of Sonora, a top boss of the 4C's had been unjustly jailed by the judge of the first instance of Arizpe. Mexico City urged prudence and caution.[92] At the core of the problem was Greene's dispute with his associates over the ownership of the Cobre Grande mine. Local Mexican authorities tried to intervene, apparently believing Greene's antagonists to be at least partly in the right. With fifteen or more armed Americans, Greene barricaded himself in one of the buildings and told the Mexicans to mind their own business.[93]

Ignacio Bonillas, dispatched by Hermosillo to evaluate the work in progress in Cananea, arrived at this juncture. Angry and astonished, hardly believing his own eyes, Bonillas reported that "armed Yankees of the worst sort from across the border"—"cowboys" he called them— had been brought to Cananea to oppose Mexican authority. Barricading themsleves in the company store, the armed goons had "piled sacks of flour and ore" against the windows and doors in order to resist whatever came. Authorities had to dispatch a force of thirty national guardsmen to get Mr. Greene and his *pistoleros* to bow to Mexican law.[94]

But, then, Greene had seldom permitted Mexicans to interfere with his plans. In 1895, when he was a penurious miner in Cucurpe, its weary mayor lamented: "No matter how nicely we deal with Mr.

Greene, he obstinately refuses to heed the authorities of this town."[95] The mayor had more recent cause for alarm. Greene, currently at the Mina de Sarashi, had complained to the governor that the mayor of Cucurpe had interfered with his work. At the point of a gun, he charged, the mayor had him brought to Cucurpe to explain why seven men in his employ had fled the mine to avoid serving a hitch in the military.

The mayor suspected that Greene had instigated the flight because, as Greene admitted in his letter, their absence would "have stopped my work and caused me much damage."[96] More likely than not, Greene exaggerated the episode. The Mexicans dispatched to bring Greene to Cucurpe adamantly denied using force; they said he had come of his own free will. Further, Greene, in his retort, incriminated not only the mayor of Cucurpe but the prefect of Magdalena district as well. Mr. Greene, who tolerated no interference with his designs, had a temper.

Mining entrepreneurs, if their camp was sufficiently large, usually agreed to pay a constable and, at times, to support a school. The agreement could be contractual or verbal. The Moctezuma Copper Company and the 4C's also promised to take up to five students picked by authorities in Hermosillo and to train them in modern mining techniques.[97] The Creston Colorado Mining Company also paid the *rurales* who defended the region against marauding Yaquis.

In theory, the arrangements put the choice of constable and school-teacher into Mexican hands. In practice, the company had veto power: managers could refuse to pay appointees they found unacceptable. Almost invariably the choice fell upon a local person, someone acceptable to both the prefect of the district and the company. Letters from prefects make this perfectly clear. In Cerro Blanco, the man endorsed for the post of constable by Ignacio Bonillas, then prefect of Magdalena, had previously worked for the mining company.[98] At other places, as at Nacozari, the company submitted names to the prefect. If he endorsed them—and he almost always did—he sent them on to Hermosillo.[99] Naturally, the companies picked men who could be counted on to do their bidding. Between 1900 and 1910, José B. Terán was constable (*comisario*) of Nacozari. Don Pepe, as he was known, was a friend of James S. Douglas, the boss, and a believer in rough handling for disturbers of the public order, at least as the company defined it. Above all, Don Pepe was "an employee of the company."[100]

In effect, the company picked the constable, the chief legal authority in the mining camp, and told him what to do. If it did not like his performance, its manager easily persuaded Hermosillo to appoint a different one. At the Mina San Felix, in the desert of Altar, for instance, the manager was dissatisfied with the work of the constable, who in this case was elected by the inhabitants of the nearby town. He asked the mayor of Caborca, the seat of authority, to replace the constable. With the concurrence of Hermosillo and the prefect, the mayor recommended a man in good standing with the company.[101] Management also claimed first rights on the constable's services when the company footed the bill. The mayor and the town council, as a conflict with a mining company in Santa Cruz showed, had to keep hands off.[102]

The mining companies seldom paid the salaries without strings attached: more often than not, they got something in return. The Melczar Mining Company, an Arizona outfit, in return for contributing 5,000 "Mexican silver dollars to be devoted to the interests of education," won the right to export the ores it produced "free of duties," according to its general manager.[103] Or a company might receive an exemption from a state tax. The Moctezuma Copper Company, for example, promised to pay the constable and the schoolteacher if Hermosillo would cancel the 3 percent tax on sales at its *tienda de raya*.[104]

But letting the piper call the tune had its drawbacks. In 1890, E. A. Price, the manager at La Colorada, wanted a constable appointed, arguing rightly that an officer was much needed in the community. He wanted his mining camp, then under the jurisdiction of the town council of Minas Prietas, declared a *comisaría*, a semi-independent political unit. As usual, he wanted something in return. Yes, he would pay the constable, if Hermosillo picked a person acceptable to him and, in addition, exempted him from the "municipal taxation . . . on *Hacienda de beneficio* ("reduction works") and *Tienda* and on goods and articles of same." The constable Price had in mind would also be the schoolteacher.[105] The tax La Colorada paid, however, represented approximately fifty pesos a month of revenue for Mina Prietas, which, to no one's astonishment, opposed making La Colorada a *comisaría*.[106] Price, manager of the biggest mining enterprise in Sonora, got his way. A year later, the town fathers of Minas Prietas charged that the new constable had done nothing but serve the wishes of Price.[107] As a letter from the constable himself testified, he jailed individuals at the behest of Price. According to a complaint from Minas Prietas, he also quarreled incessantly with the town officials.[108]

When Hermosillo permitted a company to make a pawn of the constable, the Americans gained another advantage: the practice discriminated against Mexicans in the mining towns and camps. Americans living in the mining communities were, for the most part, "well protected in their rights," the American consul in Nogales enthused, "owing to the fact that the companies, which are mostly American, select their own police force," making them "the indirect dispensers of justice in their camps."[109] Justice for Mexicans, on the other hand, was meted out by foreigners, Americans who were hostile to the natives' interests.

As for the pledge to aid education, on occasion the mining companies built schools, but they were segregated. The children of poor Mexican miners, in particular, never went to school with Americans. At Nacozari, there were two schools for boys: one for Americans and one for Mexicans.[110] Schools at Cananea segregated by race but not by sex. The companies completely reneged on the agreement, imposed by Hermosillo, to provide technical training. When five students, graduates of the distinguished Colegio de Sonora, arrived in Nacozari to begin their training, they had the shock of their lives. In the year there, they wrote the governor, they had endured "every imaginable vexation," concluding "lamentably that they were wasting their time." Instead of special training, the company had put them to doing "piecework," the work "of the most humble miner." They had "slept on the floor, been without beds, and told to live in a filthy room lacking a floor and a toilet . . . victims of the racial prejudice that befalls Mexicans here." No "technical instruction of any type" had been given them; at best, what they had done was to clean and oil machinery. "What we know," they said, "had been learned in our first eight days at Nacozari." If they fell sick, the company did not pay their "scholarship," twenty-five centavos a day.[111]

When asked to account for the complaint, Douglas, the company head, simply denied everything. The company had fulfilled its end of the contract, he told the governor. "We have done all within our ability to teach the apprentices a vocation," though some had "not behaved well." Still, he continued, "despite everything, we are very happy with them." They had, after all, "taken full advantage of their opportunity."[112] Whatever the validity of this opinion, the students ultimately abandoned Nacozari and the benevolence of Douglas.

Hector Aguilar Camín, author of a classic book on Sonora, notes that by asking the mining companies to pay the salaries of teachers and police, state authorities put the education of their children and the law of the land into the hands of foreigners. But, as he points out, education and the law are fundamental institutions of community life.[113] Penny-wise but pound-foolish, Mexican rulers abdicated control over the community and mortgaged the future.

The result was a foreign flag flying over Mexican soil. It was planted by aliens who carved out imperial enclaves complete with *guardias blancas* ("company police") and extraterritorial rights. These company towns of the late nineteenth century were "fiefdoms" ruled by a lord and his vassals. Their inhabitants' fate was in the hands of the foreign master. Management set the pace of life in the community, dictated its rules, and decided who would live in it. At Cananea, the 4C's provided the water the people drank, "the gas and firewood for their stoves . . . the electricity they used, the meat they ate."[114] The Moctezuma Copper Company, like the 4C's, controlled not only its workers but the people in the town as well. Its will was omnipotent, "global and totalitarian." From cradle to grave, as one writer described the sequence, the company "provided the needs of the workers," from the food sold at the *tienda de raya* to the "box in which you are buried."[115] La Colorada, at the insistence of its miners, set aside land for burial of their dead but so hard was the plot it gave them that at night "wild animals dug up the cadavers from the shallow graves." When the constable, speaking for the miners, asked the company for fencing to keep out the intruders, he was told that it would cost too much.[116] The company's regard for community needs went just so far.

VI

Armed Mexicans marched with the defenders of Greene at Cananea.[117] Association with wealthy Americans had suborned them. Their list, an extensive one, included mayors, police, judges, prefects, legislators, and even governors. In the shadow of the mining companies stood "men who in the world of politics . . . acted as the guardians of their interests." The companies amply rewarded their services. They became the kept men of the American moguls. One of them was Ramón Corral, who tarnished his "brilliant political career forever by acting as their ally." So close were Corral's ties to Greene, who was a friend of Porfirio Díaz, that the evidence suggests it was Greene who first brought Corral to the president's attention.[118] Corral, of course, eventually became vice-president of Mexico.

Corral was but one of scores who served the Yankee. In 1906, Izábal, the governor of Sonora, stood on the same platform with Greene to harangue the miners of Cananea. When the 4C's cut jobs in 1907, company officials prevailed upon Luis E. Torres to come to town to insure that disturbances did not break out. Taide López de Castillo, a *politico* of note in Hermosillo, fattened his pocketbook doing the bidding of the copper moguls in Nacozari. Antonio A. Martínez helped Greene run Cananea and acquire vast tracts of land. Not incidentally, he fared well financially.[119] At La Trinidad, the mining company picked Antonio J. Encinas for mayor, a position he held during the labor strike.[120]

Nothing he did during his term harmed company interests. And so it went.

What can be said of this era of Yankee ascendancy? Clearly, the arrogance of the foreigner and the relentless pursuit of the almighty dollar by the opportunistic turned countless Mexicans into pariahs in their own land. As their representatives fell into step with American speculators, Mexicans found themselves without anyone to speak for them. Their officials defended foreign interests. In time, the Mexican outcast began to lose faith in his officials, in Mexican law and justice, and in the system itself.

CHAPTER 6

The World of the Miner

I

When speculators, promoters, and adventurers arrived, they constructed a hostile world for the men who would work in the mines. The job offered high wages, but it imposed many tolls. It claimed miners' lives, some through accidents and others by disease. The ills of lung and bone that historically have felled diggers of ores killed some, but others were carried off by the infections that plague those living in crowded places. The Mexicans who lived in the dense, unhealthful mining camps and towns also inhabited a segregated universe designed by the Yankee.

II

Cananea epitomized this scene. Mexican miners built it, but foreigners drew its blueprints, managed it, and owned it. The town arose with the arrival of technicians, skilled laborers, supplies, and machinery from the United States. By 1902, according to the American consul, about 1,000 Americans, "nearly all . . . employees of the mining company, lived in Cananea and its vicinity."[1] Approximately five years after its founding, Cananea had 20,000 inhabitants, for the better part Mexican. It enjoyed "phenomenal growth," the consul said, so much so that it was "almost impossible to erect houses to accommodate the influx of people." Cananea had "more American subjects than the balance of the state of Sonora put together." About 4,100 Americans lived in the town and neighboring mines and ranches.[2]

For themselves the Americans took La Mesa, a stretch of flat terrain overlooking the ravines and valleys that separated it from the surrounding hills of copper ore. There they built their houses and the most impressive municipal structures. The trains that departed for Agua Prieta and the United States border went through it. Upon arrival, observed a Mexican journalist, travelers were "pleasantly surprised."[3] The principal street of La Mesa, which ran down to the railroad station, was "wide and straight, fenced on both sides by rows of American-style houses." It "resembled the main street of any middlewestern town in the United States." The municipal building, a two-storied structure, had the look of "an Iowa county courthouse, complete with clock tower." A nearby school, also of brick, "with its cupola and wood-columned front porch, carried on the pattern, as did the edifice housing the jail and town hospital."[4]

Home of the American colony, La Mesa gave lodging to the well-off. Residents of Omaha and Denver would have felt at home in these houses, some "quite elegant, built of brick and stone." These were the homes of the executives of the 4C's, the "leading businessmen," and a tiny handful of local Mexican authorities. Around them stood "smaller wood houses, brightly painted, with attractive porches, colorful flower patches, and picket fences" where the less influential Americans lived.[5]

A large, two-story house, with a shingled roof and porches to give shade, jutted out over the others. It was the home of William C. Greene, founder of the copper empire in Cananea. Built of stone cut from the surrounding hillsides, the house had a lavish stable behind it. "Mr. Greene" kept fine horses to pull his carriages or to carry riders on horseback. Wagons and carriages "and even one of those newfangled automobiles or two" were lodged in an adjoining garage. Gardens and green lawns were crisscrossed by stone walks and bordered by boxwood hedges. Greene's buildings and grounds occupied an entire block in the middle of La Mesa. Nearby were other elegant buildings, the homes of Arthur S. Dwight, James H. Kirk, L. Lloyd, and "Ignacio" Macmanus, close associates of Greene.[6]

To entertain visiting dignitaries, to hold family celebrations on Sundays or holidays, or to help its managers just relax, the 4C's built the Cananea Club, a brick building standing two stories tall. The Club catered to the powerful. A Mexican journalist, bootlicker of the ruling mafia in Hermosillo, thought the Club "particularly attractive" because of its "architectural beauty and its elegantly furnished interior." Ordinarily, only in large, cosmopolitan cities could such "good taste" be found. With the exception of "one or two comparable salons in Mexico City," no others existed in the Republic.[7]

The better hotels in Cananea, the Sonora and the Los Angeles, where visitors might stay, charged two to three pesos a day for a room while "taxis," horse-drawn carriages, cost 2.5 pesos an hour. A miner, who earned three pesos a day, could not afford a day in a hotel or a ride in a taxi. Both were set aside for the affluent, usually associates of the Americans who lived at the top of the hill.

To the west of La Mesa, on the banks of two slopes, rose El Ronquillo. Here was another world, that of the Mexican miner. On both sides of the hills, above a pathway between El Ronquillo and La Mesa, stood the houses of the workers, large in numbers but tiny in size. Built of cheap lumber, they were one-room shacks that accommodated not only miners but their families as well. As the mayor of Cananea said, El Ronquillo was a shantytown of hastily built hovels, some worse than others, where Mexicans lived crowded together.[8] Fires regularly burned them to the ground.[9]

Filth and cold invited disease. Each year a virtual epidemic of pneumonia from April to June claimed scores of lives. Influenza raged in the winter months, while typhoid fever, born of foul water and food, was the daily companion of the poor. Malaria, carried by the mosquitoes that infested pools of stagnant water, killed many. In 1902, smallpox spread even to the Americans who lived on the hill. Unless the inhabitants of El Ronquillo, "who obstinately insisted on living there," changed their way of life, predicted the mayor, himself a physician, illness and death would strike again and again. He spoke of steps being taken to improve the quality of the drinking water, the source of digestive ills.[10]

Adjacent to El Ronquillo lay Cananea Vieja and Mesa Sur, the next largest Mexican *barrios*. Beyond them, virtually on top of the mines themselves, were smaller slums: La Demócrata, La Chivatera, Buena Vista, Pueblo Viejo, and La Campana. Home to nearly 6,000 workers, like El Ronquillo they were "totally lacking in comfort and hygiene."[11] Recalled Esteban Baca Calderón, a legendary figure in the labor history of Cananea, "Mexicans lived in pitiful conditions."[12] These shantytowns were incubators for rebellion. The Mexicans who organized the Unión Liberal Humanidad, forerunner of the union that called the strike, and picked Baca Calderón for its secretary, met in Buena Vista. El Ronquillo nourished the organizers of a political club, companion to the groups who hoisted the banner of rebellion against Porfirio Díaz.[13]

Segregated from the Americans by geographic elevation and distance, and, worse still, by class and race, Mexicans lived in a world apart. Even schooling separated them from their foreign bosses. A primary school opened in 1903, managed and taught by American women, remembered one of its first pupils, admitted only the children of the American employees. By 1906, enrollment in the English school stood at over 100. Another school, with an unreported enrollment, accepted the Mexican children. With a wonderful touch of hypocrisy, Americans denied they discriminated. As long as places were available in the English school, they pointed out, Mexican children could attend. In practice, of course, this seldom occurred. Tuition, to begin with, was "three dollars per month."[14] Segregation left its mark on every activity, including the celebration of holidays, attending church, and getting drunk in saloons, a popular pastime with both nationalities.

In Nacozari, redoubt of the Moctezuma Copper Company, Mexican workers suffered similar conditions. A small colony of perhaps fifty Americans had the best of everything. With the spur line to Douglas, they had easy access to their homeland, a privilege equally available to their countrymen in Cananea. Two towns existed in Nacozari, a Mexican town at the foot of a ravine and an American colony above.[15] The geography of the place perfectly mirrored the social and economic relationships of its inhabitants. The top, "the odd 100 feet before the topography came to a sharp point," Ralph M. Ingersoll remembered, "was reserved for the American quarter." A "path which degenerated into a stairway led on up through two lines of white houses, with gardens fenced off from the roving burros." Each house was set aside for an American family. Everyone had a magnificent view of the valley below because, as Ingersoll described the scene, "so steep was the slope that the floor of one house was on a level with the roof of its neighbor down the hill."[16] At the pinnacle of this little kingdom was the home of James S. Douglas, the superintendent, reported a Mexican journalist, a dwelling "simple in design but pretty," and next to it were those of "Sres. Williams and Ayers, equally pretty."[17]

To speak of the American colony meant calling the roll of the executives and key personnel of the Moctezuma Copper Company. Most of the *jefes* ("chiefs"), as the Mexicans knew them, were married. To these families went the "attractive . . . little houses lining the fashionable thoroughfare up the hill known as Pershing Drive," explained Ingersoll, each "with its minute, irrigated garden in front" and "almost-green grass and peach and fig trees." For single men, the company built a "big dormitory at the top of the hill," where they "ate at a common mess, and slept on a broad veranda which circled the building."[18] The lucky bachelors spent hours on the veranda visiting with the single American women who worked as teachers, nurses, or clerks in Nacozari. To keep their employees happy, the company put up a tennis court and, later, laid out a six-hole golf course.

Below this idyllic commonwealth in the *barrio* to the south, dwelt the Mexicans, the labor force. Just one group lived farther down: the

Chinese, who cultivated vegetables and fruits for the local kitchens.[19] In its heyday, Nacozari had about 5,000 Mexicans, attracted by the promise of jobs and higher wages.[20] Yet living conditions, especially when contrasted with what the Americans enjoyed, were abominable. Malnutrition stalked Mexican families. The children of the workers, recalled Ingersoll, "died like flies at the least cold, or continued heat." Company officials, he believed, attempted to teach the practice of "safety first" and gave medical service yet "paid little or no attention to living conditions of the so-called healthy." The company built some houses for the workers, but they could be judged adequate only by comparison with what the Mexicans constructed for themselves. Company houses "were one-room shacks about fifteen feet square," an improvement over the others only because their inhabitants did not crowd more than one family into them.[21]

For the most part, Mexicans resided in houses they built with their own hands. Of wood, mud, or discarded sheet metal, or a combination of all three, the houses reflected the poverty of their owners. Photographs of the time show that they were squalid, unhygienic, and small. On close inspection, as Ingersoll recognized, they were not in the least "picturesque." Ingersoll described one of the hovels. It was an adobe hut with a roof of discarded "iron fire doors from an old mine, salvaged from some dump heap." Its owner had put up a chimney with "coffee cans telescoped one in another and raised . . . in a sort of haphazard spiral." Openings consisted of a door and two windows, so dirty that one could not see out. The shack's one room had for furniture a "dissolute-looking iron bed" in a corner, "a sort of cot in another," and an "unused" and "battered washstand . . . and two heavy chests of drawers." A small stove standing between the chests served as the kitchen while a wooden table and worn chairs "completed the furnishings." Trying to mitigate the ugliness, husband or wife had pasted "yellowed cuts from American Sunday newspapers" and added "bright-colored lithographs of vacant-looking deities with eyes raised to the cobwebbed ceiling" as if fearful that the makeshift roof "would come down on their worshippers."[22]

Given this picture, it was no wonder that Mexicans fell ill and "died like flies." Lacking the most elementary necessities required for good health, such as waste disposal and adequate drainage, the conglomerate of shacks served as a breeding ground for diverse diseases. Fresh from his studies at Yale, Ingersoll found conditions "appalling" even "to the most casual humanitarian." Its inhabitants, he said, lived "in their own filth, horribly overcrowded" and fell "easy victims to disease, which would sweep through the camps like wildfire." He spoke of summer months filled with "a continuous procession on the road to the graveyard, of funerals, in which the little blue coffins of babies predominated." The healthy dwelt alongside those sick with contagious diseases, "common to an unbelievable extent," while under the ground labored Mexican miners covered "with hideous sores." Mexicans, he observed, had virtually no resistance to illness or disease; "the simplest disorders snuffed out their lives like candles in a breeze."[23]

This scene was played out over and over again in other mining camps on a smaller scale. In La Colorada, E. A. Price and his successor, Howell Hinds, lived outside of town in a valley lying between two rocky hillsides. They had built elegant homes with a core made of rock and adobe, and encircled by wide porches, in typical mid-western fashion. At the center stood a small patio. Outside, the owners planted fruit trees and shrubs, which were fed by water brought by metal pipes from the mining camp over the hill. The Mexican dwellings lay across the road from the mines and mills: they were adobe shacks lacking sanitary facilities. Hot boxes in the summer, they barely tempered the cold during the winter months. The *barrio* of La Colorada and the one at Minas Prietas up the road resembled those of Nacozari and Cananea on a reduced scale.

Barrios, housing, and the nature of segregation varied in detail from one mining camp to another: they were more or less alike. So common was the model that it raised no eyebrows. The workers dwelt on the other side of town, a Mexican sycophant remarked uncritically, of the town built by the Banco de Oro Mining Company.[24] So it went, whether it was the Mineral El Tiro in Altar or the mines of the Melczar Mining Company at El Copete in Ures.[25] The rich and powerful *gringo*, Mexicans had long ago come to understand, lived in *colonias*, separate and distinct from the *barrios* of the Mexicans. Mexican workers had always been poor but never before segregated by race from their employers. With the coming of the white speculator from across the border, they were.

III

The world of the mining camp was unfamiliar to the workers in other ways. It brought together diverse people, groups previously unknown to each other, from every corner of Sonora and, not infrequently, from other states. To employ a discredited historical cliché, it was a melting pot. Whether they were from the hill towns of the eastern sierra, the desert hamlets of the west or, in the case of the Yaquis, from the southern river valleys, the workers left behind safe, familiar communities more conducive to family life. In their old homes, where people ordinarily lived out their entire lives, the extended family retained close ties and everyone knew the neighbors. In times of distress, family and friends came to one's assistance. The mining camp harshly altered the domestic world of the miners and their families. If it did not totally undermine family life, the mining camp *barrio* certainly drained it of much of its vigor. The high wages, particularly in the northern districts, did not compensate for what was lost in the transition from hill town, southern village, or even "city" to the crowded mining camp or town full of strangers and run by foreign speculators interested only in profits. When the worker exchanged the benefits of small-town life for the questionable advantages of an industrial-age job, he likely lost more than he gained.

Mining was a dangerous way to earn a living. It left behind women without husbands, children without fathers, and parents without sons. From the start, fatal accidents occurred, increasingly during the golden age of mining in the first decade of the twentieth century. Accidents happened in every corner of the state. That their frequency and severity frightened miners and their families cannot be denied. The death of a miner cast a gloom over the mining camp. One reason for the 1906 labor troubles in Las Chispas, a camp in Arizpe, for instance, was the recurrence of accidents. Equally significant was the fear among the miners that company negligence lay at the root.[26] That fear, at Las Chispas and elsewhere, had solid justification because, as one American student of mining observed, "the callous attitude of some companies went beyond belief." During many of these years, he pointed out, the companies valued a human life at fifty pesos ($25)—"the customary compensation for fatal accidents" in the mines.[27]

Accidents, fatal or not, exacted their toll. A goodly number were fatal, and others maimed or incapacitated workers for life. In the years 1906 and 1907, by company count alone, neither highly accurate nor fully complete, fifty-one miners perished in the *municipios* of Cananea and Arizpe. Of that number, all but four occurred in Cananea. In La Colorada, the company reported seven deaths in its mines. Others, those reported to Hermosillo, occurred in Magdalena and Alamos. But deaths represented a mere fraction of the accidents. In 1909, the 4C's reported eighteen deaths but 769 accidents, forty-seven of them "serious." Over a third had occurred in the mill and ore concentrator, testifying to the danger of working with the machinery in vogue, which more often than not totally lacked safety equipment.[28] News of accidents at small mines, the wildcat operations, rarely reached the ears of authorities in Hermosillo.

No reports exist of the number of men who lost a limb or who fell ill because of poor working conditions, some never to have a job again. The circumstances of the work place, after all, were deplorable even in neighboring Arizona. At the Copper Queen Mine, like Nacozari a Phelps Dodge enterprise, the "air was so foul that a miner's candle had to be laid down or carried horizontally to be kept alight." Water dripped from the walls of the stopes and drifts, while just across the way it was so hot that, as one miner put it, "the sweat came out of the tops of your shoes." Safety devices, crude and inadequate though they were at that time, were conspicuous by their absence.[29]

Though mine accidents occurred during the colonial days, modern equipment, by making it possible to bore more deeply into the subsoil, multiplied both their number and severity. Official awareness, even concern, appeared early. In 1885, a year on the edge of the mining boom, when secretary of state Ramón Corral learned that a miner had suffocated to death, he kept the mine closed until the cause of the death had been eliminated.[30] A few years later, Corral, now governor, dispatched a special agent to investigate a disaster at the Mina del Socorro in Ures. Owned by Mexicans, the mines had employed eighty men. Twenty perished in the disaster, leaving behind twenty-five orphans. The miners had been underground when a sudden burst of water blocked their exit tunnel. The agent dispatched to ascertain the company's responsibility found it innocent of wrongdoing.[31] At approximately the same time, Mexican workers with the Imuris Mines Company blamed a careless locomotive engineer for the derailment of their mine train. Corral told the prefect of Magdalena to order its manager, the Englishman "Federico" Seymour, to replace the engineer. If he refused, the prefect was to stop the train from running.[32] The prefect, Ignacio Bonillas, did as he was ordered. Surprisingly, Seymour replaced the culprit, an American.[33] But all of this was before foreigners got so powerful that they did not hesitate to disobey Mexican officials.

That official concern, however, was in the beginning, before the boom got into gear. In the heyday between 1900 and 1910, that solicitude already had passed into the history books. While companies had to report mine accidents, Hermosillo only displayed a cursory interest in them. The reports were just for the record. No investigation of any significance appears to have been carried out.

Yet accidents multiplied. The reports of prefects frequently included news of a mining tragedy. Between 1906 and 1909, stories of mining misfortunes at La Colorada went out with remarkable regularity. There was a laconic tone to these reports: Pedro Carranza, "upon climbing the ladder going from the fourth to the fifth level, had a boulder fall on his head, severely hurting him"; as Atilano Rodríguez, José

Angel Amarillas, and Juan Jaquis "dug with their picks, they hit an unexploded charge of dynamite, which killed the first and seriously injured the others"; yesterday, went another report, "the cage of the shaft of the Creston mine struck Manuel Contreras, who is dying"; "today, in the afternoon, as Dolores Gurrola went about measuring holes just drilled, he . . . fell twenty-five or thirty feet and died instantly"; a miner "fell from the lift and plunged 300 feet to his death."[34]

Reports for other mines sounded a similar lament. At Nacozari, death perpetually stalked the miner. In 1909, during the month of November, three men died in the space of two days: one was killed while working with dynamite, the other two died in falls down mining shafts. One, the report said, "fell 200 feet to his death." Another account related, "a slide instantly killed Alfredo López, deep in the underground"; three Japanese miners were handling dynamite and it exploded, "killing one and injuring the others."[35] At Cumpas, a boiler of the Transvaal Mining Company exploded, "killing one and gravely burning his three companions."[36] When an explosion occurred at El Tigre, only "the shattered bodies of workers could be found."[37] At the Buckeye mines, a large slide "buried two men, killing one."[38] Victims of fatal mining accidents at La Quintera in Alamos in 1906 and 1907 included Alfonso Ontiveros, age eight, and Vidal Salazar, age five.[39] In Río Chico, gunpowder stored in a warehouse blew up, "killing Alberto Chávez, Jesús Cabanillas, José Esparza, and Lorenzo Armenta. No one can explain why it went off."[40] It would require a large book to catalog the mine accidents after 1900. Nobody knows how many miners died.

Unexpectedly, a folk hero emerged out of this nightmare. Jesús García, a "simple Mexican worker," saved the town of Nacozari from being blown to bits. His true story became a tale that eloquently captured the danger that was the worker's constant companion, and celebrated the feat of the miner who confronted that fear and conquered it. Symbolically, the tale represented the victory of the Mexican over a monster created by the Yankee outsiders. García's act of heroism underscored for Sonorans their own strength, dignity, and character.

García, not yet 24, had a job on one of the narrow-gauge trains that ran to Pilares. He had worked his way up from simple railroad worker to fireman to his present position as locomotive engineer. On that fateful day in 1907, nitroglycerine newly arrived from Arizona had been transferred to cars of the mine's train. The cars stood in the railroad yard in the scorching sun awaiting a clear track up the hill to Pilares. Either because of the heat or a stray spark, a fire broke out near the cars loaded with the explosives. García, who had just returned from a run to Pilares, instantly saw that if the fire reached the nitroglycerine it would blow up the town. So he quickly coupled his locomotive to the endangered cars, now on fire, and pulled out of the yard. Half a mile away the nitroglycerine exploded, taking his life.

Luis Monzón, the teacher in the Mexican school and a future rebel, delivered the funeral oration for García. He used the occasion to lambaste Porfirio Díaz, who thought that American capital could save Mexico. With 5,000 pesos from the Mexican government, and donations from private citizens and the Moctezuma Company, the town erected a monument to its hero, a single column of gray granite thirty feet high. At its base, the bronze plaque carried a likeness of Jesús García, under the Mexican coat of arms.[41]

IV

Heady bouts with strong drink—and besotted workers—were not new to this era. The Spanish did their share of drinking to nurse the spirit. Still, evidence strongly indicates that the noxious habit gained fresh vigor in the mining camps. By 1910, archival records show, the Mexican in his cups had become an issue. The jail where he slept off his drunks was a common sight, no matter how tiny the hamlet. The popular drinks were *mezcal*, the distilled fluid of the agave plant and a distant cousin of tequila, and *aguardiente*, a cheap liquor. Bacanora, a *mezcal*, rated tops among drinkers; a town in Sahuaripa even bore its name. Moonshiners, clandestine distillers of *aguardiente* and *mezcal*, meanwhile, infested the hill towns.

Aware of the popularity of demon drink, Hermosillo, like its superiors in Mexico City, had put a tax on its manufacture and sale.[42] Hermosillo got good prices for permits it sold to individuals giving them the right to share a percentage of the tax. Sales of permits were especially brisk in mining districts such as Alamos. In 1888, Jesús P. Salido, one of the Alamos clan, paid 1,000 pesos annually in return for the opportunity to collect the tax on liquor sold.[43] Alamos district, likewise, paid the highest share of the federal tax on booze. Arizpe, on its way to becoming a key mining region, was next in line.[44]

A permit to sell liquor in a mining camp was a fabled prize. Both the 4C's and the Moctezuma Copper Company fought hard to keep out competitors. So intense was the rivalry for liquor permits that it led to open clashes among neighbors. In Ures district, two natives of France, owners of the *tiendas de raya* in the mines of La Sultana and El Copete, even went to the governor to plead their case against each other. The Sultana proprietor, who enjoyed the monopoly, adamantly refused to permit his countryman to share it.[45]

The heavy sale and use of booze had unwelcome repercussions in the mining camps. Not only did workers who wasted their wages on drink suffer; so did their wives and children. Alcohol victimized the family and undermined its members' respect for the husband and father. Many who came to work in the mining camps, especially from nearby communities, left their families at home. A sizable percentage of these lonely men drank away their wages and, more than likely, their lives. Likewise, it exacerbated the woes of poverty.

Demon drink distorted the contours of life in the mining town. Fights and quarrels, often bloody, marred the public scene. The miners at Nacozari, perhaps because they spent a good part of their life alone, in the dark, beneath the surface of the earth, and in danger, "enjoyed life to its fullest."[46] These men, observed Ingersoll, had "a taste for strong spirits . . . almost a mania." At the Nacozari mine, "every day in the year one man out of every five was off drunk" or, in the Mexican vernacular, sleeping off the *cruda*, the hangover. To Ingersoll, the drinking of alcohol had become "a force in everyday existence."[47] The miners sometimes drank beer but, more likely than not, headier stuff such as *tesquín*, a fermented corn gruel, as well as Bacanora, *mezcal*, tequila and *tenampa*—all distilled from the agave plant. To drink and talk they frequented saloons with such names as *Me Estoy Riendo* ("I am laughing at life") and *Así es la vida* ("that is how life is"), mute testimony to the Mexican's fatalistic acceptance of death or injury in the bowels of the earth.[48]

Cananea, the colossus of the mining towns, not unnaturally had the biggest number of saloons. Men from Mexico, the United States, France, Germany, Italy, Greece, Turkey, Japan, Spain, and China had come together in Cananea, their diversity matched by the kaleidoscope of *cantinas*. Bars and "other centers of entertainment" catered to many tastes. In the *cantina*, the Mexican consoled himself, "drowning in alcohol his weariness and his poverty."[49] While Yankees and other foreigners drank in more elegant saloons, Mexican workers spent their wages in dingy bars whose owners, Mexican or foreign, waxed fat on their sales.[50] In 1907 alone, J. M. Gibbs y Cía., American merchants in cahoots with the 4C's, had liquor sales totaling 57,473 pesos, a formidable profit.[51] Men in Cananea drank heavily, even company executives, as the English sign on one saloon testified: "Where one finds the finest cocktails. Where the best drinker cannot withstand three of the cocktails served in this cantina."[52]

If drink alone failed to offer solace, the miner had other distractions. Gambling, disguised as billiards, dominoes, or card games, said a city councilman, invited the worker to spend time and money.[53] That failing, he could go in search of the bordellos or of the streetwalker plying her trade on her own. Cananea had a plethora of these. The town's authorities early on took steps to monitor the health of the prostitutes, constant companions of lonely men with money. So many of these women were in Cananea by 1902 that the town jail had a special office to handle their cases. The police took care to supervise the bordellos— which were rapidly turning into centers of vice and crime—in the hope that "with opportune measures the daily orgies and public disturbances" might be reduced in number. To try to stamp them out entirely, the mayor emphasized, was out of the question. Every day people "from everywhere and of distinct nationalities" arrived in Cananea, he complained, and among them were the "dross of society who jeopardized the safety and welfare of hard-working and honest men." Because of these newcomers, it had been necessary to build a jail and to add police.[54] When the 4C's shut down in 1907, the prostitutes, like the miners, fled to other parts, among them Arizpe town. The postal inspector reported that the women promptly set up business in a hotel, "awaiting customers at all hours of the night."[55]

That drink and its corollary, the public disturbance, corroded life wherever mining flourished, the litany of complaints from prefects, judges, mayors, and constables leaves no doubt. Their chorus of indignation echoed up and down the land. In Aconchi, a town where workers from the nearby mines lived, the prefect of Arizpe lamented, "dwell individuals with nothing to do but drink, provoke disorders, and commit bloody crimes."[56] Among the men at Cerro Blanco, a mining camp, declared the mayor of Imuris, "were drunks and gamblers . . . paid good wages who went down to the Switch and spent days boozing and getting drunk." Most people found in mining camps, he added, were generally "wild and rowdy."[57] When mining operations began in Santa Elena, newcomers looking for jobs arrived in adjacent Banámichi; the unlucky ones who did not find work, said the prefect of Arizpe, "turn to drink and scandalize the community."[58] At the mining camp of Santa Ana in Magdalena district, the governor, angry over reports of damage done to homes and business houses by drunks, banned the sale of liquor.[59]

Drinking interfered with mining and with other types of labor. The *San Lunes*, the Monday morning hangover, kept many a worker from his job. One owner in Santa Ana told the governor that prolonged drinking sprees by his workers had made it impossible to run his mine. At La Sultana, heavy drinking by the workers caused enormous financial losses to the company.[60] The celebration of Independence Day in San Francisco, customarily one long drinking spree, according to the prefect of Altar, one time "lasted so long that it shut down the mine." Over a week later, with his men still not back to work, the American mine manager asked the constable to stop the sale of liquor.[61] In Arizpe, the prefect ordered the mayor of Bacoachi to ban the sale of liquor because of the harm done to mining in the vicinity.[62] As railroad construction approached Río Chico, the celebrated mining enclave in Alamos, the governor, determined to put an end to "public drunkenness and outrageous behavior," prohibited liquor sales and the holding of dances and fiestas in the adjacent towns. As he explained, their promoters used these events to sell hard drink.[63]

Gambling never failed to thrive in the mining camp, most especially on payday. Just before payday in La Casita, a camp in Sahuaripa, "a horde of gamblers . . . arrived there to ply their vocation."[64] So many "disreputable and rowdy individuals" loitered in El Tigre that its constable, in fear of losing his life, wanted rifles to keep order.[65] With or without guns, he apparently failed to rid the place of its disturbances. By 1910, hardly a day went by without "a public tumult" at the bar and whorehouse of don Antonio Murrieta on the outskirts of El Tigre Mine.[66] When labor troubles erupted in Las Chispas in 1908, the prefect closed all the bars on payday. Before he took that precaution, miners who had walked off the job got drunk, while the inebriated constable had been beaten up and lay in bed.[67]

At Agua Prieta, the entrepôt for Cananea and Nacozari, "gambling banned by law" thrived while local Chinese ran an opium den. In the dingy bars catering to the boisterous from both sides of the border, dancing until the wee hours was an everyday affair, with the sounds of music punctuated by noisy, drunken brawls and the bark of gunfire. A letter chronicling these activities was sent by the authorities in Hermosillo to the constable in Agua Prieta, demanding to know why the disorder was allowed to continue.[68]

Thievery, particularly of mining company property, became a troublesome problem. At least as reported by company stalwarts, the upsurge in thefts was a "constant headache" that rendered the use of Mexican labor more costly than expected.[69] For a minority of workers, "ore stealing" was an "acceptable practice." At La Colorada, the constable claimed, "petty pilfering of ore took on the character of a daily occurrence."[70] What the miner failed to get in wages he made up in theft. For him, these petty crimes were a symbol of his power to flout the law.

But there were also more serious crimes. Minas Prietas had a number of troubles. Merchants regularly acted as fences for silver bullion stolen from La Colorada. In a dramatic episode, thirty-two armed men captured the Grand Central mine, terrorized the miners, and took two tons of silver ore on the backs of burros. The culprits, identified by the miners, lived in Minas Prietas. Again, merchants there openly purchased the stolen ore.[71] In Las Chispas, a special detective identified the priest of nearby Banámichi as a buyer of stolen ore and the priest in the church in Cananea as his outlet.[72] For the most part, thefts victimized Americans because, as the owners of the mines, they had money to lose. But the Americans themselves commonly tried to circumvent the law. A new law had to be enacted to punish those who exported metals without paying the duty. It declared these ores contraband. If caught, their bearers were subject to a stiff punishment: triple duty, another monetary penalty, and a thirty-day stint in jail.[73]

Lawlessness, however, transcended petty theft, robbery on a grander scale, and the failure to pay duties. Behavior condemned by society took on fresh dimensions in the mining town. A report at the turn of the century on Alamos district by Conrado Pérez, lawyer and judge of fine repute, made this abundantly clear. With about 50,000 inhabitants, Alamos, the largest district in the state, had the most crimes and the highest crime rates. Pérez found a direct correlation between mining and, as he called it, "criminal behavior" in Alamos. It had more crimes not because it was the largest district but because it was a mining region.[74]

With the exception of three or four *municipios*, the entire district had links with the mining industry. Río Chico, Minas Nuevas, Promontorios, and Aduana survived on mining, while Rosario, Barroyeca, Macoyahui, and Alamos city partly depended on mining. The four mining *municipios*, along with Alamos, suffered the largest number of crimes. Their rates were matched only by those of Navojoa and Huatabampo, both rapidly becoming hubs of commercial agriculture and both heavily populated by Yaqui and Mayo wage workers. *Municipios* inhabited by dirt farmers, meanwhile, had the lowest rates of criminal behavior. Why? Because, explained Judge Pérez, the mining *municipios*, along with Alamos, enjoyed the highest wage scales and offered "more opportunities" for "dissipation." Lonely miners with money in their pockets, shut up in isolated camps and doing hard and dangerous work, "blew off steam." They found escape, as Pérez said, in "dissipation." They and their money also attracted an army of unsavory characters.[75]

Pérez's analysis of Alamos shows that the mining towns were unique in the repetition, over and over again, of certain types of crimes. Crimes against *buenas costumbres*, the accepted social norms, occurred often, especially against women. Rape and abduction by force or deceit were committed repeatedly. Drunkenness was common. Murder occurred only sporadically, usually committed by outsiders who had had too much to drink. But assaults with bodily injuries were frequent, committed by "inebriated elements of the lower class, using both knives and pistols."[76]

A plaintive letter from the mayor of Aduana laments that on Saturdays and Sundays the entire world, even the inhabitants of Alamos city, visited his town. Aduana, a town of about 2,000 people in 1898, turned into a three-ring circus on weekends, its streets littered with drunks, its peace disturbed by public brawls, and its citizens terrorized. The mayor wanted funds to build a decent jail with doors strong enough to hold prisoners behind bars. It had to have at least three rooms, he said, one for criminals, another for drunks who had gotten into trouble, and a third for female miscreants, whom he wanted to isolate. When men and women were locked up together, he emphasized, "shockingly immoral acts had taken place." He also wanted a shaded patio where he could put "Indians and other drunks." Now, he said, they were "sprawled out in the streets, obnoxious spectacles" that barred "families of good standing from leaving their homes without stumbling over prostrate bodies."[77] The people of Minas Prietas, a mine superintendent from the United States stated, "were perfect candidates for the army because, without doubt," they were "good for nothing else, being *coyotes* ("cheats") and thieves who steal what is not theirs."[78]

Drink, the *cantina*, disorderly conduct, and crime antedated the mining boom, but the world of the mines made the problem worse. The shift of countless dirt farmers from rural village to mining town, from tilling the soil to digging for ore, undermined traditional foundations. Family and home declined in importance in the mining camp. By coming to work in a mine, the worker often severed himself and his family from links with parents and grandparents, uncles and aunts, and dear friends, and from the place where he grew up, with what was familiar, and, in short, from what he counted on in time of need. The shift to mining camp or town populated by strangers set the worker and his family adrift in a stormy sea. From now on, they were on their own, in a world dramatically different from the one they had abandoned. With danger a steady and faithful companion, the worker sought solace in drink, gambling, and, when he could afford them, prostitutes. Parasites with no intention of doing manual labor set themselves up to prey on the poor and ignorant in the mining towns. They were the gamblers, petty thieves, *coyotes*, sellers of hard drink, and pimps. As mining flourished, so did this world, to the detriment of the Mexican miner.

CHAPTER 7

The Making of a Working Class

I

Ever since colonial days, mining had been the backbone of wage labor. Yaquis who left their lands and the Spanish missions in the southern valleys to labor temporarily in the mines of Alamos laid the cornerstones for what eventually became a wage-working class. In time, they were joined by others, Mexicans and Spaniards from the interior of New Spain. With the perpetual Spanish hunt for silver and gold, from Alamos to Sahuaripa, then up the Río Sonora, and finally north to Arizpe and Moctezuma, that class grew.

Until the late nineteenth century, it was both miniscule and marginal. Mining provided Sonora with its major export but employed only a fraction of its population. The overwhelming majority of the poor tilled the land for a livelihood, either as dirt farmers or as *labradores* ("laborers") on *haciendas*. Not until the later mining boom did a modern labor class totally dependent on wages emerge. The mining speculator gave life to a labor element usually found only in the industrial nations. Foreign investment, mostly Yankee money, encouraged the growth of an industrial proletariat in a province largely rural, without cities of note and with only marginal industry. Mining for industrial ores, copper essentially, integrated the workers of Sonora into the global manufacturing economy. For better or for worse, their welfare, specifically their jobs, depended on the ups and downs of international capitalism.

By 1910, these laborers, unemployed in many cases, were an important part of the economy of Sonora. Miners from Cananea, Nacozari, and diverse camps, resentful of the foreigner and bitter at the Mexican establishment that courted him, joined the rebel cause by the thousands.

II

From the start, this working class was heterogeneous, its members drawn mainly from the far corners of Sonora but also from diverse parts of the Republic. To Nacozari, the first of the great copper enclaves, men in search of jobs arrived from neighboring Cumpas, Arizpe, San Pedro, and Batuc, and from the adjoining states of Sinaloa and Chihuahua.[1] The majority of them were of simple stock. Barely literate at best, they left small agricultural communities behind. Nacozari and Cananea both attracted a species of migrant worker: dirt farmers who labored in the mines in the seasons when the land lay dormant. Alongside them were Yaquis driven from their homes by the relentless push of Mexicans and Yankees hungry for fertile lands. Drawn by high wages, carpenters, blacksmiths, mechanics, and other skilled laborers filled out the work force. When the ores petered out, the miners moved on and joined other camps.[2]

Mining, the harbinger of good times, helped bring about a demographic explosion at the turn of the century. By 1910, according to census figures, Sonora had 265,383 inhabitants, nearly 45,000 more than a decade before.[3] A rise in the birth rate was largely responsible for this increase; less than 5 percent of the population had been born outside the state. As the population grew, so did the mining camps, the way stations springing up along the railroad, and, in the years just before 1910, the settlements in the Mayo and Yaqui valleys. Significantly, these burgeoning centers were linked to markets in the United States. A majority of their inhabitants were wage earners. They were miners, workers with jobs tied to the railroad or commerce, or day laborers on the commercial farms in the southern valleys.

Between 1891 and 1910, the work force, roughly 30 percent of the population, grew by 30,000 people. In 1910, at the end of over two decades of sizable investments of foreign money, especially in mining, Sonora had nearly 80,000 economically active inhabitants. Of this number the mining industry claimed between 13,000 and 14,000, about 17 percent of the people with jobs. Adding perhaps another 4,000 in commerce, transportation, agriculture, and "manufacturing,"

Sonora had a wage-labor group of approximately 18,000, or 22.5 percent of the job holders. Additionally, there were nearly 600 teachers and fellow employees in public education who, poorly remunerated, literate, and often aware of class inequalities, might expect to close ranks with the worker.[4] By 1910, therefore, a significant percentage of men with jobs belonged to what, loosely speaking, could be termed an industrial proletariat. Even if these workers were not aware of their status, they belonged to a class dependent upon wages either paid by foreigners, in the case of mining and railroading, or, as in commerce and the cash-crop farms, by Mexican employers joined to business interests abroad. No matter what, Americans, both as buyers and sellers, had a hand in their fate.

Mining paid the highest wages of any job, not just in Sonora but in the entire Republic. This phenomenon dated from the last decades of the nineteenth century. With the industrial metals boom, particularly in copper, wages had shot upward. Mining in the north of Sonora had its wage spurt early. By 1891 the Imuris Mine Company, a silver and gold operation in Magdalena, already paid most of its workers 1.25 pesos a day, with a minority getting up to 2 pesos.[5] While silver mining in Alamos district, in the south, paid better than agriculture, its wages lagged behind those in the copper industry. A decade later wages were uniformly higher in the northern districts. At El Tigre, the wage scale started at 2.6 pesos and went up to 5 pesos for skilled labor.[6] In Oputo, also in Moctezuma, a miner earned 3 pesos for a day's labor while other mines in the vicinity offered from 2 to 3 pesos.[7]

By 1910, even menial labor in the mining camps paid, on a national average, 1 peso a day, twice that of three or four decades earlier. Most men who worked in the mines earned from 1 to 3 pesos daily. Judged by the 50 centavos or less of the field hand, miners earned good pay. Wages in the northern states and along the Pacific coast usually topped others in Mexico.[8] A mine worker who shifted from laboring in the pits to working in the mill or reduction works got more money.

The big operators generally paid the highest wages. The Cananea Consolidated Copper Company, with its 3 pesos or more a day, had the highest in Sonora and, perhaps, in the Republic. Mine operators in other parts of Mexico, some authors maintain, even asked Porfirio Díaz to ask the 4C's to reduce its wages.[9] In Nacozari, wages of 2 pesos or more were the rule.[10] As at other mining camps, Mexicans often labored on a piecework system at Nacozari. They were paid so much for a ton of ore no matter how much time it took to produce it. Under that system, an American superintendent in Nacozari enthused, Mexicans would "work with a vigor which is remarkable."[11] The physical toil, however, exacted a heavy toll on the human body.

Wages in mining, while uniformly higher, did vary by region. They were highest in the northern districts. Cananea's wage structure, while the best, was not too far out of line with those in Altar, Arizpe, Moctezuma, and even Magdalena. The Bonanza Mining Company of Magdalena, for instance, had wages of 3 pesos a day, while the Transvaal Copper Company in Moctezuma offered 2.75 pesos, according to Mexican authorities. By company statistics, the rate was from 3 to 3.5 pesos.[12] In Altar, at El Tiro, El Plomo, Cerro Colorado, and Cajón de las Amarillas, the mining companies paid 3 pesos a day while in nearby Caborca the prevailing wage was 2.5 pesos.[13] At Cananea and other major northern camps, therefore, workers generally earned about 3 pesos a day.

To the south, wages dropped, although not always dramatically. In Hermosillo district, wages at La Colorada were 2.5 pesos a day, but only 1 peso at Charles Butters and Company in Amarillas.[14] Wages in Ures district ranged from a low of 1.75 at the Yaqui Smelting and Refining Company in Toledo to 3 pesos in Tuape.[15] Minas Prietas paid 1.5 to 2 pesos. In Alamos district, wages varied from a high of 2 to 3 pesos at Mulatos to the 1 peso paid by the Quintera Mining Company in Aduana.[16] Most of the Alamos mines paid about 2 pesos. In Sahuaripa, the average fell below 2 pesos. La Bufa Mining Company at La Trinidad, as late as 1906, paid only 1.5 pesos for a day's work.[17]

Mining in Sonora, unlike other parts of Mexico, was almost entirely men's work. The mining companies hardly ever employed women and they used only a scattering of boys. Most of the children received meager monetary rewards. The mines at Zambona and Minas Nuevas in Alamos, not terribly out of line with their competitors, paid their boys 35 centavos for ten or more hours of toil.[18] The Transvaal Company in Cumpas, on the other hand, reported wages of 1.5 pesos for its boys.[19] Women, only a tiny band in mining, fared no better; in fact, they could earn less than the children.

At a superficial glance, Mexican miners seemed to belong to a pampered minority, an "aristocracy of labor." By comparison with other laborers, they seemed well off. But appearances were deceiving. Most of the mining camps suffered from exorbitant costs of living.[20] Everything from food to clothing to shoes had to be brought in, either from the hinterlands or from across the border. Two important dietary items, wheat flour for tortillas, the staple of the workers' diet, and meat cost much more than they did elsewhere. This was particularly so along the border, especially in isolated places like Cananea and Nacozari which imported not just clothing from the United States but also food.

Miners nearly always had to build their own dwellings. Hovels though they were, they still required materials for their construction.

At times, land on which to build had to be bought or rented from the mining company. With the house up, there was a stove to buy, and a bed, tables, and chairs. Winter weather in the north, and even in the mining camps of Alamos and Sahuaripa, called for the extra expense of heavy jackets. Countless saloons, gamblers, and "ladies of the night" awaited the workers, always ready to take their money on payday. On these "sins," miners spent liberally.[21] In the city of Hermosillo, on the other hand, a sales clerk who earned 50 pesos a month—less than the top-paid miners—could "put on airs," wear coat and tie, and eat the finest meal in a "splendid restaurant."[22] A master bricklayer who never earned over 1.75 pesos a day in Hermosillo, may have been, because of his low cost of living, better off than the miner in Cananea.

The prosperity of mining, and the advent of the railroad also encouraged the growth of a working class in the cities and towns. Money injected into the economy helped expand commerce, trade, and industry. As these sectors grew and prospered, so did the number of jobholders. When the Triumvirate fell from power in 1910, Sonora probably had about 4,000 of these jobholders, over a third of them in the districts of Guaymas and Hermosillo, with the next largest number in Arizpe and Ures.[23] Some labored in flour mills, the oldest and, after mining, the most important industry in the state. On the eve of the mining boom, Sonora already had sixty flour mills. Likewise, Mexicans in Alamos, Guaymas, Hermosillo, Nogales, and Santa Ana labored in shops turning out cheap shoes for miners. A brewery, a lumber mill here and there, bakeries, brickyards, and small *talleres* ("factories") turning out cheap cotton shirts and trousers employed others. As the cities and towns grew, workers in the building trades—carpenters, bricklayers, and masons—multiplied. Men occupied most of these jobs, but women and even children could be found in shops requiring light labor. They did such jobs as rolling cigarettes, making straw hats, or baking bread. The number of these jobs swelled in the cities and towns blessed by the railroad and, not by accident, in those linked to the mines.

Again, wages for these jobs tended to be higher in the north. The high cost of living, inflation in a sense, probably accounts for the better pay scales. Arizpe district, home of the 4C's, paid best; naturally wages in Cananea itself were high, but also in such towns as Arizpe the scale ran from 1.5 pesos a day for work in the flour mill to 3 pesos for carpenters and wagon makers.[24] Wages in Altar and Magdalena were similar, with blacksmiths reported earning the same 3 pesos a day as carpenters.[25] At the turn of the century, the city fathers of Hermosillo had gardeners working for 1 peso a day, laborers for 75 centavos, and men without any skills for 15 pesos a month.[26] In the southern districts, wages ranged from as low as 37 centavos a day for labor in the flour mills of Alamos to 1 peso in the shoe "factories" and 2 pesos for carpenters and blacksmiths.[27] As wages in the skilled trades indicated, supply and demand helped to determine pay levels. Sahuaripa, one of the poorest and most isolated districts, for example, paid better than Alamos, because skilled workers were scarcer.[28] By comparison with the tillers of the soil, the industrial laborers in cities and towns fared well, though they earned less than their compatriots in mining.

In Sonora, even the labradores ("farmhands") had wages above the average for other parts of Mexico, with those in the northern districts earning even higher pay.[29] Debt peonage (indentured laborers) had a marginal existence. At the close of the initial decade of the twentieth century, *haciendas* and *ranchos* in Magdalena paid, on the average, 1.5 pesos per day; in Altar, wages fluctuated between 1 and 1.5 pesos.[30] They dropped to 1 peso or less in the district of Hermosillo, with women earning half that.[31] In Ures, the pay scale rose to 1.25 pesos for a man working in the fields and to 75 centavos for women.[32] In the valley of Guaymas, *hacendados* and *rancheros* paid men 75 centavos and women 50 centavos, wages similar to those in Alamos district.[33] But in the Mayo valley, a part of Guaymas district, wages fell to 37 centavos a day on the hacienda of Jesús M. Salido.[34] In short, though field hands were better off in comparison with Mexicans elsewhere, they fared poorly. A sizable gap existed between *labradores*, and miners, the labor elite.

III

The industrial working class made its bow in a hostile climate. While advocating economic growth, upper-class Mexicans opposed any change in the social structure. As in the industrial nations, labor was just a commodity. What benefits existed, the employer dispensed at will. "Blessed were they," to paraphrase a biblical psalm, "who put their trust in him." Employers who risked their capital provided jobs and, as was their prerogative, set wage scales. Laborers, the sweat and toil of the enterprise, had no rights but the right to move on if they were unhappy. Reflecting the Liberalism of the day—an offshoot of capitalist dogma in the United States and Western Europe—Mexico's national charter, the Constitution of 1857, banned labor unions and, most emphatically, strikes. To advocate changes in the wage structure or to impede the "free interplay between industry and labor," either by physical or moral force, meant risking a heavy fine at the very least or, more likely, a jail sentence. The rulers of Sonora took that message to heart, as Ramón Corral made clear to the strikers in La Trinidad. North and south of the border, the same gospel reigned in the mining camps. In the copper empire at Bisbee, Phelps Dodge ran an open shop with no place for labor unions.[35] James Douglas, who controlled affairs in Nacozari, shared this philosophy, as did William C. Greene in Cananea and the bosses in the lesser camps.

To the sorrow of these social Darwinists, however, workers had a club to hold over the head of their employers. Almost since the days of the Conquest, Sonora had suffered a chronic shortage of labor. During the chaotic years before 1870, that shortage was exacerbated by the flight of as many as 16,000 Sonorenses to California and Arizona.[36] The mining companies paid "high" wages because they had to. The labor shortage, old on the *ranchos* and *haciendas*, plagued mining operations from the beginning. Cheap and docile labor—part of what lured investors to Mexico—often proved absent in Sonora. Because of the scarcity, laborers, formerly available "for 50 centavos or 75 centavos per day," wrote the American consul in 1890, "now are paid 1 peso and 1.25 pesos."[37]

Mining relied on adult male labor, the most sought after.[38] The lack of hands held up the construction of the mill and ore concentrator at Nacozari; in Cananea in 1906, it prevented Greene from recruiting scabs to break the strike.[39] The shortage hit all sectors. An attempt to build a road between Huépec and Opodepe, the gateway to the Río de Sonora valley, faltered for lack of workers.[40] To some extent, and similarly, commercial agriculture bloomed late in the Yaqui valley.[41] As late as 1908, businessmen were complaining of the "scarcity of labor" while in the farm belt of Ures, the leading newspaper, a mouthpiece for local *hacendados*, thought the shortage most severe for agriculture.[42] Ures, like the mining camps, was a focal point of discontent by 1910.

The shortage reinforced an old Spanish habit that might be labeled a form of class oppression or conflict. Since colonial times, wealthy town fathers had been in the habit of drafting the poorest local citizens to get "public tasks" accomplished. Very often the task was the building or maintenance of roads. In Altar in 1887, for instance, in order to upgrade roads the *ayuntamiento* ("municipal government") demanded that the men of the town give six days of unpaid work or the equivalent in money.[43] Two years later, the officials of Cumpas and Moctezuma towns had men doing road work and cutting trees for the telegraph line to Banámichi in adjacent Arizpe.[44] When the Companía Minera de Oro Grande, recent buyer of the mines in Mulatos, asked Hermosillo to help lay a road to Estación Torres, it got free labor from Sahuaripa.[45]

The labor shortage had other repercussions. First of all, it led to an influx of foreign workers. For example, 200 American blacks were brought in to lay track for the Sonora Railway. Along with them came Chinese coolies, initially to help with the construction of the railroad, and Japanese to labor in the mines. From across the border came more Americans, not just to do skilled labor but also, because of the high pay, to work side by side with Mexicans in the most menial jobs. The mechanization of mining, first with steam and later on with electricity, came partly in response to the ubiquitous labor shortage, a fact of mining life to the very end of the boom, as the testimony of Governor Rafael Izábal shows.[46]

But the employers' need for strong backs, while a sort of club in the hands of the worker, scarcely changed attitudes toward labor. That club turned out to be more stick than cudgel. Not only did management hold firm in its ill-treatment of workers, so did don Porfirio and his legion of Mexican sycophants. The two groups collaborated to make sure nothing changed. The worker dwelt, after all, said an American sage, in a world where "every man is wanted and no man is wanted much." As Esteban Baca Calderón, an oracle of labor, exclaimed, he "wished that miners could see the dictatorship as their worst enemy," doubtlessly referring to don Porfirio's political philosophy and its kinship with mining company policy.[47] In spite of their "high wages," the miners were unhappy, and an embryonic spirit of class consciousness began to emerge. A clash with management and, given the shape of national policy, with Mexico City and Hermosillo was unavoidable.

IV

That the best paid would be the first to go to the barricades against their employers was inevitable as well as logical. To quote Leon Trotsky's famous dictum, rebellion arises not in the souls of men crippled by hunger and want but, to the contrary, in those who have tasted the bitter fruit of change. Dashed hopes for a beneficent future or a sudden loss of hard-won gains underlie rebellion. Given this axiom, it should surprise no one that workingmen joined hands to protect their interests. Hard times lead to labor agitation and strikes.

The outburst that rocked Cananea in 1906 was the most visible protest, but it was hardly the first time labor tried to organize. Attempts at labor unity dated back at least to 1873, with the birth in Alamos of the Sociedad Mutualista de Artesanos, a mutual insurance group.[48] A similar organization, known as the Sociedad de Obreros de Hidalgo, had its headquarters in Hermosillo in the 1880s.[49] Guaymas, the port city, had not one but four labor units: La Sociedad de Artesanos y Obreros del Porvenir, Sociedad Mechor Ocampo, Unión de Mecánicos, and Sociedad José María Morelos.[50] The Artesanos del Porvenir, under a banner proclaiming the virtues of "work, responsibility, and union," ran a primary school, offered night classes for adults, and, in 1888, prevailed upon Governor Ramón Corral to distribute lots for homes to workers in Guaymas.[51] A Comité Obrero Guaymense, a kind of central labor council, coordinated the activities of four groups, the Unión de Mecánicos, Unión de Aprendices de Mecánicos, Unión de Calderos, and the Artesanos del Porvenir.[52] One early workers' society had as a goal, its brochure announced, "wiping the tears from the eyes of the anguished worker."[53] In Nogales, others organized the Sociedad Hidalgo de Artesanos Unidos, dedicated to gaining strength through self-help in order "to withstand the bitter disappointments of life."[54] But Mexican workers did not just organize and talk. They walked off jobs, they went on strike, and they shut down mines.

The first of the labor troubles against the foreign proponents of "progress" exploded in 1889 in, of all places, the isolated Sahuaripa district. In the mining town of La Trinidad, a mecca for silver speculators, workers struck against a company that "paid the highest wages in Sonora." This strike, in an age that judged capital sacrosanct, challenged not just the power of the foreign speculator but the authority of his Mexican allies.

The mines of La Trinidad, largely silver, antedated Mexican independence. Until the 1880s Matías Alsúa, their Mexican owner, had fattened his purse with profits taken from them. Upon his death, the mines, "considered the most valuable of any in Sonora," were sold to some Londoners for a reputed $1.5 million, at that time "the largest mining sale . . . ever . . . in northern Mexico."[55] The English began to dig deeper tunnels, to erect a reduction works with the aid of Americans from California, and to build a sawmill to provide lumber for the mine. They opened a wagon road leading from the mine to Estación Torres on the Sonora Railway.[56] One and all in Trinidad, its mayor solemnly affirmed, stood ready "to do all we can" to help the company get under way, believing that in the long run everybody would gain.[57] A euphoric report by Loreto Trujillo, prefect of Sahuaripa, predicted a cornucopia of plenty with the reopening of the mine. (The report also contained thanks to the management for helping Trujillo prepare it.)[58] Unfortunately for Trujillo's dreams, the English went bankrupt, abandoned the enterprise, and left behind a mountain of unpaid debts.[59] But before the bumbling Englishmen departed, La Trinidad, a community of 4,000, became the stage for the drama of the first labor uprising in Sonora.

There were some rumblings earlier, but the worst of the labor troubles exploded in February. Obviously unimpressed by the trumpeted "highest wages" in Sonora, the miners boldly defied their English bosses. They called for more money and for a change in their relations with management, although the exact nature of this demand is not entirely clear.[60] When the Englishmen turned down the demands, a band of miners stopped working. Edmund Harvey, the outspoken general manager, was aghast. As he told Mexican authorities, this was "the second time" the miners had defied him. Unless taught a lesson, the Mexicans would surely repeat their action with "dire results" for everyone.[61]

At the time the conflict erupted, the company, true to its boasts, had indeed been paying "good wages," at least by comparison with others. Miners toiling in the tunnels below earned 1.5 pesos per day, and those above ground, 1 peso. *La Constitución*, the official journal in Hermosillo, wondered how miners could strike when they earned the fabulous sum of 1.5 pesos for a day's labor. But the English played tricks, taking back with one hand what they offered with the other. Instead of paying cash on payday, La Trinidad Limited gave its workers *boletos*, paper chits, redeemable, the company promised, at any store in town. To the anger of the miners, half of the local merchants, clearly of little faith in the English enterprise, refused to accept *boletos*. They wanted cash for their merchandise.[62] According to the company, the miners had money to spend; the merchants, however, declared them penniless. The workers, not unnaturally, asked for their wages in pesos.

More than money was at stake, though. The confrontation was developing nasty racial overtones. The agitators of the strike, charged the company's Mexican lawyer, had attempted to "pit natives against foreigners." "No one can deny that many of the Mexican miners . . . think of these criminals as martyrs battling for a just cause." With shouts of "*gringos cabrones*" ("Yankee devils"), he went on, the agitators had endeavored to win support of miners of like bent.[63] *La Constitución* agreed that troublemakers from the outside had stirred up the miners.[64]

The troubles, the recalcitrant English maintained, lay with the "native element." As the American superintendent, Richard R. Hawkins, Harvey's superior, put it, "for some time now" the Mexicans had been "growing ugly and outspoken in their hatred and denunciation of foreigners in general and the employees of the company in particular." "But," he asserted, "we propose to run this business ourselves"; the Mexicans would not dictate terms. With this in mind, Hawkins and Harvey had brought in Yaqui scabs, "Indians and outsiders," leaving "strikers and their friends . . . out in the cold." It was then that the strike grew violent. To exacerbate matters, Hawkins complained, native hostility had "culminated . . . in as glaring an outrage as ever disgraced the annals of any civilized country."[65] To what did Hawkins refer?

The episode took place late in February. One night during the strike, so Hawkins told the story, as he and five of the "mine bosses and carpenters" were sitting "quietly conversing" on the veranda of his house, "a gang of half-drunken natives" had "come along" and hurled insults at them, the term "*gringos* and *cabrones* being the mildest employed." When the Mexicans were asked to move on, their "hatred and rage long accumulated broke all bounds" and they began to bombard the foreigners with rocks. The bosses fled to the shelter of the house. Before barricading themselves, Harvey and the others fired "a few shots in the air to summon assistance." Then, continued Hawkins, "it seemed as though all Hell had broken loose." The mob, its ranks swollen to "hundreds," rained more rocks against the house, shattering doors and shutters, while "the floor of the sleeping room and the beds were literally covered with boulders." Still, as Hawkins wove his tale, "the little band of pale, determined men," grasping "their revolvers," stood firm, "ready to sell their lives dearly."[66]

To their immense relief, Harvey, "all available foreigners," and the town police came to their rescue. The "mob was soon dispersed" and "the ringleaders as had not escaped . . . captured and lodged in jail." Still, upon returning "to the scene of the devilish outbreak," Hawkins went on, "we were [once again] saluted with a rock volley fired from somewhere."[67] What he refused to see was that the strikers had a throng of sympathizers in the community. The company, he maintained, had "always treated their native employees in an exceptionally kind and liberal manner." Not only did it pay "higher wages than elsewhere in Mexico," after the strike it had opened a general store where workmen could purchase "supplies of every description at . . . cost, . . . an excess of liberality unparalleled in Mexican mining history." He thought "the treatment of the men . . . really patriarchal" and the outbreak "consequently inexcusable."[68]

Harvey judged the strike leaders "the worst class of men" who "can possibly exist in *any* country." He did not want them back in La Trinidad where "we are compelled to go about armed, and on nearly every occasion if any of us should . . . go through the town after dark we are saluted with volleys of large stones." To make matters worse, in Harvey's view, the mayor of the town failed to punish the chief culprit, Manuel Pablo Encinas, who also headed the town council. Harvey, calling the mayor, "an inoffensive man . . . who can be turned around

the little finger," wanted a more vigorous man in his place.[69] Or, to put
it more accurately, Harvey wanted a man sympathetic to the company.
Still as he acknowledged, even a new mayor would not solve all the company's woes. Even though the strike had been broken, the workers were
continuing a more quiet resistance. "The men work two days and remain idle the rest of the week," he said, keeping "our machinery going
at half capacity more than half the time."[70] The mayor, Miguel Avilez,
had a slightly different version of the labor difficulties. He said his conciliatory efforts had faltered because of the intransigence of both managers and workers, a difficult situation made impossible by the decision
to bring in *esquiroles* ("scabs").[71]

In the meantime, wishing to apply pressure on Mexican authorities,
the company appealed to the government in London. Lord Salisbury,
the British foreign minister, asked Mexico City to investigate the complaint. According to his note, the company was suffering greatly because of "frequent strikes by its miners, encouraged . . . by persons
well-known in the community." His letter reminded Mexicans that
wages paid by La Trinidad Limited represented nine-tenths of the income of miners in Sahuaripa district. Salisbury also pointed out the
company's nominal capital of 750,000 pounds and heavy investment in
the mine.[72] His note got immediate results. From Mexico City, Porfirio
Díaz, a disciple of the virtues of foreign capital, told Governor Corral
of Sonora to stop the strikes and to protect, "within the law," as he defined it, "the interests of the company."[73]

Díaz need not have written his epistle. Corral had already taken steps
to end the labor dispute. Corral proudly informed Mexico City that he
had ended the strike, jailed its ringleaders, and restored the company's
confidence in Mexican law. "My government, aware of the importance
of private capital in the development of the country's natural resources," Corral wrote, protected all companies doing business in Sonora, regardless of their nationality, "taking special care . . . on behalf
of La Trinidad Company."[74] Earlier, replying to a bitter letter from Edmund Harvey, Corral apologized "for the troubles caused by a few malcontents." However, perhaps thinking of the possible political repercussions, Corral refused to draft the strike leaders into the army, as
Harvey wanted, claiming that the punishment did not fit the "crime."
Nonetheless, he informed Harvey, he had ordered the prefect of
Sahuaripa to watch over the interests of the company. Come what may,
it could count on his support. If the company would pay its workers in
cash, that and the punishment meted out to the agitators would restore
peace to La Trinidad. As to Harvey's request that the troublemakers be
driven from town, Corral urged the Englishmen to take his case to the

judicial authorities who, he thought likely, would comply. But to get men to work more than a day or two a week, the company simply had to recruit others.[75]

The report of Loreto Trujillo, the prefect, made one thing clear: the strike had the sympathy of the town. On orders from Hermosillo, he had arrived with twenty-five armed men, ready to put down the disorders. He knew beforehand that the issue was money (the paper chits) and that the company, unwilling to raise wages, had hired scabs from the outside. Still, by the next day, he too concluded that "certain individuals" had encouraged the miners not to go back into the pits if their demands were unmet.

In an attempt to find a compromise, Trujillo called a meeting of labor and management. To his disappointment, nothing came of it. During the meeting, Pablo Encinas, a town councilman, said that he spoke on behalf of the "people" of La Trinidad. To get the mine going again, he insisted, the company had to pay better, pay in cash, and pay by the week. The company, for its part, merely offered to get local merchants to accept the *boletos* as money for purchases. The superintendent wanted Encinas punished but, Trujillo told Corral, no evidence linked him to the outbreak of the strike. Nonetheless, he wondered, might it not be prudent to remove Encinas from the town council and to get him out of town?[76] Corral, likely offended by Harvey's arrogance, would not go along with the idea.[77]

Corral, a fickle friend of labor at best, laid down the law. All men in La Trinidad who were not working or did not own property had to find a job or be punished as vagrants. Anyone bringing any trouble upon the company, or seeking to change the wages of miners, or to undercut the laws of supply and demand would be jailed promptly.[78] Significantly, the mayor, who needed the support of Encinas and knew that public opinion favored the strikers, delayed enforcing these dictates.[79] Not until Trujillo threatened to report him to Hermosillo did he carry them out.[80] The six miners considered the ringleaders of the strike were jailed in Sahuaripa.[81] The Trinidad Mining Company made one concession: it established a *tienda de raya* where, said Trujillo, a firm believer in the benefits of foreign capital, the miners could buy articles at cost. He acknowledged that the measure kept the miners earning *boletos*, and hurt the merchants of La Trinidad, all of them Mexicans. But the workers of La Trinidad, the company superintendent assured him, were now "very happy."[82]

So ended the labor strike at La Trinidad. Foreigners, with the support of Mexican officials, locally and in Hermosillo, had gotten their way. The heralded "progress," however, never materialized. The company ultimately folded when the silver ore petered out. Sahuaripa was denied the long-awaited taste of modernity. By 1905, a mere 561 inhabitants, most of them poor, dwelt there.[83]

The little-known saga of the strike at La Trinidad, a portent of things to come, lies buried in the historical records. The strike at Cananea nearly two decades later, in contrast, has a prominent place in the history books about Sonora, the Republic, and the Great Rebellion. To many Mexicans, the strike was the forerunner of the upheaval of 1910. The salient national political event of 1906, the strike halted work in Mexico's major mining center. It was troubling because it erupted in what was considered the "progressive sector" of the economy, in an industry regarded as a key to the modernization of Sonora. Cananea, the biggest city in the state, enjoyed one of the highest rates of growth in Mexico and basked in the limelight of the copper bonanza. Its terrible aftermath, years of unemployment, came with the decline of the market for copper, mainly in the United States.

Why the strike? The powder keg at Cananea exploded for multiple reasons. Mexican workers, first off, had the semblance of an organization and a bit of leadership. By 1906, Esteban Baca Calderón, Manuel M. Diéguez, and Francisco Ibarra, the "agitators," had helped to establish in Cananea a branch of the radical Partido Liberal Mexicano of Ricardo Flores Magón, an advocate of labor rights, as well as a Unión Liberal, a reformist political club. Baca Calderón, to crown all, urged the formation of a countrywide Liga Minera de los Estados Unidos Mexicanos and support for Flores Magón.[84] Interestingly, these outspoken champions of the rank and file sat behind desks. Diéguez, for example, earned 7 pesos a day, over twice the wage paid miners.

A decision by the 4C's to cut costs ignited the tinderbox. In late May, the company suddenly announced, labor at the Oversight mine, one of the biggest, would be paid differently. No longer would the miners be paid by the time they spent on the job; instead, they would be paid according to the amount of ore they dug out of the ground. The harder a miner toiled and the more copper he delivered, the greater the profit to the company.[85] Such was the thinking behind the new wage system. Undoubtedly, the 4C's meant to adopt it in the other mines as well. Based on past experience, the miners knew the policy meant fewer jobs, harder toil, and larger profits for the labor contractors, the Americans at the Oversight mine who were the intermediaries between them and the company.

Equally ominous, Greene and his subordinates granted a pay increase to the American workers, who made up 34 percent of the labor force in 1906.[86] The discriminatory pay hike galled the Mexicans.

Many of the Americans, already enjoying higher wages, performed the same work as Mexicans: not every Yankee had a master's job. The Mexicans wanted more pay, a minimum of 5 pesos a day, and a workday of eight hours. Had they gotten their way, one noted Mexican believed, the fact that pay scales favored Americans would not have unduly disturbed them.[87] This view flies in the face of the evidence. More and more, Mexicans had come to resent the discriminatory pay structure. Mexican *barreteros*, men who worked with a crow, wedge, or pick, earned 4 pesos for a day's labor while Americans doing the identical job earned $3.50. The exchange rate stood at 2 pesos for a dollar so the American was earning the equivalent of 7 pesos, but the buying power of the dollar was even higher. American carpenters made 4 dollars a day but Mexicans 4 pesos.[88] From the start, Americans making dollar wages earned over twice as much.

To aggravate matters, the Yankees had the best jobs. Most *barreteros*, among the better paid of the workingmen, were Americans, while the labor bosses and the office staff, almost invariably recalled Baca Calderón, were Yankees. "I never saw a single Mexican," he charged, "with a job that called for intelligence."[89] The Yankee bosses often asked Mexicans to work longer hours, or under cruel and arrogant foremen; the miners demanded, for instance, that two vicious foremen be fired. The 3 pesos a day of Mexican miners, exalted as the best in the Republic, actually compared poorly to the paycheck Americans carried home.

Wage differences, as Mexicans knew, were old hat in Sonora. They existed wherever Americans and other foreigners could be found. The inequalities at Cananea were part of a larger picture: in Sonora and elsewhere in their own country, Mexicans simply made less money than foreigners. For example, the Moctezuma Copper Company, an American enterprise, took care to reward its own, paying Yankee workers two or three times more than Mexicans in its employ. The Transvaal Copper Company in Cumpas, in addition to its mechanics and machinists, had tappers and weighers—jobs requiring little skill but always set aside for Americans—making from 4 to 6 pesos a day. Its foremen, rarely Mexicans, made 7 pesos.[90] On the Sonora Railway, Mexican workers earned the lowest wages.[91] On the spur line between Minas Prietas and Estación Torres, the better paying jobs, often reserved for Americans, paid 100 pesos or more a month, while the pick-and-shovel brigades earmarked for Mexicans and Chinese paid only 45 pesos.[92] When Corral brought in Americans from California to help construct the Palacio de Gobierno in Hermosillo, he gave carpenters 6 dollars a day, their assistants 5 dollars, and roofers slightly less, wages out of reach of Mexicans.[93] Corral and his friends, by going along with discriminatory wage scales, revealed their own class and racial prejudice.

When William C. Greene curtly rejected their pleas, Mexicans at Cananea, unwilling to accept no for an answer, went on strike. Before they returned to work, half a dozen Americans would lose their lives while thirty Mexicans would be killed by the defenders of Greene— bootlicking Mexicans and Americans, as well as a troop of rangers who crossed the border from Arizona. The invasion of Mexican soil by rifle-toting Yankees raised a hue and cry in the Republic. The strike, according to a memorandum to Díaz, tested "the extent and quality of the forces" at the disposal of his enemies. Its author, Rafael de Zayas Enríquez, a trusted confidant, urged Díaz "not to look upon the affair at Cananea with indifference, but to accede to public demand . . . to investigate," his advice continued, "and to demonstrate, that the government was fully justified in its actions, thus dissipating doubts, calming fears, and satisfying public opinion." Díaz had "to effectually countenance the laborers insofar as their demands are just."[94] In their support of the foreign speculator, Mexicans in power, implied Zayas Enríquez, had gone too far. It was time to bring a sense of balance into the picture, to rectify the worst inequalities.

The sparks of labor's discontent burned fleetingly at Cananea and La Trinidad. But they also burned elsewhere. In Las Chispas, a mining camp notorious for its strip searches, Mexican miners went on strike in 1906 after their pleas for more money were rejected.[95] That same year, miners at San Francisco in Altar district stopped working when their American bosses refused to pay them 3 pesos a day. The constable, a lackey of the mining company, jailed the strike leaders, four dissident Mexicans who, he asserted, "had disturbed the public order," and he barred others from entering the mine. The company, he told his superiors in Hermosillo, did not want the agitators to return to San Francisco.[96]

The economic debacle of 1907 added more fuel to the fire, worsening relations between workers and management. As more and more mines closed, the numbers of unemployed rose, and so did the ranks of men waiting for paychecks for work they had done earlier. The list of the unpaid grew by leaps and bounds, as the official correspondence of the time demonstrates. Since February, to quote a letter dated April 23, 1908, from the prefect of Moctezuma to Hermosillo, the mining company in San José de Nacozari had not paid its workers.[97] In the same district, the Transvaal Mining Company, having stopped operations a year earlier, left its workers to fend for themselves, paying some with *giros* ("drafts") merchants refused to accept. So angry were the workers that the mayor of Cumpas feared riots might break out.[98]. When the Lista Blanca and Calera mines near Caborca fell on evil days, their general manager, John Henderson, fled without paying his miners—or his debts to local merchants—a complaint to the governor testified.[99] Even financial agreements with guards hired to watch over the shut-down mines were not always honored, according to a complaint against the Trinity Mining Company.[100] Managers of the mines, almost always American, often simply took as much as they could while the ores flowed, fled when things turned sour, and gave no heed to the plight of their Mexican workers.

V

By 1910, a working-class consciousness had begun to emerge. The miner, in banding together with others to carry out strikes, had recognized that he and his companions stood at odds against their American employers and their allies, the Mexican upper class. A proletariat had taken its first step up the ladder to political maturity. *Regeneración*, the pugnacious journal of the Flore Magón, circulated widely among the workers.

Of no less significance, men had begun to speak out for the workers. Literate men, willing and able to voice the lament of the workers at Cananea, had challenged Greene, the Yankee master, and his Mexican allies. One such man was Luis G. Monzón, a native of San Luis Potosí, a teacher by trade and a socialist. Run out of his home state because of his labor militancy, he had come to Sonora and taught school in Cumpas, Moctezuma, Nacozari, and Cananea, the heart of the copper belt. A born malcontent, Monzón had whetted his intellectual appetite reading Kropotkin, Bakunin, and Proudhon, joined the Club Verde protest in Hermosillo at the turn of the century, and spent time in jail in Agua Prieta and Douglas for his advocacy of the Magonistas.[101]

Juan G. Cabral, an instigator of the strike, later bore arms against the Old Regime. The cashier of the lumberyard in Cananea, Cabral had spent his adolescence in the mining hamlet of La Colorada, gone to school in the Colegio de Sonora, and turned critic of Díaz at the ripe age of seventeen.[102] Esteban Baca Calderón, who labored in the foundry of the 4C's, had his eyes opened in Santa María del Oro in Nayarit by a teacher with a nationalist view of Mexican history. All people had immutable rights, Baca Calderón learned, but in Mexico when it came to the use of national resources the rights of Mexicans ought to supersede those of foreigners.[103] Lázaro Gutiérrez de Lara in 1902 was a lawyer who arrived in Arizpe town, where he edited a newspaper. Moving to Cananea in 1905, he sided with labor and took part in the strike of 1906.[104]

CHAPTER 8

Consequences of a
Dependent Bourgeoisie

I

Alamos, the oldest town in Sonora, gave birth to a fledgling commercial elite. *"Caballeros* ("gentlemen") and . . . merchants," recalled Manuel Corbalá Acuña, the bearer of one of the town's distinguished family names, had given Alamos its character. Under the guiding hands of don Domingo Terán de los Ríos, one of its merchant founders, the commercial entrepôt of Alamos had stamped its imprint on the rest of Sonora.[1]

Yet later, when foreign investment flowed into Mexico, the rulers of Sonora hastened to tie their fate to Western capitalist nations, particularly the United States. They turned their backs on these native merchants, who might have been able to construct a stable economic edifice in their own country. By courting foreign capitalists, buying manufactured goods from them, and linking commerce to markets north of the border, the leaders helped to dismantle this fragile edifice almost before it was built and to create, instead, a bourgeoisie dependent on the whims of foreigners.

II

Until late in the nineteenth century, the situation was quite different. Local inhabitants rarely purchased American goods. What few articles they bought usually bore a European imprint, either English or

French, lamented the United States consul. Despite the presence of these foreign import houses in Guaymas, the consul admitted that Mexicans still "sold most of the goods." This local merchant order, a nascent bourgeoisie, was "mostly in debt" and had "no capital."[2] However, the merchants had native roots and, equally important, some of them handled goods made in Mexico—textiles, for example. Outside Guaymas, Hermosillo, Ures, and Alamos—the "cities" of Sonora—markets for luxury articles hardly existed and merchants were rarely foreign.[3]

Trade between the smaller towns was limited, but the exchange of goods between town and country, at times handled by merchants, was alive and well. Without many good roads or wagons to transport their grains and beef to distant markets, *rancheros* and *hacendados* more often than not sold them close to home. They did not get fabulously rich but they made money. The townspeople were the buyers of farm and ranch products. It was an exchange of goods characterized by necessity and self-sufficiency. *Ranchos* and *haciendas* produced meat, milk, cheese, wheat, corn, rice, garbanzos, and fruits, and purchased wheat flour, candy, *mezcal*, and other goods. Hermosillo and Ures towns became known for *panocha*, cubed brown sugar, and the Pinacate for its salt.[4] In the towns, an artisan would build simple chairs, tables, and chests of drawers on the request of a buyer, who might be a town resident or a nearby dirt farmer or *hacendado*. The towns had butchers, invariably a blacksmith, here and there a saddle-and-harness maker, cobblers, perhaps a carriage or wagon shop, and always a *tienda mixta*, the general store.

Of industry, only the most fragile of foundations stood in place. Industry arrived tardily, hampered by the scarcity of population, the huge expanse of territory, and the absence of good roads, as well as by the lack of capital and know-how.[5] Nonetheless, a tiny start had been made. Almost every town of any significance had a flour mill. The surplus flour, a major export out of state, sold up and down the Pacific Coast, principally in Sinaloa and Lower California. Additionally, small factories produced brooms, *petates* ("straw mats"), soap, pants and shirts of cheap cloth (*mezclilla*) for field hands and miners, straw hats to shade out the hot sun, and cigarettes. A cotton textile mill, the first in the state, was established in 1839 in Los Angeles by Manuel Ruiz Iñigo.[6] Some three decades later, it operated sixty-four looms.[7] Owners and workers, as well as the buyers of its cloth, were Mexican.

Trade and the mercantile business, unlike industry, had a venerable heritage. With Alamos as the model, urban communities emerged in diverse corners of the state, acting largely as commercial centers for the surrounding hinterland. For the merchant founders of Alamos, like their later disciples, civilization and culture withered away outside of the towns, a view they inherited from the Spaniards.[8] The towns sheltered merchants, along with tradesmen, artisans, and, here and there, a petty bureaucrat, but also *labradores*, the tillers of the soil. On the northern fringe of Sonora, the inhabitants customarily erected dirt walls around their towns to guard against Apache attacks. These "urban" enclaves were walled towns, in certain respects resembling the bastions of medieval Europe. The town, the bedmate of commerce, appeared early in Sonora.

At least four towns, cities they were called, had climbed to eminence by the 1850s. Founded in the colonial era, Hermosillo was the largest and most prosperous. The small quantity of luxury goods and machinery imported from Europe by way of Guaymas port, as well as articles from other parts of Mexico usually found their way to Hermosillo, the focal point of commerce in the state. Goods from the hinterland of the Río Sonora, from the north and northwest, arrived in Hermosillo before being shipped to Guaymas.[9] Large wholesale firms handled these transactions. By 1850, Hermosillo could boast of public buildings, an assayer's office, the state mint, a public school, and a prison. Ures stood to the east on the banks of the Río Sonora. A colonial town with intellectual pretensions, Ures was the capital city. *El Sonorense*, a vociferous journal, was published there. The town included commercial firms, a sugar mill, retail stores, a school, a large church facing the square, and a jail. Guaymas, the chief port, was a trade center, with *almacenes*—warehouses for goods brought in by ship—mercantile houses, and stores.[10] Alamos, a social hub of the state, controlled the trade and commerce of the mining towns of the south. The business deals of its merchants had repercussions everywhere in the state. Alamos, Hermosillo, and Guaymas all had rich agricultural hinterlands, which were both markets for goods and suppliers of food. All of these centers had a commercial sector, a tiny native bourgeoisie that was relatively independent.

Beyond these commercial depots lay smaller ones. Along the Río Sonora and in the south especially, some had emerged as towns from *reales de minas*, *villas* or *presidios* of colonial origin. They served as economic centers for their back countries. Moctezuma, Altar, and Sahuaripa retained a legendary air dating from colonial days. During the final decades of the eighteenth century, the Golden Age of New Spain, colonists from the Iberian peninsula settled in Sonora, attracted by its peace and prosperity. By 1810, over 70,000 had built their homes in the old intendency of Arizpe. A nucleus settled in the town, converting it into a marketplace of note. Moctezuma and, to the west, Magdalena and Altar had similar histories.[11]

Determined to sink their roots into their adopted land, the colonists brought with them urban traditions from the towns and cities of northern and eastern Spain they had left. Entrepreneurs by habit and custom, they established commercial houses, engaged in trade, invested money and labor in mining, and, in the nearby valleys and deltas, developed small farms, *ranchos*, and *haciendas*. Jealous of their independence, they set up *municipios*, corporate political bodies, to keep the *hacendados* from meddling in their affairs. It was primarily the merchants who led this drive to confer on the town a political life of its own.[12] No matter how poor the town, the visitor "could usually find one or two comparatively rich men with an inkling of the outside world."[13] Despite the growing importance of merchants, however, Sonora remained rural, with political power basically in the hands of *hacendados*, who frequently had commercial stakes of their own, usually a flour mill.

III

Over the course of time, the doyens of the large commercial entrepôts, particularly Hermosillo and Guaymas, gradually began to displace the rural power brokers. Whether urban merchants or maverick *hacendados* with business links, these ambitious men heralded the transformation of society. The urbanites were feeling their oats; they wanted a bigger share of political power. The change signaled a transfer of economic power from the sierra, the old colonial bailiwick, to the flatlands of the western desert. The climax came with the shift of the capital from Ures to Hermosillo, where merchants ruled. The war with the United States, in which Mexico lost its northern territories, as well as the Gadsden Purchase (*Tratado de la Mesilla*) in 1853, speeded up the transition. With the flowering of the American Southwest, Mexican merchants began to forge trade ties with their northern counterparts, especially in Tucson.

On both sides of the border, trade and commerce prospered. In Mexico, foreigners began to introduce modern managerial techniques and reinforce nascent capitalist values. A few married into the elite of Alamos.[14] Slowly but surely, Mexican merchants and businessmen, and *hacendados* joined to them by family ties, began to prosper by their links to the outside world. They increasingly judged these links to be indispensable to their well-being. They came to identify the development of Mexico—or rather their own economic ascendency—with capitalism and the industrial nations of Europe and, eventually, the United States. Foreign investment, they concluded, meant economic growth. Not much later, cattle ranchers in the north and planters in the Mayo and

Yaqui valleys, both wanting to exploit markets across the border, joined this school of thought. What really was taking place was the growth and ascendency of a dependent bourgeoisie, at the expense of local economic interests.

The victory of Ignacio Pesqueira, a native of provincial Arizpe who was educated in Europe, over Manuel María Gándara, a conservative caudillo, epitomized this transition. The defeat of Gándara, who was identified with the interests of *hacendados*, opened the doors to a new epoch. Pesqueira's triumph was mostly the work of the merchants of Guaymas port, who were aided and abetted by merchants and mining entrepreneurs in Alamos. With his victory, more power fell into the hands of the western towns, home to the nascent bourgeoisie. Pesqueira's rise capped the struggle of nineteenth-century Liberals to pull Sonora into the capitalistic age, to cut the power of the landowners, and to get the military back into the barracks. Cast in political terms, it meant more independence for the *municipio*, and for its dominant group, the merchants. Although beholden primarily to merchants and miners, Pesqueira could not blissfully turn his back on ranchers and *hacendados*. The ambivalent character of his support, typified by Pesqueira himself, a cattle rancher and *hacendado* with commercial interests, ultimately led to his downfall.[15]

Pesqueira's rule from 1856 to 1876, the eventful years from Ayutla to La Reforma to the French Intervention, opened wide the political doors to small but powerful merchant houses in the west. Their names survived the nineteenth century: the Monteverdes and José Aguilar in Hermosillo; a brother of Aguilar in Guaymas; and an Aguilar cousin in Ures. Also, new names, unheard of until then, suddenly loomed important: Cirilio Ramírez in Hermosillo; and Wenceslao and José Iberri, and Torcuato de la Huerta in Guaymas. Relative newcomers from abroad also climbed the ladder of success: John R. Robinson and Thomas Spence, American residents of Guaymas; and, in Hermosillo, the Spaniards Celedonio and José Ortiz; and the French Camou clan— Juan Pedro, Francisco, Pascual, Pedro Andŕes, and José. These merchant capitalists, dabblers in mines and land too, wanted political stability. As they saw it, the political chaos of yesteryear had hurt commerce. Unfortunately, the decades of Pesqueira's rule also brought onto the political stage another generation of military caciques.

With the encouragement of his merchant backers, Pesqueira spent time and money trying to create a climate hospitable to their interests. He built wagon roads; he urged American merchants to come to Sonora. International trade grew. Convinced that business and commerce required literate and trained men, Pesqueira advocated public education and set aside funds for schools. Mining was revitalized as

American speculators began to venture south. An infant economic boom, the first in a long time, began to unfold, particularly in Hermosillo and Guaymas. Its benefits spread to the northwest, especially to Magdalena.[16]

Not all of Sonora enjoyed good times. Ures failed to prosper while Alamos had mixed results, primarily because the Yaquis and Mayos stood their ground. Without the development of the Indian valleys there could be no prosperity.[17] Ironically, when Pesqueira raised taxes to pursue his wars against the Indians, the merchants of Alamos, Hermosillo, and Guaymas, along with dissident soldiers, revolted and toppled Pesqueira. Pesqueira's tax policies, which eventually helped the elites of Alamos and Guaymas, paradoxically led to his undoing.

IV

Nothing better typified this era than the transformation of Guaymas port and, along with it, the nature of its merchant elite. Roughly speaking, 1870 marks a watershed in the history of Guaymas. Until then, the port languished. Its tiny merchant bourgeoisie was largely Mexican and relatively independent, although infiltrated by foreigners, reported the American consul.[18] During the latter half of the century, before the arrival of the railroad, the port thrived. Its merchants enjoyed abundance as middlemen by importing foreign goods and by exporting minerals. Exports of garbanzos through Guaymas port went out mainly to Spanish and Caribbean markets but also to American buyers. Because it bought and sold foreign articles—more and more often of American manufacture—and profited from the shipment of raw materials abroad, the health of the port city came to rest on foreign customers, Americans by and large. Those who handled the transactions, the middlemen, eventually came to form a dependent bourgeoisie.

Until 1824, so unimportant was Guaymas that it had no customs house. The establishment of such a house and the designation of Guaymas as a *villa* (small town) occurred simultaneously. With a bay ringed by hills, Guaymas was the finest port on the Pacific, but its limited trade with other Mexican and foreign ports hardly mattered. Exports consisted mostly of wheat flour. The port stagnated. With skimpy shipping facilities (just three small wharves), and no good roads to other parts of Sonora, the port and its population stood still.[19] Travelers judged Guaymas "a poor stopover point"; the surrounding hills kept the waters placid, shut out breezes, and turned the heat into "a veritable furnace."[20] At mid-century, things took a turn for the better. Steamships with greatly enlarged carrying capacities lowered the cost of ocean transport, while the discovery of gold in California, and the subsequent rush to exploit it, turned Guaymas into an important harbor.[21]

The replacement of sailing ships by steam transformed Guaymas into an international port of call. As in colonial or neocolonial countries, foreigners controlled the shipping. The American Pacific Mail Company ran ships from the Mexican west coast to San Francisco, with a stopover in Guaymas. The Newbern, a coastal ship carrying passengers and cargo, docked there too. Other steamship lines included the Campañía de Vapores de California, Lineas Aceleradas del Golfo de Cortés, Compañía de la Costa del Pacífico, and the Canadian, Mexican Pacific Steam.[22] Just one was Mexican, the Compañía Naviera del Pacífico, brainchild of Luis Martínez, a Guaymas tycoon related by blood to the Pesqueiras. With an ear attuned to current politics, he named his ships after noted Mexican Liberals, among them Benito Juárez, Ramón Corral, Bernardo Reyes, and José Limantour. An entrepreneur with many irons in the fire, he was one of the owners of the lumber firm in Guaymas and a stockholder in the Banco de Sonora.[23]

Guaymas profited in multiple ways. When a French company began to exploit the copper deposits at Santa Rosalia on the peninsula of Lower California, ships from Guaymas carried its food and other articles. Because of its location near the mouth of the Yaqui River, Guaymas also profited as a supply depot during the wars against the Yaquis. Afterwards, Guaymas became the port for goods entering and leaving the towns of the Yaqui River delta, and enjoyed a monopoly of the trade with Sahuaripa.[24] Lumber from Oregon and Washington bound for mines in Bisbee entered through the port.[25]

With the mining boom of the 1880s, the economy of Guaymas really took off. By 1910, Guaymas disputed Hermosillo's economic supremecy in the state. Its commerce was two and a half times that of Hermosillo; it had more municipal revenues; and its population of 12,333, though about the same as of its rival, was growing at a faster pace.[26] Guaymas district, in the interval, had outstripped Hermosillo district in population. The two cities were quite unlike. Although important commercially, Hermosillo was also a cattle and farming district, and a mining emporium.[27] Guaymas district, while profiting from an increasingly important agriculture, especially in the Mayo valley, still relied primarily on its port. Of its five *municipios*, that of the port was the largest and wealthiest.

Ships docking at the port brought goods into Guaymas to be resold at a profit by its merchants, while others made money by handling exports. By 1907, about 10 of the nearly 14 million pesos' worth of goods imported by the state entered through Guaymas, and 6 of the 15 million pesos exported left through the port.[28] Not all merchants profited equally; only certain import houses reaped a bountiful harvest. The firm of García Bringas had annual sales of 480,000 pesos; that of Pedro Cosca, 420,000 pesos; G. Moller y Cía, 460,000 pesos; Arturo Morales, 410,000 pesos; and the Compañía Industrial de Maderas, a venture with capital of Luis Martínez, 370,000 pesos. Of the approximately 150 enterprises in the *municipio* of Guaymas, just thirteen had yearly sales above 100,000 pesos; sales of seven more ranged from 20,000 to 81,000 pesos. None of the rest made over 13,000 pesos a year; and most made less than 3,000 pesos.[29] A select coterie was monopolizing the fruits of dependency.

The rich of Guaymas were the import merchants. They were Morales, Moller, Martínez, the brothers Astiazarán, the Cosca family, and Iberri among others, heads of business houses buying, for resale, hardware, machinery, lumber, tools, clothing, and French wines, and perfumes, and cheese.[30] When asked to name the leading businesses of Guaymas in 1898, Ramón Corral picked several firms selling general goods, a lumber store, a haberdashery, and a tannery.[31] At the turn of the century, of the three richest men in Guaymas, two were importers and the other was a banker, Aguayo Hermanos, a financial mainstay of commerce.[32] By 1910, the merchant oligarchy stood at the top of Guaymas's economic ladder above the *hacendados*, powerful figures in their own right.

Below merchant and *hacendado*, at times one and the same, a middle class still in its infancy went about its business. Aping the rich in dress and manners, its members hoped to blur the lines between themselves and their patrons, the merchant elite. The class was ill-defined and often its members were unwilling to acknowledge they belonged to it. Roughly, it included men with professional degrees, lawyers and physicians primarily, and accountants, office clerks, and bureaucrats in customs or the port authority. At the bottom were the clerks in the stores, all men; no women held these jobs. Their dress code, modeled on the European, called for a black suit and, no matter how hot the day, for a coat and tie. In the eyes of the men who wore it, this outfit endowed their jobs with "importance and respectability." The coats cut from French cassimere hung low, almost to the knee, while the style had been imported from "Tucson or California."[33]

Service to the merchant elite heaped rewards on a tiny minority. Guillermo Robinson, a lawyer of standing in the community, worked for the Southern Pacific railroad, a link in the chain of Guaymas's trade, as did Isaac Rivers, a physician. Victor M. Venegas exercised his strident voice in *El Correo de Sonora*, a paper he published for the merchants of the port. The director of the Colegio Guaymense, "el profesor" Fernando F. Dworak, carved a niche for himself in the social register by teaching the sons of the city's rich. The lawyer Ernesto Peláez, editor of *El Comercio*, a journal avowing the importance of trade, earned extra income by "clearing up" dubious titles to mining properties.[34] On the Avenida VIII, the Wall Street of Guaymas, the heads of the credit institutions for the port city—Banco de Sonora, Banco Occidental, and Banco Nacional de México—hobnobbed with the merchant plutocracy. Whether they were well-off or simply penniless but snobbish, the members of this middle class, like their patrons, depended for their purple and fine linen upon outsiders, either customers or manufacturers, primarily in the United States.

As the merchants tardily learned, dependency hardly permits fortunes to be built on foundations of bedrock. When manipulated by outsiders, the mercantile structure teeters precariously at the least breeze. By 1910, ill winds were threatening the upwardly ambitious of Guaymas. The railroad, once viewed as the salvation of Guaymas, had altered the nature of trade. As more and more goods crossed the border, the northern customs houses of Nogales, Agua Prieta, Sásabe, and La Morita profited at the expense of Guaymas. In 1883, Guaymas monopolized 45 percent of the imports into Sonora but, a few years later, only 12 percent. At this juncture, 78 percent of the imports and almost the entire export trade went through Nogales and La Morita. The value of goods entering and leaving Guaymas still climbed but more slowly now, particularly in comparison with trade figures for the border customs houses. Guaymas merchants continued to make money, but on smaller scale. With the mining bonanza in the north and commercial farming gaining a foothold in the Mayo and Yaqui valleys, the oligarchs in Hermosillo, ever mindful of the political winds, gave less heed to Guaymas. The rise in trade with the United States, bringing with it a substantial increase in total imports and exports, ironically damaged Guaymas. As Sonora became more dependent on its northern neighbor, the Guaymas merchants lost standing.[35] Despite its relative decline by 1910, Guaymas encapsulates the ascendancy of the dependent merchants and their allies.

Meanwhile, to encourage trade and commerce, the Triumvirate erected an infrastructure: roads, telegraph, and telephone lines, and a rail line south from Guaymas to Sinaloa.[36] To lay the foundations for a healthy business climate, Ramón Corral introduced a uniform system of weights and measures, spelled out rules for professional degrees, erected schools to teach modern values, and constructed jails to keep the disorderly off the streets. To open the Mayo and Yaqui valleys to commercial farming, the Triumverate relied on guns and soldiers. However, as a prefect of Altar told Corral, "It was easier said than done."[37]

V

More than Guaymas, the city of Hermosillo, a trade depot and the chief beneficiary of both the mining bonanza and the opening of the railroad to the border, came to symbolize the new order. Its designation as the capital of the state in 1879 trumpeted the ascendancy of the merchants and their followers.[38] Even the Catholic archbishop, a seasoned political weather vane, moved his seat from Ures to Hermosillo. Like Guaymas, Hermosillo thrived in the later years of the nineteenth century but, unlike the port, Hermosillo had an economic boom that gave no sign of letting up. More and more jobs opened up, and demands for articles with labels from the United States grew apace.[39] By 1910, the chronic imbalance in the state's budget was remedied.[40] The merchants were enjoying the lion's share of wealth and income. As these multiplied, either directly or indirectly through ties with foreign capital, markets, and goods, so did Hermosillo's political clout.[41]

The ascendancy of merchants and bankers in Hermosillo, partly at the expense of their rivals in Guaymas, dramatically changed the flow of exports and imports. Until the advent of the railroad, two-thirds of Sonora's foreign trade had been by sea with England and France, entering and exiting mainly through Guaymas. After that, it was with the United States, as its consul noted, by way of Hermosillo. The thriving copper industry in Cananea and Nacozari further undercut the importance of Guaymas and favored Hermosillo. By 1910, exports from Agua Prieta, mainly copper for American smelters over the border, had a value ten times greater than those of Guaymas port.[42] The development of refrigeration, which allowed the export of beef and vegetables by rail, increased Hermosillo's trade with the United States.[43]

The rise of the merchants and their lot to the pinnacle of power, the upshot of dependency on the United States, upset the economic balance. The era of prosperity favored the inhabitants of cities and towns but played favorites among them. The more ties to mining a place had and the closer it was to the railroad, the bigger its rewards. Hermosillo and Guaymas benefited most, but so did way stations on the railroad, colonial towns like Magdalena and upstarts such as Nogales and Navojoa. At the close of the century, the towns monopolized nearly 88 percent of property values in Sonora, 80 percent of mercantile capital, and 72 percent of municipal revenues. With their budgetary surpluses, civic fathers began to remodel their towns, establishing schools, piping water into the community, paying for public lighting, building jails, adding police, and laying out parks and tree-lined avenues.[44]

As the commerical, banking, and political center of the state, with ties to the mining empire, Hermosillo profited most. The city represented "much of the wealth and intelligence of Sonora," reported the American consul in 1903.[45] Profits from sales in Minas Prietas and La Colorada, mining camps in its vicinity, filled the coffers of its merchants and bankers. Men with an eye for pecuniary gain began to see Hermosillo as a mecca. Corral built a flour mill there, the biggest in the state, and sold electricity generated by its plant to the city. George Gruning and Albert Hoeffer, Germans who settled in Hermosillo, put up the largest brewery. The eminent stores included the Ciudad de Paris, which sold French shoes, hats, and fabrics; La Mercería de la Paz, a haberdashery; and the Compañía Ferretera, a hardware store. L. J. Pavolovich y Hermanos, an export firm, shipped oranges from orchards around Hermosillo to the United States and Canada.[46]

In the pattern of Guaymas, a tiny band of firms monopolized the business of the city. Of the 326, only six had yearly sales of 100,000 pesos or more. The biggest enterprise, Corral's flour mill, had sales of 582,000 pesos. Of the twenty-five leading enterprises, just five, including a shoe "factory" owned by Chinese, and the flour mills of Corral and Abelardo G. Noriega, had no direct ties with foreign capital or markets.[47]

The merchant moguls and their allies in banking and mining dictated life in the "City of the Oranges." They ate, talked, and concocted business deals at the exclusive Casino Club, reserved for the "100 most distinguished men." They sent their sons to study in the United States and Europe, bought their wives fashions from Paris and New York, spoke English, and built elaborate abodes. The home of Luis E. Torres, who loved to entertain the rich, had "a distinctly Oriental flavor," while Guillermo Domínguez, a lawyer for the Cerro Prieto Mining Company, had a home in "French Nouveau style," complete with a library adorned by huge paintings of Corral and Díaz.[48] When Corral, then vice-president of the Republic, paid a visit to Hermosillo and Guaymas, the elite who honored him with banquets served "French food" and printed their menus in French. Culture and customs among the plutocracy—taking a cue from the origins of their prosperity—had foreign trappings.

VI

Economic growth nourished by foreign capital and markets exacerbated old imbalances between towns and cities and between regions. Not everyone had an equal slice of the pie and no other district had helpings the size of Hermosillo's and Guaymas's.[49] Towns and districts that were cut off from cheap transportation languished, becoming virtual colonies of the more developed regions. This phenomenon is known as "internal colonialism." Merchants in the foresaken towns and districts became the retailers of merchandise purchased from wholesalers in Hermosillo or Guaymas. Yet no matter how scanty the profits to be had, each town or district had a tiny merchant plutocracy exercising a monopoly over the economic returns available. At worst, the merchants divided the spoils with ranchers and *hacendados*.

No town had a more quixotic fate than Alamos. Well into the nineteenth century, Alamos, the town that "welcomed outsiders with open arms," rode a wheel of fortune spun by foreigners who were exporting silver.[50] The merchant elite flourished: while they might also own *haciendas* or *ranchos*, the merchants' wealth grew out of commerce. In singular cases, some made fortunes by speculating in mining. Antonio Goycolea, Angel Almada, Quirino Corbalá, and Tomás Robinson Bours, among the richest men, were merchants. Just one *hacendado*, Homobono G. Lamadrid, Alamo's wealthiest citizen, had more money than Goycolea, the richest merchant. Yet compared with the big commercial houses in Hermosillo and Guaymas, local retailers faired poorly.[51] The *tiendas de raya* in La Aduana and Río Chico, foreign-owned mining camps, had the biggest sales in the district.[52] Outside Quiriego and Rosario, also mining enclaves, no store in the outlying towns sold more than 3,000 pesos of goods a year.[53] The drop in silver prices, as well as the decision of the railroad builders to bypass Alamos, led many on its social register to find a new haven in the Mayo valley.

Circumvented by the railroad, Ures city underwent a similar decline. Yet parts of Ures district that were crossed by the railroad enjoyed good times. In Horcasitas, for instance, the key firm of Abascal y Cía. had sales of 22,000 pesos a year.[54] The iron horse also linked the traditional breadbasket regions—the river valleys of San Miguel, Matapé, and the southern corner of the district—to new markets. With bigger profits in mind, farmers added to the land under cultivation. Ures district gained inhabitants but the town lost residents, dropping from 8,600 in 1884 to 6,000 in 1907. Its tiny commercial order (no single merchant sold over 8,000 pesos annually) had no monopoly on wealth, having to share it with powerful *hacendados* connected with the port of Guaymas.[55] The merchants supported the clique in Hermosillo, and generally stood at odds with the *hacendados*, who were led by the brothers Paulo and Francisco Morales.[56] One merchant, Francisco G. Aguilar, the leading retailer of Ures, was prefect of the district for years.[57]

To the north of Hermosillo, railroad and mining opened up new commercial enclaves, Nogales on the border and, farther south, Imuris, Santa Cruz, and Magdalena. With a population of about 3,500, Magdalena town, the hub of the river valley, had a bevy of prosperous merchants, some foreigners. Miguel Latz y Hermanos, the largest enterprise, had sales totaling 200,000 pesos in 1906. A German who migrated south from California, Latz had been mayor of the town and prefect of the district. Next in line were Fenner Hermanos y Polizer, with sales of 100,000 pesos yearly, and Fon Qui with 28,000 pesos, all foreigners. By comparison, Francisco Estrella, the heavyweight among Mexican merchants, with annual sales of 20,000 pesos fared only moderately well.[58] At Santa Cruz, local branches of Miguel Latz and Fon Qui monopolized commerce, while in Imuris Latz and Chinese storekeepers had things their way.[59] Both Magdalena and Imuris sat on the rail line, and Santa Cruz was just a stone's throw away from it.

Commercial interests even established a new town, with the local elite totally dependent upon trade with the other side of the border. Until 1882 Nogales had been but an empty desert, recalled Corral, with only the tents of Mexican customs agents to mar the landscape.[60] The railroad transformed Nogales into the "gateway to the west coast of Mexico," joining it with Hermosillo and Guaymas.[61] From the start, Nogales had a population half Mexican and half American, with just a street serving as a buffer against the American town on the opposite side, also named Nogales.[62] John T. Brickwood, a resident of the American side, had a saloon that straddled the border. An early settler, he built the Brickwood Hotel and married a woman from Guaymas, Guadalupe Cañez, whose mother ran a boarding house and restaurant in Nogales, Arizona.[63]

Nogales grew rapidly as an inland port until 1900, when the establishment of Naco, a town north of Cananea, cut into its commercial supremacy. Like Agua Prieta and Sásabe, western entrepôts on trade routes running north and south, Naco had no life of its own. By 1910, Nogales had nearly 4,000 inhabitants, having grown three times faster than its sister town across the border.[64] Built in a narrow valley, Nogales was pressed for land, and real estate was an expensive commodity. As early as 1890, lots for houses sold for 300 pesos, high for that time.[65] An overnight phenomenon, Nogales was mostly a shantytown clinging to hillsides. So poorly built were some houses that less than a decade after its founding the town fathers were writing Hermosillo about the deplorable and dangerous condition of some of them.[66] Without a drainage system of any kind, heavy rainstorms threatened to wash away the town. But the Sonora Railway, its tracks running through the heart of Nogales, opposed attempts to dig any drainage canal that "endangered" its property.[67] Nogales was a frontier trading post shorn of life's amenities but with a cost of living beyond that of "Indianapolis or

Washington" because, the American consul explained, "practically nothing" was raised there.[68]

From the start, Nogales existed as an emporium run by merchants. Their livelihood, indeed their very survival, depended with rare exceptions on trade with "the other side." They were a classic dependent bourgeoisie. None were longtime residents. They had arrived from every corner of Sonora, from Jalisco and Sinaloa, and from countries as far off as China, determined to cash in on Nogales's proximity to Arizona.[69] By 1890, merchants, office workers, and clerks represented the largest segment of the economically active population, with wage workers forming the next largest group. Only a handful labored in the fields.[70] The trade brokers, *agentes aduanales*, included Manuel Mascareñas, José Pacheco, Próspero and Aurelio Sandoval, Ismael Padilla, and Cirilio Ramírez, the leading men of business in Nogales. Mascareñas and other brokers handled exports of raw ores, livestock, oranges, and grains, with a value of over 10 million pesos by 1910.[71] Imports, also managed by these traders, totaled over 5 million pesos.[72]

A handful of merchants, usually agents for American firms, had a monopoly on commerce. The biggest store in Nogales, Horvilleur y Cía., sold 40,000 pesos' worth of imported clothing in 1907, nearly twice the sales of Benjamin Schwab, its closest rival. Four firms with yearly sales of 17,000 or more had the lion's share of commerce, selling their merchandise not only locally but also in Hermosillo and Guaymas and along the border from Arizpe to Altar.[73] Stores on the Arizona side, moreover, sold their goods in Nogales and farther south. The Boston Clothing House had branches in Hermosillo, Guaymas, and Cananea. It advertised "the finest and most complete stock . . . of Gent's Furnishings." Goods imported from the United States to be resold: this was the business of Nogales. Additionally, Nogales had become a center for the developing livestock industry. There Mexican ranchers sold their cattle to American buyers.[74] The cultural tastes of the merchant capitalists of Nogales, like those of their brethren in Hermosillo and Guaymas, ran to imitation. The Teatro Ramírez, the "finest in Sonora," had been designed in the "gentlemanly style of Louis XIV" and decorated with iron ornaments from the United States.[75]

The benefits of merchant ascendancy had their limitations. Not every corner of the state benefited. Prosperity of the type enjoyed by Nogales made a detour around the valley of the Río Sonora, isolating the towns of Baviácora, Aconchi, San Felipe, Huépac, Banámichi, and Sinoquipe. Their 10,000 inhabitants lagged behind, despite their farms, cattle, and even mineral ores, because they had no road leading to Hermosillo. Farmers and ranchers could not sell their beef and foodstuffs easily, and merchants in the communities only with difficulty brought goods in from the outside.[76] Arizpe and Moctezuma towns, both seats of rich mining districts, and Cumpas did better.[77] Altar, formerly the lodestar of its district, on the other hand, went into a tailspin in the 1890s, falling behind Caborca and Pitiquito, which were richer in commerce, agriculture, and mining. The price of flour fell and, to compound matters, the McKinley Tariff cut into the exports of cattle to markets in Arizona. Both products were mainstays of Altar, and its economy faltered. Without an economic base of its own, Altar survived off others, according to a report of 1891.[78] In Caborca, meanwhile, the merchants Francisco Morineau and Juan Luna had a monopoly on commerce. With yearly sales of 35,000 pesos, Luna's business stood at the top, with Morineau's just below. Their word had been law in Caborca since the 1890s.[79] Luis P. Serrano, their rival in Altar, had sales less than half of Morineau's.[80]

To finance their business dealings, the leading merchants of Sonora banded together in 1897 to establish the Banco de Sonora, which affiliated with banks outside the state. Until then, credit had been tight, granted only by branches of Mexico City banks or by large commercial firms, and granted only to a tiny coterie of big merchants.[81] If business and commerce were to expand, Governor Corral told his legislature, a local system of bank credit had to be established.[82] Among the principal stockholders of the Banco were the brokers Sandoval and Mascareñas of Nogales, Corral, and Martínez, the Guaymas magnate.[83] By 1910, from its seat in Hermosillo, the Banco exercised control of credit through branches in every major center of the state. In Cananea, at the same time, the 4C's had its own bank with an entirely American board of directors.[84]

The merchant capitalists and their American partners, however, largely failed to build a native manufacturing industry, the bedrock of a national bourgeoisie. To 1910, Sonora continued to buy most of its manufactured articles from the United States.[85] So little was done to develop industry that until quite late in the nineteenth century Altar, with just a flour mill and little else, ranked among the four top industrial centers of the state.[86] At the head of the list of native industries were the flour mills, about eighty in number, half of them powered by steam. All but a score antedated the heavy influx of American capital at the turn of the century.[87] Among their owners were the well-known merchants or *hacendados*: Goycolea, Morales, Latz, Camou, Corbalá, Almada, Morineau, and Corral.[88] Just a handful of "industries" had made their appearance: a brewery here, a cracker plant there, and "factories" of the Chinese turning out cheap shoes for workers. With the second largest amount of foreign capital invested in any state in Mexico, Sonora lagged far behind the so-called industrial states of the Republic.[89]

VII

A debate over the right to profit from the sale of American goods split the merchant capitalists into warring camps. For years, the inhabitants of the northern towns had purchased their goods duty-free in stores on the other side of the *linea*, thus spurring the growth of Arizona border towns. Recognizing the inevitability of this trade, the Mexican government in 1884 established a *zona libre* ("free zone") extending sixty kilometers south of the border. People living in this region did not have to pay customs duties on imported goods.[90] The *zona libre* legitimized the contraband trade of the early merchant importers and brokers in Nogales, among them Mascareñas and Sandoval. Before long, nearly every item sold in this border town, and later in Naco and Agua Prieta, bore an American label. Worse still, imported goods had a way of filtering south beyond the *zona libre*.

Naturally enough, merchants in such places as Magdalena and Santa Cruz were quickly up in arms. Their complaints were joined by those of farmers and the makers of wheat flour, cigarettes, lard, butter, dried fruits, and cheese. The indignant Mexicans claimed the free zone hurt their business. The products they sold were also imported from the United States and for sale in the free zone at prices lower than theirs. Rather than buy from them, potential customers chose to ride the train to Nogales and purchase the same goods—duty-free—for less.[91] To pour salt into the wound, Nogales also had manufacturers, supposedly Mexican enterprises, who made furniture and clothing out of duty-free raw materials from across the border. They shipped their finished articles to markets south of the *zona libre*, where they sold at lower prices than authentically Mexican products did.[92] These "factories," nineteenth-century versions of the *maquiladores* (assembly plants), made their profits off cheap Mexican labor. Merchants in Nogales also shipped south imported articles that had come in duty-free. Handicapped by the *zona libre*, their rivals wanted the free importation of articles stopped. It was a family quarrel; at stake was not the defense of Mexican national industry, despite the bitterness of Mexican foodstuff producers. At issue was the right of merchants to compete on equal terms for profits from the sale of American goods.

But for Mascareñas, Sandoval, and like middlemen, the *zona libre* spelled the difference between prosperity and total ruin. Without it, no merchant order—or the white-collar structure it fed—would exist in the border towns. Their inhabitants would simply buy what they needed on "the other side." To Mascareñas, commerce spurred population growth and building construction, provided a market for the vegetables, grains, and beef of nearby farmers and ranchers, as well as jobs for workers, and, in the bargain, raised property values. Without the *zona libre*, Nogales and sister towns would stagnate. Everything would be on the American side, including jobs for workers. As Mascareñas and his companions bluntly put it, Mexicans could not compete on equal terms with the American's capital, his spirit of enterprise, or his technical knowledge. Only the *zona libre* and, of course, the "incompatibilities of race" kept the imbalance between the two sides of the border from tipping too heavily in one direction.[93] To quote Corral, the only choice was whether to legalize imports or to make them part of a huge network of contraband trade.[94] Such were the views of the dependent merchants and their spokesmen in Hermosillo.

CHAPTER 9

The Errant Cattle Industry

I

Cattle ranching, as native to Sonora as its giant flour mills, matured into an industry largely because of Yankee ranchers and American cattle markets. The transformation took place mostly in the twentieth century, around the same time farms in the Mayo and Yaqui valleys were turning into commercial agricultural enterprises and mining was booming in Cananea and Nacozari. A few Mexicans profited. By 1910, the cattle industry was supporting rich Mexican cattlemen in the north while southern ranchers, equally Mexican, who raised beef for home consumption had fallen on hard times. In the topsy-turvy world of dependency, the foreign sector profited most.

II

Yet the *vaquero* and his horse had colonial roots, and the rich panoply of livestock terms and lore were of Spanish origin. The first cattle to arrive in Mexico came with the Jesuit missionaries to such places as Mátape, from where the herds were driven south. To each of the missions he established, Eusebio Kino brought cattle, sheep, and goats, to be raised for food and for profit. The money was for the upkeep of the missions and their inhabitants, the conquered Indians.[1] From the missions the practice of raising livestock spread. By the eighteenth century, Spaniards spoke of a cattle industry, particularly in the northwest, where ranches of horses and cattle spread across the landscape.[2] The hope of profit from the sale of beef brought more Spaniards and Mexicans to the region, and slowly raised land values.

In Sonora, cattle ranches thrived best in the districts of Arizpe, Moctezuma, Magdalena, and Altar, and, to the southeast, Sahuaripa. Arizpe led the lot with Moctezuma and Altar next in line. Cananea and the valleys of the San Miguel, Sonora, Moctezuma, Nacozari, and Bavispe rivers were particularly good. Every town on the Río Sonora had cattle ranches of varying size. This was open-range, high-mesa country with plenty of pasture. Except in times of drought, the cattle survived on grass and water from shallow wells and intermittent streams. However, droughts, never too far away in this arid land, often wreaked havoc. During these periods, when the grass withered and the wells dried up, starvation and dehydration would kill from 10 to 20 percent of the herds.[3]

In Mexican hands, the livestock industry hardly flourished. Up to 1885, Apache raids kept the northern plains skimpily settled.[4] Not until the coming of the railroad, moreover, was a potentially large market for Mexican beef opened up.[5] It was a primitive industry, poorly organized, with scarcely any fencing to distinguish one ranch from another. Herds were of poor quality. Even the practice of branding steers was not yet fully developed. Cattle sold as beef on the hoof, generally in small numbers, in Arizona or New Mexico. Still, in 1891, Sonora, along with Chihuahua and Coahuila, the kingpins of the ranching states, already had 3 million head of cattle. Two decades later, Sonora had 7.6 percent of Mexico's cattle and the lion's share of the quality breeds. Only Chihuahua and Jalisco had more cattle.[6]

III

American markets and capital, if not solely responsible for the numerical increase, certainly explained the growth of the cattle industry. Cheap land, good pasture and water, plus railroad access to buyers as far away as Kansas City and Chicago, brought Texas cattlemen, often wealthy and willing to speculate, to Sonora, Coahuila, and Chihuahua. With an initial investment of under $50,000, a rancher could earn $25,000 or more yearly.[7] By 1886, just four years after the completion of the Sonora Railway, Americans were buying up land "near the border of Arizona" for stock raising. Americans owned, according to their consul in Guaymas, "at least 1 million acres of land . . . for stock raising and grazing purposes."[8]

A lucky few had ranches on both sides of the border. "Guillermo"

Barnett was one such entrepreneur. With his Rancho La Arizona in Magdalena district and his Rancho Babocómari in Arizona, in the back country of both towns named Nogales, Barnett moved his stock back and forth over the border. When regulations in the United States jeopardized profits from sales of his Mexican beef on the hoof—a quarantine on Mexican cattle, for instance—Barnett simply took his animals to Arizona.[9] Barnett might have been a character in a Wild West novel. He had come to Mexico early, certainly by the 1870s, when, legend has it, he hid the young Ramón Corral, then being hunted by Pesqueira, in a warehouse. Corral, an enemy of the *caudillo*, had attacked Pesqueira in a newspaper published in Alamos. From that time on, Barnett had Corral as a friend, and later Celedonio Ortiz and Manuel Monteverde, both rich and influential men, befriended him. Barnett took an immediate liking to Sonora, settled there, married twice to Mexican women, and fathered nine sons and two daughters. His ranch, La Arizona, located about twenty-five miles southwest of Nogales, covered 100,000 acres of land. The state of Arizona later took its name from Barnett's property. Besides raising steers for sale across the border, Barnett cultivated wheat, corn, vegetables, sugar cane, and fruit trees. He established a tannery and soap factory, a tiny sugar mill, and a canning plant. Workers wove sarapes on hand looms at his ranch, and leather workers made saddles and harnesses.[10]

Barnett probably acquired his ranch through trickery, perhaps with the help of Corral, by then governor of Sonora. La Arizona, according to the records of a legal dispute in 1887, had a Mexican owner, either Jesús Moreno Villaescuso or Antonio García. Both claimed title to it. Moreno asserted that he had purchased the ranch in 1846, while García alleged that the ranch had been in his family since 1814. He said his father had acquired it then, only to abandon it precipitously in 1876 because of Apache raids. Some time later, Barnett occupied the ranch with his cattle and laid claim to it. But, as García's lawyer argued, Barnett had no legal right to it; unless they had the consent of the president of the Republic, Mexican law barred foreigners from owning property within sixty miles of the border. García appealed to Corral to order Barnett to move on.[11] Corral referred the matter to Mexico City, which replied that it was up to Hermosillo to decide the issue.[12] Legally or not, Barnett kept his ranch.

Barnett was but one of scores of American adventurers who got an early start in the cattle business. A. J. Martin, an American of little note, lived out his life as a cattle rancher in Nacozari and died there in 1883.[13] At about the same time, the mayor of Sinoquipe in Arizpe reported a sale of cattle by "Eduardo" Donahue, an American, for 4,500 pesos, a "formidable sale of cattle" for those years.[14] At the Rancho del Alambre near Cananea, its American owner hired Texas cowboys to tend his herds. Even Englishmen could be found in the cattle business in Sonora.[15] The Hagan brothers, "Tomás" and Daniel, British subjects and residents of Magdalena district, owned a ranch about thirty miles from Santa Cruz. They sold their cattle in the United States.[16]

Around the turn of the century, a different breed of Yankee speculators entered the cattle scene in Sonora. These were men with more grandiose plans. One of them was William C. Greene, the copper magnate. With an eye on the expanding market for beef across the border and in his booming mining town, Greene organized the Cananea Cattle Company. Its pasture lands, lying on a fertile mesa to the east of the mining site and in the mountain valleys to its west and south, were 100 miles long and forty miles wide. Greene ran 40,000 head of Herefords, "most of good quality. They were Mr. Greene's cattle."[17] It became a tradition for the prefect of Arizpe district to attend the annual roundup of the Cananea Cattle Company, when the strays of other ranchers were picked up.[18] The town of Naco, dating from 1902, stood on land belonging to the Turkey Track Cattle Company, another of Greene's enterprises. Wages for the cowhands of the Cananea Cattle Company in 1906 were two pesos a day, less than what Greene paid his miners and not a penny more than what cowboys took home in Altar district in 1887, but over three times what they earned in Hermosillo district.[19]

Greene's cattle kingdom did not rule unchallenged. It had rivals, among them the Sonora Land and Cattle Company, an American operation with 533,535 hectares in the districts of Arizpe and Moctezuma. Dating from 1887, the company had promised to subdivide the land and to sell it in smaller parcels, but failed to keep its pledge. Its manager, Frank M. Watts, lived in La Cuesta, a suburb of Nacozari, where he enjoyed the life of lord and master of a vast domain. With its home base in Oshkosh, Wisconsin, the company raised steers for sale to American buyers and, periodically, cut down trees to be converted into lumber at its sawmill. Francisco R. Almada, a dean among Sonora's historians, accused Watts and his patrons of operating "as if in conquered territory, of relentlessly trying to get around state and municipal authorities."[20]

Among the other beef empires were the Alamo Cattle Company, the owner of 3,640 hectares; the West Coast Cattle Company with 92,250 hectares; the Cabullona Cattle Company in Agua Prieta; and the Santa Rosa Cattle Company in Bacoáchi. A hop, skip, and a jump away, the Transvaal Copper Mining Company, operating out of Cumpas, ran cattle on three ranches, two of which it owned outright (Piedras Negras with 6,500 hectares and Cloud with 5,000 hectares) and on one it shared jointly (San Nicolás-Tolentino with 10,000 hectares). Other

American ranchers of note were M. M. "Mariano" Sherman, J. Dowdle, and "Senor Williams."[21]

The Americans turned the native industry upside down. They invested capital and began to make cattle raising big business. To get their cattle to market, they drove them to the railheads on both sides of the border and then shipped them by train. As early as 1888, stockmen began to import high-grade bulls from the United States and to cross them with native herds to improve the quality of their cattle.[22] By bringing in Herefords, Greene did most to upgrade the industry in Sonora.[23] Rival American companies followed suit, as did a small but growing band of Mexican ranchers. The improvement in quality could not have taken place without the barbed-wire fence, which Greene and other Americans used to enclose their pasture lands, keeping their stocks pure. By 1906, every ranch in the *municipio* of Cananea used wire fencing, and the practice was copied by Mexican cattlemen elsewhere. Manuel Elías, owner of the Rancho Gallardo and scion of a noted clan, for instance, fenced his entire property.[24] To solve the problem of water scarcity in times of low rainfall, cattlemen, both Americans and Mexicans, dug deep wells and installed windmills or steam-driven pumps to get the water to the surface.[25] Taking their cue from "how it was done in the United States," Mexican ranchers built tanks in which to bathe their cattle, in order to kill range ticks.[26]

By 1910, the cattle industry of the northern ranges, where the Americans had their ranches, led the state. Elsewhere, the industry, usually in the hands of Mexicans, lagged behind, relying on outdated methods and low-grade herds.[27] Its beef, sold on the domestic market, produced marginal profits. Despite the development of refrigeration, a technique that transformed the meat industry in such places as Argentina and Australia, Sonora had just two meat-packing plants. Greene had a large one in Cananea that allowed him to export chilled beef to the United States. A small one in Hermosillo was Mexican-owned and sold meat only to local customers.[28]

In the cattle industry, international boundaries hardly mattered. Whether Mexican or American, the stockmen of northern Sonora had tied their fortunes to the world beyond the border. Apparently indifferent to nationalist sentiments, this international industry embraced pasture lands on both sides of the border. As herds multiplied in number, particularly on the American-owned ranches, their owners drove "their cattle across the line for the purpose of grazing." When confronted by American officials, they explained that they "did not know where the line begins and ends."[29] More and more, they did this by having separate ranches on either side of the border. Colin Cameron, for example, owned the Rancho Batepito in the district of Arizpe and the Rancho San Rafael de la Zanja in Arizona. In the summer of 1891, he drove 250 head of cattle to his Bapetito ranch and later returned home with their "natural increase," in all, 922 animals.[30] Manuel Almada, a Mexican of similar proclivities, had a ranch in the district of Magdalena and one not far from Tucson. Both Almada and Cameron drove cattle across the border at Nogales without paying the Mexican export tax, arguing that they were merely transferring animals from one of their properties to another.[31]

In time, cattle ranching in northern Sonora came to depend almost entirely on the American economy. Even cattle for the Mexican market, specifically Mexico City, had to be taken across the border, either by rail or on foot, then shipped by railroad car, in bond, virtually the full length of Texas to enter Mexico again at Laredo.[32] By the same token, the railroad consolidated the cattle trade with the American consumer. Until 1882, few cattle had been exported north; but by 1885 Mexican cattle bound for sale in Arizona and New Mexico had become "quite an important item of the exports of Sonora."[33]

IV

Mexicans and Americans alike raised beef for sale to American buyers. So high was the possibility of profit in this trade that middlemen appeared, agents who scoured the northern districts for cattle to buy for resale across the border. Both Mexicans and Americans participated in this business. Colin Cameron, for example, was annually buying 500 to 600 steers in Magdalena to take back to Arizona, plus employing an American to look for cattle to buy in districts from Altar to Arizpe and south to Ures and Hermosillo.[34] Mexican ranchers in Bacoáchi banded together to sell their cattle to George Spindle, who drove them to "the other side." He paid the Mexicans nine pesos a head.[35] At other times, Mexicans might buy or take cattle on consignment from local ranchers for sale in Arizona, sometimes moving over the border with the animals of an entire district. One of these was the entrepreneur Miguel López, a native of Arizpe town and its mayor.[36] Cipriano Ortega, a cattle broker in Altar, took his herds into Arizona by way of Sásabe and sold them in Tucson.[37] Sásabe eventually became a keystone in the cattle trade with "the other side."[38] Gabilondo Hermanos, by 1907 one of the principal Mexican beef merchants, shipped cattle to American buyers from ranches in Cuchuverachi, Bacoáchi, and Bavispe, towns in Arizpe and Moctezuma, through Agua Prieta, a much traveled border station.[39]

On the eve of the enactment of the McKinley Tariff in 1891, about

10,000 head of cattle from Mexico were sold annually in the United States.[40] Of the steers taken over the border by Mexican ranchers, every one of them went as beef on the hoof—still alive—to be fattened in Kansas City, Chicago, or other stockyards. Had Mexican cattlemen exported chilled beef, the product of packing plants, or fattened steers for immediate sale on the American market, their profits would have been greater.[41] As it was, American corporations, the buyers of Mexican cattle, reaped the biggest rewards.

Without customers on the other side, the Mexican cattle industry would not have taken off. The domestic market was just too small to sustain a thriving or modern cattle industry. Sonora, after all, had a mere 265,383 inhabitants, and most of them were too poor to buy high-grade beef. But stockmen in Sonora had rivals on the American markets. They had to compete with ranchers in Chihuahua and Coahuila, and with their counterparts in the United States, particularly Texas, which was growing as a producer of quality beef. The lean and tough Texas Longhorn had long ago made its last bow. From then on, there was stiff competition for the Yankee client.

The free-for-all came to a head with the McKinley Tariff of 1891. By levying a duty on beef imported into the United States, the tariff dealt a heavy blow to the Mexican cattle industry, which had just been getting underway. It was the "kiss of death," lamented Ramón Corral. Since its passage, he went on, Sonora had failed to export "a single steer to the neighboring Republic." Denied that market, "our cattle industry cannot continue to grow." The livestock business, particularly along the border, fell into a depression that threatened to leave it a shambles. The future looked bleak unless Washington were to lower the duties on imported beef. "What made this situation especially frustrating," Corral moaned, "is that we can do nothing about it." No matter what, Mexicans could not "influence the politics of the Republic to the north." The McKinley Tariff, by raising duties prohibitively, had cost Mexican cattlemen their major source of income.[42]

At the time of the tariff bill, the cattle industry was the staff of life for many a northern town. Not a few of them had no other means of support. Cut off from customers on "the other side," the cattle business and the towns that depended upon it faced "imminent ruin."[43] That prophecy came true by the summer of 1891 in Altar district, where, a report proclaimed, the "wretched (*malhada*) McKinley law" had "killed the livestock industry."[44] Despite eventual modifications in the tariff, Mexicans were still blaming it for the decline of the cattle business as late as 1907. As one of them said, the business "had been shipwrecked in the heavy seas of the tariff."[45] Yet, the American consul, naturally more inclined to look the other way, still spoke of a "considerable growth in the number of cattle raised" and of the "large increase in the number placed on the market." In 1909, that meant sales of beef with a value of \$438,780, more than twice that of a year before.[46] By 1910, cattle exports picked up to about 20,000 head, just about double the figure of 1891. The McKinley Tariff seriously hurt the Mexican cattle industry but, despite the cries of anguish of Mexicans, did not stop its growth altogether. Profits had simply taken a turn for the worse.

Apart from the tariff, Americans had still another club to wield. It was the cattle quarantine, an arbitrary tool that sent shivers up and down the spines of Mexican cattlemen. It could be imposed either by Washington or by authorities in the Territory of Arizona. In theory, the quarantine was intended to keep cattle infected with hoof and mouth disease (aftosa) or ticks off the American market. In practice, the quarantine often was used to block imports of foreign beef. The decision to impose this arbitrary device rested solely in American hands. Mexicans had no say whatsoever. In 1887, for example, the governor of the Territory of Arizona abruptly declared a ninety-day "quarantine against all cattle of Europe and Mexico." Given Arizona's location, he clearly had Mexican cattle in mind. The quarantine, wrote the American consul, "caused much surprise to the people of Sonora," particularly since it occurred at a time of the year when cattle were "fat and saleable." Although "no contagious disease" was "known to exist among the cattle," reported the consul, the ban "stopped" their shipment into Arizona.[47] When rumors of another such quarantine came to his attention, he made it clear to his superiors that it would injure "both sides of the border."[48] A decade later, nonetheless, federal inspectors in Arizona imposed yet another quarantine, this time a limited one, confined to cattle from Moctezuma district, who were judged sick with a contagious disease.[49]

The Texas fever scare of 1908 best illustrates the dimensions of the quarantine's impact. On this occasion, United States authorities had imposed a ban on cattle because of a disease known as Texas fever, carried by the *garrapata* or tick. The quarantine covered the entire state of Sonora. So alarming was the news that Governor Luis E. Torres convened a special meeting of the recently formed Junta de Ganaderos ("cattlemen's association") to discuss ways to deal with the calamity. In Torres's opinion, a view shared by the livestock men, the quarantine "threatened to destroy one of the richest industries in the state." The meeting, which took place in February 1909, brought together the leading cattlemen of the state, Mexicans and Americans alike. One of the Americans who attended was William C. Greene, while the list of Mexicans read like a *Who's Who* of the big ranchers. After much discussion, however, the ranchers could only conclude that they had to comply with American demands despite evidence that the tick had not infected all the cattle on the northern ranges.[50]

Mexicans also learned that quarantines, like a doubled-edged sword that's dull on one side, did not always cut both ways. Inspectors in Arizona judged that the tick found in cattle belonging to American ranchers in Moctezuma district was not contagious. They allowed these approved steers across the border, but banned animals belonging to Mexicans. The Mexicans cried foul. In their eyes, authorities on the other side of the border should treat all cattlemen equitably, "without regard to nationality."[51]

Proximity to the border also encouraged cattle rustling. It was lucrative and simple to drive cattle to buyers in Arizona who, as everyone knew, never asked questions. Both Mexicans and Americans dealt in this clandestine trade. It occurred time and time again. Mexicans sold cattle stolen from Fronteras, for instance, or gangs of Americans made off with steers from Magdalena district. It happened so often, the prefect of Magdalena complained, that the thefts had "demoralized livestock men."[52] Cattle rustling in Arizpe district in the 1880s was so commonplace that Governor Corral virtually had to beg General Angel Martínez, the commander of the northern military zone, to station "a detachment of cavalry to patrol" the area. That appeared to be the only way to end the cattle thefts commited with "impunity" by *bandidos texanos* ("Texas bandits"), who fled over the international line when they were pursued by Mexican authorities.[53] Soon after, Corral called on the rural police to prevent stolen steers from being taken across the border, while the prefect of Magdalena appointed a special sheriff to keep out cattle rustlers.[54] Corral might have spent his time more profitably keeping his own house in order. According to *El Independiente*, a newspaper published on the Arizona side, José V. Escalante, brother-in-law to Corral and prefect of Magdalena district, had a habit of rounding up "stray" cows and horses, over the protests of their owners.[55]

By the turn of the century, whatever the merits of Corral's military plans, rustling had a firm grip on Arizpe, the major cattle district, especially in the vicinity of Fronteras. Ranchers stole steers from one another, and either put their brands on them or butchered them and sold the meat in the mining camps. Rustlers of both nationalities masqueraded as miners staking out ore claims, but instead of hunting for metals they stole cattle from nearby ranches. Farmers killed their neighbors' cattle, usually to put meat on the table for their families.[56] As late as 1910, Ignacio Pesqueira, a rancher of note in Arizpe, was accusing *texanos* of taking his cattle while Manual Mascareñas and others complained that rustlers in Magdalena stole steers and sold them in Arizona.[57] The Mexican consul in Tucson spoke of rustlers on both sides of the international line who took cattle over the border to their ranches in the other country.[58] In Altar district, its prefect charged, "individuals of dubious reputation" turned rustling into an everyday phenomenon.[59] The culprits were Mexicans and Americans. Where cattle meant money, the border knew no laws. The expected rewards on the American market helped turn rustling into an institution.

V

As exports of beef on the hoof multiplied, so did the wealth of the elite Mexican cattlemen. Their ranches or haciendas stretched from Altar to Arizpe, sometimes extending alongside the big American cattle spreads. Like their Yankee rivals, whose practices they copied, they depended on buyers across the border. Without American customers paying dollars for beef the Mexicans did not prosper. Like the merchants of Guaymas and Hermosillo, Mexican cattlemen in the north came to depend on their Yankee neighbors; the richer the Mexicans got, the greater their dependency. They were making money in the short term but jeopardizing their future.

Their interests, as the testimonials of Corral and Torres showed, increasingly helped dictate policy along the northern tier. The Mexican cattlemen were a powerful group by 1910, although they numbered no more than two dozen or so. Foremost among them were men such as Manuel Mascareñas, Rafael Gabilondo, Antonio Martínez, Miguel Molina, Ignacio Pesqueira, Francisco Chiapa, and Ignacio Elías.[60] Both Chiapa and Elías were prefects of their districts, while Mascareñas and Martínez were mayors of Nogales.

These Mexican magnates, for all intents and purposes, had turned their backs on the domestic market. In their view, it was too small and poor to nurture a modern cattle industry. Yet statistics do not entirely bear this out. The domestic market was small, but it was expanding. Cattle butchered for domestic consumption in 1899 numbered 43,604; that number had risen to 54,435 by 1905; to 59,359 two years later; and to 66,357 in just one year more. Small ranchers, particularly in Sahuaripa district, had supplied that market.[61] This group could not afford the innovations of their northern neighbors; their cattle were ill-kept and of poor quality. Though large in numbers and important in the small towns, these most Mexican of cattlemen were, ironically, the poorest.

CHAPTER 10

Saga of the Valleys

I

While the minerals of the earth were fueling the mining boom, the fertile valleys of the south underwent a striking metamorphosis. Along the deltas of the Mayo and Yaqui rivers, where nature had united water and rich alluvial soil, an agriculture for export had begun to prosper by 1910. Like its mining counterpart, this new commercial agriculture, the offspring of venturesome Mexicans in the Mayo valley and Americans in the Yaqui, depended on markets in the United States.

II

The transformation of the valleys, the Mesopotamia of Mexico, was partly responsible for tolling a death knell for an older age. The agricultural upsurge came as Alamos, the old colonial bastion of yesteryear, was declining. The culprit was the price of silver, on a downhill slide since the end of the nineteenth century. By 1910, Alamos town had stopped growing, as had Promontorios, Minas Nuevas, and La Aduana, the oldest of the mining *municipios*. When the railroad builders failed to run their track through Alamos, they sealed its fate. The inhabitants of these dying towns began to migrate to the nascent farmbelt triangle outlined by the hamlets of Etchojoa, Huatabampo, and Navojoa, which in 1907 was a way station on the railroad line.[1]

The refugees found jobs building the railroad from Guaymas to the border with Sinaloa, and then turned to cultivating crops, first wheat and finally the garbanzo, or chickpea, the miracle crop. The town fathers of Navojoa, seeking to take advantage of the influx of immigrants, were working on plans for a Pueblo Nuevo ("new city").[2] So spectacular was the growth of the town's business since the coming of the railroad, that state officials in 1907 asked Mexico City to establish a post office there.[3] In like manner, the railroad infused life into a host of settlements in the Yaqui valley that at first were mere way stations: Cruz de Piedra, Mapoli, Pithahya, Oroz, Pótam, Vícam, Lencho, Bácum, Carrales, Esperanza, Fundición, and Cajeme.[4] These towns repopulated the valleys. Once home to the Mayo and Yaqui Indians, "white" Mexicans covetous of their fertile lands had killed or driven off many of their aboriginal owners.

The rape of the Mayo and Yaqui was part of the rush to acquire lands in the valleys as the railroad approached. With the defeat of the Indians in the nineteenth century, their lands, in time-honored tradition, went to the conqueror. In the beginning, the old families of Alamos got them. Some of these families, such as the Almadas, made rich by the Quintera mine near Alamos, invested money buying "idle lands, such as the Rancho de Agiabampo and, in union with the Richardson Company, acquiring 3,500 hectares in the Yaqui valley and, additionally, in an *hacienda* near Navojoa.[5] General José Tiburcio Otero, a parochial *politico* and hero of the wars against the Mayos, made himself the owner of 7,000 hectares on the outskirts of Huatabampo in 1890. With water taken from the Mayo river, Otero put 1,200 hectares under cultivation, calling his enterprise the Hacienda Jupateco. Angel García Peña was a colonel and member of the military body allegedly appointed to distribute parcels of land to the defeated Mayo and Yaqui. In company with Jesús Morales, he got his hands on 13,000 hectares. He called his land grab the Hacienda Juarez—in honor of the Indian president of Mexico.[6] A majority of the "*hacendados*"—really just planters, especially in the Mayo valley—acquired their lands from the ministry of fomento (development) in Mexico City, for between two and fifteen pesos a hectare, a bargain at that time.[7] These were the days of the laws of idle lands (that is, lands without owners and not under cultivation) and of windfalls for those who surveyed them. That was how Antonio Goycolea, an Alamos stalwart, made off with 5,000 hectares in the *municipio* of Navojoa in 1907.[8] In those bountiful times, it was still possible to rent land from local planters, most of whom had far more than they could use, and quickly turn a profit.[9]

Of the planters, none left a larger stamp on the agriculture of the valleys than the Salido family. They introduced the cash-crop farm to the valleys, particularly at Rosales, their most lucrative hacienda, where they cultivated 800 hectares of irrigated land and annually produced 5,000 bags of corn and an equal amount of wheat for their flour mill. The three Salido brothers were the first to dig the irrigation canals that ultimately crisscrossed the landscape of the valleys.[10] The success of the Salidos, wrote Héctor Aguilar Camín, whetted the "greed of the whites" for remaining Indian lands.[11] The Mayos, fortunately for the Salidos and their cohorts, stayed in place as cheap labor for the conquering planters, something the Yaquis failed at times to do.

The Salidos, a venerated Alamos family, came into the Mayo valley on the heels of the defeat of Cajeme, the stubborn Yaqui chieftain. The Salido brothers—Martín, José de Jesús, and Juan—struck it rich immediately. Their hacienda Santa Barbara paid off its original cost, 60,000 pesos, with profits from its first harvest.[12] Water, a scarce commodity in arid Sonora, in combination with fertile soil brought about that miracle. The Salidos' first irrigation canal, about twelve kilometers long, brought water from the Mayo river to their hacienda Tres Hermanos. With an investment of 75,000 pesos, the Salidos dug the canal, built their first flour mill, and set a pattern to emulate. Others quickly followed, not just the Almadas, but also Francisco Orrantia, Pedro S. Quiroz, Crispín Palomares, and Jesús Valderráin, all stalwarts of Alamos.[13]

Though the achievements in the Mayo valley were impressive, it was in the valley of the Yaqui that the dreams of the elite bore fruit.

III

The Yaqui river, almost 700 kilometers long, begins its journey to the Pacific in the sierra of neighboring Chihuahua, just south of Ciudad Guerrero. Known there as the Río Papigóchic, the Yaqui enters Sonora by way of Moctezuma and Sahuaripa. Along its path to the sea it collects the waters of diverse streams, the Mulatos, Sátachic, Nácor, Bavispe, Sahuaripa, and, near the end, the Tecoripa. The acclaimed Yaqui valley begins at a place known as Buena Vista.

When news of the arrival of the railroad in the Yaqui reached Mexico City, its journalists predicted that the river would become the Nile of Sonora. At that time, Cajeme, the valley's hub-to-be, was but a stop on the route of the iron horse. The prediction of the prophets proved true, largely because the Yaqui valley, "the most fertile in Sonora," included "choice alluvial lands." The total land area was roughly 1,685 square miles; nearly a third of it had prime soil.[14]

Developments in the Yaqui followed those in the Mayo by about a decade. Unlike the earlier venture, mainly the work of the Alamos clans, the promoters in the Yaqui were outsiders for the most part. It was entrepreneurs from north of the border who coaxed the Yaqui soil into yielding its wondrous harvest, and who transformed Indian lands into an agricultural empire linked by capital and markets to the United States. The change began in 1880, when *políticos* in Mexico City appointed a Comisión Geográfica Exploradora under Colonel Angel García Peña to survey, subdivide, and colonize the Yaqui and Mayo valleys. García Peña "gave" the Yaquis tiny parcels of land and put them under the watchful eye of soldiers. This act, Mexico City naively believed, would transform the Yaquis into dirt farmers. Having returned a bit of the stolen land to the Yaquis, the government distributed the bulk of it to other Mexicans. In fact García Peña, with the help of Felipe Salido, then an engineer in the army, merely subdivided the ancient *ejidos*, the Yaquis' communal lands, in the mistaken belief that everything would turn out well once the Yaquis became dirt farmers.

García Peña formally set up seven Mexican towns, already largely Yaqui and originally founded as missions in the sixteenth and seventeenth centuries. He assigned approximately 7,500 hectares of land to each town, with the stipulation that the plots, held as private property by individuals, would not be sold for five years. Cócorit, Bácum, San José, Tórin, Vícam, Pótam, and Guirivis, the towns of García Peña, also included non-Indians. The object was to pacify and control the Yaquis by having whites, who were also given lands, live among them. García Peña carried out a similar program in the Mayo valley, founding San Pedro, Etchojoa, (a Mayo community), and Moroncarit.

The Yaquis failed to see the logic of the government's design. The subdivided land, after all, had belonged to them. Not unnaturally they fought on, often abandoning the plots "given" them. In 1892, Mexico City appointed a second committee, again under García Peña. Unlike the first, this one had orders to open up the Yaqui and Mayo valleys to everyone. The quaint idea of colonizing the Yaqui valley with bitter Yaquis had been discarded. Mexcians, *los blancos* ("the whites"), as they were called, would do the colonizing this time. At one point, Mexico City even concocted a scheme to get "whites" to homestead in the Yaqui valley by offering seeds, tools, money, and rifles to some Hermosillo artisans—illiterates when it came to farming.[15]

At this juncture "Carlos" Conant, the son of a Yankee father and a Spanish mother, made his appearance. An American by character and training, Conant, the initial "developer" of the Yaqui, was born in Guaymas in 1842. Educated in California, he returned "home" to work with his brother don Benito in the mines of Alamos, eventually becoming superintendent of the Santa Eulalia mine of the Alzua family in Pinos Altos, Chihuahua. When its miners stopped work in 1883, Conant declared martial law, jailed the strike leaders, and, as president of a court-martial, put to death five of its leaders—and would have killed twelve others had not higher authorities intervened. During his early life, he took up arms against Ignacio Pesqueira and had the good sense to turn Porfirista. As a reward, Mexico City blessed his ambitious plan to survey, subdivide, and colonize the lands south of the Yaqui river, including those of the Mayo and Fuerte, the last in northern Sinaloa. The government also granted him the right to a third of the water of these rivers. Conant sold his ideas to capitalists from New York, and established the Sonora and Sinaloa Irrigation Company, organized under the laws of New Jersey. As security, Conant mortgaged the 500,000 hectares of land granted him by Mexico City.[16]

His blunders, exacerbated by the unwillingness of the Yaquis to accept their rape peacefully, eventually led his American backers to withdraw their captial, compelling him to sell undeveloped land to Mexican speculators. Thus appeared the first planters in the Yaqui, with Conant at the head of their list. Despite his mistakes, he managed to keep 26,084 hectares for himself. José María Parada came next with 13,407 hectares, followed by Albino Almada with 2,500, and Jesús A. Salazar with 1,400. Domingo Pérez and Jesús Valderráin also received healthy slices of land. The new planters tapped the waters of the Yaqui with irrigation canals, brought in machinery and modern equipment, planted corn, beans, melons, wheat, and garbanzos, raised cattle, and built flour mills. The commercialization of the Yaqui was under way. Nearly all of the Mayos, as well as the Yaquis who stayed behind, became tillers of the land, the wage workers of the *hacendados*.[17]

With Conant's bankruptcy, the Richardson Construction Company of Los Angeles took over, getting rights from Mexico City to irrigate and sell off 176,000 hectares of land.[18] Recognizing the Richardson Company as a surveying venture under the laws of idle lands, the grant limited activity to the Yaqui valley. The Richardsons were just a few of many American land speculators who came south at the turn of the century, often aided and abetted by powerful local families. These companies generally had to promise to "develop" and sell idle lands to private buyers, who turned out to be speculators or farmers from California and Texas.

The prime promoters in the Yaqui, the Richardsons came south during the 1880s. Natives of Los Angeles, three of the four brothers were originally active in mining in Sahuaripa. David, who was of administrative bent, handled finances; William, an engineer, had railroads in his blood; while Louis, also an engineer, served as the mining expert. In 1902, they purchased La Bufa, a mine in Sahuaripa, incorporating their enterprise in Arizona under the title of the Bufa Mining, Milling, and Smelting Company. The mines were thought to be rich in gold, silver, and copper. The Richardsons, so mining lore had it, spent $300,000 on a mill, foundry, concentrating plant, ovens, and diverse equipment to update their mines. They also brought in a spur line from Estación Corral, just south of Guaymas, that, following the banks of the Yaqui river, wound its way upstream past Buena Vista, Tónichi, and Colorada. Had it been completed as planned, it would have joined with the railroad running between Naco and Cananea, "Mr. Greene's railroad." It was baptized the Ferrocarril de Cananea, Río Yaqui y Pacífico. The trunk line, built by the Southern Pacific, ran for 154 miles, linking the Yaqui valley to Guaymas and, perhaps of more significance for the future, to markets north of the border.[19]

When the Richardsons bought out the bankrupt Conant in 1904, they acquired thousands of hectares of land and partly completed canals. They set about finishing the canals. They mapped out blueprints for an irrigation system for 750,000 acres of land, to include storage dams, reservoir, diverting dam, intake gates, and a network of feeder canals. In 1904, at the time of the purchase, only 3,750 acres were under cultivation. Less than a decade later, the Richardsons had irrigated and planted 27,000 acres. By 1910, furthermore, they had dug twenty-five miles of main canal plus forty-five miles of feeder canals. In the bargain, the company subdivided its lands into lots, 300 of them of ten hectares, and began to sell them to Americans.[20]

The lands of the Yaqui found enthusiastic buyers in the United States. The "lands are selling rapidly," reported a jubilant American consul, "and a great number of Americans looking for land are continually arriving." Were the shoppers to buy, a "large increase in the American population" of the state would follow.[21] As an article in *Sunset Magazine* testified, describing "empire . . . building" in the delta of the Yaqui, the visitors did buy lots. "Several hundred Americans, young, hustling and aggressive," had staked their future in the Yaqui. Some 50,000 acres, the author of the article wrote, had already been sold "and the demand is such that this part of Sonora promises to make a good American state in a mighty short time." Profits "as high as $300 an acre from tomatoes and onions," for shipment to Los Angeles or eastern markets, had lured the Americans, according to the *Sunset* article.[22]

But the success of the Richardsons enticed more than farmers from the north. It also encouraged land buying by other speculators, including John Hays Hammond, a mining engineer with years of experience in Mexico. In company with Harry Payne Whitney, son of the late tycoon William C. Whitney, and Leigh Hunt, an Iowa College professor, Hammond received a concession from Mexico City to take water from the Yaqui river to irrigate manifold acres of land that, stressed the *Sunset* writer, "will grow anything." The Yaqui Valley Land and Irrigation Company, another Los Angeles venture, controlled over 200,000 acres of delta soil.[23]

So began the influx of Americans into the Yaqui valley and the development of commercial farming for export. The long-imagined dream of the Alamos elite—bringing "whites" with go-getting ideas into Sonora—was finally taking shape.[24] To the surprise of the elite, many native Sonorenses, including some planters in the valleys, did not take kindly to the flood of intruders from north of the border.

Water was the wellspring of the growing conflict. Though they had similar goals, by 1910 Americans and Mexicans in the Yaqui stood at loggerheads over how much water each had a right to use. By then Luis E. Torres, the key *politico* in Sonora, had come to doubt the conventional wisdom that foreigners were always the bearers of progress. When the Richardsons asked Mexico City for the authority to construct a large dam on the Yaqui to store water for the dry season, a project opposed by Mexican landowners, Torres urged caution. He wanted both the property and the water of the Mexicans safeguarded.[25] Of like opinion, the governor of Sonora asked Mexico City not to grant the subsidy of 10 million pesos the Richardsons had requested. The company, he wrote, would be the "sole beneficiary" because, apart from the Indian *ejidos*, it owned virtually all the land on both banks of the river.[26]

The political winds had shifted. Now they were blowing against the Americans and against the idea that private enterprise alone could open the doors to the future. The new tack was that only Mexico City, the federal government, could unlock those magic doors. The 10 million pesos, the governor pointed out, would be put to better use if the government were to build irrigation works of its own. The projects of the Richardson Company, he declared, had "not benefitted Sonora" because the prices it set for the sale of its lands were beyond the means of Mexican dirt farmers. Only foreigners were able to purchase the lands. Not only did the company exercise a monopoly on the land of the left bank of the Yaqui river, as the concession of 1906 had stipulated, but to the anger of Mexicans it had come to use nearly all of the water on the opposite side. The Richardson Company's control of the lands and water of the Yaqui, the governor warned, jeopardized the sovereignty of the state of Sonora. Under no circumstances should Mexico City relinquish control of the Yaqui river.[27]

Hermosillo made its turnabout in response to local sentiment. Mexican planters in the Yaqui, never enthusiastic about the Richardson venture, had come to view its operations with jaundiced eyes. To expand their own plantings, they needed not just more land but more water for irrigation. That Mexican farmers wanted greater access to the waters of the Yaqui river, their petitions to Mexico City abundantly testify.[28] Juan Bojórquez, a malcontent in the making, sent one such request, as did Juan R. Orcí, who made a petition for himself and for other Mexicans, pleading for a larger share of the Yaqui waters.[29] An article by Enrique Monteverde, scion of the Hermosillo clan, published later but quite likely voicing current opinion, asked for access by municipal and state governments to the waters of the Yaqui. That way, he argued, the waters could be kept out of the hands of "greedy foreigners such as the Richardson Company."[30] For their part, the Richardson brothers hardly endeared themselves to the Mexican community, not only because of their monopoly of land and water, but because of a petty behavior.[31]

IV

Over on the Mayo, meanwhile, Mexican planters had fallen to fighting among themselves over water rights. The clash pitted the small planters against the barons of the valley. Until 1910, there were only eighteen major irrigation canals, all of them in the hands of the big planters, among them the owners of the *haciendas* Tres Hermanos, Rosales, Santa Barbara, and San Pedro. When an outsider attempted to add one more canal to the list, the establishment families—the Salido, Almada, and Salazar clans—took a hostile view of the endeavor.[32]

Commercial agriculture, made possible by the railroad link with markets in the United States, fostered urban growth in the valleys. Navojoa, Huatabampo, and Etchojoa, the key *municipios*, grew rapidly, adding 9,000 inhabitants in the decade from 1900 to 1910. By 1910, Huatabampo had over 2,000 people, and Navojoa, the commercial entrepôt for the Mayo, had over 3,000. As these *municipios* mushroomed, they undermined the predominance of Alamos city, which was still home to an elite with ties to the power brokers in Hermosillo.

Standing astride the "valleys of the Mesopotamia of Sonora," Navojoa had pioneered the way. At the close of the nineteenth century, it was already a "significant business center" renowned for its "undeniable progress."[33] By 1909, just two years after the arrival of the railroad, Navojoa had become a leading *municipio* of the state, with an annual budget of 25,000 pesos. Within its boundaries could be found a host of flourishing *haciendas*, among them San Pedro and Rosales of the Compañía Agrícola de Río Mayo, a Salido enterprise. Not far away were the *haciendas* of Jesús Morales and Angel García Peña, names to be reckoned with. However, as local farmers knew, not all of the land in the haciendas was planted with crops; much of their fertile soil lay fallow.[34]

The town of Navojoa, in the interval since the railroad's arrival, had shot up around the depot of the Southern Pacific, just steps away from Navojoa Viejo, its original site. One early settler, Carlos Valenzuela, put up a hotel; José Auerelio Ross, of the Ross family of Alamos, set up *El*

Furgón, an eatery that became a gathering spot for the town gossips; and another intrepid adventurer, Jesús Ruy Sánchez, established the first general store. Formerly a clerk with the mining companies in Promontorios, Sánchez came to Navojoa after the mines shut down. Other stores were opened, oftentimes by planters or their relatives. This group included Angel and Pedro Quiroz, Antonio and Jesús Morales, and Germán Bley, a German with Mexican citizenship.[35] As extensions of the *haciendas*, these stores were just another plum in the hands of the planter, giving him the means to control the prices of his wheat and garbanzos. A monopoly of sorts took root early. Flour mills, a carriage shop, two brickyards, and a lime pit made up the "industrial" sector of Navojoa. Its most successful business, a *tienda mixta* or general store, had annual sales of nearly 5,000 pesos; none of the rest had sales topping 4,000 pesos.[36] Business, while good, had not yet advanced too far.

A collection of wooden buildings on unpaved, rectangular streets, Navojoa had the look of a frontier town. Its inhabitants, a motley group, were of humble origin. With the exception of the tiny business and planter elite, usually one and the same, most of the inhabitants of Navojoa were wage workers, just as in the mining camps and towns. Such was their affluence on payday, however, than an army of bar girls and just plain prostitutes had invaded Navojoa by 1909. The town fathers ordered monthly health inspections for the women and built an infirmary to shelter the sick among them. To pay for this medical service, the good fathers levied a monthly tax of five pesos on the women's earnings.[37]

Huatabampo dated from 1890. Originally under the jurisdiction of Navojoa, it became a *municipio* just eight years after its founding, so remarkable was its population growth. Among those who petitioned Hermosillo to declare Huatabampo a *municipio* were the Obregóns—Carlos, Francisco, and Lamberto. Lamberto was once a constable of the town.[38] Alvaro, still another brother, was destined to enshrine the Obregón name in Mexican history. He would later settle in Huatabampo. Like Navojoa, Huatabampo evolved as the hub of a rich farming delta, especially with the digging of canals in 1893 to tap the waters of the Mayo.

V

To the north, the towns of the Yaqui valley also made headway, although they never were a match for the settlements in the Mayo. Founded as missions, most sheltered both Yaquis and Mexicans. Pótam and Medano, two of these towns, evolved as key business centers for the Yaquis. Non-Indians, nevertheless, had a corner on its commerce. Among the entrepreneurs were Francis McDonald, the owner of a flour mill, and the future *político* Salvador Alarado, a merchant in 1907. The first plantings of rice in the valleys were on Pótam's communal lands, which had been allocated by the Comisión Geográfica. Luis Cong Si, manager of a Chinese shoe shop in Guaymas, planted the crops there as an experiment. He later purchased land in Huatabampo, where he planted rice that eventually was sold everywhere in Sonora.[39] Tórin, an agricultural town that at one time was second only to Cananea in population, served as headquarters for the army employed to "pacify" the recalcitrant Yaquis. It also had the military hospital serving Sonora, Sinaloa, and Baja California. In its plaza, where the "white" conqueror held sway, stood a bust of Benito Juárez, Mexico's Indian president. In a fine irony, Angel García Peña, a colonel in that army, owned the biggest flour mill in Tórin.[40]

Cócorit, a less important town, had just started to bloom. With a plaza at its center, and wide streets laid out in rectangular fashion, Cócorit had housed the offices of the Sonora and Sinaloa Irrigation Company, Conant's ill-fated venture. Planning for the first canals in the Yaqui took place there. Conant's hacienda Los Gitos stood there, as did the Hacienda Guadalupe of Jesús Valderráin, an Alamos stalwart. Nearby, Jesús Antonio Parada, a *notable* of politics and society, cultivated but a fourth of the 4,000 hectares of his Hacienda La Esperanza, a commonplace occurrence in the region. One of the finest, the *hacienda* of Domingo Pérez, grew cotton and grapes for wine. Pérez, who also operated a cotton gin, arrived in Cócorit in 1904 from La Laguna de Tlahualillo in Coahuila, a cotton belt with water problems of its own. Cócorit was less Yaqui and "more Mexican," especially because many of its inhabitants had come from Quiriego, the colonial mining town in Alamos. The town became the social hub of the Yaqui valley and gained reknown for the beauty of its women.[41]

Bácum, another of the Yaqui towns and an agricultural center, had lands planted in tomatoes. In 1908, American promoters who financed and supervised their cultivation shipped 133 boxcars of tomatoes to markets north of the border. The value of tomatoes shipped from the port of Guaymas multiplied threefold between 1908 and 1909. Unfortunately for the promoters, however, frosts destroyed the tomato crops in 1910 and 1911, temporarily putting an end to their cultivation in the Yaqui.[42] Médano, the leading commercial town for the Yaqui tribes, served as a kind of port because of its location near the mouth of the Yaqui river. From Médano, merchandise was carried to Pótam and from there shipped to other towns. Vícam, a political and religious shrine for the Yaquis, had farms and a tiny business enclave.[43]

VI

The "green revolution," offspring of an export agriculture, altered the demographic and physical contours of the valleys.

No crop better exemplified the metamorphosis taking place than the garbanzo or chickpea. Like sugar in Cuba or coffee in El Salvador, the garbanzo helped dictate the economic and social structure of the Mayo valley. Life revolved around the planting, harvesting and sale of the garbanzo. To the population of southern Sonora, the chickpea was the new treasure, replacing the silver of yesteryear. Navojoa, Huatabampo, and Etchojoa, centers of the garbanzo industry, took over from Alamos, La Aduana, and Río Chico, names from the illustrious silver-mining past, as the most important towns of the south. But like the sugar and coffee planters in Cuba and Central America, the Mexicans soon learned what it meant to tie their fate to the caprice of foreign buyers. The garbanzo cultivators, some of whom had made the journey from silver mines to agricultural fields, found they had exchanged one fickle commodity for another.[44]

The golden age of the garbanzo, like that of copper, unfolded because of events beyond local control. True, with the help of the military the planters themselves ousted the Mayos, robbing them of their lands. They irrigated the valley, and now its fertile soil nurtured the garbanzo. Still, the demand for the crop came from abroad. Spanish merchants in Alamos, Hermosillo, and Mazatlán had encouraged its cultivation. In 1909, Carmelo Echeverría, manager of Ramón Corral's flour mill in Hermosillo, paid Alejandro Lazy to buy up the garbanzo crop in Guaymas district. His price of five pesos a *fanega* (1.6 bushels), twice that paid by competitors, was a pot of gold to farmers. Until then, the garbanzo had been used mainly for cattle feed. By 1910, with a bag of garbanzos selling for sixteen pesos or more, the value of the year's crop reached 1 million pesos.[45] All the same, the good times of the garbanzo could not have occurred without the arrival of the railroad in the Mayo, or the collapse of mining in Alamos, which left countless workers looking for jobs. Fortuitously, both events coincided.

Mother Nature, too, had a hand in events. When the early planters began to till the soil of the Mayo, few paid much attention to the chickpea. They planted corn, beans, and especially wheat, profitable because it could be milled into flour. By 1901, the Mayo valley had six flour mills; the oldest, on the Hacienda Tres Hermanos of the Salidos, dated from 1865. However, wheat fared poorly because of fungus diseases and insects. Its decline hurt the flour mills, compelling their owners to look for other sources of income. For a time cotton seemed to offer a way out, but its rewards also proved ephemeral. The garbanzo made its entrance at this juncture, first on the Hacienda Los Rosales, property of the Salido brothers. Eventually, garbanzo plantings occupied 60 percent of the cultivated land.[46]

International demand for the garbanzo, especially from Spain, Cuba, and the United States, kept its price up. In 1909, a bag of garbanzos sold for 12 pesos; a year later, the early harvest went for 13.5 pesos a bag and, as the supply dwindled, for 16.5 pesos. As one author wrote, "a veritable avalanche of buyers fell upon Sonora," encouraging planters to cultivate nothing but garbanzos. Its success in the Mayo carried it elsewhere, to plantings in Bácum, Pótam, Tórin, and Cócorit in the Yaqui valley, and north to San José de Guaymas and Hermosillo. In 1910, of the 145,000 hectoliters harvested, (about 406,000 bushels), 84,500 came from Alamos and Guaymas, the core districts of the garbanzo empire.[47] The garbanzo harvest of 1910 sold for 2 million pesos, putting Sonora at the top of the world's list of producers.[48]

The financial needs of the planters brought bankers into the picture. Offices of the Banco de Sonora went up in Navojoa and Alamos, and, of no less importance, the banking firm of Tomás Robinson Bours y Hermanos of Alamos, agents for the Banco Occidental de México.[49] The bankers lent money to plant the bean, to harvest it, and to ship it abroad, the bulk of exports going from Guaymas port where, to quote a local newspaper, "the number of ships entering and leaving astonished."[50] But credit, as complaints revealed, did not flow freely to one and all alike. First, it went to the big planters; then, if still available, to the lesser planters but never to the dirt farmers at the bottom of the totem pole. The not-so-big needed more money and, especially, long-term loans.[51] Some of the disenchanted later bore arms against the bankers and their friends in Hermosillo.

The tiny chickpea gave birth to a complicated agro-industrial complex of planters, bankers, shippers, and, significantly, an army of wage workers. Not everyone got an equal helping of the profits, least of all the workers. A small contingent of planters cornered most of the profits. In Huatabampo, the hub of the garbanzo empire, of the thirty leading planters only nine had a harvest of over 1,000 bags a year. Of that elite group, two planters towered over the rest: the Salidos with 8,000 bags and José Tiburcio Otero, the old *cacique*, with 4,000. The next largest producers, the Valderráin brothers, harvested 3,000 a year. The brothers Ross produced 2,500 bags. Of the 21 lowest-ranking planters, none produced over 800 bags, and most produced less than 400. By comparison, Alvaro Obregón, an up-and-coming planter with 700 bags annually, had little to complain about.[52] A similar situation existed in Navojoa, with Morales and García Peña at the top with 3,000 bags each, followed by a plethora of brothers: Salido, Campoy, and Amparán, natives of Alamos town.[53] In Guaymas, four planters, one of them Francisco Maytorena of the future rebel family, sat at the tiller.[54]

The Indians, often as wage laborers, tilled the lands they had once called their own.[55] As field hands they were poorly compensated, earning on the average no more than seventy-five centavos for a day's toil. The Salidos, niggardly tycoons, paid even less: men in their fields earned thirty-seven centavos and women, when they employed them, twenty-five centavos. They were paid only for the days they worked, of course, and each May after the harvest was in, the jobless tillers of the soil were left to fend for themselves. Like the mining regions, the valleys turned into a series of camps or towns where men and women of diverse origins had recently settled. Untold numbers, of course, migrated from the mining camps of Alamos, but that district had never had a homogeneous population. Others ventured south from the copper kingdoms of Cananea and Nacozari, which were crippled by the economic crisis of 1907, or from the mining camps of Altar, Magdalena, Ures, and Hermosillo. The Yaquis, resentful and hostile while serving the planters, were the core of the cheap labor force. It was a social structure that had not jelled. The people in it were tenuously pulled together only by jobs and the hope for profit.[56]

The repercussions of this world in flux, like those in the mining camps, were predictable. At Esperanza, one of the towns of the Richardson Company in the Yaqui valley, Mexicans and Americans led separate lives. East of the railroad tracks lay the tiny American colony with the better homes and the hospital. On the west side dwelt the Mexicans, in shacks of "sticks and mud called *horcones*" and in huts of wood and adobe. Beyond them stretched open space, lots for those who wanted to put up *ramadas, jacals* ("huts") made of brush.[57] At times, swarms of mosquitoes, so thick they turned day into night, made life miserable, while rattlesnakes, ubiquitous in the Yaqui, turned labor in the field into a test of courage. "Above all the rattlers" a later immigrant from the hill towns recalled of trials in the valley. "What a nightmare, to turn over a dead mesquite only to encounter a nest of rattlesnakes . . . [and] to feel their poisonous fangs bite into the sticks we used to move them."[58]

At Cócorit, where Yaquis and *yoris* ("white" Mexicans) dwelt side by side, police arrived early. They were brought there by necessity, wrote a group of its citizens, the consequence of a population "heterogeneous by inclination and custom" and prone to crime.[59] The drinking of strong liquor, especially among the Yaquis, had nearly universal appeal. Yaquis, believed an army physician, "loved to get drunk."[60] Determined to put a stop to the "drunken orgies," the mayor of Cócorit asked saloonkeepers to close their doors on Sunday afternoons. Local planters, it appears, had complained that alcohol imbibed on Sunday kept men out of the fields on Monday.[61] The Richardson Company went further, asking Hermosillo for a monopoly on liquor sales in the entire valley, so the company could control its use. With the influx of people into the Yaqui, the Richardsons explained, unscrupulous men had a golden opportunity to "open saloons, gambling parlors and bordellos," to the detriment of company goals.[62] Actually, that had already begun to take place, as an order from Hermosillo testified. The prefects of Alamos and Guaymas districts were ordered to "take steps to put the use of alcohol beyond reach of the working class."[63] It did not, however, grant the Richardsons a liquor monopoly. At Navojoa, "drunken Mexicans," if the report of the prefect can be believed, clashed with American engineers of the Southern Pacific, leading the town luminaries to ask Hermosillo to enlarge the police force, a request it granted immediately.[64]

VII

Change also blessed the valleys with an intermediate class of entrepreneurs with a foot in both agriculture and business. They were well-off but less affluent than the old planters. In comparison with the Richardson brothers, they fared poorly. In the course of events, some of them not only saluted the banner of rebellion but helped raise it aloft. Among the most successful was Benjamín Guillermo Hill Salido, planter, flour merchant, and town father of Navojoa.

A maverick by blood and temperament, Benjamín Hill was the offspring of doña Jesús Salido of Alamos and William Hill, who had been a physician with the Confederate forces during the Civil War in the United States. With the defeat of the south, the elder Hill ventured into Mexico, becoming a rancher after failing as a mining speculator. His ranch, Yori Tamegua, stood on the edge of Navojoa, not far from the *hacienda* of Martín Salido. He married doña Jesús, sister of Martín. (Another sister, Cenobia, was mother of seventeen children by a rancher at Siquisiva named Espiridion Obregón. Her youngest, baptized Alvaro, would become a garbanzo planter at Huatabampo and a rebel.) In his early adulthood, the Hills' son, Benjamín, wasted little time trying to upgrade the family ranch, dedicating himself instead to becoming a "playboy and gambler."[65] His father, however, did send his son to study in Europe, where he spent nine years. In Italy, Hill Salido went to school with Enrique Caruso of operatic fame. He returned home, one of his neighbors wrote, a "gourmet," a bon vivant with a taste for good food, a legacy of his years in Italy and Germany.

When the old Hill died, in the manner of the *gran patrón* he bequeathed 2,000 pesos to the poor of Alamos.[66] Hill eventually matured and returned to the life of a planter in Navojoa. There he cultivated forty hectares of irrigated land. It was choice property but not among the largest farms—that honor belonged to the holdings of the Salidos, Morales, and García Peña. Relying on the laws of idle lands, Hill added 2,494 hectares to his property in 1909.[67] But Choarca, as the new land was called, lacked water. Its owner would have to find a way to dig a canal, a formidable task given the competition for water. Additionally, Hill ran a flour mill, one of three in Navojoa. The largest belonged to Morales and García Peña. Powered by steam, Hill's mill, called Mochibompo, produced up to 1,500 hectoliters (5,745 bushels) of wheat flour a year, in good times amply compensated. To run it, Hill employed six men and paid them from fifty to sixty centavos a day, no more and no less than other mill owners dispensed.[68]

Hill was not just one more petty entrepreneur. By family ties, he was a Salido, a distinguished name in the social registry of Alamos, where he maintained a home. He was on good terms with the big planters of Navojoa, especially Angel Quiroz. With a sense of humor, he referred to members of the ruling circle in Hermosillo as *pícaros* ("rogues"), but made certain to accompany Luis E. Torres, the *compadre* ("godfather") of politics, whenever Torres visited Navojoa.[69] Torres treated Hill amiably, almost as a friend. Following the normal progression, Hill eventually found himself a *regidor*, one of the four members of the town council of Navojoa. But in January, 1910, he resigned abruptly. The mayor, in urging Hermosillo to accept the resignation, said Hill had a "dogmatic personality" and labeled him an "enemy of the government."[70]

Hill, indeed, had embraced views antagonistic to the circle in power. He won his seat on the council because he was not intimately identified with Jesús Morales, the political boss of Navojoa. He thought it would be a mistake to reelect Porfirio Díaz, and return the Triumvirate to Hermosillo. In a letter to *La Voz de Juárez*, a Mexico City newspaper, he urged the election of men divorced from the ruling cabal. So highly did Hill rate the book *La Sucesión Presidencial*, an attack on don Porfirio by Francisco I. Madero, an *hacendado* from Coahuila, that he had 200 copies printed and distributed in the towns of the Mayo and Yaqui. When Madero chose to challenge Díaz at the polls, Hill and his companions established an Antireelectionist Club in Navojoa; others who backed the club included the Bórquez brothers, Flavio, Arnulfo, and

Ventura, as well as Inocente Amparán. All were planters or merchants; not one was a penniless worker. When Madero arrived in Navojoa during his campaign for the presidency, Hill met him at the train station —with his *peones* ("laborers").[71]

Why the turnabout? If one or two reasons could explain the change in Hill, they would be water and land. A disaster in January 1907, though a common-enough occurrence, was the proverbial straw that broke the camel's back. It rained steadily for seventy-two hours in Navojoa; water covered the fields and the town.[72] If it were to escape the yearly floodings, Navojoa would have to move upstream, away from the surging waters of the Mayo. Pueblo Nuevo, on higher grounds, would be safe. The town council, with an Almada serving on it, chose this moment to award the right to "develop" land in Pueblo Nuevo to an Almada relative. Baldomero A. Almada, head of a Compañía Colonizadora ("land speculators"), would develop the tracts fronting on the railroad station—the most valuable lots in town. By terms of the agreement, Almada would sell the lots to private individuals, keeping for himself 60 percent of the sale price. On top of that, he would build homes to put on the market. Some 450 lots with a value of 70,000 pesos were involved. The town council also relinquished its right to sell lots on its own and required no financial guarantee of any kind from Almada. Hill, Flavio Bórquez, and others, apparently with real-estate ambitions of their own, urged Hermosillo not to approve the transaction.[73] Their pleas fell on deaf ears. Almada and his backers kept their lucrative business deal.[74] The episode, however, alerted Hill to the importance of politics.

Flavio Bórquez, Hill's political ally and also a budding rebel, was a native of Quiriego, the old mining town in Alamos. Along with Hill and Alvaro Obregón, he mastered the three R's at the knee of Guillermo Bracamontes, a local teacher who later headed the Instituto de Niños in Alamos. A Liberal in the mold of Benito Juárez, Bracamontes upheld the separation of church and state, believed in the republican form of government, and worshiped the virtues of free enterprise. He taught these ideas to his students.[75] Bórquez was related through his mother to Jesús Valderráin, the planter in Huatabampo. As a young man he had gone off to Chihuahua to make his fortune. He became a merchant and, as secretary to the *cacique* of Matamoros, whetted his appetite for politics. From Chihuahua he returned to Alamos, then moved to Navojoa, where he established himself as a grain merchant.[76] Later he helped topple the power of the Triumvirate in Sonora.

In the town of Huatabampo dwelt Ramón Ross, a native of Alamos, and, like Hill and Bórquez, destined for prominence in the post-Díaz era. With Ildefonso Ross, he owned El Huichaca, one of the better *haciendas* in the *municipio* of Huatabampo. He employed forty men to plow and plant his crops. Never one to pass up a peso, he also ran a profitable general store.[77] Of a pliant disposition—so much so that some thought him "disingenuous"—Ross got along well with his neighbors.[78] With a penchant for politics, Ross was elected a *regidor* of the town council in 1894 and then mayor of Huatabampo. A loyalist until the end, he signed a pledge of allegiance to don Porfirio. Bórquez, who knew him well, recalled that Ross had been Obregón's "buddy" since the 1880s.[79] Eventually, Ross joined Obregón's war against the old regime.

Also in Huatabampo lived Pedro J. Almada, a native of La Quintera, the Alamos mining town. Through his father, he was related to the Almada *camarilla* ("power group"). He had come to Huatabampo and, like Obregón, gone about acquiring land and planting garbanzos. He fared so well, he would later boast, that his profits made it possible for him to buy out the bakeries in town and to gain a monopoly. Beyond that, he ran the *rastro*, the town slaughterhouse, and was the agent for Singer Sewing Machines in Sonora. When Obregón became mayor of Huatabampo in 1911, he named Almada its chief of police.[80]

Had men such as Hill and Bórquez bided their time, they doubtlessly would have climbed the political ladder. But it might have taken years because in the Mayo and Yaqui, as in the rest of the state, a small knot of men controlled affairs. In Alamos sat Francisco A. Salido, prefect of the district. Still another Almada, Ignacio L., was mayor of Alamos, while on its town council were another Salido and a Palomares, both local bluebloods. In Navojoa, José A. Morales, of the "eternal" Morales family, was mayor, and Jesús L. Almada and Antonio Quiróz *regidores*. Nearby, in Huatabampo, José Tiburcio Otero, *cacique*, landlord, and ally of Ramón Corral, dictated events, including his own election to mayor in 1910.

These wealthy potentates hobnobbed with the cabal in Hermosillo and looked with favor upon a system increasingly linked to capital and markets in the United States. By 1910, Navojoa, the home of Hill and his recalcitrant companions, had become a hotbed of antireelectionist sentiment.[81] Yet the elections, a triumph for the circle in Hermosillo, passed quietly.[82] Had Madero not decided to rebel, Hill, Bórquez, and Ross probably would not now figure in the history books as rebels.

The transformation of the Yaqui and Mayo valleys into an export paradise had asymmetrical consequences. Their ancient owners, the Yaqui and Mayo Indians, lost most of their lands. They often became wage laborers, the tillers of the soil for big planters, Americans and

Mexicans cultivating cash crops for export to the United States and Europe. A cabal formed by planters, merchants, and bankers, not infrequently related by blood, came in for a big share of the profits. That ties to markets north of the border helped this cabal, few will dispute; that they resulted in disaster for the poverty-stricken majority is equally evident.

But even the Mexicans who profited became part of a dependent class, a kite tossed by the heady winds from the north. And much of the land itself fell into the hands of Americans.

CHAPTER 11

The March of Civilization

I

When the political factions settled accounts, peace and order, the heralded signposts of civilization, made their bow in much of Sonora. But to the chagrin of the *camarilla* in power, Indians were blocking the blueprint for progress. In the south, Mayos and Yaquis controlled the best lands; on the northern frontier, Apaches harassed miners. To open the southern valleys to commercial farming and entice foreigners to exploit mineral resources, the authorities had to deal with the Indian "problem." Civilization—or, rather, economic growth—required the conquest of the Indian, the "savage" of popular lore. This homegrown racial antagonism was heightened by the arrival of the Americans who helped fuel the fires of prejudice and discrimination.

II

Long before the advent of the Triumvirate in Hermosillo, the "whites,"—the Mexicans who claimed Spanish ancestry—had confronted the Indian in every corner of Sonora. The inhabitants of Alamos, along with their neighbors in Guaymas valley and the sierra of Mazatán, had been fighting Indians since colonial days. Rare was the Sonoran who could not recall a death in the family at the hands of Yaqui or Mayo. For these people, wrote Luis E. Torres, the subjugation of the Indian was the top priority.[1] By the late nineteenth century, the white Mexican's racism was barely hidden. Carlos Plank, a darling of the reformers of 1910, for example, could not tolerate the company of any Indians, his father having died at Indian hands. The ghost of his father, he thought, would rise from the grave were he to befriend an Indian.[2] Along the northern border, stories of Apache atrocities were legion. The name of Gerónimo, an Apache chieftain, was synonymous with cruelty, rape, and death.

Yet the Indians had long lived in Sonora. Some linguists believed that even the name of the state had an Indian derivation, from the word *sonotl* (*oja de maís* or "ear of corn") in the language of the Opata, one of the local tribes. Since the days of the Spaniards, Sonora had ranked among the provinces with the largest number of Indian tribes. On the eve of the invasion by American speculators in the late nineteenth century, tribal Indians made up about a third of its population.[3] With the exception of a fraction of people of undiluted Spanish background, according to the American consul, Sonora's inhabitants were "mixed bloods," mestizos with racial bonds to both Europe and America.[4] Among the tribes, the Yaquis, numbering between 20,000 and 25,000, were the largest, followed by the Mayos, with 10,000 to 15,000 people.[5] By 1910, the Yaqui population, decimated by three decades of warfare and deportation to the henequen plantations of Yucatán, stood at 15,000 and that of the Mayos at 6,000. A fourth of the Yaquis had perished.[6]

The dominant culture attached a stigma to being Indian. Ever since the conquest, the Spaniards had treated the Indian as an inferior. In Sonora, to be "white" or Spaniard meant one belonged to the superior race. To be Indian meant one was a member of an inferior race as well as an inferior class. As late as 1926, over 42 percent of Sonora's inhabitants classified themselves in a census as whites—utter nonsense even if "purity" of blood could be measured after three centuries of sexual mingling.[7]

The need to be considered "white" went back a long way. It responded to a harsh truth: miscegenation had long ago blurred racial lines, to the despair of the Sonorenses who wanted to be called white. As far back as the eighteenth century, the people the Jesuits labeled Spaniards, those living outside the missions, were really mixed bloods. True Spaniards were but a tiny core. To the Jesuits, secular society was "really a Spanish-speaking non-Indian world that included many mestizos." As early as the seventeenth century, there were only 500 true Spaniards—mostly miners, farmers, and storekeepers—living in Sonora.[8] Racial miscegenation, the coupling of Spaniard and Indian, rather than the segregation of the races was the rule. In Ures *mestizaje* ("racial mixing") had gone on for so long that when its prefect, on request of Hermosillo, attempted to find authentic native artifacts, he could not do it.[9]

Still, Spaniards and creoles—those born in Mexico of Spanish parents—made up a larger fraction of the population in Sonora than they did in southern Mexico. *Mestizaje* had taken root unevenly in Sonora. It was most common in the former Pima and Opata homelands, the Sahuaripa district, and in Alamos. The Mayo and Yaqui valleys, on the other hand, sheltered the largest groups of unassimilated Indians. Ironically, in this southern cone, Alamos, the oldest city in Sonora, had the distinction of being the "whitest."[10] At the inauguration of the Mexican Republic in 1821, half of the Europeans in Sonora, 6,280, lived in Alamos.

In southern Sonora, two distinct groups, Spaniards and Indians, confronted each other across barricades of class and race. It was the brown man, or bronze as Mexicans were wont to say, against whites. A similar situation prevailed in the north, where Apaches faced Mexicans. Mutual fears and opposite goals led whites and Apaches to bear arms against each other: the Indian to defend his property and the whites to stop Indians from barring development of mine and farm. Sonora, with only occasional periods of peace and order, became an armed camp where the rifle ruled. Scores of its leading citizens climbed the ladder to prominence by bearing arms to kill Indians.[11]

Out of this situation evolved a virulent racism, publicly denied but privately practiced, particularly in the selection of marriage partners, in a society where the idea of family lines was important. By the late nineteenth century, "purity of race," if not a publicly endorsed doctrine, guided the thought and behavior of key segments of the population, particularly the elite and the ambitious. In their bastion in Alamos, the venerated families, boasting of their Spanish ancestry, enjoyed the fruits of the good life. Proud of their whiteness, they blocked the marriages of their daughters and sons with dark-skinned Mexicans.[12] The inhabitants of other parts of Sonora walked a similar path. In a contest to select the most beautiful women of Guaymas in 1887, the three finalists, boasted a scion of the merchant clique, were "young, tall and blue-eyed" and "of clear, smooth, white skin."[13] To their way of thinking, the whites, were the *gente de razón* ("the civilized") as a prefect explained. The Indian, in contrast, was a "savage."[14] It was a hierarchical society split along racial and class lines where, a foreign traveler concluded, one had "to protect the dog from the Indians; the Indians from the Mexicans; and the Mexicans," after the Yankee had made himself at home in the Sonora, "from the Americans."[15]

Yet there was a strange ambivalence toward the Indian in this often hypocritical universe. Cuauhtémoc, the hero of ancient Tenochtitlán, was a national symbol in a country that, in a gesture of native pride, forbade the bones of the conqueror Hernán Cortés, one of its founders, to be buried in its soil. But the Mexicans who laid a wreath at the feet of the Indian warrior who fought the Spaniards also decreed war against the Yaqui and the Mayo.[16] These same Mexicans, charged Esteban Baca Calderón, with much logic, allowed foreigners to gain "racial hegemony" in Sonora.[17]

The Yaquis, one author declared, epitomized the "Indian plague." They had "not permitted a moment of tranquility," he said, and only added to the woes inflicted by Apaches and other heathens.[18] The wars against the Yaquis, declared a Mexican historian, gave every sign that their instigators wanted to exterminate the Indian.[19] The uprising of the Yaquis in 1885, the biggest of their wars against whites, even united squabbling Mexican *politicos*. "Given current conditions," pontificated *La Opinión*, an Alamos newspaper, "everyone, absolutely everyone must rally behind our government to combat the common enemy, who is, at the same time, the enemy of civilization and mankind." *La Opinión*, ordinarily an opposition journal, was referring to Yaquis.[20] Ramón Corral, the author of essays praised for their magnanimity towards the Indian, considered Tetabiate, the successor to Cajeme, the legendary Yaqui chieftain of the Yaquis, "idiotic and stupid."[21] Or to cite a judge of Alamos, the "savage hordes of the Yaqui and Mayo Indians" had unleashed the gods of war. Some Sonorenses found the Yaquis barbarous and "child-like" at the same time. When asked why he allowed Yaquis to drink in the town, the constable at Estación Pesqueira replied that he did not think its citizens would mind. Only after drunken Yaquis had started fighting among themselves did he step in, because, he said, they might "hurt each other."[22]

To the ruling cabal, the Yaquis blocked progress. Sooner or later they had to submit or die, and "the sooner the better."[23] That attitude was deeply entrenched in the circles of power and among federal army officers fighting the Yaquis.[24] It led to wanton acts of cruelty, acts amply repaid by the Indians. One specific episode, the massacre of Indians at Bácum, stands out. A large group of Yaquis who wanted peace had approached Colonel Próspero Salazar Bustamante but, not trusting them, he took them prisoners. The colonel had the 450 Indians locked in the church at Bácum and then had his artillery bombard it. One hundred Yaquis died in the massacre.[25] In this vicious war against the Yaqui, both the peaceful (*mansos*) and the rebellious (*broncos*), the "guilty" as well as the innocent, perished at the hands of the military. Luis Medina Barrón, a commander of the *rurales*, slashed his way into the record books of barbarity by hunting down Yaquis "with hatred and tenacity." His tortures of the Yaqui were acts of wanton cruelty that bloodied the history of race relations.[26]

Medina Barrón's torture of Dolores Buitimea, a Yaqui field hand, documents the scope of that cruelty. Suspected of aiding the *broncos*, Buitimea had been turned over to Medina Barrón by a planter. To punish him and learn more about the *broncos*, Medina Barrón had his soldiers tie a rope around Buitimea's neck and pull it over a branch of a mesquite tree.

"*¿Sabes?*" ("What do you know?"), the commander demanded.

"Nothing," Buitimea answered.

Angered by the response, Medina Barrón told his soldiers to pull the rope, briefly allowing the Yaqui to dangle by the neck. He had him lowered and then repeated the question.

"*¿Sabes?*"

"Nothing."

Again the man was pulled up, this time for longer.

"*¿Sabes?*"

"Nothing."

Once again, Medina Barrón ordered the Yaqui hung, for a still-longer period, and then had him lowered.

"*¿Sabes?*"

"Nothing."

This performance was repeated over and over again but always with identical results. The victim's son, Jesús Buitimea, standing just steps away, watched the entire drama without batting an eyelash. At last a bored Medina Barrón had the Yaqui hung for good. When the man was dead, the commander turned to Jesús. Known as a brave man who knew the region intimately, Jesús spoke *Cahita*, the language of the Yaquis, and by reputation was a friend of the "whites." Medina Barrón was impressed by his stoic acceptance of his father's fate and offered to make Jesús an officer in the army. But Jesús refused, daring Medina Barrón to hang him as he had his father. So in anger Medina Barrón complied, hanging the son alongside his father on the same mesquite tree.[27]

Medina Barrón's cruelty was not unusual. Ignacio Pesqueira, who ruled Sonora until the advent of the Triumvirate, won renown killing Yaquis. As governor, Rafael Izábal took special delight in torturing Yaquis, including *mansos*. On one memorable occasion, he went off to hunt Yaquis as if they were wild animals, and like a proud safari hunter returned with a photograph of the fruits of his gruesome deed. Loreto Molina, a renegade Yaqui doing the bidding of the whites, burnt down Cajeme's house and raped his wife. To honor the veterans of the Yaqui wars, the state legislature, prodded by Governor Lorenzo Torres, had silver decorations cast in their honor—for the officers, that is. Luis E. Torres, Corral, and General Angel Martínez, ringleaders of the wars, got gold medals.[28]

The embittered Yaqui reciprocated, taking out his revenge on *yoris* ("whites"), repaying their cruelty with a barbarity of his own. That wrath, to cite a perceptive comment, turned into an "implacable hatred for the white man." It was the Yaqui woman, reported inhabitants of the valleys, who kept alive that hate, transmitting it from one generation to the next.[29] Partly because he believed that women carried the germ of hatred for the *yori*, Governor Izábal deported not only Yaqui males but their mothers, wives, and daughters as well. To eradicate the Yaqui menace meant expunging the entire household. Cruel and misguided as he was, Izábal did not err because the Yaqui was determined that his "valley was for the Yaqui and for no one else."[30]

III

At the time of the Spanish conquest, about 200,000 Indians dwelt in the Sonoran desert, the region from northern Sinaloa to Arizona. Perhaps up to 70 percent had their homes in the south, mainly in the Yaqui, Mayo, and Fuerte river valleys. The early Spanish missionaries estimated the Yaqui population to be about 30,000.[31] For the most part, Yaquis farmed for a living, planting corn, squash, beans, cotton, and tobacco. Their biggest settlements were Bácum, Cócorit, Tórin, Vícam, Ráum, and Pótam. While Spanish towns dated from the sixteenth century, not until the next century did the Spaniards "conquer" the Yaquis and occupy their valley. Jesuit missionaries, who spearheaded the conquest, built their first mission in the Yaqui valley in 1617, on the heels of an earlier one in the Mayo. A decade later, the good padres claimed to have baptized the Yaquis and settled them in eight missions.[32] From the beginning, therefore, as General Luis E. Torres argued, neither the Yaquis nor the Mayos could be thought entirely savage, because they "baptized their children, married in the Church and attended Catholic services."[33]

Whatever the merit of Torres's utterance, the Yaquis, spurred on by the religious zeal of the padres, who often took their side against lay Spaniards, adapted to life on the missions. A compromise had been worked out. For three days a week the Yaquis tilled the fields and tended the ranches of the missions; during the rest of the week, they cultivated food crops on land assigned to them for their own subsistence. The missions, in the course of time, came to control the best-irrigated lands, a fact of no little consequence. Given the rudimentary farming techniques and the scarcity of water, cultivable soil stood in short supply. But during the period that no one but padres intruded on the lands, Yaquis and Spaniards lived in peace.

This idyllic picture, if Spanish accounts are to be believed, began to crumble in the latter half of the seventeenth century with the discovery of silver in Alamos. Lured by the promise of easy wealth, more and more Spaniards arrived. Most headed to the mines of Alamos but, to the despair of both padre and Yaqui, some took up farming, first in the Mayo valley and then in the Yaqui. The white man's invasion of the valleys had started. According to the Jesuits, as Spanish interlopers multiplied and more and more land fell to them, the Yaqui turned belligerent and then rebellious. The Yaqui uprising of 1740, the first of many to come, however, had multiple causes. The farms in the Yaqui, secular and clerical alike, had begun to grow corn and wheat for the miners of Alamos and for the padres who set out to found new missions in the Río Sonora and Baja California. The Yaquis complained of heavy workloads, of having to produce and transport grains and cattle for the missions in California, largely at their own expense. The Yaquis wanted to sell their surplus produce for their own profit and to work in the mines, something the Jesuit fathers did not readily accept. In addition, floods had led to famine, encouraging hungry Yaquis to plunder mission granaries and other Spanish holdings. And on top of this, the Spanish governor, Manuel Bernal de Huidobro, was trying to bring the missions to heel.[34] When the uprising broke out, the Jesuits, with the aid of Spanish soldiers, put it down with rifles. Nevertheless, the rebellion weakened the hold of the padres over the Yaquis and, more significantly, temporarily halted the whites' invasion. No other Yaqui rebellion challenged Spain's rule in the valleys.

Independence in 1821, a mixed blessing for other Mexicans, made life worse for the Indian. Under the Crown, Indian *pueblos* had enjoyed a measure of freedom. They were allowed to elect their own officials, overlook the obligation to pay taxes, and to retain communal lands outside mission control. Under the Constitution of 1824, the Indian became a citizen of the Mexican Republic, no longer a ward of the state. Along with the other citizens, he now had to pay taxes, obey Mexican political bosses, and guard his lands as best he could, often from avaricious local officials. With the coming of independence, the Yaquis wanted sole ownership of the former mission lands, insisting that the entire valley belonged to them. Mexican republicans had a different set of blueprints.

The initial clash of wills occurred in 1825, when the Yaquis refused to shoulder arms against the Apaches. Determined to punish the disobedient Yaquis, the Mexican commander, General José Figueroa, dispatched soldiers to the Yaqui valley, killing a number of rebels at the battle of Ráum. But when the troops departed, other Yaquis fell upon the nearby *haciendas* and *ranchos* looking for food and loot. The Mexican governor, less inclined than Figueroa to assume a bellicose stance, convinced the Yaqui rebels to return to their villages, but ignored their demand that "the Yaqui people be recognized as the sole and absolute owners of land." Figueroa, however, set about to punish the recalcitrant Yaquis, thereby inviting the rebellion of Juan Banderas, the first of the famous Yaqui chieftains. With the help of the Mayos, who joined his defiance of the Mexicans, Banderas compelled Figueroa to acknowledge the Yaquis' demand for land to "all classes of indigenous people." Banderas held out until 1833, when he was captured and shot, but not before he set aflame the river valleys and the mines, *ranchos* and *haciendas* on the outskirts of venerable Alamos.[35]

In 1828, new legislation called for the "union and equality" of whites (*blancos*) and Indians. To get Mexicans to settle in the valleys, the law exempted them from paying taxes for six years and put Mayo and Yaqui *pueblos* under the supervision of the Mexican *ayuntamiento* of Buenavista. Another state law of that year subdivided the communal lands of the Yaqui *pueblos* into tracts of private property, precisely what the Indian most feared. That the degree ordered the restitution of lands stolen from Indians mattered little, for it also encouraged the sale of the old mission lands to whites. The first law limited their independence, and the second broke up their communal lands, or, as they saw it, took the lands away. To the Yaquis, the two were connected: unless they kept their autonomy, they would lose their lands.[36]

From the 1830s to the 1870s, factional quarrels kept Sonora in turmoil, as Federalists turned Liberals battled Centralists become Conservatives. Both sought out the Yaqui for support in their interminable wars against each other. The Yaqui, for his part, cared not a whit for political doctrines; he only wanted to know who would respect his autonomy and lands. By their bellicosity, their ability to pick the winning side, and, of course, the unwillingness of Mexicans to settle their bickering, the Yaquis held onto most of their lands for the time being. They generally sided with Manuel María Gándara, the Conservative caudillo, even when he turned against Benito Juárez to back Maximilian's imperial dreams in the 1860s. They usually fought against the Federalists-turned-Liberals. These were the authors of grandiose schemes to populate the valleys with white Mexican farmers and to develop mining and commercial agriculture, both of which would depend on cheap Yaqui labor. Ignacio Pesqueira, the Liberal caudillo who eventually replaced Gándara, attempted, off and on for twenty years, to assimilate the Yaquis and develop agriculture in the Yaqui and Mayo valleys. One of his party suggested: "Why don't we make Mexicans out of Yaquis?" But the Yaquis resisted efforts to integrate them into Mexican society on the whites' terms. After all, as a famous Mexican general said, colonization, the term euphemistically employed, meant robbing the Yaqui of his lands.[37] The ambitions of Pesqueira and his allies provoked violent confrontations with the Yaquis and Mayos.

Pesqueira's fall from grace, and the resulting peace, opened an onslaught on Yaqui lands. Until then, as Corral noted, squabbles between Conservatives and Liberals, with both wooing the Yaqui warrior, had kept Mexicans out of the valleys.[38] Peace under the Triumvirate gave politicians, war heroes, planters, and mining entrepreneurs the chance to acquire land, their appetites whetted by the approaching railroad. With the invaders at their doorsteps, the Yaquis rebelled again, this time under the famous Cajeme. The cruel and bloody War of the Yaqui, as it came to be known, lasted from 1885 to 1886, and ended with a terrible defeat for Cajeme and, ultimately, his death.

A decade later, hostilities broke out again, concluding with the Peace of Ortiz (1897), the last of the major treaties with the Yaquis. Signed by Tetabiate, the principal Yaqui chieftain, the Peace attempted to "repatriate" the Yaquis. According to its author, Luis E. Torres, then the federal military commander, the Yaquis were to return to their homes in the valley, with the federal government giving each adult male a private plot of 4.5 hectares to farm. The Yaquis would help colonize their own valley. Tetabiate, to the anger of Hermosillo, adamantly insisted that no Mexican colonists or troops be permitted in the valley. While willing to accept Mexican control, the Yaquis wanted the land to themselves, to farm and rule as they saw fit. When Torres failed to abide by their wishes, the Yaquis of Bácum and Vícam rebelled after two "peaceful years as farmers." The Yaquis, clearly, did not want to cultivate private plots of land, live side by side with *yori* colonists, and abide by the law and order of troops stationed nearby.[39] Thus ended the attempt to colonize the Yaqui valley with Yaquis.

Repatriation, moreover, had not sat well with northern mine owners and *hacendados*, the employers of cheap labor. Their mutterings of discontent were soon heard in Hermosillo. To their way of thinking, the Peace of Ortiz promised nothing. To the contrary, repatriation had left employers without workers. More to the point, repatriation hurt severely *hacendados* and ranchers, Mexicans unable to compete with the higher wages paid by foreigners in the mines and railroad. Other workers, both Mexicans and foreigners, held better-paying jobs in mines, railroads, and commerce. To worsen the picture, by 1905 the burden of Hermosillo's folly fell most heavily on agricultural entrepreneurs, the Mexican element, while favoring foreigners, the owners of mines and the railroad.

The failure of repatriation convinced Mexicans in Hermosillo and Mexico City that only outsiders with resources of their own could colonize the valleys. The time was propitious, for soon the railroad would join the valleys to the rest of the Republic and to the United States. Economic opportunity beckoned, so the Yaqui guerrillas had to be dealt with. In truth, Yaqui resistance after Tetabiate hardly won the lands back for the Indian, but it did seriously hamper efforts to make the Yaqui valley bloom with settlers, while keeping much of the state in turmoil.

The Yaquis were the white man's chief adversary, but at least five other tribes also kept him at bay. The Mayos belonged to the same group as the Yaquis, sharing customs, beliefs, and, with minor variations, the Cahita language. In 1885, the Mayos, next-door neighbors of the Yaquis, occupied towns on the left bank of the Mayo river, including Navojoa and Etchojoa. Just a small colony of whites lived in Navojoa. Like the Yaquis, the Mayos defended their lands with arms but stopped fighting after 1886, the year of their last uprising.[40] Renegade bands of Mayos, however, kept stealing cattle and horses from the white settlers in the valley, and, occasionally, killed some of them.[41] As a group though, the Mayo had made his peace with the conqueror, and not infrequently turned to drink to find solace.

The Opatas, once hostile like the Yaquis and Mayos, ultimately proved receptive to the white man's advances.[42] "As lissome as a hazel wand," these Indians won the plaudits of the whites. To Corral, the Opata were the model for "good" Indians, those willing to assimilate. They were "docile," "hard-working," "brave," and "peaceful," and served as soldiers under Mexican *caudillos*. By 1903, the habits, clothing, and food of the 6,000 Opatas, most of whom farmed marginal lands, were identical to the whites.'[43] A similar fate befell the Pimas, who also bowed before the conqueror, so much so that by 1885 it was difficult to distinguish them from their Mexican neighbors. Where assimilation had not totally triumphed, pockets of Pimas still survived, particularly in Sahuaripa. Initially unfriendly like the Opatas, the Pimas had won the white man's confidence, becoming, said Corral, a "civilized" people. The last of the incorporated Indians were the Pápagos of the desert of Altar.[44] Once in a while the Pápagos defied the Mexican's rule, stealing his cattle and, in 1888, even attacking a detachment of troops, killing one soldier.[45] But by and large, the Pápagos had come to terms with the whites, even submitting to Hermosillo for approval their choice of *gobernadores*, their tribal chieftains.[46]

The Seris, on the other hand, refused to assimilate, leading Corral to label them "savages" and to attempt to confine them, North American fashion, on reservations. A tiny band who dwelt mostly on Tiburón

Island and at Tastiota, a settlement on the Gulf of Baja California, the
Seris had a habit of killing invaders of their lands. More than once, the
Mexicans organized military expeditions against them, one under
Izábal. After an uprising in 1880, the ruling clique put them on a reser-
vation just outside Hermosillo, but the Seris rebelled and fled, taking
up arms again in 1883 and 1884. By 1885, perhaps no more than 300
Seris survived, living a life of abject poverty.[47]

The "civilized" inhabitants of Sonora reserved their strongest invec-
tives for the Apaches, the pariahs among the "savages."[48] Fighting to
hold onto their homeland, the northern mountains, valleys, and flatlands, armed Apaches had more than once taught the whites to stay
away. For over a century, the blood of Apache and Mexican killed in
combat stained the northern lands. Every village in Sonora, recalled
one of its noted chroniclers, could recall the death of a neighbor at the
hands of this "barbarous tribe."[49] The Apache, a guerrilla fighter,
struck and ran, taking refuge across the border in the Chiricahua
mountains outside Douglas.[50] He was a shadowy enemy "who killed
without being seen . . . escaping whatever trap was laid for him, to surface again where least expected." To Corral, the Apache topped the list
of "traitorous enemies, crafty, indefatigable, bloodthirsty, bold but with
an audacity tempered by prudence."[51]

More to the point, the Apaches had blocked the full development of
mining in northern Sonora. So long as the Apaches could strike at will,
only the foolhardy ventured forth. Until the 1870s, the Apaches kept
miners and *rancheros* in mortal fear for their lives. Only in the southern
districts, relatively free of Apaches, did mining prosper. Elsewhere it
was a no man's land, where miners labored with a constant eye out for
the Apaches. One of the few battles where the Apaches stood their
ground to fight Mexicans on their own terms occurred just outside
Nacozari, the future site of the Phelps Dodge copper kingdom.

Like most conflicts, the confrontation between Apache and Mexican
had not suddenly burst forth. It dated from the days of the conquest.
Partly because the Apaches were such implacable and resourceful warriors, the Spanish advance "stalled and finally retreated." Yet at the beginning of contact with the whites, the Apache had not lived by the
sword, having, one scholar stressed, "peaceful avocations." But years
upon years of "abrasive contact with Spanish imperialism" changed the
Apache, compelling him "to specialize in the art of border warfare, first
in self-defense and later as an alternative means of making his livelihood."[52] Near the close of the seventeenth century, the confrontation
"erupted into a wave of rebellions" lasting until the eve of the twentieth.[53] Occasionally, Spanish bribes kept the peace. Between 1780 and
1820, the Spaniards spent $18,000 to $30,000 yearly on what they
labeled "supplies" for the Apaches. In return, the Apaches left Spanish

settlements alone. After independence, when the bankrupt Mexicans failed to pay up, the Apaches went on the warpath, nearly depopulating northern Sonora with their reign of terror. Fearful Mexicans abandoned their homes, leaving lands untilled and mines unworked. Settlements turned into ghost towns, with only adobe walls remaining to remind travelers of what had once stood there.[54]

The theft by the United States of Mexico's northern lands in 1848 and their settlement by Americans exacerbated the conflict. The growth of the Southwest took more land away from the Apaches, driving them southward. Matters took a turn for the worse when Americans, coveting more lands, put the Apaches on reservations. According to Mexicans, the Apaches used the reservations as a haven to take refuge from pursuit, only to arm themselves again with Remington rifles and Winchester carbines for more incursions into Sonora. Unscrupulous Americans in Arizona, New Mexico, and Texas, meanwhile, not only sold them the latest weapons but purchased ill-gotten goods stolen from Mexican settlers.[55]

In his essay on the Indians, Corral chronicled month by month, and almost by the day at times, what he called Apache depredations. Between November 1866 and February 1869, he wrote, the Apaches "killed seventy-eight men, eleven women and seventeen children and wounded thirty-seven persons, of whom ten had died." In 1870 alone, 123 Mexicans lost their lives at the hands of Apaches. The litany of Apache killings lasted into the 1880s.[56] So fierce were Apache raids in 1882 that federal troops had to be summoned to halt a veritable invasion of the borderlands.[57] Not until the death of Mangas Coloradas, a noted Apache chieftain, and the capture of Gerónimo in 1886 did the attacks decline. A treaty signed that year between Mexico City and Washington, permitting troops of both countries to cross the international line in pursuit of Apaches, helped restore peace.[58] The fighting left a legacy of communities armed to do battle and a virulent racial hatred for Apaches in particular and for Indians in general.

IV

To complicate matters, the Opatas, Pimas, Mayos, and, most of all, the Yaquis provided much of the labor for the mines and farms of Sonora. In the towns, they were the masons, carpenters, tanners, weavers, and cobblers. Of the Indians, no one worked harder or better than the Yaquis. They kept the economy alive. The Yaquis as well as the Mayos, conceded Corral, did the labor in the fields, walked behind the plow, and descended deep into the bowels of the earth to bring out the ores. They were the best sailors, the finest pearl divers, and the most reliable laborers in town. A Yaqui or a Mayo, declared Corral, could do twice

the work of the best laborer of the "white race," an opinion earlier
voiced by General Bernardo Reyes.[59] Colonel Francisco B. Cruz, a vet-
eran of the Indian wars, said the Yaquis were "the finest workers in Sonora." To cite a Yankee mine foreman, "one Yaqui laborer" was "worth
two ordinary Americans and three ordinary Mexicans."[60]

Despite eulogies to his prowess, the Yaqui ranked high as a hewer of
wood and a drawer of water mostly because he toiled for low wages. In
labor-scarce Sonora, the Yaqui was the major source of cheap labor.
Without him, the economy would have come to a standstill, shutting
down mines, hampering work on cattle ranches and *haciendas* and, in
towns and cities, curtailing work that called for strong backs. The Yaqui
was indispensable; he could not be replaced. That reality, complained
Governor Izábal, himself bent on ridding Sonora of the Yaquis, had
led planters and miners to employ them without bothering to ascertain
if they were *mansos* or *broncos*.[61]

Since the middle of the eighteenth century, Jesuits and settlers had
relied on the cheap labor of the Yaquis and Mayos. At first, their young
men ventured forth from their homes in the valleys to seek temporary
work in the mines of Alamos. With rare exceptions, they returned
home; work in the mines simply supplemented their income. By always
returning home, the Indians kept intact their ties with their communities and their lands.[62] By doing so, they stopped short of becoming simply wage workers, although by the time of Mexican independence they offered the most important source of "labor of hand kind,"
as the American consul referred to it. As of the 1870s, "the Yaquis and
other Indians," he reported, were selling their toil for six to eight pesos
a month plus a "small ration of beans and corn."[63] Yaquis could be
found in the mines of La Colorada and Minas Prietas and as far north
as Cananea, Nacozari, and Imuris, where, lamented the mayor, they
also signed complaints against management.[64] On the *haciendas*, the
Yaquis labored everywhere, in the valleys and in Hermosillo and Ures
districts, tilling the soil for the Morales clan as well as for Izábal's
Hacienda Europa.[65] Given the scarcity of cheap labor, some planters
had fallen back on the *tienda de raya* and debt peonage in order to keep
the Yaqui on their *haciendas*. Among this group were the Mascareñas
in Magdalena, Albino and Simón Almada, Arnold Esquer, and Jesús
Antonio Parada, all bearers of distinguished family pedigrees.[66]

V

To their eventual sorrow, the Yaquis and Mayos possessed the richest,
best-watered lands in the state. Their value increased when the railroad arrived in Guaymas port and later journeyed south into the valleys. Their lands, wrote Governor Carlos R. Ortiz, a rich merchant and

planter, were "the finest in the state, because of their fertility and water."[67] Crops of diverse types, Corral promised, could be grown on them. All that was required to make them bloom was to "pacify the tribes" and apply to the land "the industry and intelligence of civilized man." Were Mexico City to station troops in the Yaqui valley, Corral enthused, "decent and educated men would flock there in such numbers that in no time they could defend themselves against the Indians." Then the Yaqui and Mayo valleys, "today unproductive and a redoubt for rusticity and cruelty, would become the richest part of the state."[68] Beyond that, the new cabal in Hermosillo had another goal: by pushing Yaquis and Mayos off their lands, the government would increase the pool of cheap labor to build the railroad and to work in the revitalized mines and in the developing fields of agriculture and commerce.

Most of the "unexplored frontier that awaited civilized man"—as *La Constitución* called the Indian lands—had fallen to him by the 1880s. Only the Yaqui lands were still held by their ancient owners.[69] Their conquest, however, Washington's consul in Guaymas gleefully reported, was close at hand. Mexico City was about to "take possession of the lands . . . and open them up to settlers."[70] When the Yaquis adamantly refused to relinquish their lands, the consul assured Washington that the government in Mexico City proposed "to adopt more vigorous measures to capture the hostile bands who," he lamented, had "neutralized . . . colonization efforts."[71] With the defeat of the Yaquis, the *Examiner* of San Francisco gloated, "a cruel and devasting war" had ended but, more importantly, it had thrown "open to settlement a vast and fertile region." And, the journal emphasized, "to the prospector" it unlocked the door of "one of the most valuable mineral regions in the entire world."[72] By not cultivating their lands, Yaquis and Mayos had lost their right to them. Yet these critics spoke with "forked tongue," carefully forgetting that their wars had made it impossible for Yaquis and Mayos to till their lands.

Whites had already nibbled away at the Indians' lands, here and there establishing an *hacienda*, José María Almada and the Salidos among them. With the triumph of Pesqueira, more invaders appeared, first Ignacio del Campo and then Colonel Crispín S. Palomares, a faithful acolyte of the *caudillo*, who stayed to become the *cacique* of the valleys. Pesqueira, who wanted colonists, also resettled the valleys with Mexicans who had returned home from sojourns in the United States.[73]

With American capital flowing into mining just after the arrival of the Sonora Railway, the quest for lands in the Mayo and Yaqui was renewed. In 1882, Governor Ortiz, wanting to enlarge his holdings in Navojoa, appointed his brother military commander of the district: the brother made the double blunder of attacking Cajeme, the Indian chieftain, and of failing to defeat him. That disaster, combined with his challenge to the Torres clique, cost the governor his job.[74] Before he fell, Ortiz gave his blessing to a plan of Corral, then president of the state legislature, to get Mexico City to dispatch 1,000 soldiers to stop the Yaqui and Mayo "atrocities" and to open the valleys to settlement by whites.[75] Without the soldiers, the Sonorenses could not conquer the Yaquis. The Ministry of War in Mexico City at first rejected the plan but Corral and his sympathizers ultimately prevailed, though in a roundabout way. A plot hatched by Torres and Corral to pit Yaqui against Yaqui backfired, provoking instead a huge Indian uprising led by the legendary Cajeme. When state authorities could not quell the rebellion, Porfirio Díaz dispatched General José G. Carbó to "restore order."[76] It was just what the ruling clique in Hermosillo wanted, convinced as they were that only outside force could bring the Yaquis to their knees.[77] So began the inglorious War of the Yaqui and Mayo, pitting the nation's army against the Indian. Halfway through the campaign, Carbó died. His place was taken by General Angel Martínez who finished the job a year later, in 1886.

But Mexican occupation of the valleys, as General Bernardo Reyes, the federal commander in 1881, pointed out, would lead to tragedy if the "appetite of everyone who had put in a claim for ['idle land'] were satisfied." The claims far exceeded the amount of available land in the valleys. To grant them all, he explained, would leave "the luckless Indians without even the means to earn a living."[78] With these declarations, Reyes brought down upon himself the wrath of Corral, who, Reyes thought, was implicated in the land schemes. Reyes lost his political battle. He was transferred to San Luis Potosí as a punishment, according to his son, for his unwillingness to fight Yaquis and Mayos.[79] With the defeat of the Yaquis, the influx of "settlers" began, reported the American consul, "with . . . cattle to establish themselves there, and cultivate the land."[80]

The assault on the Yaquis, according to witnesses, involved more than a simple plot to steal lands. The temptations for profit from graft and "commissions" on the sale of food and supplies for the federal soldiers in the Yaqui, were too powerful for merchants and politicians to resist. That was the opinion of John Kenneth Turner, whose *Barbarous Mexico* stirred the souls of Americans.[81] Albert K. Morowetz, the American consul, partly concurred. Writing in 1905, when sporadic guerrilla fighting by Yaquis still plagued Sonora, Morowetz said the wars had dragged on by design, to enrich officials in pursuit of personal gain. The government of Sonora, he believed, had "made millions of dollars out of the money . . . sent for the purchase of rations, horsefeed and other supplies." He wanted an end to the killing because it endangered American lives and property.[82] Esteban Baca Calderón voiced similar views, but not out of regard for Americans; he believed it immoral to profit from killing Yaquis.[83] In Ures, *La Bandera Sonorense*, a newspaper unhappy with Hermosillo, put the blame for the war on the "greed of a rich and powerful cabal."[84] On the other hand, the newspaper's backers, the *hacendados* of Ures, had lost workers because of the persecution of the Yaquis.

Whatever the truth, Mexicans did profit. A few of them, "heroes" of the wars, retired to *haciendas* in the valleys, including Luis E. Torres, José Tiburcio Otero, and Lorenzo Torres. Colonel Lorenzo Torres, a former governor who apparently enjoyed fighting Yaquis more than running affairs in Hermosillo, carved out for himself a tiny empire. He survived the wars with 15,000 hectares, part of which he sold to an American real estate dealer in Guaymas, who subdivided the land and sold it to farmers from California. With his Hacienda Guamúchil, Torres took over lands set aside for the Yaqui village of Ráum, while lands earmarked for Cócorit, Bácum, and San José went to other *yoris*.[85] Crispin S. Palomares, who also acquired real estate, had fought the Yaquis fervently, as had the Salidos and Almadas.[86]

Also profiting were merchants. Colonel Francisco Peinado, sent by Mexico City to restore peace in the Yaqui (a region never really tranquil in the days of the Triumvirate), thought the "businessmen of the state" chiefly responsible for the wars, an opinion shared by General Angel Garciá Peña. Even Corral, no enemy of merchants, believed "agents" in Guaymas sold arms to the Yaquis.[87] Manuel Balbás, author of the classic *Recuerdos del Yaqui*, put the matter more bluntly. A doctor with federal troops in the Yaqui campaigns, Balbás described how the army spent its budget in Guaymas. War was a godsend for the town's merchants. To keep their profits up, the Guaymas merchants fanned the martial spirit, selling arms and munitions to the Yaquis. When soldiers searched the body of a Yaqui killed in the battle of Buatachive, they found letters from merchants in the port offering to sell him war supplies.[88] Merchants big and small bloodied their hands in this nefarious business. The arrival of federal troops bound for the front in the Yaqui, recalled a son of the old merchant families, brought "tears of joy to Guaymas."[89]

VI

The Yaqui question gradually brought into public debate the American role in Sonora. Thoughtful Mexicans, more and more, began to take into account the disparity between the way the ruling cabal in Hermosillo handled foreigners and the way it dealt with the Yaquis who, whatever might be said of them, had native roots. Mexicans, lamented the *Diario del Hogar,* a Mexico City daily, openly embraced the foreigner, conferring on him their best lands and every courtesy. At the same time, the unlucky Indian was "cruelly [being] deprived of his lands."[90] To the consternation of Izábal and his circle, even journals north of the border expressed shock. Yaquis, the *San Francisco Examiner* pointed out, resented "the influx of American . . . mining prospectors, who have been coming into Sonora in greater numbers each year" and getting a hearty welcome from its government.[91] While the Richardson Company had thousands of hectares handed to it on a silver platter, complained Alfred Breceda, Mexican farmers had to cut through mountains of red tape and pay 7.50 pesos a hectare for rocky soil unfit for agriculture.[92] Or to cite Balbás, the laws of idle lands blessed foreigners.[93]

Unexpectedly, the never-ending Yaqui fighting embroiled its architects in conflicts with Americans, whom they had welcomed with open arms. To begin with, the Richardson brothers wanted peace and order in the Yaqui valley and loudly made their unhappiness known when they failed to get it. American miners, menaced by armed bands of roving Yaquis, sent letter after letter of complaint to Hermosillo and, when that failed to bring results, to their own diplomats. When Yaquis killed two Americans of the Mina Grande Mining and Milling Company in Minas Prietas, its chairman took his bitterness to Washington. The Yaquis had virtually shut down operations at a mine that, he stressed, had been purchased from the prefect of the district.[94] The Yaqui Smelting and Refining Company pleaded with the U.S. ambassador in Mexico City to get Mexicans to protect Americans in Sonora.[95] Atrocity stories that put the Mexican government in a bad light began to appear in newspapers in the United States.[96] To the Mexican consul in San Francisco, these articles had but one purpose: to picture the war as inhumane and to tarnish the prestige of Mexico's rulers.[97]

VII

The Yaqui wars, the curse of the Porfiriato, left a terrible legacy behind. Along with the rebellions of the Maya Indians of Yucatán, these cruel and unjust wars sapped the ruling circles of their moral authority. The wars paralyzed the economy of the Yaqui valley and left state revenues in a shambles. Beginning in 1885 and lasting virtually until the fall of the Porfiriato, the wars cost the Mexican government over 50 million pesos.[98] Just the uprising of Cajeme in 1885–1886 cost Sonora 150,000 pesos, which, along with money it spent on battling the Apaches, left its treasury bare.[99] By 1904, Sonora faced a major economic crisis because of the deficit. It was only partly overcome as late as 1908.[100]

The bloody wars are recorded in many ambivalent chronicles. Valiant Yaquis, so goes the folk story, fought bravely, defending themselves in a cruel and harsh war. On the clash of Yaquis and whites, the literature is vast, though often repetitive and shallow. When federal troops, using Mauser rifles for the first time, put down the explosive uprising of Cajeme, the tide turned. The Yaqui warrior, not infrequently armed with bows and arrows, proved no match for the repeating rifle. From that time on, the Yaquis were "merely hunted."[101] Brave and resilient, the Yaqui fought on but only to die, as Francisco P. Troncoso vividly documents in *Las guerras con los tribus Yaqui y Mayo*. A soldier's story, his account along with that of Fortunato Hernández, an army doctor, left no doubt about the fate of the vanquished Indians. With their defeat, as Hernández vividly depicts the scene, the banks of the Yaqui river stood "deserted, bereft of Indians, unless captured or humbled." The Yaquis who escaped entrapment or death, fled into the sierra, "where hunger and the rigors of the winter's cold awaited them."[102]

With the defeat of Cajeme in 1886, the Mayos put down their guns never to fight again. The Yaquis, however, proved more recalcitrant, rising up in arms once more under Tetabiate, the last of the Yaqui cheiftains. After his death, they fought on as guerrillas. Their hit-and-run tactics, like those of the Apaches before them, hampered mining and agriculture until virtually the end of don Porfirio's rule. To put down the raids proved nearly impossible because the *broncos*, the warriors, blended in with the *mansos*, the peaceful Yaquis. Though they did not bear arms, the *mansos* supplied their brothers with food, clothing, and guns.[103] From the Sierra del Bacatete, where many armed Yaquis hid, the *broncos* periodically came down to attack hamlets.[104] So fearful had Mexicans become that in 1905 the inhabitants of Soyopa preferred to stay home and starve rather than venture forth in search of food and risk an encounter with the Yaquis.[105]

Before the curtain fell on this drama, the *yori* inflicted one last penalty. With the rebellion of Tetabiate—labeled a betrayal of the Peace of Ortiz by the *yori*—and the refusal of Yaqui guerrillas to lay down their arms, don Porfirio and his allies in Hermosillo decided to rid themselves of their nemesis once and for all.[106] Every Yaqui, whether *bronco* or *manso*, would be deported. A leading Mexican historian suggests that it was Joaquín Redo, a wealthy planter in Sinaloa, who fathered the plan, which Mexico City and Hermosillo implemented with alacrity.[107]

Deportation, whatever Redo's role, was not a new idea. Earlier, Pesqueira, an exponent of economic growth, had tried to deport rebel Yaquis to labor on mines, ranches, and *haciendas* lying outside their home territory. General Martínez, angered by his failure to capture elusive rebel leaders, escalated Pesqueira's plan, and urged Díaz to deport all Yaqui rebels out of state. Díaz, who knew his Indians better than Martínez, refused, convinced that the Yaqui would fight until death to avoid this fate. During the campaigns against Tetabiate (1895–1897), the federal army, with the approval of Mexico City, had shipped captured rebels to southern Mexico, later drafting them into the army. Women and children had also been deported, how many no one knows. State authorities required *mansos* to carry identification papers (passports). Their employers had to keep records of Yaqui workers and to turn in suspected rebels. General Torres had begun to deport captured rebels. While undoubtedly exaggerated, Torres' claims that he deported thousands were partly for foreign consumption, meant to allay American investors' fears about the unrest in Sonora.[108]

After 1900, state authorities charged with the task of mopping up the remaining Yaqui guerrillas expanded earlier surveillance programs. As Torres had before him, Governor Izábal recognized that the key to pacification lay with the *mansos*. He put restrictions on where they could live. No Yaqui was permitted to live outside of the districts of Hermosillo, Ures, and Guaymas, and those in the towns had to stay in designated *barrios*. Any Yaqui found in the wrong place or without proper credentials was arrested. By these methods, Izábal thought, he would isolate the *mansos* from their *bronco* brothers.

All the same, marauding Yaquis stepped up their raids, particularly in the districts of Hermosillo, Ures, and Guaymas. Though they probably numbered no more than 500 by 1905, the guerrillas plundered *haciendas*, villages, and the *tiendas de raya* of mining camps and railroads. To the chagrin of Hermosillo, Yaquis freely exchanged the required credentials; Mexican soldiers found the credentials in the clothing of dead Indians. *Hacendados* and other employers of cheap labor who needed the Yaquis did not cooperate with the government, preferring to ignore Yaqui violations of regulations.

But the battle was almost over. Izábal's plan of separating *bronco* from *manso* paid off, forcing rebel Yaquis to find arms, ammunition, and food on their own. After 1904, Mexico City and Hermosillo redoubled efforts to put down Yaqui depredations. Authorities in the capital dispatched *rurales* and a battalion of infantrymen, led by Luis Medina Barrón, to help with the task. By 1907, supposedly conciliatory attitudes toward the Yaqui had turned hard and uncompromising. More and more, officials labeled Yaquis "savages," as they had called Apaches earlier. By this time, few Yaquis labored in the mines and railroads run by foreigners. Earlier, American employers had argued that government policies left them without workers. Now, to the delight of Hermosillo, they uttered not a whisper of protest at the loss of their Yaquis.[109]

Why this turnabout? The key most likely lay in the economic climate of the time. The depression of 1907 had brought the sector most closely linked to Yankee markets and capital to its knees. As mines shut down, the ranks of the unemployed grew dramatically. By 1908, northern Sonora, the region most identified with the United States, had a glut of labor. No longer was the Yaqui worker indispensable; the foreign entrepreneur could do without him. Only agriculture, largely a Mexican enterprise, needed him.

It was against this backdrop that the final drama, the deportation of all Yaquis from Sonora, unfolded. By 1907, total deportation had the sanction of both Hermosillo and Mexico City. All Yaquis, *bronco* and *manso*, men, women, and children, were taken from their homeland, shipped to Yucatán or the Valle Nacional in Oaxaca, and sold to planters. Torres, Izábal, and Corral all soiled their hands in this infamous business, actively encouraged by Olegario Molina, Díaz's minister of Fomento and a big henequen planter in Yucatán. (Molina had earlier given a huge grant of land in the Yaqui valley to the Richardson Construction Company.) Deportation reached its peak in 1908. How many Yaquis were deported is anyone's guess. By some estimates, perhaps as many as 15,000 were deported between 1902 and 1908; more likely, only half that many felt the cruelty of exile.[110] The economic downturn of the day, however, eventually spread to Yucatán, helping to put an end to the sale of Yaquis from Sonora to henequen planters. Unfortunately, the depression came too late to save the Yaquis; by 1908, the backbone of their resistance had finally been shattered. Prominent Mexican *hacendados*, who felt dearly the loss of cheap Yaqui labor, were eventually to turn on the Old Regime. Among them were the Maytorenas of Guaymas and the Morales of Ures.

The grotesque episode raised a hue and cry everywhere. The more Yaquis Izábal deported, the louder the outcry; but, John Kenneth Turner knew, the protests were "to no avail." Izábal assured his legislature that he had the backing of bankers, planters, cattlemen, and merchants. On occasion, soldiers took Yaquis right before the eyes of the planters, who "begged" their captors to release them. Some of the planters, notably Eugenio Morales and Manuel Gándara of Ures, even followed their Yaqui workers to Hermosillo, hoping to get them released.[111] "Barbarous, cruel and inhumane," Mexican writer Fernando A. Galáz called deportation. He remembered watching armed "Yaqui soldiers" ironically "guarding men, women, and children of their own race on the road to the penitentiary."[112] Amado Nervo, the poet laureate of Porfirista Mexico, wrote an ode to a Yaqui woman who, compelled to live in Yucatán, starved herself to death rather than live away from her lover. Meantime in Hermosillo, the culprits shed crocodile tears. The families of Izábal, Alberto Cubillas, Francisco Chiapa, and Jacinto Padilla went so far as to take "abandoned" Yaqui children into their homes.[113]

Yankee speculation, the railroad particularly, and the lure of markets across the border affected the Yaqui wars, but did not cause them. Sooner or later the *yori's* hunger for fertile, well-watered lands would have led him to take them by force. The arrival of the Yankee, both as speculator and customer, merely advanced the timetable. With the entrance of the Southern Pacific Railway into the valleys, the opportunity for profit was at hand. The rush to capitalize on it revived an ancient struggle and brought a latent racism to the surface.

The bloody wars, by one of those odd quirks of history, left behind a saving grace. The sons of the culprits, perhaps seeking atonement for their fathers' deeds, helped forge the legend of Cajeme, the valiant Yaqui leader. Brave and incorruptible, so goes the tale, Cajeme fought in a romantic, even noble cause but could not stem the march of civilization, the transformation of the valleys into redoubts of big agriculture. The Yaquis lost the war, but in defeat they gained a hero, a man of whom all Sonorenses could be proud.

Born in Hermosillo in 1837 and baptized José María Leyva, Cajeme as a boy of twelve years hunted for gold with his father in California. Not finding it, they returned home. Unlike most Yaquis, Cajeme's parents had lived among the *yoris*. The mother, whom Corral once met, although "rustic," was a woman of intelligence and energy.[114] Cajeme went to school in Guaymas, where he learned reading, writing, and the rudiments of arithmetic. When he grew up, he soldiered in the federal army until 1875. Cajeme fought in the defense of Guaymas in 1854, when the French adventurer Gaston Raoussett de Boulbon attacked the port. He fought with the troops that captured Maximilian, the puppet emperor, and rose through the ranks to captain. Angered by the wanton attacks on his people, Cajeme in 1875 forsook the army to help the Yaquis resist Governor Pesqueira's plans. At the pinnacle of his power, Cajeme could rightfully claim to have organized a "separate republic," independent of authorities in Hermosillo. He fought hard, long, and heroically, but, inevitably, he met defeat and death— shot "for attempting to escape." The Yaquis recovered his body and laid it to rest with honors.[115] Today, in the pantheon of local heroes, Cajeme sits with the mighty whites of yesteryear, the harbingers of "civilization."

CHAPTER 12

Face to Face

I

The ills of dependency are legion. But to be both poor and dependent and to share a common border with one's rich and powerful master is perhaps the quintessence of the malady. Mexicans living on the perimeter of Arizona day by day watched the American territory grow wealthier, more populated, and more powerful than Sonora. To make matters worse, this was the Imperial Age, when chauvinists in Washington, London, and Paris judged sacrosanct the "rights" of their countrymen in foreign lands. At the border, Mexicans met the Yankee face to face.

II

An artificial boundary of about 400 miles stood between Sonora and its neighbor to the north. From 1885 to 1910, the border was poorly marked at best. On the route from Agua Prieta to San Luis, the sister hamlet to Yuma, only stone pillars put up here and there pointed out the boundary line to travelers. Until the late nineteenth century, "no towns of any importance" lay "near the boundary on either side."[1] The borderlands were sparsely settled. On the United States side, just 10,000 people dwelt in Tucson, Prescott, and Yuma. In this region, home to a population widely scattered, agriculture had scarcely begun while hostile Indians and pistol-toting thugs often defied the law.[2]

Copper mining and the railroad changed that, ushering in a new era for Arizona just as they did for Mexico's northwestern rim. The transformation of the Territory of Arizona also reshaped Sonora.

The Sonora of that time had just started to change. Like their Yankee neighbors, its inhabitants were dispersed, their communities isolated. Mexicans still rode on horseback from town to town or, on occasion, in a carriage pulled by horses. The mayors of the northern towns, when need be, could follow a trail days old with the deft touch of a bloodhound. "After I found the spot where the murder of the Americans took place," reported the mayor of Santa Ana, a village south of Magdalena, "I came across the tracks of two men on horseback, one riding a horse with its four hooves shod . . . the two killers had ambushed their victim from different sides."[3] In 1888, Ramón Corral, then governor, told his legislature of a train robbery, the holdup of a stagecoach, and an attack on two French engineers foolish enough to undertake a journey by carriage in the desolate frontier. To Corral, the *frontera*, the borderlands, was a "vast desert where bandits went openly about their business due to the absence of any kind of police force." He wanted funds set aside for rural police to catch the criminals and to halt the "demoralization taking root among the inhabitants of our borderlands" which, he explained, was just beginning to attract new people. The region, he went on, was no longer "a desert where savages alone ventured forth."[4]

Living next door to a powerful neighbor had never been easy. The Gadsden Purchase of 1853 cost the state the northern half of its territory. The filibustering expeditions of Gastón Raoussett de Boulbon and Henry Crabb, both from across the border, left bitter memories. When Americans began to settle in Arizona and to look for adventure and fortunes to the south, they stirred old fears among Mexicans. As Corral, then a fledgling congressman, told his colleagues in 1881, Mexico had to increase its population along the border and give the inhabitants the means to a better life, to protect the nation from the United States. Without economic prosperity, he warned, Mexico could not deal with the rush of Americans who were making their presence felt.[5]

Nationalism, the sentiment behind Corral's plea, flowered partly as a response to the growth of Arizona and the infiltration of the borderlands by Yankee adventurers. By 1889, scores of Americans had settled in Sonora as merchants, cattle ranchers, or miners, often acquiring property by hook or by crook. The *zona libre*, the free zone, was designed to ward off competition of business houses *del otro lado*. Corral believed the zone would help Mexican businesses grow, and in turn, help the cattle and mining industries thrive. The prosperity of the merchants would provide jobs and bring Mexican settlers north. Without the *zona libre*, Corral predicted, more Americans would come south, buy up mines and lands, and, in time, take control.[6]

While relying on the *zona libre*, itself of doubtful patriotic value, to defend national integrity, the cabal in Hermosillo, like the one in Mexico City, favored foreign colonization. To the leaders' way of thinking, Americans and Europeans brought technical know-how and capital, and, though this was more quietly acknowledged, they were thought to strengthen the racial stock. To settle within sixty miles of the border, however, foreigners needed special permission from Mexico City, and, to get it, Mexicans had to vouch for their integrity and financial standing. So foreigners came south, Americans largely, aided and abetted in their hunt for lands and mines by letters of recommendation from Corral, Torres and their cohorts, nationalistic utterances notwithstanding. When William Barnett, Corral's benefactor, in company with other Amricans asked Mexico City for the right to buy property in Arizpe and Magdalena districts, Corral wrote a glowing letter describing them as "honorable and trustworthy."[7] Until 1906, foreigners' requests for exemptions multiplied rapidly, and helped fill copious files in Mexican archives.

III

Xenophobia blossomed with the influx of Americans. Always just below the surface in the borderlands, it had flourished before. It dated back to Spanish fears of the English, the War of 1846, the Gadsden Purchase, and two filibustering expeditions. Add to that mix proximity, unequal development, and racial animosity, and the reasons for Mexican distrust and hositility become clear. At the border, two races and two ways of life met head on. As early as 1872, with just a handful of his compatriots living in Sonora, the United States consul in Guaymas, blind to the lessons of history, could not fathom the "strange antipathy to Americans" among Mexicans. "The good which we have done them is forgotten," he lamented, "whilst the smallest injury is carefully notched upon the tally."[8]

As more Americans made their appearance, the Mexican's antipathy multiplied. Two decades after the complaint by his predecessor, the consul in Guaymas explained the hostility as a class issue, with some logic. Because Americans were "more numerous than other nationalities," he reasoned, the "lower class of Mexicans look[ed] upon them with greater jealousy," becoming "annoyed very often on slight or no pretext."[9] His successor, on the other hand, more disturbed by what he saw, judged the antipathy not just as a matter of class but a national characteristic. "Among the many sections of the globe which our nation has provided with consular representation," he bemoaned, "there are none, I believe, where American citizens more frequently need the special intervention and protection of our government than in this portion of Mexican territory."[10] One citizen of Indiana, a friend of an American on trial for a mining violation, even alleged that Mexican law dealt more fairly with other foreigners than it did Americans.[11]

Antipathy to Americans had many causes. As the American consul believed, it had a class slant, for those who were denied a share of what Hermosillo called progress. Not unnaturally, those denied access to the "benefits" brought by Yankees who settled Mexican lands, exploited Mexican mines, and received a royal welcome from Mexcian authorities displayed little enthusiasm for Yankees. Governor Rafael Izábal, a fervent Yankeephile, admitted that the hostility surfaced quickly among the strikers at Cananea; indeed, it underlay the labor conflict.[12]

Conversely, those who benefited had less reason to fear the intruder. Nonetheless, some of the rich also revealed signs of the malignancy. Southern planters and northern *hacendados*, as Héctor Aguilar Camín points out, resented the warm embrace given their American rivals. Even officeholders were not immune to the disease of anti-Americanism. The Mexican mayor of Nogales wrote that Morgan R. Wise, the American consular agent, "by character is . . . peevish and a liar, and of poor repute among those who know him well," while "the educated thought his surname a joke."[13] The constable in La Casita went so far as to jail the American consul from Guaymas. John S. Gibson, the diplomat in question, had gone to La Casita, where he had money invested in a mine and a younger brother running the company store. The constable, Tomás Rico, went to the company store to buy a pair of shoes only to learn that his size was unavailable and that the storekeeper, Gibson's brother, knew little Spanish. Rico lost his temper and insulted both Gibsons. John Gibson joined in the shouting match and hit Rico, according to reports. The brawl ended with Rico briefly putting Gibson in jail along with the American owner of the mine. He accused them of resisting the law. Rico placed the blame on Gibson's arrogance and Gibson on Rico's. Whatever the truth, the clash had racial overtones. For their part, Corral and Izábal, the authorities in Hermosillo, fired Rico and asked the prefect of his district to replace him with someone "who will safeguard that important mining enterprise which is doing so much to improve the local economy." The brawl at La Casita did not end until it had become an international incident, with Washington protesting the jailing of Gibson.[14]

The hostility was not merely symbolic or psychological; it frequently had specific causes. More often than not, the ill will stemmed from a clash of interests, what Mexicans labeled "unfair competition." One such case, brought to the attention of Mexico City by Corral, involved American traveling salesmen. According to Corral, ever since Sinaloa and Chihuahua had levied a tax on their goods, large numbers of the salesmen could be found in every town in Sonora. Since they didn't have to pay duties there, the Americans enjoyed an advantage over Sonorans burdened with a state tax. The wholesale merchants of Guaymas and Hermosillo, who supplied the goods sold in the towns, not only paid the state tax but a federal one as well. Clearly the instigators of Corral's letter, the merchants wanted a tax levied on the American salesmen lest they monopolize local commerce. Yankee knights of the road, in brief, endangered the monopoly of Mexican merchants in Hermosillo and Guaymas.[15] The conflict pitted Mexican and American merchants against each other; ironically, both were selling goods of identical manufacture on the same market.

In contrast, the death of Consul Alexander Willard in 1891, less than a decade before the controversy over the salesmen, prompted days of mourning in Guaymas. Willard had spent many years in Sonora, and had scores of admirers among the merchants and shippers of the port city. Willard had not spent his time simply attending to diplomatic niceties. He had his hand in mining, land, and commerce but, the evidence indicates, always in partnership with Mexicans. Upon his death, "business houses in the city closed" while "flags on municipal, state and federal offices" flew at half-mast. When a special train carried Willard's body north, "40 or 50 of the most distinguished citizens, including the Governor . . . and other high officials of the state" were aboard.[16] Unlike the salesmen, Willard had not competed with Mexicans. To the contrary, he had used the influence of his office to help Mexicans make money. In the eyes of Mexican merchants, Williard had been a "good" American.

The need to populate the border with "patriotic" Mexicans, meanwhile, acquired urgency as Arizona continued to grow. In the north, the sixteenth of September, Mexico's Independence Day, was not just another holiday. To the mayor of Altar, the celebration was significant because the town sat on the battle line, as he put it. Like other *pueblos fronterizos* ("border towns"), Altar stood on the ramparts "that separates us from the United States." It was up to its inhabitants to hold aloft "our flag before that" of the neighboring Republic.[17]

International incidents could occur at any time. For example, when police in Nogales, the American town "on the other side," tried to capture a fleeing Mexican army officer who had gotten into trouble, Mexican soldiers fired on them. The shots fired into Arizona alarmed

Americans, and brought out into the open the underlying jingoism on both sides. Luis E. Torres, then governor, rushed to the border town to calm tempers.[18] A military court in Guaymas found the Mexican officers guilty of the "outrage committed on United States soil," to cite Willard, and sentenced them to death.[19] To the delight of Mexicans, authorities in Mexico City reduced the sentence to a jail term. When a United States sheriff crossed over to "the other side" to arrest Jesús García for disturbing the peace in the American Nogales, the "bad blood" on both sides boiled over. Mexican sovereignty, Mexicans pontificated, had been violated.[20] When a Mexican policeman handed over a wanted Mexican to American sheriffs, a furor went up from Nogales to Hermosillo.[21]

Confrontations of this type took place again and again. On Independence Day 1908, at the mining camp of Cerro Prieto in Magdalena, an American with too much to drink insulted the Mexican flag. According to Mexican witnesses, the American took a flag on display and galloped off on his horse with it, "mocking and ridiculing it." The locals were outraged.[22] At Agua Prieta, the constable alleged that while Mexico permitted Americans sick with tuberculosis and other contagious diseases to cross the border for visits, American health inspectors barred Mexicans with similar ills from visiting Douglas. That double standard, he insisted, injured public health in Agua Prieta.[23]

While Americans had forgotten the War of 1846, Mexicans had not. To Americans the Treaty of Guadalupe Hidalgo, which gave them half of Mexico, was simply history. For Mexicans, the memory of the defeat lingered. From time to time, as in 1887 in Altar, Mexican fears of another invasion surfaced. There were rumors that a gang of bandits from Arizona stood poised to invade Mexico by way of Altar and Nogales. Though without foundation, the news led Hermosillo to station a detachment of troops along the border. So ill-equipped were the Mexican soldiers, however, that Hermosillo even had to borrow a saddle for the officer in charge from the inhabitants of Saric, a tiny border town. The "invasion," (actually a fear that Mexican *politicos* might attempt to topple the cabal in power,) never materialized, fortunately for the Mexicans. As the prefect of Altar told Hermosillo, it would have been "difficult to ready 10 men willing to fight."[24] So much for the vaunted patriotism of border Mexicans.

IV

American merchants, usually men of standing in the Mexican border communities, occasionally made life hectic for public officials. One such individual was J. B. Storman, a resident of Magdalena town since

1880 and owner of commercial houses there and in Santa Ana. His Magdalena store, the largest and best stocked in town, sold both foreign and domestic articles. His American goods included Deer Company plows from Chicago, wagons made by Fish Brothers, explosives from the Giant Powder Company, and oil and kerosene from the Waters Pierce Oil Company. Among the Mexican manufactures were candles and soap from the factory of Terrazas and Britingham in Chihuahua. Storman also handled hardware, lumber, paint, shoes, perfumes, linen, and ironware. Store advertisements appeared in newspapers as far away as Altar town.[25]

Headstrong, tactless, and accustomed to getting his way, Storman had a penchant for getting into trouble. At times, he displayed scant respect for Mexican law. What most annoyed him was having to pay municipal taxes. That led to his troubles with the mayor of Santa Ana in 1890. To stop tax evasion, the mayor had decreed that recipients of goods arriving by railroad had to notify municipal authorities before transporting them to their places of business.[26] When "Julio" Cashier, the American in charge of Storman's flour mill, failed to do so, the mayor levied a fine on him. When Cashier refused to pay it, the mayor put him in jail. Storman complained to Hermosillo that the mayor had acted arbitrarily.[27]

Storman, however, omitted to mention Cashier's behavior. The mayor indignantly explained that Storman's employee consistently flaunted his American citizenship, claiming that he "did not have to obey either laws or authorities because of his foreign status." He had also let it be known that he had friends in high places, among them the prefect of the district.[28] Officials in Hermosillo, perhaps offended by the disrespect Cashier and Storman displayed for Mexico, upheld the mayor.[29] That episode, nevertheless, failed to dampen Storman's enthusiasm for circumventing Mexican law. A decade after the tax business, Storman, in partnership with "Enrique" Barnes, was working a mine in Estación Llano, a train stop south of Santa Ana. The only problem was he had no title to the mine. He was found out by another prefect, who, perhaps no longer a friend, put a stop to it.[30]

Storman's major escapade, surely the scandal of the decade in Nogales, led to a public confrontation between its mayor, Ignacio Bonillas, and the prefect of the district, Vicente A. Almada, and eventually to intervention by Hermosillo. Bonillas, whose career culminated in 1920 with his candidacy for the presidency of Mexico, felt at home on both sides of the border. Born in San Ignacio, a spot on the map not far from Magdalena, he moved to Tucson with his parents, and went to school there. To his good fortune, he met the governor of the Territory of Arizona while shining shoes on the streets of Tucson. The governor took a liking to the boy and got him a scholarship to the Boston

Institute of Technology. Graduating as a mining engineer, Bonillas returned to Sonora where, for years the only Mexican in his field, he
climbed the ladder of success.[31] Along the way, he helped draw up
plans for the Mexican towns of Nogales, Santa Ana, and Minas Prietas,
established ties with wealthy Americans, and grew rich himself.[32]

For a time, Bonillas was a federal mining agent. He was also once
mayor of Magdalena, a judge of the first instance, and prefect of the
district of Magdalena, a post he resigned in 1892. His political star,
linked to that of Manuel Mascareñas, had begun to fade by 1900. Like
Storman, Bonillas had a way of getting trapped in bewildering predica-
ments, including libel trials, as in Guaymas when *El Imparcial* printed
a story about him that he found slanderous.[33]

The scandal that squared off Bonillas and Storman took place in
1889. Storman, so the story goes, had a house, a wife, and a mistress
in Nogales. The mistress, a woman by the name of Francisca Jacome
de Camou, the last a surname of note, and the wife knew of each other
only by hearsay. On a certain day in March, Francisca, better known as
"La Jácome," met Storman's wife on the street by chance. Venting her
jealousy, the mistress insulted the wife and, in the words of Bonillas,
set off a "public uproar." Something of a prude, Bonillas had La
Jácome jailed and held *incomunicada*, a harsh penalty given the nature
of the offense, in the opinion of Almada, prefect of the district.
Whether because he was more tolerant, or, more likely, because he disliked Bonillas or had business links with Storman, Almada permitted
Storman to visit his mistress in her jail cell. Bonillas unexpectedly paid
the jail a visit, and discovered Storman in bed with La Jácome. At this
juncture, the scandal broke.

Bonillas accused Almada of infringing on his role as mayor and,
worse still, of moral turpitude. Almada replied that Bonillas had
abused his authority, and that he had had no right to lock up La Jácome in solitary confinement. When the mutual recriminations
reached Corral's desk, he was annoyed and refused to take sides, telling
both to behave. Calling the affair "scandalous and morally repugnant,"
Corral wanted all parties punished, lest respect for law and morality
be undermined. Despite Corral's order, Storman, the culprit, went un-
punished.[34] In the border towns, important people, whether Mexicans
or foreigners, seldom felt the wrath of the law, no matter what their
behavior.

As Storman's dalliance with La Jácome reveals, Americans were not
always pillars of respectability. Lured by the promise of adventure and
easy wealth, Yankees of diverse stripes went south. The lucky struck it
rich, but others were not so lucky. Scores died owning only the clothes
on their back. That was the fate of "Jorge F. Lake, age twenty-six and

a native of Texas, the victim of cirrhosis of the liver." The Mexicans buried him in his faded cowboy hat and the clothes he wore, his sole possessions.[35] Another *gringo*, a chronicler of Guaymas recalled, had come to work on the railroad but took to drink, selling chairs and tables he made to pay for his habit. For clothes, he wore "overalls, with one suspender unbuttoned and nothing else."[36]

V

Violence in the borderlands was often the work of Americans. Time and again Mexican officials were called upon to deal with crimes by Americans, including murder. That Americans in Sonora killed one another and swindled each other archival records amply document. In Nogales, Edward Clinton languished in jail for shooting a Mexican, along with Clarence Henderson, jailed for smuggling.[37] Over in Nacozari, Bill Brock shot and killed the constable and then fled across the border.[38] William Jacoby, known as Frank Briggs in Cananea, was wanted for murder in Illinois.[39] One day in 1907, again in Cananea, three Americans drinking in a bar quarreled and split up, with two going off together. The next day, still in their cups, the three met in a rooming house and renewed their dispute. One killed the other two with a pistol.[40] "I want to report the death of Anton Swenson, an American citizen," began a letter from the United States consul in Nogales. He had died at the hands of "Newton Brown, his partner" in a mining venture. A short time earlier, Brown "had sold their joint property and then spent the proceeds . . . without Swenson's knowledge."[41] At Cumpas, near the Buckeye mines, one American killed another, while at El Tigre, "L. F. Tuly" would have killed his American boss if the Mexican constable had not stood in the way.[42] A short time later, again at El Tigre, one American and two Mexicans shot and wounded three Mexicans, one of them the constable.[43]

From the start, bandits, smugglers, and ne'er-do-wells infested the borderlands. Smugglers, a breed endemic to international boundaries, had a heyday. As early as 1885, the value of the illegal traffic in goods going south, according to one estimate, stood at $100,000.[44] To check the flow of contraband, Mexico City built customs offices along the boundary line, but they hardly stopped it. The smugglers even took to killing customs agents, four of them at one time in Cumpas.[45] Others smuggled in goods by stage, hiding them in their luggage, or by train through Nogales, bribing customs agents. The border, to employ a cliché, leaked like a sieve. What value contraband traffic had in 1910, even officials could not estimate, but that it was high no one doubted.

When Mexican lawmen were not looking for smugglers, they chased after bandits. The borderlands were a haven for thieves. Criminals wanted in Arizona fled to Sonora; on occasion, entire gangs crossed the border. When Mexican police tried to capture them, they simply went back to the United States. Bandits roamed freely in Arizpe district, "outlaws known as cowboys who robbed and killed on both sides of the border."[46] At San Ignacio, bandits broke into the home of don José María Salazar, robbed its inhabitants of their money and jewelry, and then fled to Arizona, where one of them lived. The same gang fell upon Huépac and Bacamuchi, both in Arizpe. Huépac's defenders had a gun battle with the outlaws, with over 300 shots fired, but the bandits, smugglers by trade, escaped back across the border. Eventually, Mexican authorities found a part of the gang in Tucson and Tombstone and had them extradited.[47] At Agua Zarca, masked outlaws robbed the train, while others stole money belonging to the Moctezuma Concentrating Company, stopping its wagon on the run between Nacozari and Bisbee, and killing the driver.[48] At Fronteras, police captured a gang that practiced its craft with equal aplomb on both sides of the border.[49] *Bandolerismo*, as Mexicans referred to it, survived at least until 1910, declining in frequency but never disappearing entirely, as the robbery of the offices in Fronteras of the Moctezuma Copper Company by armed bandits in 1910 attests.[50]

Something else was taking place. The Mexican border towns were growing up, but not as their more respectable inhabitants had planned. Instead, they were becoming sanctuaries for "sin." Saloons, gambling halls, opium dens, and bawdyhouses proliferated. With the exception of drug parlors run by Chinese, Americans patronized them all; in fact, brisk American business explained their presence in the border towns. All these dens of vice attracted unsavory individuals. At La Morita in 1892, "daily rhubarbs" broke out in the streets, gambling flourished, and "drunks shouted insults to law-abiding citizens and police alike."[51] Bullets fired at Agua Prieta crossed into Douglas, from a saloon on the main street fronting on the boundary line. Rowdy Mexicans from Agua Prieta and Douglas, who quarreled and fought with one another, patronized the saloon, a "place of ill-repute" frequented by prostitutes.[52] At Naco, a drunken American caught beating a prostitute in a whorehouse shot and wounded three Mexican police who tried to stop him. Officials in Hermosillo ordered the bordellos of Naco closed, saying they were "dens of iniquity and immorality."[53]

Between 1885 and 1910, the trials and tribulations of Fronteras probably best epitomized the drama of the border towns. A railroad stop, Fronteras never lacked for cowboys and miners hungry for "booze and women." Saloons, gambling, and prostitution, the ingredients for disorder, were ubiquitous. "Today at 4:30 in the afternoon," began one laconic lament from Fronteras, "young Bernardino López shot Apolonio Escudero, killing him instantly."[54] At a religious festival in Cuguárachi, an event popular with people from Fronteras, the constable asked three "worshipers" to help keep the hard-drinking celebrants in order. As they were attempting to subdue a woman in her cups, a drunken American came to her rescue, so the peacekeepers beat him to death.[55]

With "heavy drinking going on constantly, daily fights, homicides" and "disgraceful and shameful behavior," the situation was out of hand by 1895. Determined to end the "immorality," the governor told the prefect of Arizpe to put a stop to the disorders.[56] When he arrived in Fronteras, the prefect found to his digust that it was impossible to distinguish between culprits and "law-abiding" citizens. Everyone, it seemed, drank all the time. When he called a meeting of the "businessmen and peaceful citizens" of the town, everyone explained that nothing could be done. As he was told, "here everyone is alike; when one person gets drunk, everyone gets drunk; when one fights or quarrels, the others follow suit." The lawbreakers, furthermore, had fled on his arrival, taking refuge on the American side "just five hours away." When Hermosillo insisted that he do something, the prefect stated bluntly that only the governor could do anything. In Fronteras, he said, no one wanted to assume the obligations of public office, thinking them burdensome, beyond their capabilities, and dangerous to boot.[57]

Other types of disorders, meanwhile, had cropped up in Fronteras. When Eduardo Camou, heir to the lands of the *ejidos* of Frontera, attempted to sell them, the community rose up in arms. The prefect, on orders from Hermosillo, had to intervene in order to avoid a pitched battle.[58] A decade later, after new *ejidal* plots had been assigned, the town's citizens accused the mayor and a councilman of keeping the best for themselves.[59] To manipulate the elections that year, the mayor had armed thugs watch over the voting booth.[60] A year later, the town council indicted the mayor for not paying for firewood he had cut on *ejidal* lands, leading the embittered prefect to throw up his hands in despair.[61] Such were the conditions in Fronteras. A town just a hop, skip, and a jump from the international line, its life had been altered drastically by the mining and ranching booms and by its proximity to Douglas. From a sleepy, stable hamlet, Fronteras turned into a raucous meeting place for the displaced, the lonely, and the rowdy.

But the border, where two cultures met, had a way of keeping ancient Mexican customs alive. One of these institutions, of special note in Nogales, was that of the *cacique*, the entrepreneur turned political bigwig. Manuel Mascareñas, one of these *caciques*, had arrived in Nogales with the railroad. A resident of the state since 1869, he made his start as a merchant in Hermosillo. From there he went to Nogales, where he purchased a ranch to raise cattle and grow pasture to sell. Along with Antonio A. Martínez of the Guaymas dynasty and Prospero Sandoval, Mascareñas ran affairs in Nogales. When he grew old, his sons, Manuel, Jr., and Alberto, took over. When the Southern Pacific Railroad dared trespass on his property in 1908, Manuel, Jr., carried his complaint to Governor Luis E. Torres. A worried Epes Randolph, boss of the Southern Pacific in Tucson, had to ask Torres to help him out of his difficulties with Mascareñas.[62]

With the political winds wavering in Magdalena, Manuel, Jr., and Martínez, the prefect of the district, quarreled openly. Knowing he had the upper hand, Martínez, with the help of the mayor of Nogales and the chief of rural police, fell upon the Rancho Santa Barbara, the property of Mascareñas, ostensibly to look for cattle thieves. Martínez took prisoner ten cowboys working for the Mascareñases and charged them with stealing cattle from his ranch, from the Cananea Cattle Company, and from ranchers in Santa Cruz. Mascareñas complained to Torres but Martínez got his way.[63] From now on, he thought, he would dictate events in Nogales; by March of the following year, however, Martínez was no longer prefect of Magdalena.[64] Not long after Manuel, Jr., embraced the critics of the cabal in Hermosillo.[65]

VI

It was not just American people, markets, and capital that helped reshape the contours of the borderlands; ideas and customs usually identified with Yankees did too. As time took its toll, the region became less Mexican and more American. One French traveler in 1909 called its inhabitants the "Yankees of Mexico."[66] In this border universe, the fabled "American way of life" changed local values. To quote a spokesman for the Mexican version of rugged individualism, "if you did not want to work, Sonora had no place for you." The state, he added, opened its doors to men of enterprise who, with "a strong and bold spirit," would exploit its resources "to their benefit and that of society." Few spots on earth, he maintained, offered richer rewards to those who wanted to "build homes and to carve out modest fortunes by dint of hard work."[67] Or, to cite another Americanized Sonoran, a councilman of Cucurpe declared that he favored law and order, swift punishment for delinquents, and a "scrupulous respect for property rights."[68]

A young man soon took note of what his father asked of him, remembered Fernando A. Galáz, a chronicler of Hermosillo. He had to know what it meant to hold a job, to earn one's money, and to understand that *huevonía*, ("laziness") made men unhappy.[69] As for government, pontificated two officials in Hermosillo, its role was "to stimulate the spirit of enterprise in useful and hard-working men," to fling wide the doors to "private enterprise."[70] For its part, the state constitution, taking a leaf from capitalist dogma, declared "sacred the right to private property, to be set aside only by reason of public utility but with absolute regard for the law and with prior indemnity."

American influences began to be felt in other ways. Imitation of Yankee customs and a fervent belief in Yankee ingenuity and skills became commonplace. Old colonial buildings fell, replaced by structures in the American style, often under the direction of American workmen. The Hotel Arcadia, one of the finest in Hermosillo in 1904, advertised itself as "a large, elegant hostelry, complete in its appointments in the American style." Its owners boasted that it compared "favorably with the best hotels in the U.S."[71] When Governor Corral decided to build a Palacio de Gobierno, he assigned the job to L. W. Mix, an American real-estate promoter who claimed the credentials of architect and engineer. The owner of the General Agency for Lands and Mines in the American Nogales and of two ranches near Imuris, Mix imported lumber, ironware, and carpenters from California for the governor's building.[72] By 1905, according to *La Bandera Sonorense*, an American engineer, J. F. Stultz, had built most of the flour mills in the state.[73] The Knights of Pythias, an American mutualist society, had a lodge in Cananea with a membership that included Mexicans.[74] To help the victims of the labor strife in Cananea in 1906, the local branch of the Society of Saint Vincent de Paul asked for donations; its president was Aida Bernstein and its secretary Manuela M. Márquez.[75]

Nothing better illustrated the Yankee impact on Sonora than baseball. In 1877, when an American merchant ship docked at Guaymas, its sailors chose up sides to play baseball. When they left, the boys of Guaymas began to play the game, using balls of string, bats made of sticks, and gloves cut of cheap cloth. From that beginning, Guaymas evolved into the cradle of baseball for northern Mexico. In 1890, the first game between teams from Guaymas and Hermosillo took place, and two years later Guaymas won the state championship, defeating teams from Hermosillo, La Colorada, Nogales, and Cananea. A "squat American who wore a long mustache" played shortstop for the Guaymas team in 1894. By 1909, every town had its baseball team while Hermosillo had turned into the capital of Mexican baseball. The new game, to the dismay of tradition-minded Mexicans, undercut the popularity of bullfighting. Attendance at the Plaza de Toros, inaugurated in 1910, fell off and eventually it had to close. Even the popularity of cockfighting declined, as Hermosillenses more and more spent their Sundays either playing or watching baseball.[76]

In the rest of Mexico, the Spanish words for water pitcher were *cántara, bocal*, or, if one wanted precision, *vasija de barro para llevar aqua*. In Sonora, the word was *pichel*. The Transvaal Company in Cumpas baptized a mine with the name *La Ultima Chanza*, "the last chance." When they played baseball, Mexican youth spoke of *picher, cacher*, or, if they were purists, *jardinero* for "outfielder." The English invasion, which modified not only the Spanish language but the way people thought, had begun. Before long, Sonorenses would lead the nation in the use of "Mexicanized" English words. The substitution of American words thought to be chic for native words judged inferior was particularly noticeable along the border. With a peculiar poignancy, the phenomenon exemplified the meaning of dependency.

CHAPTER 13

Politics of Law and Order

I

Mindful of the turmoil of yesteryear, the new apostles of economic progress called for law and order. *Libertad y Constitución* ("liberty and constitution"), the slogan stamped on official correspondence, lost its meaning, retaining only token importance in daily life. Making Sonora over in the Western mold, lest foreign capital fail to appear, paradoxically called for a return to an all-powerful state reminiscent of the Spanish Crown. Building a capitalist society meant forging, by whatever means necessary, a tough leadership in Hermosillo that would be able to guarantee "the conditions for unimpeded trade" and able to open markets. Barriers blocking the exchange of goods had to fall, uniform systems of coinage and of weights and measures had to be designed, and a modern infrastructure had to be put in place.[1] Ideals that stood in the way, the freedom to elect public officials to call to mind but one, would have to await a more propitious time.

II

The flow of foreign capital into Sonora made law and order top priorities, at the same time that its presence helped justify the implementation of stricter laws. The more the economy picked up, the more peace and order became indispensable. If factional turmoil, until only recently a mainstay of political life, were to return, it might kill the golden goose. With the economic upturn brought about by mining, more Mexicans had jobs and, by comparison with others, the new jobs were better-paid ones. The money put into circulation by mining, and later by cash crops in the Mayo and Yaqui valleys, expanded the market for imported goods, giving a shot in the arm to commerce. Revenue from the sale of goods and the export of ores filled empty coffers in Hermosillo as well as the pockets of mine owners and of planters, cattlemen, and *rancheros* who supplied the food and meat.

With glaring deficits only a bad dream of the past and balanced budgets almost a reality, city fathers built *mercados*, ("markets") elaborate post offices, huge jails of mortar and stone, and municipal *palacios* in the image of buildings in Europe and the United States. By doing so, they put more money into circulation. Until early in the twentieth century, the formula of economic growth coupled with law and order kept the peace, with just sporadic outbreaks of dissent. The collapse of the economy, as the strikes of the time bore witness, unraveled the carefully woven formula that had lasted since the days of Ignacio Pesqueira.

The requirements of economic growth, not illogically, stifled democracy. The politics of order, partly justified on the pretext of guarantees for foreign capital, wrecked the nascent experiment in self-government of the years of chaos. *Municipios* had weathered the turbulence, mastering along the way knowledge and skills vital to an independent political life. When American capitalists arrived, they helped to distort the nature of the economy and the character of politics. Local autonomy, embodied by the independent *municipio* that had been emerging on the political horizon, was but one casualty.

III

Apart from brief interludes when they fell from power, "urbanites" always had run politics in the desert kingdom. The leading families of Hermosillo, Guaymas, Alamos, and Ures—the largest towns—controlled the state legislature. There were thirteen *diputados* ("representatives") in the body, representing the nine districts in the state. The districts of the four major towns, each with two *diputados*, had eight, a clear majority, of the thirteen seats. Since the *cabeceras*, the key towns of the principal *municipios*, had the upper hand in their districts, they picked the *diputados*. From the start, an urban gentry, usually the merchant upper crust, employed politics for its own ends.[2]

Quarreling between Federalists and Centralists—a forerunner of the split between Liberals and Conservatives—briefly upset urban domination in the late 1830s and early 1840s. The *notables* took sides against each other. In Alamos and Guaymas, the Federalists wanted to exploit the lands of the Yaqui valley and to put an end to Apache depredations. At the opposite pole stood the Centralists, inhabitants of the lower Río Sonora and the Moctezuma valley. Led by Manuel García Gándara of Ures, they were *hacendados* and *rancheros*. To them, it made no sense to spend tax revenues, which they had to pay, on Indians wars of dubious benefit. North and south, nevertheless, did not always stand poles apart; merchants in Guaymas with business ties to Hermosillo and Horcasitas, for example, backed Gándara. Gándara, who spent years fighting with José Urrea, a *notable* of Alamos and a Federalist, eventually tarnished his reputation by siding with the French invaders who ousted Benito Juárez from Mexico City.[3]

For all intents and purposes, Gándara's romance with the French, which he vehemently denied until he died, shut the political door on the Centralists-turned-Conservatives. Earlier, his policy of helping the *hacendados* and *rancheros* of the center and north—backed by the Mayos and Yaquis to some extent because it did not endanger their lands— had alienated the merchants of Guaymas port and the miners of Alamos. They complained that Gándara did nothing to improve the roads, so important to their business, while his tax policies burdened them while favoring others. The conflict boiled over during the 1850s, prosperous days for the merchants of the port city.[4]

The victory of the Federalists or Liberals over Gándara, by a strange twist, installed in power Ignacio Pesqueira, a northern *hacendado* from Aripze. Educated in Spain and France and by marriage a member of the Jesús García Morales and Rafael Angel Corella clans, Pesqueira was a Liberal. Having sided with the Revolution of Ayutla, the favorite cause of the Liberals, and later fighting for the Reforma of Juárez, another Liberal landmark, Pesqueira had the backing of the urban gentry, advocates of business and law and order. The Liberals, Pesqueira's friends, spoke for the merchants in ascendancy. This tiny band of urban professionals, usually aspiring entrepreneurs, more and more resided in Hermosillo, Guaymas, Magdalena, and Altar, the districts with the lion's share of demographic and economic growth. In 1866, Pesqueira and his allies drove the French out of Sonora. The French Intervention set back business and commerce, delayed the advent of public schooling, and blocked foreign investment.[5]

Pesqueira was the *caudillo* of Sonora for two decades, staying in office until 1877. His durability alone eventually got him into trouble, especially with such young and ambitious office seekers as Ramón Corral, Luis Emeterio Torres, and the Alamos clans.[6] Eager to "develop," as he put it, the Yaqui and Mayo valleys, Pesqueira, like Gándara before him, taxed merchants and miners to raise funds for his Indian wars. The taxpayers did not take kindly to the revenue measures, especially in Alamos, where the *notables* accused Pesqueira of depopulating the state with his taxes. Critics also cried foul at the *caudillo's* attempts to portion out to his followers the lands in the fertile valleys, lands very much on the minds of the Alamos and Guaymas elites. The first rebellion, that of the Alamos speculator Carlos Conant in 1873 failed, but not that of 1875–1876. Pesqueira's fall from grace coincided with the rise of Porfirio Díaz. By the time of Pesqueira's final bow, the cornerstones for peace and order stood in place.

The triumph of the opposition over Pesqueria, nevertheless, failed to halt factional squabbling entirely. General Vicente Mariscal, sent by President Miguel Lerdo de Tejada, successor to Juárez, to discipline the Pesqueiristas and their foes, chose to back the military coup of Tuxtepec that elevated Díaz to the Mexican throne. From that time on, the die was cast. Whoever ruled in Sonora had to be a porfirista and, of course, a Liberal. The only issue was who would govern. When Mariscal abandoned Sonora, his place fell to Francisco Serna, now the governor and a rich merchant, miner, and landowner with roots in Hermosillo, Guaymas, and Altar. The son of a miner and merchant-*hacendado*, he had rejected the rural world for the glamor of Hermosillo, eventually leading the revolt againt Pesqueira in 1875. As prefect of Altar, Serna headed a group at odds with the cabal from Ures and the northeast.[7]

For a while, the political waters hardly stayed calm. Carlos R. Ortiz, successor to Serna, was an heir to Alamos wealth, who was educated in Germany and had backed the campaigns against Pesqueira and Mariscal. Governor Ortiz ruled from 1881 to 1883. He had climbed the ladder of success by collaborating with Torres and General José Guillermo Carbó, who replaced Mariscal as chief of the military zone. Bright and innovative, Ortiz eventually fell into disrepute with Torres and his gang because of designs on the lands of the Mayo, according to his critics. Those designs were at variance with the aspirations of José María Maytorena, an hacendado with plans of his own. Whatever the truth, Carbó, with the help of Torres, Corral, Maytorena, and perhaps General Bernardo Reyes, the new military chief, toppled Ortiz.[8]

From this turmoil, Torres emerged governor of Sonora. The day of the Triumvirate had dawned. Its ascent to power coincided with don Porfirio's return to office in 1884. The age of the Porfiriato and the Triumvirate, heyday of the Liberals, would be one and the same, a period of law, order, and "progress." Much remained to transform those sacred words into reality. On the local scene, the political bickering and the ouster of Ortiz helped bring the economy to its knees. Merchants suffered losses, miners stopped working their claims, and untold numbers of the jobless fled to Arizona.[9] But a new day was dawning on the horizon; as Ortiz fell, the Sonora Railway was making its way from Guaymas to Nogales. The mining boom, the child of American capitalism, was about to begin. And Torres and his cabal were making an entrance onto the political stage, promising safeguards for foreign capital.

The formula, the traditional Liberal dogma, called for stability and continuity in politics. Article 70 of the State Constitution of 1877 prohibited a governor from succeeding himself but allowed, after an interval, his reelection to office a second or third time, or, as a matter of fact, indefinitely. *Diputados* to the state legislature could serve multiple terms. Justices of the state supreme court, the highest tribunal, had four-year terms but could be reappointed by the governor. The constitution provided for a *vice gobernador* elected on the same ticket with his running mate.[10] A *secretario de estado* signed laws, decrees, regulations, and orders dictated by the chief executive who appointed him. In practice, the *secretario*, whose duties were perfected by Corral, often ran the political apparatus of the state. Corral eventually came to appoint a majority of public officials, from prefect and judge of a district down to constable, the lowest post on the political ladder. That state control evolved with the politics of law and order at the expense of municipal autonomy.

From the start of the Triumvirate, the legislature as well as the supreme court acted as virtual rubber stamps.[11] After all, the families of the *notables*, in cahoots with the governor, especially in the four major towns, picked the candidates for the legislature. Their roster included the names of the social "400"—Almada, Salido, Monteverde, and Elías—and, ultimately, those of rich upstarts such as Camou and Robinson. The *diputados* routinely approved the budget, endorsed bills from the chief executive, and did whatever else he asked. They paid themselves small salaries, met only briefly each year, did not overwork themselves, and were stingy with state funds.

Between 1879 and 1911 the people of Sonora "elected" sixteen legislatures but they only infrequently selected new *diputados*. Vacancies occurred mainly because of death or promotion to higher office or, once in a lifetime, because a maverick bit the hand that fed him. To the anger of the non-anointed, the *diputados* represented with equal aplomb the nine districts of the state, regardless of their place of residence. Just seventy-four individuals in thirty-two years occupied the 208 seats available in the 13-member legislatures, elected every two years. To top that, four of the collaborators of Torres served as *diputados* in ten or more legislatures; eight others held the post from five to nine times; and twenty-five were "reelected" on two, three, or four occasions. Just

twenty-seven *diputados* failed to be "reelected." During its days of mercantile and financial glory, *diputados* from Hermosillo dominated the
legislature. Nepotism flourished. The "reelected" *diputados* included
the brothers, cousins, and *compadres* ("godfathers") of Torres, and, to
boot, his in-laws (who were also related to Rafael Izábal); the in-laws of
Corral; and cousins of Izábal.[12] Nor did quality prevail. "Please accept
the resignation of the constable of Pitiquito," its mayor wrote to the
prefect of Altar, who had recommended that the constable be "elected"
a *diputado*. The individual, "noxious to both the people and the law,"
had "no business being a public official," the mayor explained.[13]

Although guilty of centralizing authority, the Triumvirate did not
originate the practice. It had roots as old as the colonial era. Later, both
Federalists and Centralists, now Liberals and Conservatives, tried to
curtail local autonomy. Pesqueira, a Federalist and Liberal and by
theory a believer in the popular will, had battled to beef up executive
authority on the assumption that meddling by the legislature and the
municipios set back economic growth.[14] Ironically, Torres and Corral
had applauded legislative efforts to limit Pesqueira's power. The moves
would have limited the governor to one term and allowed the election
of prefects, who until then were appointed by the governor. Pesqueira
blocked most of these measures, but the prohibition on reelection of
the governor went through. Nevertheless, he stood for another term
in 1875. Once in office, the Triumvirate, in a flip-flop, embraced Pesqueira's stance. The last challenge to the Triumvirate's authority took
place in 1887 when José María Maytorena, the wealthy *hacendado* from
Guaymas, sought the governorship for himself.

Yet the attempt to curtail municipal autonomy, arguments to the contrary, did not always undercut the popular will. Democracy—the honest and free election of public officials—had hardly ever prevailed in
Sonora. Whether the pretext for the centralization of authority was the
divine right of the Spanish Crown or the demands of economic
growth, the process usually met few obstacles. At times, the popular
will proved more fiction than fact. As the prefect of Guaymas explained
in 1884, few *municipios* had residents qualified to serve on town councils
or to hold public posts. Those elected could barely sign their names
and, once in office, not uncommonly ignored the will of the voters.[15]
Likewise, inhabitants often failed to vote, particularly in the hamlets,
as a litany of complaints from public authorities in the 1880s reveal.
On more than one occasion, celebrations of diverse types interfered
with voting. In 1892, for instance, no one voted in San Marical, a village
in Guaymas district, because the day before election day was the feast
of San Juan, the town's patron saint, and "everyone got drunk,"

reported its mayor.[16] Elections in San Juanico, Haciendita, and Carmen, hamlets in Hermosillo district could not be held because no one came to vote. The same thing happened in Arivechi, a town in Sahuaripa.[17] On other occasions, for example in Tubutama, rival bands made it impossible to hold elections.[18] Lack of popular interest in elections, especially in the small towns, did not suddenly begin with the politics of the Triumvirate. By the same token, that disinterest helped to consolidate authority. Still, election results from 1880 to 1910 reveal numerous hard-fought contests at the local level.

IV

Conflicts had flared between the *municipios* and the prefects. Before, the governor, with the approval of the legislature, had picked the prefects. The constitution of 1862 changed that, allowing them to be elected by popular vote every two years. Pesqueira wanted to return to the old system and appoint the prefects himself, viewing them as "the principal agents to do his bidding" in his efforts to control the *municipios*.[19] Independent *municipios* undermined the authority of governor and prefects. The Triumvirate, learning from Pesqueira and frightened by the challenge of Maytorena, restored the power of the governor to pick the prefects by the legislation of 1892. With a nod to local autonomy, however, the law prohibited the prefects from attending meetings of town councils unless invited or from meddling in judicial matters.[20] In theory, the prefects handled correspondence between the *municipios* and Hermosillo. Additionally, the law of 1892 gave the governor the right to name the judges of first instance, who held chief judicial authority in each district, and left the choice of constables, the *comisarios de policía*, to the prefects, subject to review by the governor. The *jueces locales* ("municipal magistrates"), who used to be elected, now were named by the town councils with the approval of the prefects.[21] Earlier, Hermosillo had permitted the prefect to handle police matters in Alamos town, a policy common to the large municipal centers.[22]

More than any other public official, the prefects were the agents of law and order; they performed their job admirably in the mining districts at the expense of labor. Most of them, whether sincerely or not, proclaimed their faith in the rejuvenating energy of foreign capital. Like their masters in Hermosillo, the prefects did the bidding of the foreigner. But with Mexicans of the "lower classes," the prefect wielded "despotic powers."[23] Obsequious before the governor, back home they ran their districts like "Persian satraps" with the help of the mayors of the *municipios*, elaborating in the course of events a *"caciquismo pueblerino,"* a petty dictatorship. When the opportunity arose, the prefects unabashedly appointed relatives, *compadres*, in-laws, and friends to political office.[24]

The prefects, especially in the isolated districts, were often omnipotent. "No doubt," concluded the American consul in Guaymas, they "abuse their position."[25] The consul had in mind Loreto Trujillo, the boss of Sahuaripa, who, on one occasion, jailed a Mexican who had become a citizen of the United States for refusing to vote for him. That the individual no longer had the right to vote in a Mexican election bothered the prefect not a bit. Trujillo, the American diplomat said, "did things with a high hand."[26] Francisco Telles, prefect of Ures in 1906, labeled "calumny" any newspaper account not flattering to him.[27] Adolfo Balderrama in Magdalena meddled in the affairs of the town councils, meted out heavy fines on whim, and allocated to himself the job of judge and juror.[28] Other prefects arbitrarily took land and water away from the dirt farmers. One such prefect, Francisco Chiapa—once a teacher of Adolfo de la Huerta, who was to become president of Mexican in 1920—put to death Severiano Talamantes and his sons, heroes of the rebellion of 1910.[29]

At times, the prefects behaved with incredible arrogance. An episode that occurred in 1892, the saga of Eduardo García Robles, prefect of Altar, is an illustration. While deep in his cups, García Robles nearly incited a rebellion of the town council of Pitiquito, its police, and "200 men, many with weapons in their hands." Armed with just a pistol, he reported, he had survived by standing his ground and then escaping to Caborca. The truth, however, had a different twist. García Robles and the judge of the district had arrived in Pitiquito one night "woefully drunk" and immediately gone off to continue their drinking spree in a bar. García Robles got into a quarrel with the bar's owner, threatening, for no reason whatsoever, to put him in jail. The judge, less intoxicated and more sensible, calmed matters but then went off with García Robles to the plaza, where the prefect, pistol in hand, became embroiled in a shouting match with the townspeople. Still under the influence, he finally rode off to Caborca, arriving there inebriated, angry, and asking for volunteers to quash the "rebellion" in Pitiquito.[30]

Powerful prefects even defied governors. Francisco A. Salido of the famous clan, as prefect of Alamos replaced the mayor of Río Chico, even though he knew that the governor thought highly of him.[31] For all intents and purposes, however, the prefects served the governor. While prefects might nominate or make appointments to public office, the governor or his *secretario de estado* had the final say. One word from either and the prefect lost his post, as Jesús A. Cano, boss of Altar, learned to his sorrow in 1908.[32] That year, Hermosillo also replaced the prefects of Ures and Moctezuma, public servants of long standing. The replacement of prefects, however, was no perfunctory decision; Hermosillo required good cause for such a drastic step. Manuel Encinas, for years boss of Sahuaripa, was never removed despite pleas from leading citizens who thought him "an old man" easily manipulated by relatives and friends. He had replaced Jesús Coronado in 1893 and aged on the job.[33] When Francisco C. Aguilar, a longtime prefect, wanted to know why residents of Ures had been asked to testify in Hermosillo, he was bluntly told that the governor did not have to explain his decisions.[34] The prefects seldom had an entirely free hand in their districts. As Francisco Morineau, a merchant stalwart of Altar, explained, local intrigues, petty rivalries, and conflicting interests undercut the authority of the prefect.[35] It appears that the "omnipotent" prefect, enshrined in the literature of his critics, may have been more myth than fact.

The politics of law and order allowed family clans or singular individuals to enjoy a monopoly of the office of prefect. In Alamos, it was the Salidos—Bartolomé in the 1880s and later Francisco A.—who stayed in office, more or less, from 1897 to 1909. If a Salido did not hold the post an Almada did; Angel Almada, for example, surrendered to the victorious rebels in 1911.[36] Vicente A. Almada was prefect of Magdalena. Francisco M. Espino, a Pesqueirista turned ally of Torres, was prefect of Magdalena from 1881 to 1883 and again in 1889, of Hermosillo in 1887, of Arizpe in 1891, and of Guaymas in 1879, 1885, and from 1893 to 1900. He died in office.[37] Francisco C. Aguilar, prefect of Ures, turned the post into a lifetime job, serving for 21 years. He died in 1906, a year after Governor Izábal replaced him. Rumor had it that the cause of death was the shame of losing his job. Once unemployed, he never stepped out of his home again, not wanting to give his former "subjects" the chance to *faltarle al respeto* ("to slight him").[38] The next prefect, Francisco J. Telles, incidentally, turned over the office in Ures to another Aguilar, the son of the old prefect.[39] In Hermosillo, Francisco M. Aguilar wielded power for years while in Arizpe, Ignacio E. Elías, offspring of the clan and a former tax collector, held office from 1902 to 1910. Balvanero E. Robles became prefect of Altar in 1893, served two years, and then went to Moctezuma, where he held the same job until 1907. As prefect, Robles won plaudits for his admiration of Yankee entrepreneurs and, from George F. Woodward, miner and hotel owner, praise for "his manly and untiring persecution" of criminals and "his lasting imprint on outlaws."[40] Jacinto Padilla, a physician more interested in politics than in medicine, became mayor of Magdalena in 1898, then prefect of the district, serving until 1908, and then mayor again. Ignacio Bonillas followed a similar political path.[41]

These prefects not only kept the peace, turning oftentimes into allies of foreign speculators but also became entrepreneurs themselves. In a nutshell, they practiced what they preached: the validity of business enterprise. Francisco C. Aguilar, related to the wealthy Aguilars of Guaymas, owned the biggest general stores in Ures and Hermosillo, and wheat lands and rich mines. So well off was he that he lent money to his district, going long periods without being paid.[42] Ignacio E. Elías had a flour mill, a cattle ranch, and *haciendas* in Arizpe.[43] A prefect with an eye for a profit, Leonardo Gámez, once held a contract to supply firewood to the Creston Colorado Mining Company and he also sold land for the railway to Estación Torres.[44] Jacinto Padilla, the physician-turned-politician, bottled and sold soft drinks, while Antonio A. Martínez, prefect of Magdalena and crony of Torres, had cattle ranches and *haciendas*.[45] One prefect of Hermosillo served as the legal representative of the Hüllen Mining Company. Like the governors, the prefects took frequent leaves of absence to attend to their "private business matters."[46]

Bringing order out of chaos meant getting the *municipios* into line. The *ayuntamientos* or town councils dated from independence; the original constitution had bestowed them on towns of 3,000 inhabitants or more. Alamos, Hermosillo, Guaymas, and Ures were among the first to have one. Each *ayuntamiento* had a mayor and *regidores* or councilmen.[47] During the early years of the Republic, when local rivalries and foreign intrigues undermined the authority of Ures and Hermosillo, the town councils had gone their own way, becoming stronger and more independent.[48] Many in the smaller communities, however, had neither the will nor the ability to carry out competently the duties entrusted to them by law. Not uncommonly, they had scanty financial resources. Revenues failed to cover expenses and appeals to Hermosillo for tax dispensations had become a regular way of meeting deficits. Petty quarrels and general apathy often made self-government a mockery.

To Pesqueira, Torres, and Corral, order called for less municipal autonomy, tighter surveillance, and the selection of mayors by Hermosillo. In their opinion, Sonora suffered from a surplus of *municipios*, many too small to justify their existence. With tiny populations, they lacked citizens able to serve in public office and a tax base large enough to support schools, police, and other services.[49] To cite the report of the prefect of Arizpe in 1887, many *municipios* not only failed to protect life and property but, in the bargain, did not bother to report crimes.[50] Attempts to reduce the number of *ayuntamientos* and to curtail their independence eventually bore fruit. In the 1870s, Sonora had 105 *municipios*; by 1900 only eighty-eight; and in 1910 just seventy. The constitutional reform of 1892, requiring a minimum of 500 inhabitants in a *municipio*, had accomplished the reduction.[51] The reform also abolished the right of the community, with the exception of its *regidores*, to pick candidates for district offices.

By controlling the prefects, Hermosillo tightened its grip on municipal government.[52] In Hermosillo, Guaymas, and Alamos, the network of old family clans lent a helping hand. The names on the *ayuntamiento* of Alamos—Salido, Almada, Palomares, Urrea, Goycolea, and Corbalá—could pass for a *Who's Who* of its social elite. Members of the key *ayuntamientos* more often than not had economic stakes to defend, either as merchants, mining speculators, and planters, or as employees of foreign companies. Not a few waxed rich off their political connections. Hermosillo allowed the loyal families a degree of flexibility, particularly in Guaymas, confident that the interests of the state and the wealthy were one and the same. The other *municipios*, Hermosillo entrusted to its prefects, with one glaring exception. In Cananea, home of Mr. Greene's empire, Mayor E. R. Arnold enjoyed a direct pipeline to Hermosillo. Unencumbered by prefects, Arnold discussed candidates for the *ayuntamiento* with Governor Alberto Cubillas and, on his own initiative, kept his town free of what he called "labor agitators."[53]

Peace and order implied permanence for the mayors. The prefects named the mayors yearly; the people "voted" for them; and their appointment was subject to the approval of Hermosillo, particularly in the cities and largest towns. To the anger of younger and ambitious men, the mayors had a facility for staying in office. The same names, constituting a sort of "plutocratic royalty," surfaced again and again at appointment time: don Vicente V. Escalante in Hermosillo; don Ignacio Almada in Alamos; don Matías Tamayo in Ures; Doctor Prisciliano Figueroa and don Arturo Morales in Guaymas; and José Tiburcio Otero in Huatabampo.[54] With the exception of Morales, these gentlemen each were "reelected" ten to fifteen times. None of these distinguished luminaries lived off his salary; all had business ties of sorts. In the countryside, His Honor the Mayor not infrequently behaved in the manner of a petty tyrant, arbitrarily blocking public roads, as at San Ignacio; levying fines on whomever he wished, a complaint of the citizens of Río Chico; or not paying taxes on sales at the general store, a pastime of don Antonio Rivera in Minas Prietas.[55] Ironically, when a mayor actually responded to the demands of his community, he could lose his job. Bernabé Robles, mayor of Fronteras, was fired when he dismissed a drunken *juez local* ("local judge") without consulting his prefect.[56]

Still, here and there, a relative degree of municipal autonomy weathered the adverse winds. Prefects dictated decisions with the blessings of Hermosillo, but occasionally they had to admit defeat. When rival bands fought for municipal supremacy, prefects kept hands off since loyalty to Hermosillo was not an issue. An official slate of candidates in districts such as Sahuaripa would sometimes lose an election to a rival group. On these occasions, prefects watched their friends lose— even though the prefects had selected them as candidates—without lifting a finger. So deep and complex were animosities, explained the prefect of Sahuaripa, a district renowned for its family disputes, that it was "impossible to know who had truth on his side."[57] Until the advent of don Matías Tamayo, mayors of rival affiliations came and went in Ures.[58] Since everyone paid homage to the Triumvirate, it mattered little who ruled.

To its despair, Hermosillo's blueprints had a habit of getting torn apart on the rocks of municipal reality. The obedience and subservience that Hermosillo demanded on more than one occasion fell before practical necessities. No matter what the rules, municipal fathers often took their message directly to Hermosillo instead of going through proper channels. By 1908, this habit had gotten out of control.[59] Additionally, not everyone coveted *el hueso* ("a political job") especially in the smaller *municipios*. The jobs paid poorly and took time away from private business matters; at best power proved ephemeral, while the headaches of public service aged the hardiest of men. Men not uncommonly were so unwilling to shoulder the burdens of municipal office that Hermosillo, bent on making them serve, resorted to threats to strip them of their rights as Mexican citizens if they refused.[60] Resignations from these posts, particularly among *regidores*, never stopped, becoming commonplace in the years just prior to the fall of the Triumvirate in 1911. The old Spanish saying, *Obedezco pero no cumplo*, ("I obey but . . ."), seldom lost its validity. Hermosillo might order, its prefects command, but *municipios*, whether out of lethargy, incompetence, or sheer orneriness, at times stood their ground.[61]

Foreign investment, the opening of markets across the border, and their attendant economic growth, failed to remedy the traditional financial malady of *municipios*. Despite added revenues in such mercantile bastions as Hermosillo and Guaymas, the good times left municipal budgets as penniless as the proverbial church mouse. The *plan de propios y arbitrios* ("budget") stayed deep in the red. Nearly always, expenditures topped revenues even in the larger *municipios*. When the foreign mining companies shut down, the nearby towns went bankrupt, not excluding Cananea. The Indian wars, especially the campaigns against the Yaquis, aggravated the financial plight of the *municipios*.

V

Nor did economic growth teach Mexicans how to govern themselves better. As fortunes were "made in a day—colossal fortunes of tainted wealth," as Rafael de Zayas Enríquez lamented, so was there corruption in political life.[62] If governors could sell rights and privileges to foreigners, why could they not also manipulate elections, distort the law, and use police and soldiers against the people they were meant to protect? At the behest of a town's citizens Hermosillo annulled elections, when convenient; when inconvenient, it ignored their pleas, especially after Corral abandoned his home for Mexico City in 1900.

Elections in the thriving towns were no less dishonest than in *municipios* untouched by economic progress. Political chicanery, supposedly a sign of poverty, plagued Nogales, a prosperous commercial entrepôt. It was indulged in by figures intimately identified with business and commerce, such as Ignacio Bonillas and Manuel Mascareñas, as the election for mayor in 1897 amply illustrated. Before the event was over, Mascareñas, a stalwart of business, employed the police to jail his opponents. For his part, Bonillas, having stacked the polls with his partisans, blocked his rivals. Antonio A. Martínez, police chief, entrepreneur, and cattle baron, on horseback with pistol in hand ran roughshod over people standing in line to vote. Over this affair presided Cirilo Ramírez, the mayor, "a wealthy man, noted broker, industrialist [and] . . . mine speculator."[63]

The good times hardly reshaped justice and law into models to emulate. Judges and constables did the dirty work of Hermosillo. Before the "reforms" of 1892, *jueces de primera instancia*, the "judges of first instance" in the district, as well as *jueces locales* ("local judges"), were elected by direct and popular vote. After 1892, the governor picked the district judges while the prefects appointed the lower judges.[64] Given the job from one to two years, judges could be reappointed, as they were more and more. The prefects appointed the constables (*comisarios*), lords of the domain on the *haciendas*, *congregaciones* (congregations), and *ranchos*; in the towns the constables were less important, and took orders from the mayor. Like their brethren, judges and constables could spend a lifetime in office. While the *ayuntamientos* named the local judges, they could not remove them; that authority belonged to the judge of first instance.[65] As a result, although they were chosen by the *municipio*, once in office lower judges could become lackeys of the district judge, himself beholden to Hermosillo, and come to be at odds with the *municipio*.

A distinctly amateur cast played in the courtroom dramas. District judges, seldom lawyers but *tinterillos* (amateurs), owed their offices to friends in the right places. The job ranked low in the bureaucratic pecking order; a district tax collector, as one judge noted, stood higher.[66] Even Hermosillo and Guaymas, the top political entities, had trouble finding qualified men for the post. Taide López de Castillo, a lawyer for the Moctezuma Copper Company, for example, refused an appointment, alleging he was too busy to accept it.[67] When the judge of Arizpe resigned in 1908, the prefect could find no qualified person to replace him.[68] Like mayors, the judges of first instance in such places as Sahuaripa often found themselves in a crossfire. Genaro Encinas, named judge in 1905, resigned three years later, declaring himself "fed up" with the hue and cry against him by a rival band.[69] Local judges were simply the "wise" men of their communities. Even in the larger towns, where at least two served, the *juez local* hardly had any legal training. Measured by the number of resignations or refusals to accept the job, he enjoyed little prestige and, perhaps more important, received trivial remuneration. As a judge of Tórin exclaimed, he had no time for himself, his family, or his business, and the job was a "daily hassle."[70] He might have added that the job paid twenty pesos a month, only slightly more than field hands earned in the Yaqui valley.[71]

The problems in law enforcement were similar. Constables, notably in the tiny hamlets, rarely had police backgrounds. At one time, *hacendados* and mining potentates, often foreigners, frequently held the job in their communities. Influential citizens urged the appointment of a friend, or perhaps the son of a crony. The nomination of José Otero, offspring of the local bigwig, for constable of Cócorit was such a case.[72] Once in a while, if the complaints multiplied, Hermosillo dismissed an autocratic constable, but it did not happen often. No one disliked by the Triumvirate, as Torres made clear in 1906, ever became a constable.[73]

VI

In the end, fittingly perchance, the politics of law and order proved the weak link in the chain forged by the Triumvirate and its admirers. Its architects, the beneficiaries of public office, were simply too greedy.

Continuity in office—the formula for keeping order—backfired. Law and order were seen as the bedrock for foreign investment, but ironically economic growth gave birth to a middle class hungry for its own share of political spoils. By inflicting heavy damage on the economic edifice, the crisis of 1907, itself a repercussion from north of the border, shattered the dreams of the young, literate, and hopeful, oftentimes offspring of the reigning family clans.

Economic growth, largely a byproduct of American capital and markets, had given hope of better days; its unexpected collapse shut the doors to upward mobility, leaving the ambitious with nowhere to climb. The politics of law and order, in addition, had turned back the clock, undercutting a municipal autonomy that had been taking shape gradually during the years of chaos. In politics, the needs of the coveted foreign capitalists, before whom Corral and his companions bowed, ultimately proved more detrimental than helpful.

CHAPTER 14

A Man for His Times

I

No one better exemplified the neocolonial mentality than Ramón Corral, a *político* who became a millionaire and won the praise of the rich Yankees he befriended. Corral did not merely preside over the political scene; he helped, probably more than any other public figure, to formulate economic policy. A man for his times, Corral worshiped at the capitalist shrine, believed foreign investors would bring about progress, and welcomed Americans to Sonora. His contemporaries, including a sprinkling who eventually joined the Rebellion of 1910, judged Corral one of the most "distinguished sons" of his native state.[1] To José López Portillo y Rojas, himself a *político* of note as well as a writer of talent from Jalisco, Corral was "clearly a gifted man of no little learning."[2] Yet once he forsook his stomping grounds to become vice-president of the Republic, he became, pathetically, a *"don nadie,"* a nobody.[3]

II

Of undistinguished family, Corral was born in 1854 just leagues from Alamos town on the Hacienda de Las Mercedes, the property of José María Almada. He was the first of seven children from the marriage of Fulgencio Corral, foreman of the *hacienda*, and Francisca Verdugo. A few years after his birth, the family moved to Palmarejo where Fulgencio became a merchant and tasted a modicum of success. From there, the family journeyed to Chínipas, a town in Chihuahua, where the father in the course of time became mayor. In Chínipas, young Corral went to primary school, his only formal education. His father, however, taught his son all he knew. He was Ramón's teacher until the days in Chínipas and, after that, "his most assiduous tutor," according to Manuel Uruchurto, Corral's biographer.[4] A storekeeper, Fulgencio inculcated his own values in his son and had a lasting influence on him.

When his father died in 1867, fourteen-year-old Ramón, as the eldest, took on the responsibility of caring for the family. He worked briefly for a mining company and later as clerk of the municipal court in Chínipas. In 1873, Corral returned to Sonora to set up housekeeping in Alamos, this time as clerk of the court of the first instance and as a part-time secretary to don Miguel Urrea, a pillar of the town's society. Urrea grew to look upon Corral as a son, and encouraged him to study on his own, giving him access to the private libraries in Alamos and introducing him to the elite. From this time on, the powerful of Alamos saw Corral as one of their own.[5]

Urrea headed the opposition to Governor Ignacio Pesqueira. Not surprisingly, Corral quickly turned into the governor's enemy as well. With his mentor's help, Corral became editor of two opposition newspapers, *El Fantasma* and *La Voz de Alamos*, where he pilloried Pesqueira in his editorials. When Carlos Conant, of recent vintage in Alamos, rebelled against Pesqueira, Corral joined him, but had to take refuge in Chihuahua when the uprising failed. With the fall of Pesqueira in 1876, Corral returned to Alamos as part of the political clan of Luis Emeterio Torres, the group that ultimately was victorious.[6]

Usually, those who took the time to know him judged Corral *simpático* ("congenial") and down-to-earth, never one to pontificate.[7] Affable in manner, he made friends easily, including in his diverse array General Mariano Escobedo, the conquerer of Maximilian at Querétaro; José Yves Limantour, the powerful minister of *hacienda* in Mexico City; and Iñigo Noriega, a rich and hated *cacique*. Corral was a man of medium height, swarthy of skin by American standards but hardly dark, with "deep penetrating eyes." He cut his hair short but sported a long, droopy mustache, black at first but then gray in later years. A powerfully built man, turning thickset over time, he was always "cheerful in countenance." Eventually, he acquired a "certain air of authority," wrote Mrs. Alex Tweedie, the peripatetic author, "and one could easily imagine him in a position of command." She judged Corral "the sort of man who would be a warm friend or a bitter enemy, a man of strong emotion and warmth of heart, a man easily beloved, and kindly in his acts." These traits, she perceptively added, were "more prominent on the surface, perhaps, than strength of character."[8]

In Hermosillo, Corral was known as don Ramón. His home, elegant but simple, was a one-story house with French doors that opened onto the street. It fronted the Calle de Hidalgo and stood next to that of Rafael Izábal. Every morning Corral walked from his house to his office, a routine he repeated in the afternoon when he returned home to eat. Along the way, he stopped to say hello to friends and neighbors.[9] Like most northern Mexicans, he was unpretentious. When asked to fill out a questionnaire, Governor Corral noted simply that he was thirty-nine years of age, married, "a public employee and resident of Hermosillo."[10] With the Alamos crowd, with friends, and, on occasion, with prefects Corral used the informal *tu* form of address. He signed his name with a flourish: it was quite illegible but unmistakably "Corral." He liked to drink and cared little for what people might say. He was often found at the bar of the Hotel Francés, a popular rendezvous for the thirsty.[11] Like many other men of his day, Corral paid visits to the brothels on Calle del Carmen.[12]

Still, above all, don Ramón was a family man. He married Amparo Escalante, a native of Hermosillo, in 1888, and she lived with him until he died. A "handsome woman," donâ Amparo and Corral had fourteen children, though five died in infancy. He counted among his *compadres* both Angel and Toribio Almada (the latter was shot by Pesqueira at Alamos). In the manner of that time, Corral thought of his *compadres*, his wife's relatives, and his *amigos* as family. To Corral, nepotism and family obligations were one and the same. Just two years after marrying Amparo, Corral got his father-in-law, Vicente V. Escalante, "elected" mayor of Hermosillo. He held the post for over a decade, despite protests by younger rivals. Vicente Escalante's brother was a relative of Joaquín Loustanau, a brother-in-law of Corral and a wheeler-dealer in politics. A son of Corral's married into the Cubillas family, another pillar of society.[13] To no one's astonishment, in 1904 when Corral, then vice-president of Mexico, paid Hermosillo a visit, family, *amigos, compadres*, and the mafia of *politicos* turned out to greet him. At a banquet at the Hotel Arcadia, with a "euphoric smile on his face," sat "don Ramón."[14]

But unlike the plutocrats around him, Corral had intellectual pretensions. He wanted to write, a proclivity he displayed early in life as editor of the Alamos newspapers. While he was a journalist of skill, Corral is best remembered as a writer for his *Obras Históricas*, ("Historical Works") essays published in the late 1880s. To the amazement of his contemporaries, Corral wrote them while serving as *secretario de estado*, acting as the right hand of the governor. These essays revealed a good knowledge of local and national history. One of his adulators, of whom he had scores, later wrote that had Corral "been born in another epoch he would have been a historian."[15]

Ignacio Pesqueira, Cajeme, and the Indians of Sonora were the topics of his essays. His study of Pesqueira, begun in 1886, was really a political and military history of Sonora during the reign of the *caudillo*. To write it, Corral did archival research. Although he was his political enemy, Corral wrote a surprisingly balanced account of Pesqueira, paying tribute to his formidable accomplishments. His essay on Cajeme reflected the admiration Corral had for this Yaqui chieftain, a characteristic also found in *Razas Indigenas* ("Indigenous Races"). Corral found time to dabble in literature, once translating the inscriptions written by the poet Juan Bautista Strozzi and the reply of Michelangelo on the tomb of the Medicis in Florence. Francisco Elguero, a literary critic of the Porfiriato, wrote in the journal *América Española* that he judged Corral's translation superior to one he had done. Corral wrote poetry on occasion, enjoyed listening to good music, and attended lectures on diverse subjects.[16] As governor, he rescued from oblivion 5,000 books languishing in government warehouses, built a library for them, and set aside funds for a curator.[17]

III

More than anything else, however, fate had decreed that don Ramón become a *politico*. He had a gift for remembering names and faces while no detail, no matter how unimportant, escaped him.[18] He knew when to speak and when to keep quiet.[19] With some justification, pundits in Mexico City looked upon Corral as simply a provincial politician, an expert on Sonoran problems but a neophyte on national issues. That Corral knew Sonora, no one disputed. From the start of his political career, he regularly had visited every corner of the state; *giras de inspección*, he called the trips. On these inspection tours, he spent days visiting with local dignitaries, the merchants, planters, and ranchers. But he also went to schools, talked to students, and, as he once did in Alamos, helped students with their work. He knew the importance of the pork barrel, seldom missing an opportunity to promise a public work for a community. He left material monuments behind: a building, paved streets, electric lighting, a municipal slaughterhouse, or piped-in water.[20] Work done well by subordinates Corral rewarded, when possible by raising their salaries, as he did for the state treasurer on behalf of his "tireless labors."[21]

Like any worthy politico, Corral learned to listen to and to obey those above him. He was loyal and circumspect with Torres and Izábal, and with Porfirio Díaz in Mexico City. As Mrs. Tweedie observed, "Corral spoke with the greatest enthusiasm of his chief . . . Indeed, it was delightful to hear his admiration."[22] Corral had kept his promise, voiced during a visit to Hermosillo in 1904, to be a "firm and devoted friend of General Díaz."[23] But then Corral had spent years cultivating the art of loyalty to one's superiors. In the 1890s he suddenly returned to Hermosillo because his replacement, the vice-governor, had backed a decree jeopardizing Izábal's water "rights" to the Río Sonora. Less than three weeks later, Corral signed a bill that left Izábal's "rights" undisturbed.[24] When don Porfirio told Corral, then still in Sonora, that he knew Corral's administration took *El Diario del Hogar,* a journal critical of the Díaz regime, Corral canceled the subscription, contritely explaining that he "never or nearly never . . . read it."[25] Obsequiousness as well as talent, undoubtedly, helped Corral climb the political ladder.

From his fledgling days in Alamos, Corral tied his star to Torres, whose clan toppled Pesqueira. Torres, Corral, and Izábal, all with ties to Alamos, formed the Triumvirate that governed until 1910. Yet Corral, as *secretario de estado,* as vice-governor, and as chief executive twice, actually ran affairs during most of the last two decades of the nineteenth century. To begin with, neither Torres nor Izábal enjoyed the daily job of managing government; both left much of that to Corral. For all intents and purposes, Corral acted as governor from 1879 to 1881 under Francisco Serna, who spent a good bit of his time attending to his farming and commercial interests; as well as under Governor Lorenzo Torres, who resigned in 1891. On his own, he was governor from 1895 to 1899. Before that, he had been a *diputado* to the state legislature, a *diputado* from Sinaloa and Michoacán to the national congress, and a senator from Michoacán.[26] Corral, who helped make the positivist doctrines of the Porfirio a reality, found a niche in the history books, according to his admirers, as the finest governor of Sonora in the nineteenth century.

From Sonora, Corral went on to become governor of the Federal District, learning of his appointment in Europe, where he had gone to find a cure for the cancer eating at his throat. Díaz named him *secretario de gobernación,* the top management spot, in 1903. The next year Corral, handpicked by Díaz as his running mate, was "elected" vice-president of the Republic and "reelected" again in 1910. If the aging Díaz were to die, his supporters thought, Corral would serve as insurance for the Porfiriato.[27] In Hermosillo, the ticket of Corral and Díaz won by a whopping margin, but not in Guaymas, a bastion of the opposition. In May 1911, in the midst of deepening civil war, Díaz tendered his resignation and Corral's as well, without consulting the vice-president. A year later, cancer killed don Ramón in Paris, where he had gone to seek medical help.[28]

As an administrator, Corral had no peers in Sonora. As *secretario de estado,* he brought order out of chaos and kept the ship of state afloat in the 1880s, when five men served briefly as governor. He mastered the art of budget-writing, accounting for every penny spent. No one knew better than he how to allocate scarce resources. Usually, he drew up the preliminary budget and wrote notes on the margins of his work sheets, later incorporating these ideas into his final draft.[29] For the first time, Sonora had the semblance of a balanced budget, with much of the revenue emanating from mining, an industry favored by Corral. During his long years in political office, Corral was a key link between Hermosillo and Mexico City. When seeking advice on matters of local importance or names of people for federal jobs, Mexico City often consulted Corral.[30] Corral acquired enormous power over federal patronage in Sonora.

A diplomat first and foremost, Corral always preferred to set confrontation aside and rely on conciliation. Meeting his foe halfway did not mean a deviation from principle, however, it was just a tactic. Unlike Governor Vicente Mariscal, who relished a fight with his legislature, Corral stood up for the assembly's independence. But, in practice, by suborning its members and having relatives and friends elected to it, Corral turned it into a chamber of sycophants. He believed in the art of co-optation, of winning over the enemy and turning him into a supporter. To do this, he gave jobs to his old foes, letting them feast at the public trough of the *municipios*. A distinguished scholar of Sonora put it another way, saying Corral dealt "justly with his old enemies," including the urban elite, regardless of political differences.[31]

With the Guaymas oligarchs, Corral took special care. He let them have control of the port city's *ayuntamiento* and the liberty to handle as best they could its trade and commerce—in return for their support. When Guaymas merchants fattened their purses with the wars against the Yaquis, Corral looked the other way and let them win commercial hegemony in the Mayo and Yaqui valleys.[32] For a while, the policy paid off. Sitting with Corral at a banquet given in his honor in Guaymas in 1904 were Carlos Maytorena, Torcuato Marcor, and Florencio Maytorena, kingpins of the local oligarchy, alongside Torres and Izábal. In company with the merchant, planter, and rancher elite of other districts, the Guaymas oligarchs benefitted from economic growth. Nevertheless, to Corral, Hermosillo remained the jewel in the crown, to be polished and ornamented with more than its share of the spoils.[33]

Corral took extra care not to step on the toes of merchants. For example, in 1885, it became necessary to increase state revenues, with much of the burden to fall on commerce, so Corral met personally with the leading merchants of Hermosillo and Guaymas in order to gain their support.[34] Again, in 1896, when the legislature abolished the old colonial *alcabalas* and replaced them with a different tax, its weight to be borne by commerce, Corral talked with the merchants of the entire state, modifying the forthcoming levy in accordance with their views.[35]

There were limits to conciliation, however. As the mouthpiece of the Triumvirate, Corral could be inflexible and unforgiving, particularly with the weak and the poor. One such episode occurred in 1883 in Moctezuma, where a brother of Lorenzo Torres, crony and ally of Luis E. Torres and Izábal, held forth as prefect. A dispute over ownership of some land had broken out. On one side stood Genaro Terán, an *hacendado* and friend of the prefect, and his mother, and on the other was Guadalupe Verlarde, who was championing the claims of the dirt farmers of Pivipa. To no one's astonishment, the courts decided in favor of Terán. When Velarde and his dirt farmers refused to surrender their lands, Governor Luis E. Torres sent troops to put down the "rebellion" and dispatched Verlarde to jail in Mexico City. The stubborn Velarde, however, returned to lay claim again to his lands. At this juncture, the governor and Corral, his powerful *secretario de estado*, had Velarde captured and shot.[36] Conciliation did not apply to dirt farmers who stood up to *hacendados* and their powerful allies.

Neither did it apply to Carlos R. Ortiz, the former governor and rival of the Torres cabal. For Ortiz, even though he was a friend of Porfirio Díaz, persecution was the order of the day. According to complaints filed by Ortiz, an *hacendado* in the Mayo valley, Torres and Corral had resorted to every trick in the book to hurt him: burning his barns, killing his workers, diverting his water, driving off his animals, shutting off credit, and generally making a mockery of law and justice. So powerful and vindictive were his enemies, declared Ortiz, that no lawyer in Sonora would take his case.[37] Corral and Torres, for their part, spread the rumor that Ortiz had lost his sanity.[38] Ultimately, Ortiz had to suffer the cruel fate of the vanquished.

IV

Corral was a man of his age. He may have been, to quote an editorial in *La Patria*, "a young man full of new ideas," but those ideas were the axioms of his time.[39] Corral upheld the accepted virtues, both of native and foreign make. He supported capitalist doctrines, as he understood them; admired the achievements of his neighbors to the north and wanted to copy them; and foresaw a better Sonora only if it were made safe for American capitalists and their European brethren. When he advocated public schooling, the building of the Sonora Railway and roads, and the telegraph, Corral had in mind an infrastructure that would link economic growth to American capital and markets. Systems of transport and communication, a literate citizenry, and law and order, he thought, would assure the exploitation of Sonora's mineral and agricultural resources by wealthy Americans. The fact that joining growth and prosperity to foreign capital and markets might endanger Mexican sovereignty and culture rarely bothered Corral.

Corral epitomized the virtues he worshiped, values dear to the hearts of the western world. Like his contemporaries, the robber barons of the United States, he was a self-made man. To Uruchurtu, his biographer, Corral was the "child of his own achievements."[40] By dint of his "indisputable talent," wrote Antonio G. Rivera, a noted author, Corral pulled himself up by his own bootstraps, conquering along the way the highest posts in Sonora and Mexico.[41] Or, in the words of an American writer, don Ramón was "a fair example of a man who by his own efforts raised himself into the upper class."[42] As an orphan who had to take on his father's responsibilities at age fourteen, Corral learned early what it meant to be self-reliant, one of his "distinctive features."[43] From his youth, Corral felt no conflict with the values of Social Darwinism, Herbert Spencer's justification for the juxtaposition of the poor alongside a tiny *camarilla* of the rich. To Corral, success was for the strong and the fit, the people who were willing to work. The others would fall by the wayside. Successful himself, he took few pains to make life better for others. Particularly after the crash of 1907, this stance made him the enemy of the striving and embittered middle class.

Like any good capitalist, Corral thought property rights sacred. Time and again he emphasized that they were inviolable, providing, of course, that they did not infringe on his rights or those of his allies. Property rights were not to be tampered with, Corral exclaimed on one occasion, even when they were at odds with the public interest. The case in question was that of Prisciliano Ruiz, a native of San Ignacio, who had purchased a flour mill run by water power. A previous owner had acquired from the *ayuntamiento* of the town the right to use water to run it. To his anger, Ruiz abruptly lost that right; the town fathers charged that he had not obeyed the original stipulations on the use of the water. In its defense, the *ayuntamiento* strongly implied that community needs—in this case, the water requirements of the town—superceded individual rights. Failing to recognize the undeniable validity of the principle under both Spanish and Mexican law, Corral found the original decision "improper and dangerous," and ordered the town to restore Ruiz's rights to the water.[44] Without law and order, property and business were not safe, Corral believed. Disorder, he thought, hampered economic growth.[45]

Bandits, criminals, and other disturbers of the public order had to be dealt with harshly, he told the mayor of Nogales. When bandits robbed and killed a traveler just outside of Saric in Altar, Corral ordered the suspension of the perpetrators' legal rights.[46] When authorities caught the bandits, they were shot without a trial.[47] Legal guarantees for lawbreakers had no place in Corral's scale of values, especially when, as in the case at Saric, they endangered mining operations just getting under way.

Under Corral and the cabal in power, individual rights had limited validity, though they were the cornerstones of the bourgeois society they wanted. Among these rights were the hallowed principle of freedom of speech and of the press to publish without fear the news that's fit to print. Writing in praise of the ruling cabal or acts on its behalf, no matter how outlandishly, were protected. Conversely, criticism that went beyond the rules of proper decorum brought down the wrath of Corral. Those who fulminated against the abuses of authority likely found themselves in jail or in exile. As Corral declared at a time of political unrest in Guaymas city in 1887, after the cabal installed its own candidate in the mayor's office, liberty of speech had limitations. When newspapers inflamed public dissent, he charged, liberty of thought had gone too far, particularly since the journals *El Sonorense* and *La Sombra de Velarde* backed the opposition. Corral ordered the culprits punished; the prefect of Guaymas jailed the "guilty" editors.[48]

On economics, Corral held to current dogmas. He defended free enterprise, spoke of competition as the bulwark of a healthy society, and linked the duties of government to the needs of business. To Corral, the interests of merchants came first; that is, if they were competing with other Mexicans. As a congressman in Mexico City and later as *secretario de estado*, he fought tooth and nail attempts to allow the importation of duty-free flour and wheat from the United States into Sinaloa and Baja California, both lucrative markets for the flour of Sonora. On these occasions in the 1880s, he turned his back on the principle of free trade and spoke in defense of Mexican planters and millers, arguing that they could not compete with flour merchants in the United States.[49] While in the state legislature, Corral sponsored bills exempting new enterprises from paying taxes in order to promote industry, and, as governor, did the same thing to encourage the production of cotton and wheat.[50] He viewed skeptically the wisdom of using taxes to raise public revenues.[51]

Corral, his admirers say, dedicated his life to promoting public education. Like Enrique Creel in neighboring Chihuahua, Corral looked upon the three R's as building blocks for the future. His *Memoria*, a report on his administration, was one measure of the importance Corral attached to schooling. Of the nearly 500 pages in Volume II, almost half dealt with education. As governor, Corral established about 100 schools and reopened the Colegio de Sonora, the center of higher learning in the state. When he was *secretario de estado*, a job that called for overseeing the entire political network, Corral took time to buy equipment, supplies, furniture, and even chalk for the schools.[52]

But Corral did not father public education in Sonora. It dated from the days of Pesqueira, who, along with his successors, believed public schooling was a tool for progress. The curriculum however, was hardly innovative; instead, it was a pale imitation of foreign models, the Lancaster school in particular. When it suited him, Corral placed individual rights over the principle of public education. At Oputo, for example, when the town fathers jailed two inhabitants for sending their children to a private school, saying the parents were violating a community promise, Corral ruled the town out of order. Whatever the agreement, it was invalid because it curtailed the rights of parents to decide what was best for their children.[53]

Corral shared the racism of his contemporaries. In writing about the Indian, a principal actor in the drama of Sonora, Corral behaved in the manner of the *patrón*, the master. He patronized. Oddly, he admired the Indian, going so far as to recognize the bravery and fighting ability of the hated Apaches. He spoke highly of Cajeme—when dealing in generalities. Yet his essay on the *Razas Indígenas* revealed a firm commitment to the defeat of the Indian in the Mayo and Yaqui valleys. Cajeme blocked their "development." When "I departed," Corral recalled after seeing Cajeme in jail in 1887, "I left with a deep feeling of sympathy for that intelligent and brave Indian, the last of the noted chieftains of that historic race."[54] But a few days later, Corral did not lift a finger to stop the military from killing Cajeme. Mouthing contemporary racist clichés, Corral referred to the Indians as "savages" and once took to the field to fight them.[55] Fighting on the battlefield apparently did not suit Corral, however, for he never risked his life that way again.

Did Corral help to hatch the nefarious plot to deport the Yaquis? If not, did he sympathize with it? The evidence is inconclusive but, whatever the truth, this episode tarnished Corral's reputation forever. His critics believed he had a hand in the deportation, one of the darkest episodes in the history of Sonora. While still conjecture, it is abundantly clear that Izábal and Torres, Corral's political *compadres*, along with Mexico City, planned and ruthlessly carried it out, and that Corral supported them.[56] Further, Corral earlier participated in the rape of the Yaquis, even fighting briefly to rob them of their lands. He wanted law and order as he interpreted them to come to the valleys, obviously at the expense of the Indian. To Cajeme's successor Tetabiate, who fought to win back the stolen lands, Corral bluntly stated that the lands now belonged to their new "owners." The Yaquis, he said, by taking up arms and fleeing to the mountains to wage battle, had abdicated their rights to the lands.[57] By 1910, the new owners were the Richardson brothers and a host of Californians who had purchased lots from them. The Yaquis, it turned out, had been deprived of their lands so that Yankees might profit. Corral, whatever his complicity in the dirty business of deportation, had the blood of the Yaquis on his hands.

The Yaqui question revealed an ambiguity in Corral. His motto, *gobernar para todos* ("to govern for everyone"), failed to withstand careful scrutiny.[58] Don Ramón may have had, as alleged, "a genuine sympathy for the lower classes" but he did nothing for them. The reality was closer to today's "trickle-down theory": prosperity, initially enjoyed by the rich, would in time filter down to the poor. Nevertheless, when Mexicans were recruited to pick cotton in Texas, Corral was disturbed, aware as he was of their exploitation in the past. He wanted contracts drawn up stipulating the hours of work and whether wages were to be paid by the day, week, or month; and guarantees of hospital care in case of illness. Unless these conditions were met, he opposed the recruitment of Mexican workers.[59]

At home, however, no record reveals that Corral ever asked a planter or mine boss to take pity on his workers. To the contrary, at Cananea in 1906, Corral told Izábal to jail the strike leaders.[60] By this action, wrote a historian from Alamos, Corral "saved" the lives of men destined to join the revolt of 1910. Clemency, the need to face political reality, ironically helped bring about the downfall of Corral and his cohorts.[61] Afterward, during his exile, frightened by the deeds of Emiliano Zapata in Morelos, Corral warned that the revolt was getting out of control.[62] The poor had to know their place in society, he thought.

Corral had a lukewarm social conscience, though he believed that *vecinos acomodados* ("the rich") had an obligation to their communities. In correspondence, he constantly urged his friends in Alamos to take part in community affairs, and applauded their willingness to serve on the school board. He prodded Ignacio Almada, Juan Rivas, and Toribio Corbalá, town bigwigs, to get their wealthy neighbors to give funds for a cemetery, telling them that it was their duty. Eventually, a new site was found and the old cemetery closed, but only after Corral talked his *compadres* into getting the work done.[63] A short time later, he cajoled them into paying for a water system by dangling before them government funding to match their contributions. If the rich cooperated, they could count on him.[64] Nearly two decades later, when Corral was vice-president, he set aside time to advise his friends on how to bring electricity to Alamos. He suggested adopting the strategy he had used in Hermosillo, and permitted Angel and Ignacio Almada to organize a company to sell electricity to Alamos. Corral had done the same thing in the state capital.[65] A civic spirit, in Corral's view, need not hamper private gain.

V

With the passage of time, Corral fell more and more under the spell of the foreigner. As he did, he began to change, to modify earlier sentiments. Like most Mexicans, he had known that dealing with the United States was like playing with fire. Unless one took special care, one got burnt. In his essay on Pesqueira, Corral accused President James Buchanan of trying to occupy Sonora and Chihuahua, on the pretext of ridding the Southwest of Apache raids. "Fortunately," he concluded, "the sinister plot . . . had not gone beyond being a bad intention."[66] But eventually, this man of Sonora, the desert kingdom renowned for its rustic simplicity, adopted the airs and manners of the outsider, as did the bootlickers around him. The banquet in his honor in Guaymas in 1904, for example, featured a menu in French. The guests toasted Corral with imported champagne and ate *"Chateaubriand à la financière, punch à la Romaine, huîtres sauce holandaise and fruits à la mayonnaise."* The ladies of Hermosillo, who met in the home of Torres for their tribute to Señora Corral, matched that menu with one of their own, also with French cuisine.[67]

Corral became, as one wag put it, a *pocho*, an Americanized Mexican.[68] He spoke "excellent English," recalled Mrs. Tweedie.[69] With Torres, Corral made a grand tour of the United States, visiting New York, Philadelphia, Chicago, and San Francisco, returning home visibly moved. On his way back, the Southern Pacific sent a special train to Nogales to pick him up, dispatching another to Benson upon his return from a trip to Europe. The Southern Pacific did not court all Mexican *políticos* so grandly. In 1903, Corral sent a son to study in Philadelphia. Among his American cronies was William C. Greene, the copper magnate. On his visit to Hermosillo and Guaymas in 1904, Corral stopped at Cananea, had a drink in the Club Cananea, and visited the offices of the 4C's. During his tour of the Oversight mine, armed men known as the Rough Riders de Cananea escorted him.[70]

Cananea was Corral's Achilles' heel, and ultimately it proved his undoing. Corral, who usually kept close tabs on local affairs, left Greene "entirely in control of the municipal government" of Cananea. From every appearance, he had a unique relationship with the Yankee baron. During the strike of 1906, Corral told Greene what to tell the press about labor conditions at Cananea, urging him not to admit that he paid Americans more than Mexicans.[71] Attuned to the shift in the political winds toward anti-Americanism, and apparently aware of Greene's proclivities, Corral warned Governor Izábal not to permit armed Americans into the mining town.[72] When he learned that his warning had arrived too late and that rifle-toting Yankees had come to Cananea, Corral ordered Izábal to deny that he had brought them in or that they had helped put down the strike. The appearance of the gunmen caught Corral by surprise, for in the same telegram he asked Izábal who these men were, how many had come, and whom they spoke for.[73]

Corral equated the coming of foreigners with progress. "I am happy to say," he wrote in his *Memoria* of 1889, "that more and more foreigners arrive every day"; that, he went on, furnished "proof that they found . . . guarantees for their person and interests and lucrative rewards for their capital and labor."[74] Soon after, he was urging landlords to subdivide their holdings and sell them in small plots in order to support Mexico City's efforts to attract foreign immigrants. Immigrants, Corral affirmed, introduced fresh ideas and brought money to Mexico.[75] He lobbied for Mexico's participation in the World Exposition of 1893 in Paris, wanting to display samples of the mineral wealth of Sonora in order to lure investors, "capitalists" who would exploit hidden riches.[76] At another moment, speaking to the American consul, Corral swore that his "major aim was to offer guarantees to foreigners who, with their capital and intelligence, would establish enterprises of benefit to our state."[77]

To Corral, the more foreigners there were, the more dollars would circulate in Sonora. Since mining lured foreigners to Sonora, it ranked at the top of his priorities. With open arms, Corral welcomed Greene, Douglas, and their crowd, all mining speculators par excellence. As he once explained to his legislature, when asking for a concession for a Frenchman who wanted to build a reduction works, "so obvious are the advantages . . . that I am sure you will readily give it your blessings."[78] But Corral wanted money of any kind, not just mining money, invested in Sonora. To get it, he did whatever it took.

George Grüning, a German beer entrepreneur, for example, wanted to build a brewery in Hermosillo. Not only would the new building enhance the architecture of Hermosillo, Corral enthused, the project also would mean more jobs for the working class. Grüning promised to train two Mexican students to handle the plant's machinery, a stipulation exacted by Corral since he equated machinery with modernity.

Beyond that, "morality" demanded the concession be granted because the brewery would help to combat rampant alcoholism by substituting beer for strong drink. As governor, Corral granted Grüning a ten-year exemption from state and municipal taxes while pledging not to give competitors a similar privilege. Of course, Corral hoped to profit himself. He bought shares in the enterprises. Additionally, the brewery had an "elegant bar with polished brass and huge mirrors"; its owner was don Ramón.[79] To build a cracker factory, an American asked that he "be free and exempt" for ten years "from State, Municipal or district taxation, and any forms of taxation whatsoever, except for the Federal tax"—not a particularly onerous one—"and that . . . the books of my company shall not be subject to the scrutiny or supervision in any manner of any individual except the Federal inspector."[80] Both state and municipal government, in a capsule, should keep their noses out of his business. Corral had the legislature approve the demands. When Edmund Harvey, boss of the mining company in La Trinidad, wanted to replace the town's mayor (he had failed to prevent a labor strike), Corral gave him a free hand. The forthcoming elections, said Corral, offered ample opportunity for the company to "select a person of its choice . . . who, if need be, could vigorously protect its interests."[81] In Corral's mind, the foreigner thanked the Lord, and Corral thanked the foreigner "for the enormous investment of . . . [these] past years."[82] Sonorans welcomed foreign capital, Corral said, "and the benefit is generally mutual."

But speculators from abroad, no matter how witless, had no interest in risking money in a nest of thieves. They wanted guarantees of a safe haven. So Corral labored for a "safe" Sonora. He tolerated no attack on foreigners. When one occurred, no matter what its nature, he spared no effort to track down the perpetrators and to punish them. In these pursuits of *malhechores* ("offenders"), Corral took a personal role, as governor sending telegrams to prefects to make sure that punishment was meted out. "I repeat," he cautioned the prefect of Moctezuma, "be circumspect and aboveboard because the affair involves a foreigner."[83] When bandits robbed a Frenchman who was exploring the feasibility of settling Germans in Arizpe, Corral did not rest until the culprits were caught.[84] The release of a Mexican accused of theft by an American mine owner brought forth a stinging rebuke from Corral for the constable who set him free. Corral wanted the Mexican arrested again and taken to Hermosillo. The mine owner, it turned out, had complained to Corral.[85] That Corral came off with flying colors in his endeavor to transform Sonora into a haven for foreign capital, the American consul in Guaymas left no doubt. "Your

acts," he wrote don Ramón in bureaucratic jargon, give "proof of the
protection which foreigners in Sonora receive at the hands of the State
Government under your charge—and which is most satisfactory to our
American citizens in Sonora."[86] The consul could have taken a lesson
in writing but his meaning was perfectly clear.

VI

Corral was not just being altruistic. When he proffered the Mexican
abrazo ("embrace") to foreigners, he had his own welfare and that of
his *camarilla* in mind. Along with the merchant elite, he had both hands
in the pie, at times for all to see. Though he held public office, he
served on the board of directors of a foreign company.[87] León and Arturo Serna, along with Dionisio Gonzáles, all of elite, affluent families,
charged in a letter to Díaz that don Ramón had splattered himself with
mud in his dealings with foreigners. They referred specifically to Corral's ties with the Creston Colorado and Grand Central Mining companies in Minas Prietas, alleging that Corral had looked the other way
when the companies turned local constables and judges into their lackeys. To make matters worse, the companies had given Corral a gratuity
for years. In return, they enjoyed freedom from labor troubles and low
taxes. Worst of all, the letter concluded, Corral had threatened merchant houses and banks with government reprisals if they had anything
to do with either the Sernas or González.[88]

Over the course of years, Don Rámon became a wealthy man, a millionaire. His fortune dated from 1885 when, with friends, he dabbled
in mining. At Minas Prietas, Corral joined Howell Hinds, speculator
and mining company boss, Juan N. Bringas, of the Guaymas merchant
family, and Jesús Cruz and his wife to exploit the mines Blanca and
Julia.[89] Corral sold his share of what became the Grand Central Mining
and Milling Company for 50,000 pesos, plus stock in the enterprise for
his part in bringing about the sale. He went to New York City to collect
his share of the booty. From that moment, his biographer Uruchurtu
wrote, Corral made up his mind to get rich, realizing that while "politics had bequeathed him pie in the sky," that is, honor and admirers,
it had given him "no money."[90]

With his profits, Corral purchased the Molino Hermosillense, which
in just ten years had become the largest flour mill in the state with
yearly sales of 600,000 pesos, and took a two-month leave of absence
to attend to business. He was half-owner of the Compañía Explotadora
de Guaymas, the big lumber store; held 10 percent of the stock in the
Banco de Sonora; and owned shares in Grüning's brewery and the bar.

To top that, Corral used the machinery of the flour mill and lumberyard to manufacture and sell, at a profit, electricity to the cities of Hermosillo and Guaymas. By 1909, he had also acquired a foundry and an
hacienda.[91]

Despite his business deals and the tasks of public office, don Ramón
found time to serve as legal adviser and consultant to foreign mining
companies.[92] Astonishingly, in 1885, he was the executor of the will of
Matías Alsúa, the millionaire Guaymas mogul.[93] While perhaps techni-
cally innocent of wrongdoing, given the flabby ethics of the age, to enrich himself Corral undoubtedly bent the law. By granting monopolies
to himself, his friends, and foreigners, Corral incurred the wrath of
those left out in the cold.

Corral died as he had lived, a rich *politico* with friends, among them
important Amerian speculators. He was the offspring of a peripheral
country during the age of the New Imperialism, at a time when the
giant next door flexed its muscles and embarked on a hunt for empire,
justifying its quest by preaching Social Darwinism. Don Ramón merely
voiced the tenets of his time, at odds with the welfare of the poor. At the
end, he was a sick and embittered man. Alienated by the rebellion of
1910, he thought Mexico a "semi-civilized country."[94] Yet, despite his
myopia, Corral had kept the politics of Sonora on an even keel. When
he departed for Mexico City in 1900, he left a void. Without him, Torres and Izábal, *politicos* of lesser talents, ran the ship of state aground.

CHAPTER 15

Affluent Malcontents

I

Why the mutiny of 1910?

Oddly, the men who toppled the edifice of the Triumvirate had fared well under its tutelage. The malcontents who embraced Francisco I. Madero, son of a rich family from Coahuila, had tasted the affluence that came with economic growth. Part and parcel of the dependent bourgeoisie, these malcontents could thank American capital and markets for their good fortune. Nourished by dollars from north of the border, the economic boom of the times had suckled them.

But there was also logic in their rebellion. Kinks in the economy, specifically the depression brought about by the Financial Panic of 1907, shut the doors to upward mobility for the young and ambitious, and triggered discontent. The Yankee role had turned full circle. American dollars and customers had given birth to good times, but they had also created the structure of modern dependency. Local economic ills, part of the international malady of 1907, impaired its robustness, and ultimately sabotaged the structure that had been put together with the help of Yankees.

II

In the age of the New Imperialism, when the colonial powers partitioned Asia, Africa, and Latin America, the structure of dependency always teetered on the brink of disaster. The Mexican boom stood on shaky foundations. The stronger the bonds, the greater the dependency, and the more precarious the relationship. Between the 1880s and 1910, the people of Sonora had come to enjoy less and less control over their own destiny, eventually becoming, in all but name, a colonial satrapy. When Yankees enjoyed good times, so did their dependent offspring—more or less. A tremor north of the border shook the Mexican edifice.

The generation of the Triumvirate endured more than one such shock. The first, in the early 1870s, occurred just as Ignacio Pesqueira and his disciples of "free trade"—a euphemism for dependency—were about to lose political clout. The economic crisis probably helped bring about his fall, though it did not unduly rock the Mexican structure; after all, dependency was in its infancy. The next major capitalist downturn, in the early 1890s, hurt more. Dependency, hurt by the sharp drop in the price of silver, Mexico's chief source of foreign exchange, led Sonora to the edge of bankruptcy, to quote Ramón Corral.[1] So bad were conditions in the southern mining *municipios* that money to pay police and operate jails could not be found.[2] For lack of funds, Hermosillo turned over control of the port of Agiabampo, gateway to the *haciendas* in the Mayo Valley, to Mexico City.[3] The McKinley Tariff, curtailing the sale of Mexican goods on the American market, aggravated the problem. The economy recovered more or less, only to fall victim to the downturn of 1901. That crisis, as one Mexican economist wrote, shook the faith of Mexicans in their government.[4]

The early debacles hardly matched the violent shocks of the crisis of 1907. As Rafael de Zayas Enríquez informed Porfirio Díaz, the financial picture was "bad all over the world, but in Mexico it is frightful." An absence of confidence paralyzed the money market; banks turned into "places of hoarding" instead of "credit-giving institutions," while a pervasive "feeling of instability" swept over the country.[5] Among the states with close ties to the Yankee economy, Sonora felt the disaster most severely. Its budget dipped into the red, compelling Hermosillo to borrow from the Banco de Sonora to cover expenditures.[6] The cost of the Yaqui wars, crop failures, and a shortage of cheap labor, Governor Rafael Izábal lamented, added to the woes.[7] The crisis placed the budget in a "truly painful situation" by 1908, and was still "very distressing" in 1910.[8]

Small business especially was harmed. In Hermosillo, storekeepers, alleging that the crisis had hurt them most and "got worse by the day," refused to close their doors on Sundays, as the clerks in the big stores were demanding. Sales to workers, free to shop only on Sunday, were a key source of income for the small storekeepers; the big merchants made their big sales during the week.[9] The Guaymas *municipio*, declaring itself insolvent, suspended its public-works projects and borrowed 70,000 pesos from the Banco Nacional; even the Fábrica Industrial, property of the fashionable Fourcade family, had to postpone payment on its taxes because of the "terrible monetary crisis."[10] Bankruptcies of storekeepers in Arizpe district piled up, while public employees in Bacoachi had to take a cut in pay.[11] Next door, the *municipio* of Moctezuma, the most important in the district, went bankrupt, as did that of Fronteras.[12] Altar, that district's key town, could not meet expenses.[13] To the south, *municipios* in the Yaqui valley, judging by the situation in Cócorit, confronted a similar predicament.[14] Towns in Sahuaripa lacked funds for the salaries of their public employees.[15]

The blows fell unevenly, hurting some more than others. As a rule, big business weathered the storm better. Wholesale merchants, the big retailers, thought 1909 a good year and predicted more of the same for 1910, while banks, reported the United States consul, did business as usual. The Banco de Sonora, as was "its custom, paid a 16 percent dividend." True, exports fell, but the outlook for 1910 was "much better" partly because "a number of companies" planned "to operate on a much larger scale." The "opening of the railroad" to the Yaqui and Mayo valleys had put local mines in closer touch with markets in the United States.[16] Governor Izábal, speaking from the perspective of the big merchants, labeled the crisis "fleeting."[17]

On the political front, the periodic ups and downs translated into trouble for the ruling clique. According to Zayas Enríquez, the Mexican situation resembled the France of 1847, when the rich reserved for themselves "the public offices, the rich sinecures, the flattery of the powers that be . . . decorations" and the "handshakes of the Bourgeois king." He called it "the reign of the grocers," a term not inappropriate for the rule of the merchants who were managing affairs in Guaymas and Hermosillo. They alone "took part in public affairs; they alone were called, and consequently they alone were chosen."[18] Meanwhile, kinship ties linked the rulers, whether merchants or *hacendados*, nearly all being "white," *gente respetable* ("respectable people"), and members of the "four hundred."

III

During earlier good times, the nascent middle class had settled for a thin slice of the pie. Hard times, beginning with the downturn of 1901 and worsening with the crash of 1907, reduced the slice, cutting down openings for the middle class in business, commerce, mining, and agriculture. Without hope of rapid entry into the political arena, the middle class had to fend for itself—as it watched the old cabal mishandle the economy. Not until the appearance of hard times did the reign of the Triumvirate, a nemesis for only a tiny coterie before, become truly oppressive to the middle class. When governors stayed in office indefinitely during an economic downturn, stressed Zayas Enríquez, it destroyed the "legitimate ambitions of . . . the rest of the citizens, who think, reasonably enough, that they have a right to . . . the management of public affairs, either for the realization of their own cherished ideals or for the fulfillment of their ambition."[19] When in 1908 Porfirio Díaz promised the middle class entry into public office, he unlocked a pandora's box in Sonora, where the ambitious wanted to climb aboard the *carro completo* ("political machine").[20] With the exception of a handful of disgruntled labor spokesmen, nevertheless, none of the aspirants championed unorthodox doctrines or a rupture of ties with American capital and markets.

Actually, the political winds had begun to blow up a storm since the turn of the century. By 1901, with Corral in Mexico City, expectations had surfaced that fresh blood might filter into government, including even the governor's office.[21] One with hopes of such a change was Alberto Cubillas, *secretario de estado* and the most likely of the out-but-in aspirants to succeed. When speaking of Corral, Cubillas referred to him as "don Ramón," a reminder that a gap divided them.[22] Corral, Luis Emeterio Torres, and Izábal represented the old guard; Cubillas, at least in his own view, signaled the future.

The spirit of discontent, oddly enough, was strongest in regions of fastest growth.[23] Both the northeast and the south, where the Maderistas enjoyed recruiting triumphs, had intimate links with American capital and markets. In the northeast, the links were through mining, especially of copper; and in the south, the Southern Pacific Railway opened markets north of the border to the commercial farms of the Yaqui and Mayo valleys. In both, growth had brought dislocations to the social structure, giving life to a dependent labor class, especially in the northeast, while in the south the displacement of the Indian and the coming of cash crops altered old contours. The mining debacle of 1906, in the bargain, rained heavy blows on the economy of the northeast, while the Yaqui turmoil temporarily blocked the dreams of planters and merchants in the valleys. Meanwhile, Yankee capitalists, the copper magnates of Nacozari and Cananea, set the political tone in the northeast, as the Richardson Company did in the Yaqui Valley.

Elsewhere, discontent was somewhat different. *Hacendados* and merchants of Ures, having earlier lost political power to Hermosillo, had to sit by and see Izábal and his allies drive out the Yaquis, their principal source of cheap labor. Ramón C. Pacheco, a newspaperman, made a name for himself in Ures on this issue, castigating Hermosillo and Mexico City, and supporting Madero.[24] *La Bandera Sonorense*, an Ures journal, published ringing indictments of Izábal's policy. Francisco de Paula Morales, an *hacendado*, and his brother, members of Ures's high society, turned against the Triumvirate.[25] On the day of Díaz's electoral triumph, demonstrations against his reeletion flared in Ures, as they did in the mining towns of Cananea, La Colorada, and El Tigre, and in Sahuaripa, too. Alamos authorities jailed anti-reelectionists.[26] José María Maytorena, an *hacendado*, led the discontented in Guaymas, joined by Eugenio H. Gayou, Carlos E. Randall, and Adolfo de la Huerta, all men tied to the commerce of the city.[27]

In time, the fabric of peace woven by Corral and Torres simply unraveled. The heavy influx of foreign capital and the rising reliance on markets north of the border destabilized the native structure. Mining had given form to a wage-labor class living in shantytowns and totally at the mercy of outsiders. The campaigns against the Yaquis, waged for the benefit of the *camarilla* in Hermosillo and its allies, alienated Mexican planters the length and breadth of the state.

The discontented divided into two main camps. On one side stood the moderates, perhaps conservative by European political standards: the Maytorenas and their followers in Navojoa and Guaymas. These were *hacendados* and dirt farmers, joined by Yaquis still dreaming of the reconquest of their stolen lands, who resented the favoritism showered on the Richardsons and other Yankee land barons. On the other side stood a more radical group of unhappy Mexicans, wage workers and their spokesmen, usually middle class, heirs of the strike at Cananea. Their supporters were in the mining towns of Nacozari, La Colorada, and El Tigre, bastions of American enterprise. A few of them read *Regeneración*, the organ of Ricardo Flores Magón and his socialist disciples. On the margins stood still another group, the *Lerdistas*, the old families who had been ousted when don Porfirio came to power: the Urrea clan in Alamos, the Elías of Nogales and Cananea, and the Pesqueiras of Arizpe.[28]

Entrepreneurs on their way up, the middle class voiced the rhetoric of the disenchanted. In their struggle to keep up appearances, the middle class just made it from one day to the next. Tiny in the 1880s, it represented in 1910 but a fraction of the total population. On a national average, the "petite bourgeoisie" represented less than 5 percent of the economically active, with bureaucrats adding another 1.3 percent.[29] In 1884, Sonora had but twelve physicians, fourteen lawyers, and nine engineers out of 110 "professionals."[30] That number, however, included twenty-two Catholic priests and fifteen telegraph operators. By 1910, that group, roughly speaking, probably had quadrupled while customs brokers, business agents, and others in that category had multiplied manyfold. But the middle class in Nacozari, for instance, also included clerks in the *tienda de raya*, two Mexicans working in the assayer's office who wore coat and tie, and the clerk of the company library.[31] Whatever its size, perhaps as much as 8 percent of the population, a middle class existed, and its members were acutely aware of every economic crisis.

By opening up opportunities to many formerly on the edges of respectability, economic growth endangered traditional class distinctions. The "newly rich," living proof of the rewards awaiting "intelligence, perseverance and thrift," to quote Corral, introduced a discordant note into high society.[32] What Corral applauded not infrequently proved distasteful in traditional social circles. To protect their status, the old families banded together in informal alliances that now added blood to the definition of class. It was not enough to be wealthy; "time in rank," "culture," and family also became important criteria.[33] To enter into high society, to gain social acceptance, the newly rich had to await their turn, unless they were foreigners. A Yankee or European entrepreneur usually found ready acceptance, to the anger of ostracized Mexicans.

For Mexicans, barriers of class often proved thorny hurdles, even in the face of monetary success. To the old families, social differences transcended money when it suited them. Known by the term *familias de pulman* ("elite families"), the snobbish believed it was better to die of hunger than to work as a clerk in an office. Their offspring had to be "lawyers, physicians, or bankers," adding a prestigious profession to their good blood lines.[34] The *pulman* families, who exemplified the hardening of class distinctions, were found in all of the colonial towns, but especially in Alamos, Hermosillo, and Guaymas.[35] Plutarco Elías Calles, for example, a *político* of the future, grew up amidst the old families of Guaymas, who held to a prudish, small-town morality. Not until much later did his family name enable him to overcome the fact that he taught school, drank too much, and failed to carve out a niche for himself in commerce. The middle class aped the elite, fearing nothing more than to lose its "social status" by rubbing elbows with the worker.[36]

For the middle class caught betwixt and between, life was never easy. It was even harder during the two economic turndowns in the early years of the twentieth century. The depression of 1907, which endured until 1910, particularly jeopardized the status and aspirations of the middle class. The office workers of the supreme court in Hermosillo put the matter succinctly when they demanded a salary boost. Until eight or ten years before, they pointed out, a government employee could live well on a monthly salary of approximately ninety pesos. Rent was eight pesos a month for a "clean and decent house" and food another thirty pesos, more or less. The rest could be spent on "the kinds of clothes in keeping with the importance and category of the job." All of that had gone by the boards: rent for a house "just a notch above a hovel" now cost over thirty pesos monthly, "and much, much more for a decent home"; food prices had "risen sky high, becoming nearly inaccessible." So costly were meat, flour, beans, fuel, and electricity that a family of four or five had to spend three pesos a day on basic necessities. Given these circumstances, an office worker had nothing left for clothes. If someone in his family fell ill, the cost of medical care bankrupted him.[37]

The staff of the supreme court was not alone in its litany of complaints. The financial squeeze was felt everywhere. In the port city of Guaymas, which had the highest cost of living in the state, it was impossible to make ends meet, as one clerk declared. A monthly salary of eighty pesos, a clerk in Magdalena explained, did not cover elementary needs.[38] Employees in such dissimilar places as Bacerac, a town in Moctezuma, and Tórin, in the Yaqui Valley, voiced identical laments.[39] Meanwhile, the municipal fathers in Cananea, until recently a boom town, dismissed public employees, among them teachers, and cut the salaries of school inspectors, nurses, clerks in the courts, and police.[40] The unemployed had to fend for themselves. In Hermosillo, at the same time, Governor Izábal granted Alberto Cubillas, _secretario de estado_, a hefty raise of 100 pesos a month.[41]

To the resentment of the strapped middle class, foreigners in mining, commerce, or cattle ranching, along with Mexicans allied with the cabal in Hermosillo, received special treatment. For example, some got tax exemptions from the state and the _municipios_ for "5, 10 or more years." Without friends in high places, the middle class had to "pay its taxes in accordance with legislation"; storekeepers had to "compete with the recipients of tax concessions."[42] Nationalism, part and parcel of the rising anti-Yankee mood, took root wherever Mexicans rubbed elbows with large numbers of well-off and powerful foreigners, particularly in the mining towns.

One exemplary case was Cananea. On the eve of the strike in 1906, Esteban Baca Calderón, a timekeeper in the Oversight mine, ended a stirring speech on the anniversary of the Mexican victory at Puebla on May 5 by appealing to the miners "not to permit capitalism to use them as beasts of burden," warning them against "capitalists who shunt us aside with their legion of blond and blue-eyed devils." Surprised and frightened by the speech, Filiberto V. Barroso, the mayor of Cananea, sent a copy to Governor Izábal. To his later regret, the governor ignored it.[43] At Cananea, too, Baca Calderón, in company with Lázaro Gutiérrez de Lara, a lawyer, and Manuel M. Diéguez, a clerk, helped found the Unión Liberal Humanidad, a worker's club. Juan G. Cabral, among the first to take up arms against the Triumvirate, was a cashier in the Cananea lumberyard.[44]

Middle-class Mexicans in town were split over the strike. Among its sympathizers were a school inspector and two teachers, as well as the mining agent and postal chief. Barroso, the mayor, thought it a mistake to use American rangers, while a physician who sympathized with the strikers had to flee across the border. In Naco, Crispín Gutiérrez, a customs agent, defended the strikers. For opposing Izábal, they lost their jobs. Not all middle-class Mexicans in town, obviously, hated Yankees or wanted the Triumvirate out of office. A Mexican constable kept order for the 4C's, while other loyal Mexican employees took refuge in the home of William C. Greene.[45]

IV

Opposition to the political status quo built up slowly during the first decade of the 1900s. This era, characterized by booms and debacles, was a tenuous time for the middle class. Protests broke out in 1901, coinciding with the economic downturn; flowered again after 1908, when the depression jarred the economy loose; and matured in 1910, spurred on by continuing hard times and by the leadership of Madero. Ties of class and age, generally speaking, tied together the currents of protest.

The protest in Hermosillo, where Vicente Escalante, Corral's father-in-law, was mayor for fourteen years, marked the initial stage. To the sorrow of the younger *gente decente* ("genteel people"), who thought the departure of Corral for Mexico City might open up some public offices, Escalante wanted to keep his job, a wish backed by the lords of commerce and banking. The dissidents backed Dionisio González, son of one of the biggest landowners in Sonora, rich since a fabulous gold strike in California. Young Dionisio, a *diputado* in the state legislature, had earlier served on the city council. His backers included Adolfo and Eduardo Ruiz, sons of the owner of La Fama, a major merchant house, a man who was also agent for the Banco Nacional de México and a friend of Corral; Arturo and León Serna, cousins of the candidate and related by blood to General Francisco Serna, a *notable*; the editors of

El Sol and *El Demócrata*; and José C. Camou, of the Guaymas and Hermosillo clan. Plácido Ríos, a Gonzalez supporter who was a writer for *El Sol*, also backed the strikers at Cananea. Jailed and sent off to fight Yaquis, he gained his freedom only when his mother convinced her friend Corral to intervene.

As one writer put it, González and his followers were from the *"clase media decente,"* the middle class with proper credentials, and many were young. When mayor Escalante and his backers called themselves the Club Colorado, González and his friends adopted the color green, becoming known as the Club Verde, a name made famous by the waltz *"Club Verde"* of Rodolfo Campodónico, a young musician. His *"Club Verde"* went on to rival in popularity *"Sobre las Olas,"* a favorite of the Díaz regime. The election of 1901, however, favored Escalante; the elder Ruiz lost his post as agent of the Banco Nacional; and the opposition, confronted with the use of force, melted away. A timid blow, nevertheless, had been struck against nepotism and the perpetual officeholder.[46]

Out of the ashes of the Club Verde rose the Reyistas (1908). Backers of General Bernardo Reyes, they established clubs in Guaymas, Hermosillo, and Navojoa. Predominantly middle class and young, the Reyistas called for no reelection, meaning Vice-President Corral would be replaced by Reyes, who ultimately would step into the shoes of the aging Díaz. Their campaign won adherents everywhere, particularly in Guaymas, where the Reyistas were headed by a physician, José San Román, with the collaboration of Adolfo de la Huerta, both of good families. Reyes proved a clay idol: he accepted exile rather than challenge Díaz. His backers then organized a Club Anti-reeleccionista, a backer of Francisco I. Madero. Led by José María Maytorena and De la Huerta, the Reyistas included Eugenio H. Gayou, Victor M. Venegas, Carlos Plank, Carlos E. Randall, and Plutarco Elías Calles. To undermine them, the cabal in Hermosillo urged the merchants of the port city to dismiss employees who joined the movement.[47]

When Reyes abandoned Mexico, the spunky Madero took up the cudgel. He too was backed by young men of good standing. Like Reyes, Madero wanted to replace Corral, then climb to the presidential chair with the death of Díaz, who was eighty years of age in 1910. His backers, former Reyistas, included Club Verde partisans. One of the anti-reelectionists was Luis Iberri, son of a prominent merchant in Guaymas. He later was briefly jailed for his role in the anti-Díaz protest.[48] To add fuel to the fires of discontent, Madero visited Sonora, arriving in Navojoa in January 1910, and going on to Alamos, Guaymas, and Hermosillo. Local authorities proved markedly hostile, reported Madero, but not the people.[49] Madero had received an enthusiastic reception from Benjamín G. Hill Salido and his friends in Navojoa, among them Flavio A. Borquez, the clerk of the town council.[50] In Guaymas, where Maytorena and his entourage waited, Madero estimated that a crowd of 3,000 had turned out to hear him, despite efforts by the mayor to prevent him from speaking.[51]

At Alamos, he was awaited by a large crowd "of diverse social classes, from young ladies of the aristocracy to humble field hands." At the reception in his honor, there were many distinguished family names: Salido, Goycolea, Urrea, Güereña, and Adrián Marcor, Madero's host in Alamos. What tickled Madero about his visit to Alamos was that anti-reelectionists included not merely "poor intellectuals, the middle class and wage workers" but the "well-off."[52] When the prefect of Alamos, Francisco A. Salido, attempted to cut short Madero's visit, Antonio and Alfonso Goycolea joined Urrea and Salido to protest his behavior to Díaz.[53] Alamos, of course, had fallen on evil days with the decline of silver; it was a dying town.

The city epitomized changes taking shape everywhere. Madero had witnessed the falling-out of the old families. Younger *notables*, eager to steer the ship of state, no longer shared the enthusiasm of their parents and older relatives for the Triumvirate. Political differences sometimes divided families. Epifanio Salido and Alfonso Goycolea, the founders of the anti-reelectionist club in Alamos, were uncles of Hill and cousins of Francisco A. Salido, the prefect and ally of Corral and Torres. Epifanio's father, Francisco Salido, a crony of Corral, had brought him into public office, along with his brother, Felipe, a high official in public education. Another branch of the Salidos, descendants of Jesús Salido, an *hacendado* in the Mayo Valley, remained loyal to the cabal in Hermosillo. The Salido Muñoz family, to which Epifanio belonged, like other *notables* of Alamos judged that change would be beneficial.[54]

North of Guaymas, Madero encountered a less hospitable climate. Authorities let Madero speak but employed hecklers to taunt him, a change in tactics authorized by Acting Governor Cubillas.[55] A mere 300 people turned out for Madero in Hermosillo; its residents, favored by the cabal, had little reason to complain. As one of them recalled, "everyone had a job, no one went hungry and a liberty of sorts prevailed."[56] Among the Maderistas were Eduardo Ruiz and his brother, Club Verde stalwarts. Others were Alfredo Caturegli, a physician; Ramón P. Denegri, a telegraph operator; Jesús Abitia, a photographer; and Cosme Hinojosa, a traveling salesman. The *notables* of Hermosillo, unlike those of Alamos, ignored Madero. From Hermosillo, Madero departed for Chihuahua, reported Cubillas, who called Madero's "political speeches in Sonora a total calamity."[57] To make certain, nonetheless, that nothing impeded the "reelection" of don Porfirio, Cubillas and his clique jailed dissidents in Cananea and Guaymas.[58]

Significantly, some of the leading spokesmen of the opposition met their tormentors face to face in early 1911. Confronted with the possible downfall of don Porfirio, General Torres, on leave from his job as governor, called together a *Junta de Notables*, a meeting of the dignitaries of Sonora, to decide on a future course. He met with Cubillas, the prefects, mayors of key *municipios*, and outspoken malcontents. About 300 individuals came together in the Palacio Municipal of Hermosillo, among them Maytorena and Randall of Guaymas, Hill and Bórquez of Navojoa, and Marcor of Alamos. With news of the uprising in Sahuaripa, the effort at conciliation collapsed.[59]

   That Torres, a lifelong ally of Díaz, should think conciliation possible with his foes reveals much about the opposition's character, politics, and goals.

                                    V

Who were these disciples of change? With only scattered exceptions, the majority belonged to the middle class and, on occasion, the upper class. They had enjoyed a relative degree of success but, with just one exception, none had struck it rich. They saw themselves as unsuccessful entrepreneurs. Additionally, many of them had dealt with American capitalists either directly or indirectly. Eugenio H. Gayou, a mining engineer, for example, had been a federal mining agent in Cananea from 1905 to 1906, a post that put him in daily contact with Greene's 4C's.[60] Surely he had an inkling of what led the miners to strike. Like Gayou a native of Guaymas, Carlos E. Randall, the son of an American father and a Mexican mother, was a mining speculator, the owner of copper, gold, and silver claims in Cumuripa and San Marcial. To his sorrow, none yielded hidden treasures. Always on the lookout for ways to fill his pocketbook, Randall owned land that had once belonged to the Sonora and Sinaloa Irrigation Company on the outskirts of Bácum in the Yaqui valley. His mining forays, and his later role as an assayer of ores, put Randall in close touch with Americans, most of them far more successful than he. He also dabbled in commerce in Guaymas, and published *El Elector*, a newspaper with a Maytorena slant. In 1909, he asked to be appointed tax agent for the district of Guaymas but, although he had important backers, he did not get the job.[61]

   Carlos Plank, the son of an American father, was born in the mining town of Baroyeca in 1876 and, as a young man, settled in La Colorado, becoming a mining speculator and traveling salesman. The decline of mining in La Colorada and neighboring Minas Prietas hit Plank hard. Whether he turned to crime because of the difficult times or not, in 1906, Plank was found guilty of forgery by the court of first instance in Hermosillo.[62]

Salvador Alvarado arrived in Sonora in the 1880s. Like his father, he had been a storekeeper in Pótam, a town in the Yaqui in Richardson Company territory; his father had been among the first to settle there. From Pótam, after a stint as a clerk in a drugstore in Guaymas, Alvarado journeyed to Cananea, Mr. Greene's bastion, where he once held the concession to employ twenty-three Yaquis to labor on Greene's Cananea, Yaqui, and Pacífico railroad. Eventually, Alvarado joined the anti-reelectionists. Juan G. Cabral, a native of Minas Prietas, an American mining town, had been a student at the University of Arizona.[63] Manuel Mascareñas, rancher, broker, and banker, had a home in the border town of Nogales. Another anti-reelectionist, Ramón P. Denegri, worked for the Southern Pacific Railroad. In Navajoa, Francisco Serrano, a bookeeper by trade, helped don Angel Almada, a merchant, sell goods to workers building the Southern Pacific line through the Mayo valley. Ramón V. Sosa, later colonel and prefect of Altar, had been mayor of Minas Prietas and sold water to the Grand Central Mining Company, both controlled by Americans.[64] Manuel M. Diéguez, an instigator of the strike of 1906, was an employee of the 4C's. Working in Cananea as a clerk when Madero's rebellion broke out was Abelardo Rodríguez, a future president of Mexico and a native of San José de Guaymas who had attended primary school in Nogales.[65] He spoke English like a native, and thought American capitalism exemplary. Severiano Talamantes, the martyr of the revolt in Sahuaripa and a native of Alamos district, had been mayor of Promontorios, an American mining sanctuary.[66]

The father of Adolfo de la Huerta, a key malcontent, held stocks in the Compañía Unión Minera of Las Prietas, an American concern. Don Torcuato's son Adolfo, an accountant by training and a singer by avocation, went to school in Mexico City, returning to Guaymas to become a teller of the Banco Nacional de México. By 1909, he was manager of the Tenería San Germán, a leather factory owned by the family of Francisco Fourcade. De la Huerta was a nephew of Adrián Marcor, an *hacendado* in Minas Nuevas, an American mining camp, and agent for the Guaymas merchant house of Francisco Seldner. Adolfo's father was for forty years a partner of the Iberri family, merchant kingpins of Guaymas.[67] Wenceslao, one of the Iberri dynasty, was the authorized agent for the Mutual Life Insurance Company of New York, the Union Assurances Society of London, and the Judson Dynamite Powder Company. His son, about Adolfo's age, backed Madero in 1910. While never directly identified with an American enterprise, De la Huerta, as merchant and banker, was beholden to a Guaymas economy dependent on markets, capital, and goods from north of the border.

His companion in politics, the *hacendado* José María Maytorena, had roots in the Guaymas valley. The clan's progenitor, don Chemalía, a nationalist first and last, spent a lifetime trying to convince the *camarilla* in Hermosillo to favor Mexicans over Yankees. As a regional *cacique*, don Chemalía twice sought the governorship, losing out the last time to Torres and Corral. When Bernardo Reyes attempted to replace Díaz, José María Maytorena, don Chemalía's son, entered politics. Don Pepe, as José María was known, attended Santa Clara College in California, and spoke English, but shared his father's nationalist sentiments.[68] He watched from the political sidelines while the Richardsons and friends of the Triumvirate acquired lands in the Yaqui valley, a stone's throw away from his Guaymas bailiwick.

The *haciendas* of the Maytorenas, moreover, had always depended on Yaqui labor. For shielding his Yaqui workers, Ramón, an older brother of José María, was sentenced to sixteen months in jail. Two other Maytorenas were imprisoned for the same reason.[69] From the start, don Pepe vehemently protested the deportation of the Yaquis, even traveling to Mexico City to confer with Díaz. Deportation, he explained, deprived his eight *haciendas* of their field hands. Angered by the indifference of Díaz and the cabal in Hermosillo to his pleas, don Pepe turned Reyista in 1908 and then backed Madero. Oddly enough, don Pepe had the confidence of the ruling cabal, who, upon his request in 1908, allowed him to import 2,000 cartridges for his rifles. Earlier, he had won election to the town council of Guaymas and gone fishing with Corral.[70]

Francisco de Paula Morales, an *hacendado* from Ures, the Athens of Mexico, headed a powerful clan. His father, Lauro, sired a family of twelve. After the merchants, the *hacendados* were the most powerful group in the state. In Ures, they helped run politics. Alberto was a lawyer while his brother Arturo owned a Guaymas hardware store, one of the town's biggest business establishments.[71] Like Maytorena, Francisco had been elected to the town council and, as an *hacendado*, had time and again protested the deportation of the Yaquis, fearing, as Maytorena did, that he would be left without workers to till his lands. Don Francisco had no stomach for a policy designed in Hermosillo to favor the cabal's supporters, Americans among them. When Madero challenged Díaz in 1911, Morales furnished nearly two-thirds of the armed men for the first clash, many of them field hands from his *haciendas*.[72]

After don Porfirio's fall, Morales, Gayou, Randall, and Maytorena, in that order, became governors of Sonora. Members of the Guaymas clan had at last tasted victory. Unfortunately for them, Madero died and Maytorena, their kingpin, fell from grace. Eventually, Ignacio L. Pesqueira, the son of the old *caudillo*, replaced them in Hermosillo. A native of Huepac, a town on the Río Sonora, Pesqueira had taught school, served as mayor of Banámichi, and made money as a merchant there, in Aconchi, and in Santa Elena, an American mining town. He put his profits into mining but went bankrupt, and had to sell his stores. In 1901, he moved to Cananea, worked briefly for the 4C's, later became a bookkeeper for a commercial house, and, in the course of time, won election to the town council in 1908.

An affable man, Pesqueira had mastered the art of making friends with a diverse lot, from Governor Izábal, who once offered to name him a *diputado* to the state legisature, to Salvador Alvarado, who despised Izábal. Pesqueira was on good terms with merchants in Guaymas, Hermosillo, and Ures and, on the American side, in Nogales, Bisbee, and Douglas. Cattle ranchers, both Americans and Mexicans, liked don Ignacio. When Corral stopped over in Cananea in 1904, Pesqueira formed part of the reception committee; in the manner of a friend, Corral gave him an *abrazo*. Pesqueira, who spoke English, had a brother—a merchant, *hacendado*, and flour mill owner—in Arizpe—who became prefect in the waning days of the Triumvirate. Yet Pesqueira, to his credit, met with Governor Izábal in 1906 to plead for the strikers. None of them, he explained, was "against the government"; they only wanted better pay and better working conditions. Pesqueira thought Mr. Greene could do more for them.[73]

The adventures of Plutarco Elías Calles, remembered by history as the rebel hero who declined to join the plot against the Triumvirate, make a tale of a different sort. Calles, of course, changed his mind later, after Izábal and Torres had departed and the dethroned don Porfirio had taken up residence in Paris. In 1910, whatever else he may have thought, Calles had no wish to turn rebel. As he told De la Huerta, his "friend and protector Alberto Cubillas" was the interim governor. Calles did not want to "hurt or disturb the man to whom he owed so much."[74] That debt included jobs as mayor of Fronteras and municipal treasurer of Guaymas. Yet once the rebels ousted the old guard, Calles embraced Madero, eventually becoming governor of Sonora and president of Mexico. The early life of this dispassionate rebel, plagued by character shortcomings and failures, on more than one occasion had been intertwined with Americans.

Don Plutarco, offspring of a family of *notables*, had old roots in Sonora. The original patriarch, Francisco Elías González de Zayas, a native of La Rioja in Spain, settled in Alamos in 1729. A rancher and farmer, he died in Arizpe, along the way having risen to captain in the militia. One illustrious descendant, José María Elías González, died with a reputation for political dexterity. In 1810, he helped quash the first outbreak of Mexican independence fever. Then he switched sides, became a hero, and ended up as governor of Sonora.

Calles, as he was known throughout his life, was born in Guaymas when it had but 4,000 inhabitants. A bastard son, the child of Plutarco Elías and doña Jesús Campuzano, Calles, after the death of his mother, was raised by Juan B. Calles, the owner of a saloon in Hermosillo with yearly sales of 1,340 pesos.[75] In gratitude, young Calles adopted his foster father's name. Yet, as he grew older, Calles rebuilt his bridges to his father and the Elías clan. In his youth, Calles taught school, served briefly as a school inspector, and resigned as treasurer of Guaymas, the job Cubillas bequeathed him, when confronted with a shortage of 125 pesos. Having lost his public post through scandal and his teaching job because of heavy drinking, Calles found a savior in his half brother, Arturo Elías, who made him manager of a small hotel in Guaymas. Calles, so the story goes, had long known the Hotel México because of its bar. A pliable *politico*, Arturo went on to become a diplomat for don Porfirio, whom he admired, and then for the men who toppled him.[76]

Tall, robust, tough of character, and hardly merciful, Calles assiduously cultivated the elite of the port city, attending fancy balls and aping the fashions of the young and the rich. In the winter, that meant wearing a black suit, a black derby, and black patent leather shoes. At age twenty-five, he married Natalia Chacón, daughter of don Andrés, chief of the harbor guard, a job of some prestige. At the urging of his biological father, Calles moved with his wife and child to Arizpe, the cradle of the Elías clan, to become boss of the Hacienda Santa Rosa, a shaky venture. Along with the 9,000 hectares of Santa Rosa, the Elías clan controlled *haciendas* totaling 25,000 hectares—all on the fringes of the Cananea Cattle Company. On these lands, the Elíases ran 16,000 head of cattle and horses. While at Santa Rosa, Calles on four occasions attempted to acquire mining properties on the Sierra La Mesteña from Mexico City. Each time, much to his disgust as a biographer said, he learned that they had been granted to an American.[77]

Santa Rosa did not reward Calles with the money he coveted. So in 1906, when James Smithers, the Guaymas agent for Smithers, Nadenhold and Company of New York, offered him the job of manager of a flour mill in Fronteras, Calles took it. He became mayor of the town as well and something of a civic spokesman.[78] Unfortunately for Calles, he proved a poor manager; the mill was bankrupt by 1909. Having failed again, Calles returned to Guaymas with Smithers to establish, in a building owned by Maytorena, the firm of Elías, Smithers y Cía., specializing in the sale of animal feed, seeds, and flour. When that too collapsed, Calles, again with Smithers, moved to Agua Prieta to establish an import business. There he became a friend of the general manager of the Moctezuma Copper Company who, according to Calles, permitted him to bring goods across the border on its private railway to avoid paying customs duties. The resale of the imported duty-free goods, handled in Agua Prieta by the firm of Elías, Fuentes y Cía., netted its owners healthy profits.[79]

That Calles was at least partly responsible for his multiple failures hardly requires proof. But it is also true that his misfortunes, at Santa Rosa as well as Fronteras, befell him during the hard times, largely of Yankee manufacturer, that followed the collapse of the mining economy. The flour mill, for one, lying between Nacozari and Cananea, was hurt immediately by high unemployment in the mining towns. Guaymas promised tenuous rewards for a grain business started in 1909, a time of poor sales. Calles failed to win the mining concession he coveted because, through no fault of his own, it was granted to an American. Ironically, the one business that paid him dividends, the general store in Agua Prieta, depended on the willingness of an American mining boss to hoodwink Mexican customs. Even so, on the eve of the demise of the Torres cabal, Calles, ever on the lookout for his pot of gold, had failed to strike it rich.

Alvaro Obregon Salido, heir of the Alamos clan, eventually joined Calles in the pantheon of heroes. That is another story. Obregón Salido, an up-and-coming garbanzo planter from Huatabampo, waited until the victory of Madero to toss his hat into the political ring. He became a malcontent only with the death of the Apostle Madero. Unlike his cousin Benjamín G. Hill of Navojoa, Obregón Salido lifted not a finger to topple Torres and Izabál.

VI

From the perspective of historical hindsight, that affluent malcontents should sink the troubled ship of state appears almost inevitable. They were legatees of a boom that was principally of American origin. When events north of the border ran the economy aground after 1906, the young and ambitious entrepreneurs turned on their patrons. The Mexicans, the Torres and Corral gang, they turned out of office; the Americans, when the economy returned to normal, they learned to live with. In their about-face, the malcontents made their peace with the Yankee capitalist, both as customer and investor. All things considered, the rebels merely replaced their old nemesis, the Hermosillo cabal, becoming, in time, another dependent bourgeoisie. The new Mexican faces on board the ship of state were appearing for the first time, but for the forseeable future the old vessel of dependency, as well as the Americans piloting it, would remain the same.

EPILOGUE

I

The Porfiriato, the years from 1880 to 1910, set in place the brick and mortar of the structure that would become modern Sonora. Much of the old colonial edifice toppled, replaced by an economy that, if not entirely new, at least had an up-to-date facade. Changes in Western capitalism largely made that possible. The shift in Europe and the United States from imports (buying raw materials and minerals) to exports (the sale of manufactured goods) altered not only the economies of the peripheral nations but the nature of their societies as well. Partly as a result, Sonora came to be a dependent society, tied lock, stock, and barrel to its northern neighbor.

II

From its early days, Sonora walked the colonial path, from the Conquest until 1821 as the child of Spain, and then in the nineteenth century as a market for articles of English and French manufacture. Nonetheless, colonial Spain was hardly a commercial or industrial giant, and the later ties with Europe were tenuous. Relatively speaking, Sonora managed to survive on its own. Its links with Mexico City after Independence hardly kept its economy alive, but that isolation went by the wayside during the years of the Porfiriato. Between the fall of Ignacio Pesqueira and the day don Porfirio departed to spend his waning days in Paris, Sonora underwent a striking transformation.

III

Bonds with Western capitalism, especially North American, left multiple benefits behind. At the top of the list, perhaps, stood the railroad, joining Arizona to Guaymas and, eventually, going as far south as Mazatlán. For Sonora, the economic good times of the Porfiriato rode on iron rails. The railroad swung open the portal to mining. Now heavy industrial metals could be shipped at a profit. With exports of copper leading the way, state revenues climbed, providing funds for public improvements. Fancy public buildings went up, electricity turned night into day in many a plaza, cities had better water systems, and schools benefited, as did a host of other ambitious schemes. Entrepreneurs laid out telegraph lines and, by 1910, here and there the telephone had made its bow.

On the heels of the mining boom in copper and, in time, other industrial metals, the fortunes of silver had a brief upsurge. Alamos, the silver metropolis of colonial society, took on new life, in part because Ramón Corral, a mighty political figure in Hermosillo, thought of it as home. During a short interlude, Alamos also waxed rich with the opening of the Mayo valley to export agriculture. For the most part, pioneers in the valley came from Alamos. By 1910, the garbanzo, sold in Spain, Cuba, and the United States, had established its hegemony in the Mayo valley. Up the road a bit, the steel plow also dug its way into the fertile lands in the Yaqui. The original owners, the Yaqui Indians, had lost their valley to the Richardson brothers and Mexicans of like bent.

Economic growth sired a middle class, small but able and ambitious. It prospered principally in the towns and cities, largely in Hermosillo, Guaymas, and Alamos, but not exclusively. In the new commercial entrepôts such as Nogales, creations of the railroad, middle-class Mexicans, sporting dark suits, white shirts, and ties, were much in evidence. Until 1907, the lads of the middle class, along with the gentlemen *notables*, celebrated the virtues of economic growth. The crash of that year gave the middle class a different perspective, turning jubilance into discontent and then outrage.

While material rewards had the starring role in this era, culture, spelled with a capital C, also made an entrance upon the stage. Beginning with Pesqueira, the moguls of Sonora equated literacy with progress, and erected schools. No matter how bare the financial cupboard, Corral always found funds for education. The state's most illustrious institution was the Colegio de Sonora, a school in Hermosillo with lofty standards, books and dedicated teachers. Although education thrived first and foremost in the cities and towns, schools existed in scores of isolated hamlets, at times for students of both sexes, an uncommon occurrence elsewhere in the Republic. Along with the residents of Chihuahua and Coahuila, Sonorans topped the list of the nation's literates. Over a third of the state's population (35 percent) could read and write. Only the Federal District, home to the nation's capital, could claim a greater proportion of literate Mexicans (50 percent). Along with Corral, men and women in towns all over Sonora bought books, built libraries to house them, and attended the theater, occasionally to applaud actors from faraway Mexico City. The adornments of urban sophistication had invaded the desert kingdom.

Economic growth and political stability went hand in glove. Until 1910, Sonora, to the delight of both foreign and Mexican entrepreneurs, enjoyed law and order. Peace, virtually absent from the departure of the Spaniards until the 1880s, reigned again. Apart from the intermittent wars with the Indians, the chaos of yesterday lingered only as a memory—that is, nearly everywhere. Stubborn borderland enclaves, Fronteras for one, still resisted pacification; however, their outlaw days were numbered. Law and order meant the politics of continuity. Scores of men, part of the entrenched oligarchy, stayed in office year after year. In Hermosillo, a Triumvirate ruled, first Luis Emeterio Torres, then Ramón Corral, then Rafael Izábal, rotating the governor's job. Of the trio, only don Ramón displayed a calling for public administration, the day-to-day handling of politics. These gentlemen almost invariably piloted the ship of state, directing everyone from the legislature to the prefects of the districts and on down to the mayors of the towns. The *municipios*, once the redoubts of local autonomy, lost much of their importance, especially outside the "big" cities. Economic growth hardly nurtured democracy; to the contrary, the requirements of foreign investment demanded stability at all costs, else the house built with outside capital and markets falls apart.

Once, in the not too distant past, historians, acting in accord with popular custom, labeled Porfirio Díaz a dictator, interpreting provincial decisions in the light of Mexico City's dictates. Most Mexican scholars, whether in Mexico City or the provinces, now believe otherwise. Don Porfirio, although inclined to manage affairs with a firm hand, knew the rules of politics. In central Mexico he might insist on getting his way, but he recognized that staying in office required a measure of flexibility. The greater the distance between Mexico City and the provincial capital, the greater the flexibility. That was the case with distant Sonora, a state loyal to Díaz but with a mind of its own. The relationship between Mexico City and Hermosillo more often than not was a marriage of convenience. Collaboration benefited both. Conflicts of interest were usually settled by mutual agreement. The record of the Triumvirate, and of the edifice it helped build, make that clear.

IV

Be that as it may, foreign investment, mainly Yankee by 1910, left an unsavory legacy. With the arrival of modern dependency, unexpected disadvantages came to light. To start with, the Mexican bourgeoisie, no matter how well off, did not control its own destiny. Neither did the infant middle class. Everyone, figuratively speaking, took his marching orders from capitalists and markets on "the other side." The consumer, a buyer in New York, Chicago, or London, called the tune. The relative self-sufficiency of an earlier day, when goods were exchanged between town and country, declined. More and more, goods passed through Nogales or Guaymas, increasingly with North American labels. Mexican merchants simply purchased for resale articles made in North American factories. Despite the flour mills, most of them antedating the arrival of Yankee dollars, industrialization never got off the ground. Little indicates that foreign capital encouraged Mexicans to build industry of their own. Without it, dependency, the need to rely on outlanders, would always be a harsh necessity.

The importance of capital, particularly by way of railroads and mining, introduced capitalism's acknowledged contradictions. Along with the flowering of a bourgeoisie, a proletariat made its entrance. The silver mining centers of Alamos district had given birth to this class of wage workers. Its rapid growth, nonetheless, had to await the coming of the copper bastions of the north: Cananea, Nacozari, and lesser camps. Class consciousness, the sense of belonging to a working sector, grew slowly, to blossom during the famous strike at Cananea in 1906. Miners not only abandoned their jobs in protest against poor pay and heartless conditions but, in the popular fashion, organized mutualist societies. Unorthodox literature circulated among the more daring, specifically the publications of Ricardo Flores Magón. Radical ideas, justifying labor unions and strikes, won adherents in such places as Cananea, where wages were the highest in Mexico.

Capitalism, in addition, helped to sabotage the remnants of Spanish colonial society. By imposing different economic relationships, it split society into antagonistic classes, pitting wage workers, the new proletariat, against foreign capitalists and their Mexican allies. Hard times, which followed the collapse of mining boom, ultimately led workers to unite with dissatisfied elements of the middle class and angry *hacendados* and to shoulder arms against the Old Regime.

The labor requirements of foreign capitalists, first on the railroads and later mining, introduced another discordant note that would come to haunt the so-called revolutionary governments. Unable to find cheap labor to lay their tracks, the railroad magnates, taking a leaf from their experience in California, imported Chinese coolies. Mostly male, they numbered no more than 4,500 by 1910, though that figure gave Sonora the biggest Chinese population in Mexico. They rapidly improved their economic status. Hard-working and ambitious, they did not long tarry doing manual toil. They quickly moved into commerce, to the unhappiness of race-conscious Mexicans, who from the first were hostile to the Chinese. Many became merchants setting themselves up as storekeepers, especially in the cities, commercial entrepôts, and mining camps. A few became owners of small "factories" turning out cheap shoes for miners and other workers. In such places as Magdalena, Chinese stores rivaled the important native business houses. Before long, envious Mexican merchants were blaming their Chinese competitors for financial difficulties. The Chinese "problem" as Mexicans defined it, further split the fabric of society, bringing out, as had the war on the Yaquis, the worst in Sonorenses.

Equally tragic, mining, the heartspring of economic growth, proved ephemeral. Once ores were dug or international demand dropped, the mines shut down. By the scores, mining camps and towns became ghost towns, mute reminders of the vanished world of the miner. As the Old Regime tottered, many of the mining landmarks were thus reduced, including lordly Promontorios, La Aduana, and Minas Prietas. With the exception of the copper kingdoms of the north, this was ultimately the fate of mining in Sonora. Even Cananea and Nacozari had their good and bad times, and neither recaptured its glory years after the depression of 1907. Mining, Sonorenses learned, could not be counted on to erect solid, enduring foundations. By relying on mining, the people of Sonora had tied their destiny to a kite.

It was inevitable that foreign capital and its bearers should sew the seeds of cultural change. Next door to an expanding Arizona economy that daily brought new arrivals from the East, Sonorenses began to copy the ways of their neighbors across the border. North American culture—modernity, some called it—reshaped local customs, habits, and even values. The Spanish language underwent modifications, adding to its vocabulary "chance," "coctel," "pichel," "sandwich," and even "gademes" and "sanabichis." Once Paris had set dress fashions, now they arrived by way of New York, Los Angeles, and Tucson. For better or for worse, the Americanization of Sonora had begun.

NOTES TO CHAPTERS

BY WAY OF INTRODUCTION

1. *Dependency and Development in Latin America*; translated by Marjory Mattingly Urquidi (Berkeley and Los Angeles, 1979), pp. xiv–xv.

2. *Ibid.*, p. xvi–xv.

3. *Ibid.*, pp. xvi and 72.

4. Samir Amin, *Unequal Development; An Essay on the Social Formations of Peripheral Capitalism* (London and New York, 1976), p. 9; Harry Magdoff, *Imperialism: From the Colonial Age to the Present* (London and New York, 1978), p. 102.

5. "The Crisis of the Seventeenth Century," Trevor Asten, ed., *Crisis in Europe, 1560–1660* (New York, 1967), p. 24.

6. Magdoff, *Imperialism*, pp. 108, 118.

7. Amin, *Unequal*, p. 161.

8. Albert Szymanski, *The Logic of Imperialism* (New York, 1981), p. 105.

9. *Ibid.*, p. 104.

10. Amin, *Unequal*, p. 163.

11. Szymanski, *Logic*, p. 112.

12. *Ibid.*, p. 104.

13. Magdoff, *Imperialism*, p. 86.

CHAPTER 1

1. Gregorio Mora Torres, "Los comerciantes de Guaymas y el desarrollo económico de Sonora, 1825–1910," Instituto de Investigaciones Históricas, *IX simposio de historia de Sonora* (Hermosillo, 1984), p. 220.

2. Jesús Felix Uribe García, "Monografía sobre la historia de las comunicaciones en Sonora, segunda mitad del siglo xix, las diligencias" (Unpublished Manuscript, Hermosillo, 1981), p. 7.

3. Beene Delmar Leon, "Sonora in the Age of Ramón Corral, 1875–1900" (Ph.D. thesis, University of Arizona, Tucson, 1972), p. 1.

4. Uribe García, *Monografía*, pp. 11, 13–14.

5. Consuelo Boyd, "Twenty Years to Nogales: The Building of the Guaymas-Nogales Railroad," *The Journal of Arizona History*, 22 (Autumn, 1981), p. 297.

6. Uribe García, *Monografía*, pp. 19–20.

7. David M. Pletcher, "The Development of Railroads in Sonora," *Interamerican Economic Affairs*, I (March, 1948), p.: 8.

8. Leonardo Gámez, Prefecto, and others to Gobernador del Estado, Arizpe, October 29, 1887, 576, Archivo Histórico de Sonora (Hereafter cited AHS); Prefecto to Secretario de Estado, Arizpe, October 8, 1887, 576, AHS.

9. Eduardo W. Villa, *Compendio de historia del Estado de Sonora* (Mexico, 1937), p. 418.

10. Ramón Corral, *La cuestión de la harina* (Hermosillo, 1881), p. 56; Mora Torres, *Comerciantes*, p. 211.

11. Stuart F. Voss, *On the Periphery of Nineteenth-Century Mexico. Sonora and Sinaloa, 1810–1877* (Tucson, 1982), p. 232; Daniel Cosío Villegas, *El Porfiriato. La vida económica*, Daniel Cosio Villegas, ed., *Historia moderna de Mexico*, 9 vols. (Mexico, 1955–1973), VII, No. 1, 504–505.

12. Claudio Dabdoub, "La economía de Sonora en 1907 y su naciente industrialización," Instituto de Investigaciones Históricas, *V simposio de historia de Sonora: Memoria* (Hermosillo, 1980), p. 214.

13. Ramón Corral, *Memoria de la administración pública del Estado de Sonora presentada a la legislatura del mismo por el gobernador Ramón Corral*, 2 vols. (Guaymas, 1891), II, 266; Hubert Howe Bancroft, *Recursos y desarrollo de México* (San Francisco, 1892), p. 133.

14. Boyd, *Twenty Years*, pp. 310–311.

15. A. F. Garrison, Vice Consul, "Annual Report," September 30, 1872, Guaymas, Mexico, Consular Dispatches (Hereafter cited CD), III– IV.

16. A. Willard, Consul, "Annual Report," September 9, 1880, Guaymas, Mexico, CD, V–VI.

17. Corral, *Memoria*, II, 265; Cosío Villegas, *Historia*, VII, No. 1, 503.

18. Ramón Corral to Diputados Secretarios del Congreso Estatal, Hermosillo, November 7, 1889, 599, AHS.

19. Pletcher, *Railroads*, p. 13.

20. *Ibid.*, p. 20.

21. A. Willard, Consul, to W. Hunter, April 4, 1880, Guaymas, CD, V-VI.

22. Cosío Villegas, *Historia*, VII, No. 2, 1078.

23. Corral, *Memoria*, II, 267; Pletcher, *Railroads*, p. 28.

24. Pletcher, *Railroads*, pp. 29–30; Osgood Hardy, "El Ferrocarril Sud-Pacifico," *Pacific Historical Review*, XX (August, 1951), p. 269.

25. United States Department of Commerce, Bureau of Foreign and Domestic Commerce, *Mexican West Coast and Lower California. A Commercial and Industrial Survey* (Washington, D.C., 1923), p. 6.

26. Pedro N. Ulloa, *El Estado de Sonora y situación económica al aproximarse el primer centenario de la independencia nacional* (Hermosillo, 1910), p. 107.

27. A. Willard, Consul, to James D. Porter, Guaymas, December 31, 1885, CD, V–VI.

28. Charles S. Aiken, "The Land of Tomorrow," *Sunset Magazine*, XXII (June, 1909), p. 569.

29. Roger Dunbier, *The Sonoran Desert. Its Geography, Economy and People* (Tucson, 1968), 343; Department of Commerce, *West Coast*, pp. 267–268.

30. Inés Herrera Canales, "El comercio exterior de México en el siglo XIX desde una perspectiva regional: Sonora de 1821 a 1910," Instituto de Investigaciones Históricas, *III simposio de historia de Sonora: Memoria*, 2 vols. (Hermosillo, 1978), I, 263.

31. Alfonso Iberri, *El viejo Guaymas* (Mexico, 1952), p. 225.

32. *Ibid.*, p. 226.

33. Alberto Noriega to Luis E. Torres, Hermosillo, November 30, 1906, 2184, Archivo Histórico del Gobierno del Estado de Sonora (hereafter cited AES); Luis E. Torres to Gobernador Alberto Noriega, Tórin, November 30, 1906, 2184, AES.

34. Luis E. Torres to Gobernador Alberto Noriega, Tórin, December 1, 1906, 2184, AES.

35. Cosío Villegas, *Historia*, VII, No. 2, 997; Pletcher, *Railroads*, p. 8.

36. Corral, *Memoria*, II, 250.

37. Héctor Aguilar Camín, *Saldos de la Revolución; cultura y política de México, 1910–1980* (Mexico, 1982), pp. 28–29.

38. Marvin D. Bernstein, *The Mexican Mining Industry, 1890–1950. A Study of the Interaction of Politics, Economics and Technology* (Yellow Springs, Ohio, 1965), p. 32.

39. Robert G. Cleland, *A History of Phelps Dodge, 1834–1950* (New York, 1952), p. 138.

40. Pletcher, *Railroads*, p. 22.

41. A. Willard, Consul, "Annual Report," September 9, 1880, Guaymas, CD, V-VI.

42. Cleland, *Phelps Dodge*, pp. 86–87.

43. Bernstein, *Mining*, p. 29.

44. Dunbier, *Sonoran*, p. 341; Cosío Villegas, *Historia*, VII, No. 1: 595.

45. Don Dedera and Bob Robles, *Goodbye Garcia Adios* (Flagstaff, Arizona, 1976), p. 26.

46. Pletcher, *Railroads*, p. 35.

47. Stuart F. Voss, "Towns and Enterprises in Northwestern Mexico—A History of Urban Elites in Sonora and Sinaloa, 1830–1910" (Ph.D. thesis, Harvard University, Cambridge, 1972), p. 486.

48. A. Willard, Consul, "Annual Report," September 9, 1880, Guaymas, CD, V-VI.

49. Enrique Contreras, *Cosas viejas de mi tierra* (Hermosillo, 1965), p. 31.

50. Pletcher, *Railroads*, p. 27.

51. Cosío Villegas, *Historia*, VII, No. 2: 1175.

52. Ulloa, *Sonora*, p. 209.

53. Palemón Zavala, *Perfiles de Sonora* (Hermosillo, 1984), p. 33; Dunbier, *Sonoran*, p. 163.

54. Joaquín Mange, "Historia del negocio del garbanzo," Raul E. Montaño and P. Gaxiola, eds., *Album del Mayo y del Yaqui; directorio comercial, 1933* (Navojoa, 1932), p. 54.

55. Héctor Aguilar Camín, *La frontera nómada: Sonora y la Revolución Mexicana* (Mexico, 1977), pp. 21 and 33.

56. Voss, *Towns*, p. 507.

57. Quong Chong Lung and others to gobernador, Tórin, Guaymas, October 3, 1907, 2258, AES.

58. Pletcher, *Railroads*, p. 41.

59. Ulloa, *Sonora*, p. 208.

60. Francisco P. Troncoso, *Las guerras con los tribus Yaqui y Mayo*, 2 vols. (Hermosillo, 1982), II: 249.

61. Aguilar Camín, *Frontera*, p. 94.

62. A. Willard, Consul, to W. Hunter, Guaymas, April 1, 1882, CD, V–VI.

63. Pletcher, *Railroads*, 42.

64. Dunbier, *Sonoran*, p. 373.

65. John H. Coatsworth, *El impacto económico de los ferrocarriles. El Porfiriato*, 2 vols. (Mexico, 1976), II: 41.

66. *Ibid.*, pp. 68–69.

67. *Ibid.*, p. 87; Cosío Villegas, *Historia*, I, 634.

68. Pletcher, *Railroads*, p. 3.

69. Department of Commerce, *West Coast*, p. 35.

70. Bancroft, *Recursos*, p. 443; Cynthia Radding de Murrieta, "El espacio sonorense y la periodización de las historias municipales," *IX simposio*, p. 77; Voss, *Towns*, p. 486.

71. Reuben D. George, Vice Consul, to Josiah Quincy, Assistant Secretary of State, Nogales, August 25, 1893, CD, 2.

72. Pletcher, *Railroads*, p. 43.

73. "Burros Too Much for a Railroad," *St. Louis Daily Globe Democrat*, January 5, 1895.

74. Department of Commerce, *West Coast*, p. 263.

75. Herrera Canales, *Comercio*, pp. 263–265.

76. Department of Commerce, *West Coast*, p. 201.

77. Angel Almada to Ramón Corral, Alamos, August 25, 1898, 767, AHS; J. A. Salido to Secretario de Estado, Alamos, June 22, 1908, 2377, AES.

78. Flavio Molina Molina, *Historia de Hermosillo antiguo* (Hermosillo, 1983), p. 196; Fernando A. Galaz, *Dejaron huella en el Hermosillo de ayer y hoy* (Hermosillo, 1971), p. 692.

79. A. Willard, Consul, to James D. Porter, Assistant Secretary of State, Guaymas, December 4, 1885, CD, V–VI; Delos H. Smith, Consul, to William F. Wharton, Nogales, February 20, 1890, CD, I.

80. Pletcher, *Railroads*, p. 43.

81. Coatsworth, *Ferrocarriles*, I, 63 and 68; A. Willard, Consul, "Annual Report," December 31, 1881, Guaymas, CD, V–VI.

82. Corral, *Memoria*, I, 341.

83. Manuel San Domingo, *Historia de Agua Prieta, Sonora* (Agua Prieta, 1951), p. 43.

84. Radding, *Espacio*, p. 18.

85. Prefecto to Secretario de Estado, Sahuaripa, May 2, 1906, 2251, AES.

86. Voss, *Towns*, p. 509; Radding, *Espacio*, p. 82.

87. A. Willard, Consul, to W. Hunter, Guaymas, November 13, 1880, CD, V-VI.

88. A. Willard, Consul, to W. Hunter, Guaymas, June 10, 1880, CD, V–VI; A. Willard, Consul, to W. Hunter, Guaymas, October 10, 1880, CD, V–VI.

89. J. A. Naugle to Gobernador Celedonio C. Ortiz, Guaymas, November 28, 1899, Referencia 24–1, AHS; Feliciano Monteverde to Gobernador del Estado, Minas Prietas, December 15, 1899, Referencia 24–1, AHS; Norberto A. Ortiz to Secretario de Estado, Empalme, June 10, 1907, 2193, AES; Secretario de Estado to Capitán Encarnación, Hermosillo, June 29, 1907, 2193, AES; Alberto Cubillas to Presidente Municipal de Imuris, Hermosillo, June 29, 1907, 2193, AES; Aiken, Land, p. 578.

90. Moisés González Navarro, La colonización en México (Mexico, 1960), p. 85.

91. A. Willard, Consul, to W. Hunter, Guaymas, August 12, 1880, CD, V–VI; A. Willard, Consul, to W. Hunter, Guaymas, August 29, 1880, CD, V–VI.

92. San Domingo, Agua Prieta, p. 217.

93. Zavala, Perfiles, pp. 33–36.

94. A. Willard, Consul, to W. Hunter, Guaymas, July 8, 1880, CD, V–VI.

95. Arturo Morales, Presidente Municipal, to Luis E. Torres, Guaymas, September 11, 1907, 2301, AES.

96. J. A. Naugle to Gobernador del Estado, Guaymas, December 14, 1899, Referencia 24–1, AHS; Secretario de Estado to Presidente Municipal de Minas Prietas, Hermosillo, December 18, 1899, Referencia 24–1, AHS; Sotero F. Navarro to Luis E. Torres, Cumuripa, December 9, 1907, 2198, AES.

97. Sotero F. Navarro to Luis E. Torres, Cumuripa, December 9, 1907, 2198, AES.

98. Pletcher, Railroads, p. 21.

99. A. Willard, Consul, "Annual Report," September 30, 1880, Guaymas, CD, V–VI.

100. Prefecto to Secretario de Estado, Guaymas, June 1, 1906, 2184, AES.

101. Alberto Cubillas, Secretario de Estado, to Gobernador Rafael Izábal, Guaymas, June 2, 1906, 2184, AES; Arturo Morales to Gobernador Rafael Izábal, Guaymas, June 4, 1906, 2184, AES.

102. Secretario de Estado to Prefecto, Hermosillo, August 26, 1909, 2525, AES.

103. Prefecto to Secretario de Estado, Guaymas, August 28, 1909, 2525, AES; Comisario de Policía to Secretario de Estado, Empalme, October 15, 1909, 2525, AES.

104. Secretario de Estado to Presidente Municipal de Santa Ana and others, Hermosillo, August 12, 1895, 671, AHS.

105. Secretario de Estado to Presidente Municipal de Guaymas, Hermosillo, Santa Ana, and others, Hermosillo, August 12, 1895, 671, AHS.

106. Gobernador Ramón Corral to Presidente Porfirio Díaz, Alamos, May 12, 1888, 586, AHS; Gobernador Ramón Corral to Diputados Secretarios del Congreso Estatal, Hermosillo, June 12, 1888, 588, AHS; H. F. Richards, Agente General Auxiliar, to Gobernador Ramón Corral, Guaymas, May 12, 1888, 586, AHS.

107. Boyd, Twenty Years, p. 316.

108. Prefecto to Secretario de Gobierno, Nogales, April 15, 1908, 2414, AES.

109. A. A. Martínez, Prefecto, to Secretario de Estado, Magdalena, May 21, 1908, 2414, AES.
110. A. A. Martínez, Prefecto, to Secretario de Estado, Magdalena, May 27, 1908, 2414, AES.
111. Ramón Corral to Diputados Secretarios del Congreso Estatal, Hermosillo, November 8, 1889, 598, AHS.
112. Silvia Raquel Flores García, "La importancia del ferrocarril en la fundición de Nogales, 1880–1884," Unpublished manuscript, Instituto de Antropología e Historia (Hermosillo, 1983), p. 193; Jorge B. Alvarez to Gobernador, Estación Torres, December 7, 1909, 2478, AES; Boyd, *Twenty Years*, p. 302.
113. Gobernador Ramón Corral to J. A. Naugle, Hermosillo, October 4, 1898, 756, AHS.
114. H. T. Richards, Gerente General, to Gobernador Ramón Corral, Guaymas, January 2, 1891, 619, AHS.
115. A. Willard, Consul, to J. D. Porter, Guaymas, December 31, 1885, CD, V-VI.
116. Corral, *Memoria*, II, 254–255.
117. Coatsworth, *Ferrocarriles*, II, 7, 24, 85, and 94.

CHAPTER 2

1. Alan T. Bird, *The Land of Nayarit* (Nogales, Arizona, 1904), p. 48.
2. Roger Dunbier, *The Sonoran Desert: Its Geography, Economy and People* (Tucson, 1968), p. 153.
3. *Ibid.*
4. United States Department of Commerce, Bureau of Foreign and Domestic Commerce, *Mexican West Coast and Lower California. A Commercial and Industrial Survey* (Washington, D.C., 1923), p. 218.
5. Bird, *Nayarit*, pp. 16 and 23.
6. Juan de Diós Bojórquez, *El héroe de Nacozari* (Havana, Cuba, 1926), p. 60.
7. F. T. Dávila, *Sonora histórico y descriptivo* (Nogales, Arizona, 1894), pp. 293–294; Department of Commerce, *West Coast*, p. 214.
8. Jesús Félix Uribe García, "Monografía sobre la historia de las comunicaciones en Sonora, segunda mitad del siglo xix, las diligencias" (Unpublished Manuscript, Hermosillo, 1981), p. 6.
9. Stuart Voss, *On the Periphery of Nineteenth-Century Mexico. Sonora and Sinaloa, 1810–1899* (Tucson, 1982), p. xiii; James E. Officer, Armando Elías Chomina, and Carmen Pellat Sotomayor, "Los hijos de Pancho: la familia Elías, guerreros sonorenses" (Unpublished Manuscript, University of Arizona, Tucson, 1982), p. 1; Manuel Santiago Corbalá Acuña, *Alamos de Sonora* (Mexico, 1977), p. 26.
10. Voss, *Sonora*, p. xii-xiii.
11. J. C. Patton to Gobernador del Estado, Moctezuma, January 18, 1890, 2323, AES.
12. Corbalá Acuña, *Alamos*, p. 39; Francisco R. Almada, *Diccionario de historia, geografía y biografía sonorenses* (Chihuahua, 1952), pp. 710–711; Officer, *Pancho*, p. 8.

13. Officer, *Pancho*, p. 2.

14. Corbalá Acuña, *Alamos*, p. 39; Almada, *Diccionario*, p. 45; Department of Commerce, *West Coast*, p. 226.

15. Eduardo W. Villa, *Galería de sonorenses ilustres* (Hermosillo, 1948), pp. 111–113.

16. ———, *Compendio de historia del Estado de Sonora* (Mexico, 1937), p. 214; Almada, *Diccionario*, p. 631; Bartolomé Eligio Almada, *Almada of Alamos. The Diary of Don Bartolome*, translated and with a narrative by Carlota Miles (Tucson, 1962), p. 2.

17. Cynthia Radding de Murrieta, "El espacio sonorense y la periodización de las historias municipales." Instituto de Investigaciones Históricas, *IX simposio de historia de Sonora:* Memoria (Hermosillo, 1984), p. 13.

18. Corbalá Acuña, *Alamos*, p. 25.

19. Voss, *Sonora*, p. 192.

20. Almada, *Diary*, p. 2.

21. Dunbier, *Sonoran*, pp. 153–154; Voss, *Sonora*, pp. 39, 191.

22. Inés Herrera Canales, "El comercio exterior de México en el siglo XIX desde una perspectiva regional: Sonora de 1821 a 1910," Instituto de Investigaciones Históricas, *III simposio de historia de Sonora: Memoria* 2 vols. (Hermosillo, 1978), 1: 271.

23. Consuelo Boyd, "Twenty Years to Nogales: The Building of the Guaymas-Nogales Railroad," *The Journal of Arizona History*, XXII (Autumn, 1981), p. 298.

24. Dunbier, *Sonoran*, p. 155; Villa, *Compendio*, p. 421.

25. Dunbier, *Sonoran*, pp. 155–156.

26. Department of Commerce, *West Coast*, p. 215.

27. Rafael Izábal, *Memoria de la administración pública del Estado de Sonora durante el periodo constitucional de 1903 a 1907* (Hermosillo, 1907), p. 176.

28. *Ibid.*; Ramón Corral, *Memoria de la administración pública del Estado de Sonora presentada a la legislatura del mismo por el gobernador Ramón Corral*, 2 vols. (Guaymas, 1891), II, 249.

29. Pedro N. Ulloa, *El Estado de Sonora y situación económica al aproximarse el primer centenario de la independencia nacional* (Hermosillo, 1910), p. 154.

30. Angel Bassols Batalla, *Formación de regiones económicas* (Mexico, 1979), p. 171.

31. Department of Commerce, *West Coast*, p. 264.

32. Cuadro Estadístico del Distrito de Arizpe en el Estado de Sonora, Arizpe, November 1, 1884, 616, AHS.

33. Antonio G. Rivera, *La Revolución en Sonora* (Hermosillo, 1969), pp. 108–109.

34. Leonardo Gámez, Prefecto, to Gobernador del Estado, Arizpe, October 29, 1887, 276, AHS.

35. Stuart F. Voss, "Towns and Enterprises in Northwestern Mexico—A History of Urban Elites in Sonora and Sinaloa, 1830–1910" (Ph.D. thesis, Harvard University, 1972), pp. 535–537.

36. *Ibid.*; Manuel San Domingo, *Historia de Agua Prieta, Sonora* (Mexico, 1951), pp. 56–58 and 69; Alfred Breceda, *México revolucionario, 1913–1917*, 2 vols. (Madrid and Mexico, 1920 and 1941), II, 55.

37. Department of Commerce, *West Coast* p. 216.

38. Prefecto del Distrito to Secretario de Estado, Arizpe, March 27, 1891, 619, AHS.

39. Prefecto del Distrito to Secretario de Estado, Hermosillo, March 9, 1888, 616, AHS.

40. Prefecto del Distrito to Secretario de Estado, Hermosillo, March 15, 1892, 620, AHS.

41. Antonio Ogazón, Prefecto, to Secretario de Estado, May 25, 1910, 2542, AES.

42. Evelyn Hu-DeHart, *Missionaries, Miners and Indians. Spanish Contact with the Yaqui Nation of Northwestern New Spain, 1633–1820* (Tucson, 1981), p. 44.

43. Claudio Dabdoub, "La economía de Sonora en 1907 y su naciente industrialización," Instituto de Investigaciones Históricas, *V simposio de historia de Sonora: Memoria* (Hermosillo, 1980), p. 208.

44. David M. Pletcher, "The Development of Railroads in Sonora," *Interamerican Economic Affairs*, I (March, 1948), p. 7.

45. Daniel Cosío Villegas, *El Porfiriato. La vida económica*, Daniel Cosio Villegas, ed., *Historia moderna de México*, 9 vols. (Mexico, 1955–1973), VII, No. 1, 239.

46. Ulloa, *Sonora*, p. 135; Healy-Genda, ed., *Directorio comercial del Estado de Sonora* (Hermosillo, 1920), p. 90.

47. Cosío Villegas, *Historia*, VII, No. 1, 250; Federico García y Alva, ed., *México y su progreso; album-directorio del Estado de Sonora* (Hermosillo, 1905–1907), p. 97.

48. J. Alexander Forbes, Consul, "Annual Report," May 1, 1893, Guaymas, CD, VIII–IX.

49. Charles S. Aiken, "The Land of Tomorrow," *Sunset Magazine*, XXII (June, 1909), p. 581.

50. Dávila, *Sonora*, p. 214; Congreso del Estado, Ley que erige en Municipalidad a Las Prietas, Hermosillo, June 22, 1889, 616, AHS.

51. Secretario de Estado to Diputados Secretarios del Congreso del Estado, Hermosillo, December 3, 1907, 2198, AES; Visitador de Hacienda, "Notas de Minas Prietas," Minas Prietas, [no date, 1907], 2304, AES; Juez del Registro Civil to Secretario de Estado, La Colorada, February 19, 1908, 2396, AES; Congreso del Estado to Gobernador, Hermosillo, December 6, 1907, 2198, AES; Gobernador to Director General de Correos, Hermosillo, December 15, 1906, 2085, AES.

52. Ulloa, *Sonora*, p. 123; García y Alva, *Progreso*, p. 162.

53. J. Alexander Forbes, Consul, "Annual Report," May 1, 1893, Guaymas, CD, VIII–IX.

54. Department of Commerce, *West Coast*, p. 230.

55. Corral, *Memoria*, II, 251; Department of Commerce, *West Coast*, pp. 221 and 228–229.

56. A. Willard, Consul, "Annual Report," September 30, 1873, Guaymas, CD, III–IV.

57. J. Alexander Forbes, Consul, "Annual Report," May 1, 1893, Guaymas, CD, VIII–IX.

58. A. F. Garrison, Consul, "Annual Report," September 30, 1872, Guaymas, CD, III–IV.

59. A. Willard, Consul, "Annual Report," December 31, 1888, Guaymas, CD, VII.

60. Armando Quijada Hernández, "Perspectiva histórica de Sonora," Instituto de Investigaciones, *IX simposio*, p. 126.

61. Marvin D. Bernstein, *The Mexican Mining Industry, 1890–1950. A Study of the Interaction of Politics, Economics and Technology* (Yellow Springs, 1965), p. 19; Ramón Eduardo Ruiz, *The Great Rebellion; Mexico, 1905–1924* (London and New York, 1980), pp. 124–125.

62. Gobernador to Diputados Secretarios del Congreso Estatal, Hermosillo, December 2, 1893, 657, AHS.

63. Carlos Garza Cortines, Presidente Municipal, Informe, Nogales, September 16, 1894, 654, AHS.

64. Diego Navarro Gil, "Los ciclos de la minería en el distrito de Alamos," *IX simposio*, p. 412.

65. J. Alexander Forbes, Consul, "Annual Report," May 1, 1893, Guaymas, CD, VIII-IX.

66. Gobernador del Estado de Colima to Gobernador del Estado de Sonora, Colima, July 20, 1893, 640, AHS.

67. A. Willard to W. F. Wharton, Guaymas, December 21, 1889, CD, VIII–IX.

68. Robert G. Cleland, *A History of Phelps Dodge, 1834–1950* (New York, 1952), pp. 116, 157.

69. Sidney Brooks, "The Coming Copper Famine," *Northamerican Review*, XXVII (April 1918), pp. 522–532; Cleland, *Phelps Dodge*, p. 158.

70. Cleland, *Phelps Dodge*, p. 145.

71. Department of Commerce, *West Coast*, p. 218; Bernstein, *Mining*, p. 5.

72. Department of Commerce, *West Coast*, p. 233.

73. Almada, *Diccionario*, p. 499.

74. Cleland, *Phelps Dodge*, p. 159.

75. Presidente Municipal, Informe, Cumpas, November 6, 1905, 2244, AES; Don Dedera and Bob Robles, *Goodbye Garcia Adios* (Flagstaff, Arizona, 1976), pp. 8, 26; Cuauhtémoc L. Terán, *Jesús García. Héroe de Nacozari* (Hermosillo, 1981), pp. 10–11.

76. Dedera, *Garcia*, p. 28.

77. Bojórquez, *Héroe*, p. 61.

78. G. Alfredo Villaseñor to Gobernador, Hermosillo, November 20, 1900, 1584, AES.

79. Villa, *Compendio*, p. 462; Gobernador to Congreso del Estado, Hermosillo, June 14, 1906, 1085, AES.

80. Gobernador to Congreso del Estado, Hermosillo, June 14, 1906, 1085, AES; Gobernador to Secretario de la Diputación Permanente, Hermosillo, September 13, 1907, 2257, AES.

81. Dávila, *Sonora*, p. 291.

82. Bird, *Nayarit*, p. 15; Francisco Medina Hoyos, *Cananea, cuna de la Revolución Mexicana* (Mexico, 1956), p. 7.

83. Ulloa, *Sonora*, pp. 78–79.

84. García y Alves, *Progreso*, p. 248.

CHAPTER 3

1. Leonardo Gámez, Prefecto, and others to Gobernador del Estado, Arizpe, October 29, 1887, 576, AHS.

2. Marvin D. Bernstein, *The Mexican Mining Industry, 1890–1950. A Study of the Interaction of Politics, Economics and Technology* (Yellow Springs, 1965), p. 49.

3. Colegio de México, *Estadísticas económicas del Porfiriato. Comercio exterior de México, 1877–1911* (Mexico, 1960), p. 400.

4. Héctor Aguilar Camín, *La frontera nómada: Sonora y la Revolución Mexicana* (Mexico, 1977), p. 110.

5. Stuart F. Voss, "Towns and Enterprises in Northwestern Mexico—A History of Urban Elites in Sonora and Sinaloa, 1830–1910." (Ph.D. thesis, Harvard University, Cambridge, 1972), pp. 533–534.

6. Cuauhtémoc L. Terán, *Jesús García. Héroe de Nacozari.* (Hermosillo, 1981), p. 19.

7. Amadeo C. Hernández, "Historia de Cumpas," Instituto de Investigaciones Históricas, *Primer simposio de historia de Sonora* (Hermosillo, 1976), p. 342.

8. Voss, *Towns*, pp. 534–535.

9. H. C. Beauchamp, Manager, to Emilo González, Cumpas, August [no day] 1907, 2218, AES.

10. Daniel Cosío Villegas, *El Porfiriato. La vida económica*, Daniel Cosío Villegas, ed., *Historia moderna de México*, 9 vols. (Mexico, 1955–1973), VII, No. 1, 303; Gobierno del Estado, Contrato, Hermosillo, August 7, 1893, 646, AHS; Gobierno del Estado, Contrato, Hermosillo, May 18, 1893, 646, AHS.

11. Ramón Corral, *Memoria de la administración pública del Estado de Sonora presentada a la legislatura del mismo por el gobernador Ramón Corral*, 2 vols. (Guaymas, 1891), II, 227; Gobernador Luis E. Torres to Secretario de Fomento, Hermosillo, October 23, 1891, 625, AHS.

12. Jesús Luna, *La carrera pública de Ramón Corral* (Mexico, 1975), p. 112; Tesorería General del Estado to Secretario de Estado, Hermosillo, June 7, 1898, 756, AHS; Secretario de Estado to Prefecto de Distrito, Hermosillo, October 15, 1895, 693, AHS.

13. Ramón Corral, Vice Gobernador, Informe, Hermosillo, May 15, 1889, 603, AHS.

14. Pedro N. Ulloa, *El Estado de Sonora y situación económica al aproximarse el primer centenario de la independencia nacional* (Hermosillo, 1910), p. 154.

15. Ismael Valencia Ortega, "Desenvolvimiento de la clase obrera en Cananea (1900–1932)," Instituto de Investigaciones Históricas, *IX simposio de historia de Sonora* (Hermosillo, 1984), p. 422.

16. Secretario de Estado to Secretario de Gobernación, Hermosillo, October 29, 1907, 2218, AES.

17. Diego Gil Navarro, "Los ciclos de la minería en el distrito de Alamos," Instituto de Investigaciones, *IX simposio*, pp. 409–410.

18. *Ibid.*, p. 411; Presidente Municipal to Secretario de Estado, Aduana, April 20, 1910, 2595, AES.

19. Prefecto to Secretario de Estado, Alamos, December 10, 1909, 2419, AES.

20. Rafael Izábal, *Memoria de la administración pública del Estado de Sonora durante el periodo constitucional de 1903 a 1907* (Hermosillo, 1907), no page number.

21. Informes of Presidentes Municipales to Secretario de Estado (districts of Arizpe, Magdalena, Moctezuma, Altar, Ures, Alamos, Hermosillo, and Sahuaripa), [no dates, 1906], 2248, AES; Teodoro O. Paz, *Guaymas de ayer* (Guaymas, [1974?]), p. 215.

22. Izábal, *Memoria*, no page number.

23. Terán, *García*, p. 17.

24. Gideon Giroux to Secretario de Estado, La Sultana, October 18, 1906, 2106, AES.

25. Ignacio E. Elías to Secretario de Estado, Arizpe, July 19, 1908, 2365, AES; Ignacio E. Elías to Secretario Estado, September 4, 1908, 2337, AES; Prefecto to Secretario de Estado, Altar, December 19, 1908, 2415, AES.

26. Presidente Municipal to Secretario de Estado, Fronteras, March 2, 1907, 2193, AES; Secretarío de Estado to Secretario de Gobernación, Hermosillo, September 12, 1910, 2584, AES.

27. Presidente Municipal to Secretario de Estado, Moctezuma, May 10, 1909, 2478, AES.

28. Francisco Chiapa, Prefecto, to Secretario de Estado, Moctezuma, January 6, 1908, 2337, AES.

29. Taide López de Castillo to Gobernador, Hermosillo, October 8, 1908, 2311, AES.

30. Francisco Chiapa, Prefecto, to Alberto Cubillas, Moctezuma, October 31, 1907, 2218, AES.

31. Ed. R. Arnold to Luis E. Torres, Cananea, September 29, 1907, 2218, AES.

32. Presidente Municipal to Secretario de Estado, Caborca, August 19, 1906, 2131, AES.

33. M. Encinas to Secretario de Estado, Sahuaripa, May 16, 1906, 2185, AES; "Un Imparcial" to Vice Gobernador Alberto Cubillas, Sahuaripa, May 26, 1908, 2253, AES.

34. Taide López de Castillo to Gobernador, Hermosillo, October 8, 1908, 2311, AES.

35. Federico García y Alva, ed., *México y su progreso; album-directorio del Estado de Sonora* (Hermosillo, 1905–1907), p. 70.

36. Presidente Municipal to Secretario de Estado, Trinidad, June 6, 1906, 2245, AES; Estado de Sonora. Distrito de Sahuaripa. Mineral de la Trinidad. Noticia Estadística, Trinidad, May 6, 1892, 647, AES.

37. Quong, Gun, Lung y Cía, to Gobernador, Alamos, April 23, 1908, 2336, AES.

38. Presidente Municipal to Secretario de Estado, Caborca, August 19,

1906, 2131, AES; M. Salcido to Secretario de Estado, Caborca, February 25, 1908, 2337, AES.

39. Alfredo Penunuri and others to Gobernador, Sahuaripa, July 14, 1909, 2519, AES.

40. L. Rozet, Presidente de la Junta Representativa del Comerio, to Gobernador, Cananea, November 4, 1907, 2116, AES; Ed. R. Arnold, Presidente Municipal, to Gobernador, Cananea, November 4, 1908, 2323, AES.

41. Siu Fo Chong y Cía. to Secretario de Estado, Guaymas, January 4, 1908, 2336, AES.

42. E. R. Arnold, Presidente Municipal, to Secretario de Estado, Cananea, October 6, 1906, 2131, AES.

43. Presidente Municipal to Secretario de Estado, Caborca, April 19, 1906, 2131, AES; Presidente Municipal to Secretario de Estado, Caborca, August 19, 1907, 2131, AES; M. Salcido to Secretario de Estado, Caborca, February 25, 1908, 2337, AES.

44. Antonio Oviedo to Tesorero General del Estado, Promontorios, September 27, 1907, 2303, AES.

45. Manuel de J. Olea to Secretario de Estado, Trinidad, October 20, 1907, 2218, AES.

46. Taide López de Castillo to Gobernador, Hermosillo, October 8, 1908, 3211, AES.

47. Liborio Vázquez to Gobernador Alberto Cubillas, Agua Prieta, May 15, 1908, 2414, AES.

48. Prefecto to Secretario de Estado, Alamos, July 29, 1909, 2475, AES.

49. Prefecto to Gobernador, Arizpe, June 15, 1908, 2468, AES.

50. M. Encinas, Prefecto, to Secretario de Estado, Sahuaripa, September 10, 1897, AHS.

51. Ignacio E. Elías to Secretario de Estado, Arizpe, July 19, 1908, 2365, AES.

52. Taide López de Castillo to Gobernador, Hermosillo, October 8, 1908, 2133, AES: Aguilar Camín, *Frontera nomada*, p. 122.

53. *Ibid.*; United States. Department of Commerce and Labor, Bureau of Manufactures, *Commercial Relations of the United States with Foreign Countries* (Washington, D.C., 1911), p. 542; Ulloa, *Sonora*, p. 157.

54. Stuart F. Voss, *On the Periphery of Nineteenth-Century Mexico. Sonora and Sinaloa, 1810–1877* (Tucson, 1982), p. 156.

55. Prefecto to Secretario de Estado, Ures, April 17, 1886, 616, AHS.

56. J. Alexander Forbes, Consul, "Annual Report," May 1, 1893, Guaymas, CD, VIII–IX.

57. *Ibid.*

58. *Ibid.*

59. Presidente Municipal to Secretario de Estado, Sahuaripa, August 3, 1906, 3348, AES; Presidente Municipal to Secretario de Estado, September 13, 1906, 2248, AES; Izábal, *Memoria*, no page number; Gil Navarro, "Ciclos," Instituto de Investigaciones, *IX simposio*, p. 410.

60. Izábal, *Memoria*, no page number.

61. García y Alva, *Progreso*, pp. 327–330.

62. Corral, *Memoria*, II, 254.

63. Antonio G. Rivera, *La Revolución en Sonora* (Hermosillo, 1969), p. 109; Presidente Municipal to Secretario de Estado, Trinidad, June 30, 1906, 2248, AES.

64. Presidente Municipal to Secretario de Estado, Trinidad, June 30, 1906, 2248, AES; Reports of Presidentes Municipales to Secretario de Estado, Alamos district, [no dates, 1906], 2248, 1906; Izábal, *Memoria*, no page number.

65. Ulloa, *Sonora*, p. 147.

CHAPTER 4

1. Marvin D. Bernstein, *The Mexican Mining Industry, 1890–1950. A Study of the Interaction of Politics, Economics and Technology* (Yellow Springs, 1965), p. 13. Daniel Cosío Villegas, *El Porfiriato. La vida económica,* Daniel Cosío Villegas, ed., *Historia moderna de México,* 9 vols. (Mexico, 1955–1973), VII, No. 1, 266.

2. Gobierno de Sonora to Secretario de Fomento, Hermosillo, May 11, 1887, 575, AHS.

3. For example, see Otis D. Crocker to Gobernador, Hermosillo, March 11, 1887, 575, AHS; Secretario de Estado to Otis D. Crocker, Hermosillo, April 22, 1887, 575, AHS.

4. Rafael Izábal, *Memoria de la administración pública del Estado de Sonora durante al periodo constitucional de 1903 a 1907* (Hermosillo, 1907), p. 176.

5. Departamento de Estadística Nacional, *Sonora, Sinaloa y Nayarit. Estudio estadístico económico social, elaborado por el Departmento de la Estadística Nacional. Año de 1927* (Mexico, 1928), p. 258.

6. Bernstein, *Mining*, pp. 20–21.

7. Harry L. Foster, *A Gringo in Mañana Land* (New York, 1924), p. 39.

8. Bernstein, *Mining*, p. 7.

9. Moisés González Navarro, *La colonización en México* (Mexico, 1960), pp. 89–90.

10. A. Willard, Consul, "Annual Report," September 30, 1880, Guaymas, CD, V–VI; A. Willard, Consul, to W. Hunter, Guaymas, April 12, 1881, CD, V–VI; A. Willard, Consul, to W. Hunter, Guaymas, April 1, 1882, CD, V–VI; A. Willard, Consul, "Annual Report," December 31, 1882, Guaymas, CD, V–VI; A. Willard, Consul, "Annual Report," December 31, 1887, CD, VII; A. Willard, Consul, to W. F. Wharton, Guaymas, December 31, 1889, CD, VIII–IX.

11. Izábal, *Memoria*, p. 148; Departamento de Estadística, *Sonora*, p. 64; Pedro N. Ulloa, *El Estado de Sonora y situación económica al aproximarse el primer centenario de la independencia nacional* (Hermosillo, 1910), p. 36.

12. Stuart F. Voss, "Towns and Enterprises in Northwestern Mexico—A History of Urban Elites in Sonora and Sinaloa, 1830–1910" (Ph.D. thesis, Harvard University, 1972), pp. 530 and 594.

13. S. Levey, Doctor en Medicina, to Secretario de Estado, Santa Elena, December 23, 1893, 654, AHS.

Notes to Pages 54–57

. Federico García y Alva, *México y su progreso; album directorio del Estado de Sonora* (Hermosillo, 1905–1907), p. 326.

15. United States Department of Commerce, Bureau of Foreign and Domestic Commerce, *Mexican West Coast and Lower California. A Commercial and Industrial Survey* (Washington, D.C., 1923), p. 241.

16. Leonardo Gámez, Prefecto, and others to Gobernador, Arizpe, October 29, 1887, 576, AHS.

17. Cosío Villegas, *Historia*, VII, No. 2, 269 and 988.

18. A. F. Garrison, Vice Consul, "Annual Report," September 30, 1872, Guaymas, CD, III–IV.

19. *Ibid.*

20. A. Willard, Consul, to J. D. Porter, Guaymas, December 31, 1885, CD, V–VI; A. Willard, Consul, to J. D. Porter, Guaymas, December 31, 1886, CD, VII.

21. A. Willard, Consul, "Annual Report," December 31, 1884, CD, VII; Delos H. Smith, Consul, to William F. Wharton, Assistant Secretary of State, Nogales, Sonora, March 10, 1890, CD, I.

22. Cosío Villegas, *Historia*, VII, No. 2, 997.

23. *Ibid.*, 266; David M. Pletcher, "The Development of Railroads in Sonora," *Interamerican Economic Affairs*, I (March, 1948), pp. 4 and 7.

24. Cosío Villegas, *Historia*, VII, No. 2, 1134; Department of Commerce, *West Coast*, p. 216; United States, Department of State, Bureau of Foreign Commerce, *Commercial Relations of the United States with Foreign Countries* (Washington, D.C., 1903), pp. 433, 436, 439.

25. United States Department of Commerce and Labor, Bureau of Manufactures, *Commercial Relations of the United States with Foreign Countries* (Washington, D.C., 1911), p. 539.

26. Beene Delmar Leon, "Sonora in the Age of Ramón Corral, 1875–1900" (Ph.D. thesis, University of Arizona, Tucson, 1972), p. 202; Antonio N. Ramírez to Secretario de Estado, Caborca, March 28, 1906, 2245, AHS; Berta Ulloa, *Historia de la Revolución Mexicana, 1914–1917. La Constitución de 1917* (Mexico, 1983), p. 101.

27. Roger Dunbier, *The Sonoran Desert. Its Geography, Economy and People* (Tucson, 1968), p. 342; Antonio G. Rivera, *La Revolución en Sonora* (Hermosillo, 1969), pp. 17 and 23.

28. Prefecto to Secretario de Estado, Arizpe, October 6, 1890, 608, AHS.

29. V. A. Almada to Secretario de Estado, Arizpe, January 6, 1885, 616, AHS; Bernstein, *Mining*, p. 57.

30. Daniel Nelson, "Fifth Column at Cananea. A Stockholder Circumvents Colonel W. C. Greene," *The Journal of Arizona History*, XX (Spring, 1979), p. 50.

31. Bernstein, *Mining*, pp. 72–73; Cosío Villegas, *Historia*, VII, No. 2, 1091; Voss, *Towns*, pp. 526–527.

32. Hector Aguilar Camín, *La frontera nómada: Sonora y la Revolución Mexicana* (Mexico, 1977), pp. 111–112.

33. W. C. Greene to Gobernador Rafael Izábal, Naco, Arizona, June 1, 1906; Esteban Baca Calderón, *Juicio sobre la guerra del Yaqui y génesis de la huelga de Cananea. 1° de junio de 1906* (Mexico, 1956), pp. 43 and 56.

34. A. León Grajeda, Vice Consul, to Secretario de Relaciones Exteriores, New York, August 14, 1906, 2077, AES.

35. See description in García y Alva, *Progreso*, no page numbers.

36. Mildred Y. Wallace, "I Remember Chung," *The Journal of Arizona History*, XX (Spring, 1979), p. 35.

37. Voss, *Towns* p. 529.

38. Robert Glass Cleland, *A History of Phelps Dodge, 1834–1950* (New York, 1952), pp. 130–131; Bernstein, *Mining*, pp. 59–60.

39. Cleland, *Phelps Dodge*, p. 114.

40. Fernando Méndez to Gobernador, Hermosillo, October 6, 1899, 682, AHS; Secretario de Estado to Fernando Méndez, September 21, 1899, 682, AHS; Cosío Villegas, *Historia*, VII, No. 2, 1091.

41. Cleland, *Phelps Dodge*, p. 133; Cuauhtemoc L. Terán, *Jesús García. Héroe de Nacozari* (Hermosillo, 1981), p. 18; Bernstein, *Mining*, p. 58.

42. Cleland, *Phelps Dodge*, pp. 91–107, 231; Terán, *Jesús García*. pp. 17–18.

43. Superintendente, The Moctezuma Copper Company, to Gobernador Rafael Izábal, Nacozari, June 7, 1906, 2184, AES.

44. García y Alva, *Progreso*, p. 322.

45. Terán, *Jesús García*, pp. 11–12; Don Dedera and Bob Robles, *Goodbye García Adios* (Flagstaff, Arizona, 1976), p. 28; García y Alva, *Progreso*, p. 323.

46. J. Alexander Forbes, Consul, "Annual Report," May 1, 1893, CD, VIII–IX.

47. Allen T. Bird, *The Land of Nayarit* (Nogales, Arizona, 1904), p. 28; Rafael Fort, Representante Legal, to Gobernador, Hermosillo, August 26, 1890, 606, AHS; Bernstein, *Mining*, p. 68.

48. J. Alexander Forbes, Consul, "Annual Report," May 1, 1893, Guaymas, CD, VIII–IX; *La Constitución*, June 3, 1897.

49. Pletcher, *Railroads*, p. 27.

50. F. H. Seymour, Manager, to Gobernador Ramón Corral, Imuris, April 2, 1891, 624, AHS.

51. Juan Duarte, Eduardo Lubas, and others to Gobernador, Cerro Blanco, August 22, 1891, 614, AHS.

52. J. Alexander Forbes, Consul, "Annual Report," May 1, 1893, Guaymas, CD, VIII-IX.

53. Bird, *Nayarit*, p. 22.

54. Diego Navarro Gil, "Los ciclos de la minería en el Distrito de Alamos, 1895–1910," Instituto de Investigaciones Históricas, *IX simposio de historia de Sonora: Memoria* (Hermosillo, 1981), p. 410.

55. Albert R. Morawetz, Vice Consul, to David J. Hill, Assistant Secretary of State, Nogales, Sonora, May 4, 1899, CD, III.

56. Presidente Municipal to Secretario de Estado, April 4, 1906, 2248, AES; Palemón Zavala, *Perfiles de Sonora* (Hermosillo, 1984), p. 42.

57. M. Encinas to Secretario de Estado, Sahuaripa, August 23, 1890, 625, AHS.

58. Prefecto to Secretario de Estado, Sahuaripa, January 3, 1890, 608, AHS.

59. Ramón Corral, Secretario de Estado, to Prefecto, Hermosillo, January 13, 1890, 608, AHS.

60. Prefecto to Secretario de Estado, Sahuaripa, February 7, 1890, 608, AHS.

61. Prefecto to Secretario de Estado, Sahuaripa, September 25, 1890, 619, AHS.

62. Bird, *Nayarit*, p. 27.

63. Manuel P. Muñoz to Secretario de Estado, Hermosillo, September 13, 1890, 606, AHS: Estado de Sonora. Distrito de Ures, Municipalidad de Ures, October 26, 1905, 2244, AES; Cuadro Estadístico del Distrito de Arizpe, Arizpe, November 1, 1884, 616, AHS; Claudio Dabdoub, "La economía de Sonora en 1907 y su naciente industrialización," Instituto de Investigaciones Históricas, *V simposio de historia de Sonora: Memoria* (Hermosillo, 1980), p. 206; Noticia que manifiesta los nombres de los lugares que forman la Municipalidad de Arizpe, Arizpe, November 10, 1905, 2244, AES.

64. Bernstein, *Mining*, p. 64.

65. H. C. Beauchamp, Manager, to Emilio González, Cumpas, August [no day] 1907, 2218, AES; Arthur Jenks to Gobernador Rafael Izábal, Cumpas, May 3, 1906, 2105, AES.

66. García y Alva, *Progreso*, p. 327.

67. Bird, *Nayarit*, p. 22.

68. *Ibid.*, p. 4.

69. Izabál, *Memoria*, no page number.

70. J. A. Salido to Secretario de Estado, Alamos, April 6, 1906, 2248, AES; Prefecto to Secretario de Estado, Guaymas, February 28, 1906, 2248, AES; M. Encinas to Secretario de Estado, Sahuaripa, May 23, 1906, 2248, AES; Prefecto to Secretario de Estado, Ures, April 18, 1906, 2248, AES; Jacinto Padilla to Secretario de Estado, Magdalena, May 9, 1906, 2248, AES; Prefecto to Secretario de Estado, Moctezuma, May 18, 1906, 2248, AES; Prefecto to Secretario de Estado, Arizpe, May 16, 1906, 224, AES; Prefecto to Secretario de Estado, Altar, March 8, 1906, 2248, AES.

71. Hubert H. Bancroft, *Recursos y desarrollo de México* (San Francisco, 1892), p. 240; A. Willard, Consul, to W. F. Wharton, Guaymas, December 31, 1889, CD, VIII–IX; García y Alva, *Progreso*, p. 7.

72. Ramón Corral, *Memoria de la administración pública del Estado de Sonora presentada a la legislatura del mismo por el gobernador Ramón Corral*, 2 vols. (Guaymas, 1891), II, 252.

CHAPTER 5

1. Héctor Aguilar Camín, *La frontera nómada: Sonora y la Revolución Mexicana* (Mexico, 1977), p. 118; Marvin D. Bernstein, *The Mexican Mining Industry, 1890–1950. A Study of the Interaction of Politics, Economics and Technology* (Yellow Springs, 1965), p. 78.

2. Cited in Francisco P. Troncoso, *Las guerras con las tribus Yaqui y Mayo*, 2 vols. (Hermosillo, 1982), 1: 104.

3. Albert W. Brickwood, Jr., Vice Consul, to Assistant Secretary of State, Nogales, Sonora, June 23, 1906, CD, IV.

4. Antonio G. Rivera, *La Revolución en Sonora* (Hermosillo, 1969), p. 145.

5. Daniel Cosío Villegas, *El Porfiriato. La vida política interior,* Daniel Cosío Villegas, *Historia Moderna de México,* 9 vols. (Mexico, 1955–1973), IX, No. 2, 708.

6. Rivera, *Revolución,* p. 126.

7. Francisco R. Almada, *La Revolución en el Estado de Sonora* (Mexico, 1971), p. 27.

8. Rufino Félix and others to Prefecto, Río Chico, May 25, 1890, 614, AHS.

9. Bernstein, *Mining,* p. 90.

10. Ralph McA. Ingersoll, *In and Under Mexico* (New York and London, 1924), pp. 37 and 45.

11. *Arizona Daily Star,* August 7, 1883.

12. J. Alexander Forbes, "Annual Report," May 1, 1893, Guaymas, CD, VIII–IX.

13. Ignacio Elías, Prefecto, to Secretario de Estado, Arizpe, August 31, 1906, AES.

14. Prefecto to Secretario de Estado, Arizpe, March 7, 1908, 2414, AES.

15. Prefecto to Secretario de Estado, Arizpe, May 28, 1909, 2478, AES.

16. Bernstein, *Mining,* p. 99.

17. *Ibid.,* p. 91.

18. Daniel Nelson, "Fifth Column at Cananea. A Stockholder Circumvents Colonel W. C. Greene," *The Journal of Arizona History* (Spring, 1979), p. 58.

19. Bernstein, *Mining,* p. 90.

20. William L. Sturgis to Enrique Monteverde, Official Mayor, San Félix, May 9, 1891, 624, AHS.

21. Ingersoll, *In and Under,* p. 139.

22. Pedro J. Almada, *Con mi cobija al hombre* (Mexico, 1936), p. 115.

23. Prefecto to Secretario de Estado, Alamos, October 11, 1892, 628, AHS.

24. Rivera, *Revolución,* p. 131.

25. Pablo Rubio, Comisario de Policía, to Secretario de Estado, Cananea, February 13, 1907, 2301, AES.

26. Secretario de Estado to Comisario de Policía, Hermosillo, February 13, 1907, 2301, AES.

27. Comisario de Policía to Secretario de Gobierno, El Alacrán, October 13, 1908, 2414, AES.

28. Joseph Sherman, Superintendent, to Willard Richards, Nacozari, June 6, 1887, 673, AHS.

29. Palemón Zavala, *Perfiles de Sonora* (Hermosillo, 1984), p. 42.

30. Rivera, *Revolución,* p. 126; Esteban Baca Calderón, *Juicio sobre la guerra del Yaqui y génesis de la huelga de Cananea, 1° de junio de 1906* (Mexico, 1956), p. 30.

31. Rivera, *Revolución,* pp. 19 and 126.

32. Alberto Calzadíaz Barrera, *Hechos reales de la Revolución; el General Ignacio L. Pesqueira . . . y surgen Obregón y Calles* (Mexico, 1973), p. 30.

33. W. Espinosa to Secretario de Estado, Cananea, February 19, 1908, 2414, AES.

34. Junta Organizadora del Partido Liberal Mexicano to Baltasar R. Rivera, St. Louis, September 1, 1906, 2183, AES.

35. Rivera, *Revolución*, p. 145.

36. César Tapia Quijada, *Apuntes sobre la huelga de Cananea* (Hermosillo, 1956), p. 56.

37. Secretario de Estado to Prefecto, Hermosillo, April 8, 1895, 702, AHS; Secretario de Estado to Presidente Municipal de Minas Prietas, Hermosillo, April 26, 1895, 702, AHS.

38. Secretario de Estado to Juan Duarte, Tomás Romero, and others, Hermosillo, September 4, 1891, 624, AHS.

39. E. Dávalos, Comisario de Policía, to Secretario de Estado, Las Cabezas, September 2, 1906, 2082, AES; Secretario de Estado to Comisario de Policía, Hermosillo, September 21, 1906, 2082, AES.

40. Ramón Gil Samaniego, Comisario de Policía, to Secretario de Estado, Cerro Prieto, August 30, 1906, 2138, AES.

41. Secretario de Estado to Comisario de Policía, Hermosillo, August 31, 1906, 2138, AES; Jacinto Padilla, Prefecto, to Secretario de Estado, Magdalena, August 31, 1906, 2138, AES.

42. Ignacio R. Encinas to Gobernador, August 2, 1907, 2323, AES.

43. Jacinto Padilla, Prefecto, to Secretario de Estado, Magdalena, September 10, 1907, 2190, AES.

44. Comisario de Policía to Secretario de Estado, Nacozari, July 14, 1907, 2323, AES; Comisario de Policía to Secretario de Estado, Nacozari, July 15, 1907, 2323, AES.

45. Antonio Ogazón to Secretario de Estado, Altar, May 22, 1909, 2478, AES; Comisario de Policía to Secretario de Estado, San Francisco de los Llanos, May 14, 1909, 2478, AES; Antonio Ogazón to Secretario de Estado, Altar, May 18, 1909, 2478, AES.

46. Antonio Ogazón to Secretario de Estado, Altar, May 18, 1909, 2478, AES.

47. Berta Ulloa, *Historia de la Revolución Mexicana, 1914–1917. La Constitución de 1917* (Mexico, 1983), p. 102.

48. Gobernador Ramón Corral to Juez de Primera Instancia, Hermosillo, July 10, 1891, 619, AHS.

49. *Ibid.*

50. Tomás Robinson Bours y Hermanos to Luis E. Torres, Alamos, October 7, 1909, 2525, AES.

51. Ramón Corral, *Memoria de la administración pública del Estado de Sonora presentada a la legislatura del mismo por el gobernador Ramón Corral*, 2 vols. (Guaymas, 1891), II: 250.

52. Gobernador to Secretarios del Congreso del Estado, Hermosillo, May 18, 1886, 682, AHS.

53. Corral, *Memoria*, II, 251.

54. Ignacio Bonillas to Secretario de Estado, Nogales, Sonora, May 1, 1900, 1584, AES.

55. *Ibid.*

56. United States Department of Commerce, Bureau of Foreign and Domestic Commerce, *Mexican West Coast and Lower California. A Commercial and Industrial Survey* (Washington, D.C., 1923), p. 216.

57. Cuauhtémoc L. Terán, *Jesús García. Héroe de Nacozari* (Hermosillo, 1981), p. 15; Federico García y Alva, *México y su progreso; album-directorio del Estado de Sonora* (Hermosillo, 1905–1907), p. 161.

58. U. B. Freaser to Gobernador Ramón Corral, Opusura, June 18, 1888, 673, AHS.

59. Edward Foster to Gobernador Ramón Corral, Opusura, June 18, 1888, 673, AHS; Secretario de Gobierno to Prefecto, Hermosillo, June 13, 1888, 673, AHS.

60. U. B. Freaser to Gobernador Ramón Corral, Opusura, June 18, 1888, 673, AHS.

61. Cosío Villegas, *Historia*, VII, No. 2, 1182.

62. F. H. Seymour, Manager, to Gobernador Ramón Corral, Imuris, April 2, 1891, 624, AHS.

63. F. H. Seymour, Manager, to Gobernador Ramón Corral, Imuris, May 18, 1891, 624, AHS.

64. Juan Duarte, Eduardo Lubas, and others to Gobernador, Cerro Blanco, August 22, 1891, 624, AHS.

65. *Ibid.*; Gobernador Ramón Corral to Presidente Municipal, Hermosillo, August 25, 1891, 624, AHS; Presidente Municipal to Gobernador Ramón Corral, Imuris, August 29, 1891, 624, AHS; Presidente Municipal to Celador de Policía, Santiago López, Imuris, August 21, 1891, 624, AHS.

66. Manuel R. Uruchurtu, *Apuntes biográficos del señor D. Ramón Corral: desde su nacimiento hasta encargarse del gobierno del Distrito Federal (1854 a 1900)* (Mexico, 1910), p. 201; Eduardo W. Villa, *Compendio de historia del Estado de Sonora* (Mexico, 1937), p. 443; Bernstein, *Mining*, pp. 40, 60; Robert G. Cleland, *A History of Phelps Dodge, 1834–1950* (New York, 1952), p. 135.

67. Balvanero E. Robles, Prefecto, to Secretario de Estado, Moctezuma, February 27, 1905, 682, AHS.

68. Rafael Izábal, "Decreto," Hermosillo, February 4, 1907, 682, AHS.

69. Glen S. Dumke, "Douglas, Border Town," *Pacific Historical Review*, XVIII (August, 1948), p. 287; Albert R. Morawetz, Consul, to Francis B. Loomis, Assistant Secretary of State, Nogales, Sonora, September 2, 1904, CD, IV.

70. Antonio Maza, Vice Consul, to Gobernador, Douglas, July 7, 1906, 2139, AES.

71. "Will Take Mine by Force," *Douglas Daily Dispatch*, July 7, 1905.

72. M. López to Gobernador, Fronteras, July 9, 1905, 2139, AES.

73. Jesús L. Arvizu, Comisario de Policía, to Secretario de Estado, La Colorada, October 6, 1890, 614, AHS.

74. Tomás Rico to Gobernador, Cananea, January 13, 1906, 2129, AES; Presidente Municipal to Secretario de Estado, Cananea, April 6, 1906, 2138, AES; Presidente Municipal to Secretario de Estado, Cananea, April 7, 1906, 2138, AES: Secretario de Estado to Presidente Municipal, Hermosillo, April 11, 1906, 2138, AES.

75. Comisario de Policía to Secretario de Estado, Mineral de Cerro Prieto, February 21, 1906, 2106, AES; Nabor Salazar to Secretario de Estado, Magdalena, December 19, 1906, 2190, AES.

76. Vicente L. Murrieta and others to Gobernador, Cucurpe, March 19, 1908, 2376, AES.

77. *Ibid.*

78. Secretario de Estado to Tesorero General del Estado, Hermosillo, December 26, 1899, 682, AHS.

79. Aguilar Camín, *Frontera*, pp. 113–114.

80. Lázaro Gutiérrez de Lara to Secretario de Estado, April 13, 1906, 2138, AES.

81. R. C. Clancy, Director General, to B. S. Pelzer, Presidente o Representante de la llamada The Picacho Gold Mining Company, Cananea, March 10, 1906, 2138, AES.

82. Ignacio Elías, Prefecto, to Secretario de Estado, Arizpe, May 9, 1906, 2138, AES; Secretario de Estado to Lázaro Gutiérrez de Lara, Hermosillo, May 16, 1906, 2138, AES.

83. Alejandro Fasabia to Presidente Municipal, Cucurpe, December 25, 1906, 2298, AES.

84. Santos Soto and others to Gobernador, Cucurpe, March 20, 1908, 2376, AES.

85. Secretario de Estado to Santos Soto and others, Hermosillo, April 11, 1908, 2376, AES.

86. Francisco Chiapa, Prefecto, to Secretario de Estado, Moctezuma, June 22, 1910, 2559, AES.

87. Leonardo Gámez, Prefecto, to Ramón Corral, Arizpe, December 4, 1884, 552, AHS.

88. *Ibid.*

89. A. Willard, Consul, to W. Hunter, Guaymas, January 28, 1885, CD, V–VI; A. Willard, Consul, to Gobernador Luis E. Torres, Guaymas, December 4, 1884, 552, AHS.

90. A. Willard, Consul, to W. Hunter, Guaymas, February 1, 1885, V–VI.

91. Prefecto to Secretario de Estado, Arizpe, July 28, 1908, 2414, AES; Prefecto to Secretario de Estado, Arizpe, July 28, 1908, 2414, AES.

92. Ignacio Mariscal to Gobernador, Mexico, April 4, 1900, 1622, AES; Ignacio Mariscal to Gobernador, Mexico, April 5, 1900, 1622, AES; Ignacio Mariscal to Gobernador, Mexico, April 8, 1900, 1622, AES.

93. C. C. Ortiz, Gobernador, to Secretario de Relaciones Exteriores, Hermosillo, April 5, 1900, 1622, AES.

94. Ignacio Bonillas to Secretario de Estado, Nogales, Sonora, May 1, 1900, 1584, AES.

95. David Fernández, Presidente Municipal, to Secretario de Gobernación, Cucurpe, October 28, 1895, 668, AHS.

96. William C. Greene to Gobernador, Cucurpe, October 14, 1895, 668, AHS; Ramón Corral, Secretario de Estado, to William C. Greene, Hermosillo, October 21, 1895, 668, AHS.

97. S. M. Aguirre to Secretario de Estado, Cananea, December 12, 1901, 1584, AES.

98. Ignacio Bonillas, Prefecto, to Secretario de Estado, Magdalena, January 1, 1892, 627, AHS.

99. Prefecto to Secretario de Estado, Moctezuma, September 30, 1897, 759, AHS; Secretario de Estado to Prefecto, Hermosillo, October 5, 1897, 759, AHS.

100. Terán, *Jesús García*, p. 20.

101. Secretario de Estado to Presidente Municipal, Hermosillo, August 17, 1891, 619, AHS; Presidente Municipal to Secretario de Estado, Caborca, August 17, 1891, 627, AHS; Secretario de Estado to Presidente Municipal, Hermosillo, September 17, 1891, 627, AHS; Ayuntamiento de Caborca to Secretario de Estado, Caborca, September 26, 1891, 627, AHS; Secretario de Estado to Presidente Municipal, Hermosillo, October 5, 1891, 627, AHS.

102. W. W. Carney to Luis E. Torres, Nogales, Arizona, September 2, 1908, 2414, AES.

103. William Melczer to Gobernador Rafael Izábal, Phoenix, Arizona, September 13, 1900, 1584, AES.

104. Fernando Méndez to Gobernador, Hermosillo, February 14, 1900, 682, AHS; Secretario de Estado to Fernando Méndez, Hermosillo, May 9, 1900, 682, AHS; Appleton H. Danforth to Secretario de Estado, Nacozari, May 19, 1900, 682, AHS.

105. E. A. Price to Gobernador Ramón Corral, Minas Prietas, February 5, 1890, 615, AHS.

106. Presidente Municipal to Secretario de Estado, Minas Prietas, February 22, 1890, 615, AHS.

107. Secretaria de Estado to Prefecto, Hermosillo, March 8, 1890, 615, AHS; Secretario de Estado to E. A. Price, Hermosillo, May 10, 1890, 615, AHS.

108. Prefecto to Secretario de Estado, Hermosillo, November 24, 1891, 620, AHS; Secretaria de Estado to Prefecto, Hermosillo, December 17, 1891, 620, AHS; Jesús Z. Arvizu, Comisario de Policía, to Secretario de Estado, La Colorada, September 13, 1892, 628, AHS; Presidente Municipal to Juez Local, Minas Prietas, December 6, 1892, 628, AHS.

109. J. T. Darnell, Consul, to David J. Hill, Assistant Secretary of State, Nogales, Sonora, July 2, 1901, CD, III.

110. Don Dedera and Bob Robles, *Goodbye Garcia Adios* (Flagstaff, Arizona, 1976), p. 57.

111. Miguel Quirós, Filizardo Peralta, Roberto Camou and others to Gobernador, Nacozari, November 12, 1901, 682, AHS.

112. J. S. Douglas to Secretario de Estado, Nacozari, December 18, 1901, 682, AHS.

113. Aguilar Camín, *Frontera*, p. 113.

114. Stuart F. Voss, "Towns and Enterprises in Northwestern Mexico—A History of Urban Elites in Sonora and Sinaloa, 1830–1910" (Ph.D. thesis, Harvard University, Cambridge, 1972), p. 529.

115. Terán, *Jesús García*, p. 19.

116. Prefecto to Secretario de Estado, Hermosillo, November 25, 1892, 635, AHS.

117. Villa, *Compendio*, p. 459.

118. Rivera, *Revolución*, p. 123.

119. Voss, *Towns*, 527–528.

120. Loreto Trujillo to Gobernador, Sahuaripa, February 22, 1889, 606, AHS.

CHAPTER 6

1. J. F. Darnell, Consul, to David J. Hill, Nogales, Sonora, July 21, 1902, CD, III; J. F. Darnell, Consul, to David J. Hill, Nogales, Sonora, July 27, 1902, CD, III.

2. W. J. Galbraith, Consular Agent, to Albert R. Morawetz, Consul, Cananea, June 9, 1905, CD, IV.

3. Federico García y Alva, ed., *Mexico y su progreso; album-directorio del Estado de Sonora* (Hermosillo, 1905–1907), p. 243.

4. Stuart F. Voss, "Towns and Enterprises in Northwestern Mexico—A History of Urban Elites in Sonora and Sinaloa, 1830–1910" (Ph.D. thesis, Harvard University, Cambridge, 1972), pp. 522–523.

5. *Ibid.*

6. Francisco Medina Hoyos, *Cananea, cuna de la Revolución Mexicana* (Mexico, 1956), pp. 6–7.

7. García y Alva, *Progreso*, p. 245.

8. Filiberto Vázquez Barroso, *Informe. El 16 de septiembre de 1902, al terminar el periodo administrativo del primer ayuntamiento de Cananea, Sonora* (Hermosillo, 1902), pp. 11–14.

9. García y Alva, *Progreso*, p. 260.

10. Vásquez, *Informe*, pp. 11–14.

11. Medina Hoyos, *Cananea*, pp. 6–7.

12. Esteban Baca Calderón, *Juicio sobre la guerra del Yaqui y génesis de la huelga de Cananea. 1° de junio de 1906* (Mexico, 1956), p. 19.

13. Medina Hoyos, *Cananea*, p. 142.

14. Minnie McClure Torrance, "La Profesora McClure," *The Journal of Arizona History*, XX (Spring, 1979), p. 42.

15. Ralph McA. Ingersoll, *In and Under Mexico* (New York and London, 1924), p. 161.

16. *Ibid.*, p. 10.

17. García y Alva, *Progreso*, pp. 317–318.

18. Ingersoll, *In and Under*, pp. 134–136.

19. Don Dedera and Bob Robles, *Goodbye Garcia Adios* (Flagstaff, Arizona, 1976), p. 26.

20. Juan de Dios Bojórquez, *El héroe de Nacozari* (Havana, Cuba, 1926), p. 52.

21. Ingersoll, *In and Under*, pp. 58, 115; Marvin D. Bernstein, *The Mexican Mining Industry, 1890–1950. A Study of the Interaction of Politics, Economics and Technology* (Yellow Springs, 1965), p. 87.

22. Ingersoll, *In and Under*, p. 113.

23. *Ibid.*, p. 119.

24. García y Alva, *Progreso*, p. 341.

25. Gustavo Torres to Secretario de Estado, Hermosillo, December 27, 1901, 1584, AES.

26. Agustín Alcocer to Secretario de Estado, Arizpe, October 18, 1906, 2184, AES.

27. Bernstein, *Mining*, p. 88.

28. Prefecto to Secretario de Estado, Arizpe, October 17, 1908, 2256, AES; Prefecto, A. A. Martínez, to Secretario de Estado, Magdalena, October 30, 1908, 2256, AES; Prefecto to Secretario de Estado, Hermosillo, October 6, 1908, 2256, AES; Prefecto to Secretario de Estado, Arizpe, October 18, 1910, 2595, AES.

29. Robert G. Cleland, *A History of Phelps Dodge, 1834–1950* (New York, 1952), p. 110.

30. Ramón Corral, Secretario de Estado, to Prefecto, Hermosillo, September 21, 1885, 552, AHS.

31. E. García Robles to Secretario de Gobierno, Hermosillo, August 15, 1890, 614, AHS.

32. Secretario de Estado to Prefecto, Hermosillo, November 25, 1892, 635, AHS.

33. Ignacio Bonillas to Secretario de Estado, Magdalena, December 7, 1892, 635, AHS; F. H. Seymour to Ignacio Bonillas, Magdalena, May 14, 1892, 635, AHS.

34. Prefecto to Secretario de Estado, Hermosillo, May 14, 1906, 2184, AES; Prefecto to Secretario de Estado, Hermosillo, December 10, 1906, 2184, AES; Prefecto to Secretario de Estado, Hermosillo, January 6, 1907, 2301, AES; Prefecto to Secretario de Estado, Hermosillo, January 9, 1907, 2301, AES; Prefecto to Secretario de Estado, Hermosillo, May 28, 1907, 2301, AES; Prefecto to Secretario de Estado, Hermosillo, October 8, 1907, 2301, AES; Prefecto to Secretario de Estado, Hermosillo, May 17, 1909, 2325, AES.

35. Francisco Chiapa to Secretario de Estado, Moctezuma, November 30, 1909, 2525, AES; Prefecto to Secretario de Estado, Moctezuma, January 28, 1910, 2644, AES; Prefecto to Secretario de Estado, Moctezuma, May 23, 1910, 2645, AES.

36. Balvanero Robles, Prefecto, to Secretario de Estado, Moctezuma, April 17, 1906, 2185, AES.

37. Balvanero Robles, Prefecto, to Secretario de Estado, Moctezuma, April 17, 1906, 2185, AES.

38. Francisco Chiapa, Prefecto, to Secretario de Estado, Moctezuma, September 27, 1907, 2301, AES.

39. Prefecto to Secretario de Estado, Alamos, November 9, 1908, 2256, AES.

40. Prefecto to Secretario de Estado, Alamos, April 1, 1910, 2645, AES.

41. Ingersoll, *In and Under*, pp. 10–12; Dedera, *Jesús García*, pp. 80 and 82.

42. Ramón Corral, Secretario de Estado, to Prefectos de Distritos, Hermosillo, January 28, 1885, 553, AHS.

43. Contrato celebrado entre el Ejecutivo del Estado y el Señor Jesús P. Salido, Hermosillo, October 13, 1888, 604, AHS.

44. Jefe de Hacienda to Gobernador Ramón Corral, Hermosillo, May 16, 1898, 756, AHS.

45. Prefecto to Secretario de Estado, Ures, February 22, 1906, 2106, AES; Julio Bannaud to Prefecto, Ures, April 17, 1906, 2106, AES.

46. Cuauhtémoc L. Terán, *Jesús García. Héroe de Nacozari* (Hermosillo, 1981), p. 28.

47. Ingersoll, *In and Under*, pp. 81 and 125.

48. Dedera, *Jesus Garcia*, p. 27.

49. Antonio G. Rivera, *La Revolución en Sonora* (Hermosillo, 1969), p. 126.

50. Voss, *Towns*, p. 524.

51. Pedro D. Robles, Apoderado del Señor F. L. Protor, to Gobernador, Hermosillo, January 27, 1907, 2216, AES.

52. *El Centenario*, May 12, 1906.

53. Regidor de Cananea to Gobernador, Cananea, May 24, 1906, 2132, AES.

54. Vázquez Barroso, *Informe*, pp. 11–14.

55. Antonio C. Negrete, Inspector Postal, to Dirección General de Correos, Arizpe, January 31, 1907, 2299, AES.

56. Prefecto to Secretario de Estado, Arizpe, March 21, 1908, 2414, AES.

57. Presidente Municipal to Gobernador, Imuris, August 29, 1891, 624, AHS.

58. Prefecto to Secretaria de Estado, Arizpe, August 16, 1897, 759, AHS.

59. Secretario de Estado to Comisario de Policía, Hermosillo, September 18, 1906, 2106, AES.

60. Francisco Telles, Prefecto, to Secretario de Estado, Ures, April 21, 1906, 2106, AES.

61. Prefecto to Secretario de Estado, Altar, September 24, 1906, 2183, AES.

62. Ignacio Elías, Prefecto, to Secretario de Estado, Arizpe, November 15, 1906, 2184, AES.

63. Secretario de Estado to Presidente Municipal, Hermosillo, March 8, 1909, 2440, AES.

64. Charles E. Hale, Consul, to Edwin Uhl, Assistant Secretary of State, Nogales, November 1, 1894, CD, II.

65. Comisario de Policía to Prefecto, El Tigre, June 21, 1906, 2076, AES.

66. Prefecto to Secretario de Estado, Moctezuma, April 21, 1910, 2645, AES; Prefecto to Gobernador, Moctezuma, October 26, 1911, 2685, AES.

67. Prefecto to Secretario de Estado, Arizpe, March 3, 1908, 2414, AES; Prefecto to Secretario de Estado, Arizpe, March 7, 1908, 2414, AES.

68. Secretario de Estado to Comisario de Policía, Hermosillo, May 3, 1907, 2190, AES.

69. Bernstein, *Mining*, p. 90.

70. Jesús Z. Arvizu to Secretario de Estado, La Colorada, September 9, 1892, 628, AHS.

71. Rosendo Mendival, Agente de Policía, to Ramón Corral, Estación Torres, December 11, 1893, 650, AHS; José Escalante, Prefecto, to Secretario de Estado, Hermosillo, August 10, 1890, 614, AHS; Gerald E. Ward, Superinten-

dent, to Secretario de Estado, Estación Torres, August 10, 1889, 606, AHS; Ramón Corral to Juez de la Instancia de este Distrito, Hermosillo, December 20, 1889, 606, AHS.

72. Información Secreta del Detective enviado para investigar robos de minerales de Las Chispas, Las Chispas [no date] 1908, 2525, AES.

73. Gobernador Luis E. Torres to Secretario de Fomento, Hermosillo, October 23, 1891, 625, AHS.

74. Conrado Pérez to Vice Gobernador, Hermosillo, October 11, 1897, 740, AHS.

75. *Ibid.*

76. *Ibid.*

77. Presidente Municipal to Secretario de Estado, April 23, 1898, 682, AHS.

78. Gerald E. Ward, Superintendent, to Secretario de Estado, Estación Torres, August 10, 1889, 606, AHS.

CHAPTER 7

1. Cuauhtémoc L. Teran, *Jesús García. Heroe de Nacozari* (Hermosillo, 1981), p. 18.

2. Ismael Valencia Ortega, "Desenvolvimiento de la clase obrera en Cananea (1900–1932)," Instituto de Investigaciones Históricas, *IX simposio de historia de Sonora: Memoria* (Hermosillo, 1984), p. 420.

3. Departamento de Estadística Nacional, *Sonora, Sinaloa y Nayarit. Estudio estadístico económico social, elaborado por el Departmento de Estadística Nacional. Año 1927* (Mexico, 1928), p. 69.

4. Calculations based on: "Padrones de habitantes" provided by presidentes municipales for the nine districts to Secretario de Estado, 1906, 2245 and 2248, AES; Linda B. Hall, *Alvaro Obregon, Power and Revolution in Mexico, 1911–1920* (College Station, Texas, 1981), p. 16; Pedro N. Ulloa, *El Estado de Sonora y situación económica al aproximarse el primer centenario de la independencia nacional* (Sonora, 1910), pp. 36, 43; United States Department of Commerce, Bureau of Foreign and Domestic Commerce, *Mexican West Coast and Lower California. A Commercial and Industrial Survey* (Washington, D. C., 1923), p. 41.

5. F. H. Seymour, Manager, to Gobernador Ramón Corral, Imuris, April 2, 1891, 624, AHS.

6. Presidente Municipal to Secretario de Estado, Moctezuma, April 2, 1906, 2245, AES.

7. Ulloa, *Sonora*, p. 93.

8. Marvin D. Bernstein, *The Mexican Mining Industry, 1890–1950. A Study of the Interaction of Politics, Economics and Technology* (Yellow Springs, 1965), p. 86.

9. *Ibid.*; Antonio G. Rivera, *La Revolución en Sonora* (Hermosillo, 1969), p. 157.

10. Don Dedera and Bob Robles, *Goodbye Garcia Adios* (Flagstaff, Arizona, 1976), p. 28.

11. Bernstein, *Mining*, p. 89.

12. Presidente Municipal to Secretario de Estado, Canandea, March 24, 1906, 2245, AES; Presidente Municipal to Secretario de Estado, Magdalena,

March 28, 1906, 2245, AES; H. C. Beauchamp, Manager, to Emilio González, Cumpas, [no day] 1907, 2218, AES; Presidente Municipal to Secretario de Estado, Cumpas, August 29, 1906, 2245, AES.

13. Presidente Municipal to Prefecto, Altar, September 1, 1906, 2245, AES; Presidente Municipal to Prefecto, Caborca, March 27, 1906, 2245, AES.

14. Presidente Municipal to Secretario de Estado, Minas Prietas, May 28, 1906, 2245, AES.

15. Presidente Municipal to Secretario de Estado, Opodepe, April 10, 1906, 2245, AES.

16. Presidente Municipal to Secretario de Estado, [no day] 1906, 2245, AES; Y. L. Almada to Secretario de Estado, Alamos, May 9, 1906, 2245, AES.

17. Presidente Municipal to Secretario de Estado, Sahuaripa, May 2, 1906, 2246, AES; Presidente Municipal to Secretario de Estado, Trinidad, April 21, 1906, 2245, AES.

18. Y. L. Almada to Secretario de Estado, Alamos, May 9, 1906, 2245, AES.

19. Presidente Municipal to Secretario de Estado, Cumpas, August 29, 1906, 2245, AES.

20. Rivera, *Revolución*, p. 157; Stuart F. Voss, "Towns and Enterprises in Northwestern Mexico—A History of Urban Elites in Sonora and Sinaloa, 1830–1910" (Ph.D. thesis, Harvard University, Cambridge, 1972), p. 546.

21. Rivera, *Revolución*, p. 126.

22. Bojórquez, Juan de Dios, *"Champ," Rodolfo Campodónico, autor de "Club Verde"* (Mexico, 1936), p. 58.

23. Computed on the basis of "Informes" from the presidentes municipales for the nine districts to Secretario de Estado, 1906, 2246, AES.

24. Reports of presidentes municipales, Arizpe district, to Secretario de Estado, 1906, 2246, AES; Presidente Municipal to Secretario de Estado, Cananea, August 25, 1906, 2246, AES.

25. Reports of presidentes municipales to Secretario de Estado, Altar, 1906, 2246, AES; reports of presidentes municipales to Secretario de Estado, Magdalena, 1906, 2246, AES.

26. Reports of presidentes municipales to Secretario de Estado, Hermosillo, June 26, 1906, 2246, AES; "Informe," Hermosillo, 1899, 779, AHS.

27. Reports of presidentes municipales to Secretario de Estado, Alamos, 1906, 2246, AES.

28. Reports of presidentes municipales to Secretario de Estado, Sahuaripa, 1906, 2246, AES.

29. Ulloa, *Sonora*, p. 169.

30. Presidente Municipal to Secretario de Estado, Pitiquito, October 24, 1906, 2472, AES.

31. Prefecto to Secretario de Estado, Hermosillo, April 25, 1909, 2472, AES.

32. Prefecto to Secretario de Estado, Ures, [no date] 1909, 2472, AES.

33. Prefecto to Secretario de Estado, Guaymas, January 11, 1909, 2472, AES.

34. Y. I. Almada to Secretario de Estado, Alamos, May 9, 1906, 2245, AES.

35. Robert G. Cleland, *A History of Phelps Dodge, 1834–1950* (New York, 1952), pp. 110–111.

36. Stuart F. Voss, *On the Periphery of Nineteenth-Century Mexico. Sonora and Sinaloa, 1810–1877* (Tucson, 1982), pp. 182–183.

37. A. Willard, Consul, to W. F. Wharton, Guaymas, December 31, 1889, CD, VIII-IX; A. Willard, Consul, to W. F. Wharton, May 8, 1890, CD, XIII-IX.

38. Federico García y Alva, *México y su progreso; album-directorio del Estado de Sonora* (Hermosillo, 1905–1907), p. 339.

39. J. J. Pesqueira to Gobernador, Hermosillo, July 11, 1900, 682, AHS; F. V. Barroso, Presidente Municipal, to Gobernador, Cananea, June 1, 1906, 2184, AES.

40. Rafael López D. to Secretario de Estado, Huépac, November 20, 1906, 2129, AES.

41. García y Alva, *Progreso*, p. 171.

42. *El Progreso*, October 15, 1892; Francisco Morineau to Alberto Cubillas, Gobernador, Caborca, May 24, 1908, 2308, AES; *La Bandera Sonorense*, July 27, 1905.

43. Ayuntamiento de Altar, Altar, November 5, 1887, 576, AHS.

44. Prefecto to Secretario de Estado, Moctezuma, October 16, 1889, 604, AHS.

45. Daniel B. Gillette, Superintendent, to Prefecto, Mulatos, December 16, 1889, 604, AHS; Ramón Corral to Prefecto, Hermosillo, December 31, 1889, 604, AHS.

46. García y Alva, *Progreso*, p. 337; Daniel Cosío Villegas, *El Porfiriato. La vida económica*, Daniel Cosío Villegas *Historia moderna de México*, 9 vols. (Mexico, 1955–1973), VII, No. 1, 295; Rafael Izábal, *Memoria de la administración pública del Estado de Sonora durante el periodo constitucional de 1903 a 1907* (Hermosillo, 1907), p. 149.

47. Esteban Baca Calderón, *Juicio sobre la guerra del Yaqui y génesis de la huelga de Cananea. 1° de junio de 1906* (Mexico, 1956), p. 24.

48. Eduardo W. Villa, *Compendio de historia del Estado de Sonora* (Mexico, 1937), p. 430.

49. Gabriel Monteverde to Gobernador, Hermosillo, October 28, 1910, 2639, AES; Fernando A. Galaz, *Dejaron huella en el Hermosillo de ayer y hoy* (Hermosillo, 1971), p. 754.

50. Horacio Sobarzo, *Episodios históricos* (Mexico, 1981), p. 199.

51. Sociedad de Artesanos Obreros del Porvenir, Guaymas, September 1, 1898, 759, AHS; Prefecto to Secretario de Gobernación, Guaymas, August 19, 1895, 760, AHS; Villa, *Compendio*, p. 424; Presidente, Sociedad de Artesanos Obreros del Porvenir, to Gobernador Ramón Corral, Guaymas, August 7, 1888, 583, AHS.

52. Comité Obrero Guaymense to Gobernador, February 17, 1910, 2639, AES.

53. Rafael González, Presidente, to Gobernador, Guaymas, January 13, 1890, 609, AHS.

54. M. Mascareñas to Gobernador, Nogales, November 29, 1890, 609, AHS.

55. A. Willard, Consul, to W. Hunter, Guaymas, December 31, 1884, CD, V–VI; Prefecto to Secretario de Estado, Sahuaripa, February 21, 1887, 576, AHS.

56. A. Willard, Consul, to J. D. Porter, Guaymas, December 31, 1885, CD, V–VI.

57. Prefecto to Secretario de Estado, Sahuaripa, February 21, 1887, 576, AHS.

58. *Ibid.*

59. J. Alexander Forbes, "Annual Report," May 1, 1893, Guaymas, CD, VIII–IX.

60. Representante General to Loreto Trujillo, Prefecto, Sahuaripa, February 26, 1889, 606, AHS; Beene Delmar Leon, "Sonora in the Age of Ramón Corral, 1875–1900" (Ph.D. thesis, University of Arizona, Tucson, 1972), pp. 167–170.

61. Edmund Harvey, General Manager, to Gobernador Ramón Corral, Los Bronces, February 26, 1889, 606, AHS.

62. Loreto Trujillo to Gobernador, Sahuaripa, February 22, 1889, 606, AHS.

63. Representante General to Loreto Trujillo, Prefecto, Sahuaripa, February 26, 1889, 606, AHS.

64. Francisco R. Almada, *Diccionario de historia, geografía y biografía sonorenses* (Chihuahua, 1952), p. 351.

65. Richard R. Hawkins to A. Willard, Sahuaripa, February 25, 1889, 606, AHS.

66. *Ibid.*

67. *Ibid.*

68. *Ibid.*

69. Edmund Harvey to Ramón Corral, Los Bronces, March 16, 1889, 606, AHS.

70. *Ibid.*

71. Loreto Trujillo to Secretario de Estado, Sahuaripa, February 25, 1889, 606, AHS.

72. Quoted in Manuel Fernández, Secretario de Fomento, to Gobernador, Mexico, January 12, 1889, 606, AHS.

73. Quoted in *ibid.*

74. Ramón Corral to Secretario de Fomento, Hermosillo, January 21, 1889, 606, AHS.

75. Gobernador Ramón Corral to Edmund Harvey, Hermosillo, March 7, 1889, 606, AHS; Gobernador Ramón Corral to Edmund Harvey, Hermosillo, March 26, 1889, 606, AHS; Loreto Trujillo to Gobernador Ramón Corral, Trinidad, February 17, 1889, 606, AHS.

76. Loreto Trujillo to Gobernador Ramón Corral, Trinidad, February 17, 1889, 606, AHS; Loreto Trujillo to Secretario de Estado, Sahuaripa, Feburary 25, 1889, 606, AHS.

77. Ramón Corral to Loreto Trujillo, Hermosillo, March 1, 1889, 606, AHS.

78. *Ibid.*; Loreto Trujillo, Prefecto, to Presidente Municipal, Sahuaripa, February 25, 1889, 606, AHS.

79. Loreto Trujillo to Gobernador Ramón Corral, Sahuaripa, February 22, 1889, 606, AHS.

80. Loreto Trujillo to Presidente Municipal, Sahuaripa, February 3, 1889, 606, AHS.

81. Gobernador Ramón Corral to Loreto Trujillo, March 7, 1889, 606, AHS.

82. Loreto Trujillo to Gobernador Ramón Corral, February 22, 1889, 606, AHS.

83. Noticia que manifiesta el numero de habitantes, Trinidad, December 21, 1905, 2244, AES.

84. Calderón, *Juicio*, p. 25.

85. Stuart F. Voss, "Towns and Enterprises in Northwestern Mexico—A History of Urban Elites in Sonora and Sinaloa, 1830–1910" (Ph.D. thesis, Harvard University, Cambridge, 1972), pp. 550–551.

86. Bernstein, *Mining*, p. 59.

87. Cosío Villegas, *Historia*, VII, No. 2, 708.

88. Calderón, *Juicio*, p. 18; Rivera, *Revolución*, p. 126.

89. Calderón, *Juicio*, p. 18.

90. H. C. Beauchamp, Manager, to Emilio González, Cumpas, August [no date] 1907, 2218, AES.

91. Consuelo Boyd, "Twenty Years to Nogales: The Building of the Guaymas-Nogales Railroad," *The Journal of Arizona History*, XXII (Autumn, 1981), p. 308.

92. Federico H. Seymour to Presidente Municipal, Estación Torres, March 27, 1907, AES.

93. M. P. Box, Milling Engineer, to Gobernador Luis E. Torres, San Francisco, November 28, 1884, 682, AHS.

94. Rafael de Zayas Enríquez, *Porfirio Díaz* (New York, 1908), pp. 236 and 241.

95. Prefecto to Secretario de Estado, Arizpe, September 3, 1906, 2184, AES.

96. Prefecto to Secretario de Estado, Altar, September 24, 1906, 2183, AES.

97. Prefecto to Secretario de Estado, Moctezuma, April 23, 1908, 2478, AES.

98. Francisco Chiapa to Secretario de Estado, Moctezuma, November 4, 1907, 2264, AES; Secretario de Estado to Prefecto, Hermosillo, June 18, 1907, 2264, AES.

99. Adolfo Noriega to Alberto Cubillas, Pitiquito, June 18, 1907, 2201, AES.

100. Felizardo Bazurto to Gobernador, Magdalena, September 28, 1907, 2264, AES.

101. Djed Bórquez, *Monzón; semblanza de un revolucionario* (Mexico, 1942), p. 9; Terán, *Jesús García*, p. 30; Héctor Aguilar Camín, *La frontera nómada; Sonora y la Revolución Mexicana* (Mexico, 1977), p. 123; Almada, *Diccionario*, p. 485.

102. Aguilar Camín, *Frontera*, pp. 122–123.

103. *Ibid.*, p. 116.

104. Almada, *Diccionario*, p. 337.

CHAPTER 8

1. Manuel Santiago Corbalá Acuña, *Alamos de Sonora* (Mexico, 1977), p. 24.

2. A. F. Garrison, Vice Consul, "Annual Report," September 30, 1872, CD, III–IV.

3. Armando Quijada Hernández, "Perspectiva histórica de Sonora, 1821–

1831," Instituto de Investigaciones Históricas, _IX simposio de historia de Sonora: Memoria_ (Hermosillo, 1984), p. 126; Hubert H. Bancroft, _Recursos y desarrollo de México_ (San Francisco, 1892), p. 491; Manuel R. Uruchurtu, _Apuntes biográficos del señor D. Ramón Corral: desde su nacimiento hasta encargarse del gobierno del distrito federal (1854 a 1900)_ (Mexico, 1910), pp. 13–14; Daniel Cosío Villegas, _El Porfiriato. La vida económica_, Daniel Cosío Villegas, _Historia moderna de México_, 9 vols. (Mexico, 1955–1973), VII, No. 1:9.

4. Claudio Dabdoub, "Panorama del sur de Sonora en los siglos XIX y principios del XX (En su aspectos económicos y social)," Instituto de Investigaciones Históricas, _Primer simposio de historia de Sonora: Memoria_ (Hermosillo, 1976), p. 253; Cosío Villegas, _Historia_, VII, No. 2, 298 and 751–752; Ramón Corral, Secretario de Estado, to Celedonio Ortiz and others, Hermosillo, December 4, 1885, 553, AHS.

5. Carlos Dabdoub, "La economía de Sonora en 1907 y su naciente industrialización," Instituto de Investigaciones Históricas, _V simposio de historia de Sonora: Memoria_ (Hermosillo, 1980), p. 213.

6. Francisco R. Almada, _Diccionario de historia, geografía y biografía sonorenses_ (Chihuahua, 1952), p. 405.

7. A. F. Garrison, Vice Consul, "Annual Report," September 30, 1884, CD, III-IV.

8. Stuart F. Voss, _On the Periphery of Nineteenth-Century Mexico. Sonora and Sinaloa, 1810–1877_ (Tucson, 1982), p. 24.

9. _Ibid._, p. 108.

10. _Ibid._, p. 109.

11. _Ibid._, pp. 24 and 47.

12. _Ibid._, p. 24.

13. Carl Lumholtz, _El México desconocido. Cinco años de exploración entre las tribus de la Sierra Madre Occidental; en la tierra caliente de Tepic y Jalisco y entre los Tarasco de Michoacán_; translated by Balbino Dávalos, 2 vols. (Mexico, 1945), I, 13.

14. Alberto Suárez Barnett, "Los presupuestos de egresos del gobierno del Estado, 1863–1910" (Unpublished manuscript, Nogales, Sonora, 1983), p. 8.

15. _Ibid._, p. 5; Rodolfo F. Acuña, _Sonoran Strongman; Ignacio Pesqueira and His Times_ (Tucson, 1974), pp. ix, xx and 16; Eduardo W. Villa, _Compendio de historia del Estado de Sonora_ (Mexico, 1937), p. 227; Voss, _Sonora_, p. 139.

16. Voss, _Sonora, pp._ 151–160.

17. _Ibid._

18. A. F. Garrison, Vice Consul, "Annual Report," September 30, 1872, Guaymas, CD, III-IV.

19. Gregorio Mora Torres, "Los comerciantes de Guaymas y el desarrollo económico de Sonora, 1825–1910," Instituto de Investigaciones Históricas, _IX simposio de historia de Sonora. Memoria_ (Hermosillo, 1984), p. 216; Inés Herrera Canales, "El comercio exterior de México en el siglo XIX desde una perspectiva regional: Sonora de 1821 a 1910," Instituto de Investigaciones Históricas, _III simposio de historia de Sonora: Memoria_, 2 vols. (Hermosillo, 1978), I, 261.

20. David M. Pletcher, "The Development of Railroads in Sonora," _Interamerican Economic Affairs_, I (March, 1948), p. 6.

21. _Ibid._, p. 6; Herrera Canales, _Comercio_, I, 261.

22. Bancroft, *Recursos*, p. 477; Cosío Villegas, *Historia*, VII, No. 2, 779; Herrera Canales, *Comercio*, I, 279.

23. Alfonso Iberri, *El viejo Guaymas* (Mexico, 1952), p. 18; Francisco R. Almada, *La Revolución en el Estado de Sonora* (Mexico, 1971), p. 24; Stuart F. Voss, "Towns and Enterprises in Northwestern Mexico—A History of Urban Elites in Sonora and Sinaloa, 1830–1910" (Ph.D. thesis, Harvard University, Cambridge, 1972), pp. 516–517.

24. Bancroft, *Recursos*, p. 455; A. Willard, Consul, to W. F. Wharton, Guaymas, February 9, 1891, CD, VIII–IX.

25. Robert G. Cleland, *A History of Phelps Dodge, 1834–1950* (New York, 1952), p. 142.

26. Voss, *Towns*, p. 514; Héctor Aguilar Camín, *La frontera nómada; Sonora y la Revolución Mexicana* (Mexico, 1977), p. 74.

27. Dabdoub, *Economia*, p. 209.

28. Aguilar Camín, *Frontera*, pp. 70, 74.

29. Presidente Municipal to Secretario de Estado, Guaymas, October 6, 1906, 2245, AES.

30. Dabdoub, *Economía*, p. 210.

31. Secretario de Estado to Consul de los Estados Unidos Mexicanos, Hermosillo, March 28, 1898, 745, AHS.

32. Estado de Sonora, lista nominal de los vecinos principales de cada población, Distrito de Guaymas, Guaymas, September 5, 1892, 647, AHS.

33. Iberri, *Guaymas*, pp. 18, 25; Juan de Dios Bojórquez, *"Champ," Rodolfo Campodónico, autor de "Club Verde"* (Mexico, 1936), p. 58.

34. Aguilar Camín, *Frontera*, p. 73.

35. *Ibid.*, p. 75; Herrera Canales, *Comercio*, I, 269, 272, 276–277.

36. Ramón Corral, Gobernador, to Diputados Secretarios del Congreso del Estado, Hermosillo, December 10, 1889, 599, AHS; Dabdoub, *Panorama*, p. 254.

37. Prefecto to Ramón Corral, Altar, September 24, 1885, 552, AHS.

38. Suárez Barnett, *Egresos*, p. 8.

39. A. Willard, Consul, to W. Hunter, Guaymas, February 13, 1881, CD, V–VI: Ramón Corral, Gobernador, to Disputados Secretarios del Congreso Estatal, Hermosillo, November 14, 1888, 587, AHS.

40. Pedro N. Ulloa, *El Estado de Sonora y situación económica al aproximarse el primer centenario de la independencia nacional* (Hermosillo, 1910), pp. 49–51.

41. Mora Torres, *Comerciantes*, p. 210.

42. Colegio de México, *Estadísticas económicas del Porfiriato. Comercio exterior de México, 1877–1911* (Mexico, 1960), pp. 487 and 499.

43. A. Willard, Consul, to Department of State, Guaymas, March 3, 1890, CD, VIII–IX.

44. Voss, *Towns*, p. 327.

45. Albert R. Morawetz, Consul, to David J. Hill, Assistant Secretary of State, Nogales, Sonora, January 17, 1903, CD, 4.

46. Dabdoub, *Economía*, p. 204.

47. Presidente Municipal to Secretario de Estado, Hermosillo, November 9, 1906, 2245, AES.

48. Voss, *Towns*, pp. 337, 473, 475 and 477.

49. *Ibid.*, pp. 327–328.

50. F. T. Dávila, *Sonora histórico y descriptivo* (Nogales, Arizona, 1894), p. 265.

51. Presidente Municipal to Secretario de Estado, Alamos, August 25, 1906, 2245, AES: Estado de Sonora, lista nominal de los vecinos principales de cada población, Distrito de Alamos, Alamos, [no date] 1892, 647, AHS.

52. Presidente Municipal to Secretario de Estado, Aduana, May 30, 1906, 2245, AES; Presidente Municipal to Secretario de Estado, Río Chico, May 26, 1906, 2245, AES.

53. Presidente Municipal to Secretario de Estado, Quiriego, August 27, 1906, 2245, AES; Presidente Municipal, Rosario, June 20, 1906, 2245, AES; Presidente Municipal to Secretario de Estado, Comoa, May 26, 1906, 2245, AES; Presidente Municipal to Secretario de Estado, Novas, May 30, 1906, 2245, AES; Presidente Municipal to Secretario de Estado, Promontorios, August 28, 1906, 2245, AES; Presidente Municipal to Secretario de Estado, Minas Nuevas, [no date] 1906, 2245, AES; Presidente Municipal to Secretario de Estado, Nuri, June 17, 1906, 2245, AES.

54. Presidente Municipal to Secretario de Estado, Horcasitas, May 24, 1906, 2245, AES.

55. Presidente Municipal to Secretario de Estado, Ures, May 26, 1906, 2245, AES: Voss, *Towns*, pp. 331–332.

56. Aguilar Camín, *Frontera*, p. 107.

57. Presidente Municipal to Secretario de Estado, Ures, May 26, 1906, 2245, AES.

58. Noticia de los pueblos, congregaciones, haciendas, ranchos comprendidos en la jurisdicción de esta municipalidad, Magdalena, October 28, 1905, 2244, AES; Presidente Municipal to Secretario de Estado, Magdalena, May 25, 1906, 2245, AES; Estado de Sonora, Modelo No. 2, Distrito de Magdalena, Villa de Magdalena, Magdalena, March 31, 1892, 647, AES.

59. Presidente Municipal to Secretario de Estado, Santa Cruz, May 24, 1906, 2245, AES.

60. Ramón Corral, *Memoria de la administración pública del Estado de Sonora presentada a la legislatura del mismo por el gobernador Ramón Corral*, 2 vols. (Guaymas, 1891), I, 341.

61. Allen T. Bird, *The Land of Nayarit* (Nogales, Arizona, 1904), p. 2·.

62. Secretario de Estado to Diputados Secretarios del Congreso del Estado, Hermosillo, May 21, 1887, 575, AHS.

63. Alma Ready, ed., *Nogales, Arizona, 1880–1980* (Nogales, Arizona, 1980), p. 30.

64. *Ibid.*, pp. 10 and 92; V. A. Almada to Secretario de Estado, Magdalena, June 27, 1889, 616, AHS.

65. Presidente Municipal to Prefecto, Nogales, March 13, 1890, 615, AHS.

66. Presidente Municipal to Prefecto, Nogales, September 12, 1890, 607, AHS; Ramón Corral to Prefecto, Hermosillo, September 20, 1890, 607, AHS.

67. J. W. Espinosa and others to Gobernador, Nogales, July 26, 1889, 604, AES; L. W. Mix to Ramón Corral, Nogales, Arizona, August 28, 1889, 604, AHS; M. Mascareñas to Secretario de Estado, Nogales, August 12, 1889, 604, AHS.

68. J. F. Darnel, Consul, to Assistant Secretary of State, Nogales, November 18, 1898, CD, III.

69. Ayuntamiento de Nogales. Padrón de los habitantes de la municipalidad de Nogales, Nogales, May 11, 1889, 616, AHS.

70. *Ibid.*

71. Voss, *Towns*, p. 332; Silvia Raquel Flores García, "La importancia del ferrocarril en la fundición de Nogales, 1880–1884" (Unpublished manuscript, Instituto de Antropologia e Historia, Hermosillo, 1983), p. 188; Colegio, *Estadística*, p. 494.

72. Colegio, *Estadística*, p. 473.

73. Presidente Municipal to Secretario de Estado, Magdalenda, May 26, 1906, 2245, AES.

74. Voss, *Towns*, pp. 470–471.

75. Federico García y Alva, *México y su progreso; álbum directorio del Estado de Sonora* (Hermosillo, 1905–1907), p. 335.

76. Joaquin Corella, Ignacio E. Elías, and others to Secretario de Estado, Banámichi, March 31, 1906, 2129, AES; Secretario de Comunicaciones y Obras Públicas to Gobernador, December 11, 1906, 2129, AES; Presidente Municipal to Secretario de Estado, Baviácora, June 26, 1906, 2245, AES; Presidente Municipal to Secretario de Estado, Banámichi, September 1, 1906, 2245, AES.

77. Presidente Municipal to Secretario de Estado, Moctezuma, August 30, 1906, 2245, AES; Presidente Municipal to Secretario de Estado, Arizpe, July 25, 1906, 2245, AES.

78. T. Ortiz to Secretario de Estado, Altar, July 30, 1891, 624, AHS.

79. Presidente Municipal to Secretario de Estado, Caborca, May 30, 1906, 2245, AES; Presidente Municipal to Gobernador, Caborca, October 14, 1911, 2657, AES; Alberto Cubillas to Francisco Morineau, Hermosillo [no date] 1908, 2308, AES.

80. Presidente Municipal to Secretario de Estado, Altar, August 24, 1906, 2245, AES.

81. Departamento de la Estadística Nacional, *Sonora, Sinaloa y Nayarit. Estudio estadístico económico social, elaborado por el Departamento de la Estadística Nacional. Año 1927* (Mexico, 1928), p. 415; José Y. Limantour to Luis E. Torres, Mexico, September 4, 1895, 738, AHS; *La Constitución*, October 1, 1897.

82. Ramón Corral to Jose Y. Limantour, Hermosillo, September 25, 1895, 738, AHS; Ramón Corral to Secretarios del Congreso del Estado, Hermosillo, December 11, 1897, 759, AHS.

83. Almada, *Diccionario*, p. 100; Almada, *Revolución*, p. 25.

84. Almada, *Diccionario*, p. 99.

85. Ulloa, *Sonora*, p. 193.

86. Voss, *Towns*, p. 469.

87. Corral, *Memoria*, II, 264.

88. Secretario de Estado to Propietarios de Molinas Harineros, Hermosillo, December 31, 1889, 603, AHS.

89. Angel Bassols Batalla, *México. Formación de regiones económicas* (Mexico, 1979), p. 177.

90. Bancroft, *Recursos*, p. 497.

91. Ramón Corral to Secretario de Hacienda, Hermosillo, November 20, 1889, 610, AHS.

92. Eduardo S. Klein to Gobernador, Nogales, March 23, 1906, 2105, AES.

93. Presidente Municipal to Secretario de Estado, Nogales, August 2, 1897, 755, AHS; R. Larralde, P. Sandoval, Amado González, M. Mascareñas, and others to Supremo Gobierno, Mexico, February 10, 1890, 610, AHS.

94. Ramón Corral to Secretario de Hacienda, Hermosillo, November 20, 1889, 610, AHS.

CHAPTER 9

1. Alfonso Trueba, *El Padre Kino; misionero itinerante y ecuestre* (Mexico, 1955), pp. 30–31.

2. Stuart F. Voss, *On the Periphery of Nineteenth-Century Mexico. Sonora and Sinaloa, 1810–1877* (Tucson, 1982), p. 23.

3. Federico García y Alva, *México y su progreso; álbum-directorio del Estado de Sonora* (Hermosillo, 1905–1907), p. 9; Healy-Genda, ed., *Directorio comercial del Estado de Sonora* (Hermosillo, 1920), p. 105; United States Department of Commerce, Bureau of Foreign and Domestic Commerce, *Mexican West Coast and Lower California. A Commercial and Industrial Survey* (Washington, D. C., 1923), p. 209; Roger Dunbier, *The Sonoran Desert. Its Geography, Economy and People* (Tucson, 1968), p. 268; R. Gabilondo to Alberto Cubillas, Agua Prieta, October 1, 1909, 2519, AES.

4. A. Willard, Consul, to J. D. Porter, Guaymas, December 31, 1885, CD, V–VI.

5. Tesorería General del Estado to Gobernador, Hermosillo, January 21, 1887, 578, AHS.

6. Hubert H. Bancroft, *Recursos y desarrollo de México* (San Francisco, 1892), p. 367; Daniel Cosío Villegas, *El Porfiriato. La vida económica*, Daniel Cosío Villegas, ed., *Historia moderna de México*, 9 vols. (Mexico, 1955–1973), VII, No. 1, 152.

7. Cosío Villegas, *Historia*, VII, No. 2, 1107.

8. A. Willard, Consul, to J. D. Porter, Guaymas, November 1, 1886, CD, VII; A. Willard, Consul, "Annual Report," December 31, 1887, Guaymas, CD, VII.

9. Guillermo Barnett to Gobernador, Nogales, January 24, 1898, 756, AHS.

10. Alma Ready and Alberto Suárez Barnett, "William Barnett, Gringo Rancher of La Arizona, Sonora" (Unpublished Manuscript, Nogales, Arizona, 1982), pp. 6 and 9.

11. Jesús Moreno Villaescuso to Gobernador, Hermosillo, May 11, 1887, 575, AHS; Antonio Richards to Gobernador, Magdalena, March 30, 1887, 575, AHS.

12. M. Fernández, Secretario de Fomento, to Gobernador, Mexico, June 8, 1887, 575, AHS.

13. A. Willard, Consul, to Vice Gobernador, Ramón Corral, Guaymas, March 11, 1888, 584, AHS.

14. Francisco Ballesteros, Presidente Municipal, to Secretario de Estado, Sinoquipe, [no date] 1898, 756, AHS.

15. Prefecto to Secretario de Estado, Arizpe, October 6, 1890, 608, AHS.

16. Tomás and Daniel Hagan to Gobernador, Nogales, February 22, 1890, 614, AHS.

17. Marvin D. Bernstein, *The Mexican Mining Industry, 1890–1950. A Study of the Interaction of Politics, Economics and Technology* (Yellow Springs, 1965), p. 58; Stuart F. Voss, "Towns and Enterprises in Northwestern Mexico—A History of Urban Elites in Sonora and Sinaloa, 1830–1910" (Ph.D. thesis, Harvard University, Cambridge, 1972), p. 522.

18. Ignacio E. Elías, Prefecto, to Secretario de Estado, Arizpe, September 29, 1907, 2266, AES.

19. Presidente Municipal to Secretario de Estado, Santa Cruz, April 18, 1906, 2245, AES; Tesorería General del Estado to Gobernador, Hermosillo, January 21, 1887, 578, AHS; Presidente Municipal to Secretario de Estado, Suaqui Grande, March 31, 1906, 2245, AES.

20. Germán Zúñiga Moreno, "Consideraciones sobre la posesión de la tierra y la propiedad privada," Instituto de Investigaciones Históricas, *Segundo simposio de historia de Sonora: Memoria* (Hermosillo, 1977), pp. 56–57; García y Alva, *Progreso*, p. 316; Francisco R. Almada, *La Revolución en el Estado de Sonora* (Mexico, 1971), p. 26.

21. Rafael Izábal, *Memoria de la administración pública del Estado de Sonora durante el periodo constitucional de 1902 a 1907* (Hermosillo, 1907), no page; H. C. Beauchamp, Manager, to Emilio González, Cumpas, August [no date] 1907, 2218, AES; Voss, *Towns*, p. 531.

22. A. Willard, Consul, "Annual Report," December 31, 1888, Guaymas, CD, VII; Voss, *Towns*, pp. 323–324; Eduardo W. Villa, *Compendio de historia del Estado de Sonora* (Mexico, 1937), p. 464.

23. Dunbier, *Sonoran*, p. 264; Ignacio E. Elías to Secretario de Estado, Arizpe, October 3, 1906, 2266, AES.

24. Ignacio E. Elías to Secretario de Estado, Arizpe, June 23, 1908, 2311, AES; Manuel Elías to Secretario de Estado, Agua Prieta, December 22, 1908, 2519.

25. Izábal, *Memoria*, p. 176.

26. P. Sandoval to Gobernador, Nogales, February 12, 1906, 2519, AES.

27. Healy-Genda, *Directorio*, p. 105.

28. Pedro N. Ulloa, *El Estado de Sonora y situación económica al aproximarse el primer centenario de la independencia nacional* (Hermosillo, 1910), p. 183.

29. Delos H. Smith, Consul, to William F. Wharton, Assistant Secretary of State, Nogales, April 25, 1890, CD, I.

30. Reuben D. George, Deputy Consul, to W. W. Rockhill, Assistant Secretary of State, Nogales, May 11, 1897, CD, III.

31. Tesorería General del Estado to Secretario de Estado, Hermosillo, March 14, 1898, 756, AHS.

32. Department of Commerce, *West Coast*, p. 208.

33. A. Willard, Consul, to W. Hunter, Guaymas, October 5, 1883, CD, V–VI; A. Willard, Consul, to J. D. Porter, Guaymas, December 31, 1885, CD, V–VI.

34. Colin Cameron to Gobernador Ramón Corral, Santa Ana, October 15,

1888, 586, AHS; Colin Cameron to Gobernador Ramón Corral, Lochiel, Arizona, October 18, 1888, 586, AHS.

35. F. A. Aguilar and George Spindle to Gobernador, Hermosillo, April 6, 1898, 756, AHS.

36. Miguel López to Gobernador Ramón Corral, Hermosillo, February 17, 1898, 756, AHS.

37. Cipriano Ortega to Gobernador, Altar, July 2, 1898, 756, AHS.

38. Antonio Ogazón to Secretario de Estado, Altar, December 12, 1909, 2475, AES.

39. Inspector de Ganadería to Gobernador, Nogales, August 8, 1907, 2298, AES.

40. F. T. Dávila, *Sonora histórico y descriptivo* (Nogales, Arizona, 1894), p. 306; Delos H. Smith, Consul, to William F. Wharton, Assistant Secretary of State, Nogales, July 17, 1890, CD, 1.

41. Ulloa, *Sonora*, p. 179.

42. Corral, *Memoria*, II, 265.

43. Secretario de Estado to Manuel Mascareñas, Presidente de la Junta de Ganaderos del Estado de Sonora, Hermosillo, January 3, 1891, 625, AHS.

44. T. Ortiz to Secretario de Estado, Altar, July 30, 1891, 624, AHS.

45. Dávila, *Sonora*, p. 184; García y Alva, *Progreso*, p. 9.

46. United States Department of Commerce and Labor, Bureau of Manufacturers, *Commercial Relations of the United States with Foreign Countries* (Washington, D. C., 1911), p. 552.

47. A. Willard, Consul, to J. D. Porter, Guaymas, September 26, 1887, CD, VII.

48. A. Willard, Consul, to G. L. Rivers, Guaymas, November 3, 1888, CD, VII.

49. Miguel López, Presidente Municipal, to Gobernador, Fronteras, July 27, 1897, 749, AHS.

50. M. Molina to Alberto Cubillas, Terrenate, October 8, 1909, 2519, AHS; Luis E. Torres to Mi estimado amigo, Hermosillo, January 30, 1909, 2519, AES.

51. Roberto V. Pesqueira to Alberto Cubillas, Fronteras, April 18, 1910, 2640, AES; Gobernador to P. G. Vega, Inspector de Ganadería, Hermosillo, April 21, 1910, 2640, AES.

52. Juan Figueroa, Presidente Municipal, to Gobernador, Fronteras, February 7, 1907, 2301, AES; José Escalante, Prefecto, to Secretario de Estado, Magdalena, February 21, 1894, 660, AHS.

53. Gobernador Ramón Corral to Diputados Secretarios del Congreso Estatal, Hermosillo, June 12, 1888, 588, AHS; Gobernador Ramón Corral to General Angel Martínez, Jefe de la la Zona Militar, Hermosillo, December 26, 1887, 585, AHS.

54. Prefecto to Secretario de Estado, Magdalena, June 2, 1888, 586, AHS; Ramón Corral to Capitán de Rurales, Hermosillo, January 28, 1889, 596, AHS.

55. *El Independiente*, November 29, 1894.

56. Prefecto to Secretario de Estado, Arizpe, July 6, 1909, 2479, AES.

57. Ignacio Pesqueira, Prefecto, to Alberto Cubillas, Arizpe, November 13,

1910, 2644, AES; Manuel Mascareñas and others to Presidente Municipal, Nogales, May 18, 1910, 2644, AES.

58. Arturo M. Elías, Consul, to Gobernador, Tucson, Arizona, September 29, 1910, 2644, AES.

59. Prefecto to Presidente Municipal, Altar, May 10, 1906, 2184, AES.

60. P. G. Vega, Inspector de Ganadería, to Secretario de Estado, Hermosillo, February 8, 1909, 2519, AES; State of Sonora, *Resolutions Passed by the Convention of Cattlemen of Sonora to Combat the Microbe Producing Texas Fever. Relative Dispositions Enacted by the State Government* (Hermosillo, 1909), pp. 1–6; Ignacio E. Elías to Alberto Cubillas, Arizpe, October 2, 1909, 2519, AES.

61. Noticia de la matanza de ganado en este Estado durante el año de 1899, Hermosillo, July 12, 1900, 1590, AES; "Informes" of presidentes municipales to Secretario de Estado, 1906, 2246, AES; Secretario de Estado to Agente Consular del Rey de Italia, Hermosillo, December 18, 1909, 2368, AES.

CHAPTER 10

1. Héctor Aguilar Camín, *La Frontera nómada. Sonora y la Revolución Mexicana* (Mexico, 1977), p. 39.

2. Prefecto to Secretario de Estado, Alamos, January 26, 1909, 2525, AES.

3. Secretaria de Estado to Director General de Correos, Hermosillo, October 8, 1907, 2299, AES.

4. Palemón Zavala, *Perfiles de Sonora* (Hermosillo, 1984), p. 37.

5. Secretaría de Fomento to Gobernador, Mexico, November 28, 1896, 730, AHS; Pedro N. Ulloa, *El Estado de Sonora y situación económica al aproximarse el primer centenario de la independencia nacional* (Hermosillo, 1910), pp. 130 and 138–139.

6. Aguilar Camín, *Frontera*, p. 31.

7. Crispín J. Palomares and others to Gobernador, Hermosillo, November 10, 1911, 2657, AES.

8. Secretario de Fomento to Gobernador, Mexico, September 27, 1908, 2302, AES.

9. Federico García y Alva, *México y su progreso; álbum-directorio del Estado de Sonora* (Hermosillo, 1905–1907), p. 230.

10. Isabel Socorro Gallareta Partida, "Las aguas del río Mayo (1900–1920)," Instituto de Investigaciones Históricas, *IX simposio de historia de Sonora* (Hermosillo, 1984), p. 395; Ulloa, *Sonora*, pp. 143 and 147.

11. Héctor Aguilar Camín, *Saldos de la Revolución: cultura y política de México, 1910–1980* (Mexico, 1982), p. 24.

12. Joaquín Mange, "Historia del negocio del garbanzo," Raul E. Montaño and Octavio P. Gaxiola, eds., *Album del Mayo y del Yaqui; directorio comercial, 1933* (Navojoa, 1932), pp. 40–41.

13. Aguilar Camín, *Frontera*, p. 23; Carlos Dabdoub, "La economía de Sonora en 1907 y su naciente industrialización," Instituto de Investigaciones Históricas, *V simposio de historia de Sonora: Memoria* (Hermosillo, 1980), p. 209; Mange, *Garbanzo*, pp. 48–49; Ulloa, *Sonora*, p. 144.

14. A. Willard, Consul, to W. Hunter, Guaymas, April 3, 1885, CD, V-VI;

United States Department of Commerce, Bureau of Foreign and Domestic Commerce, *Mexican West Coast and Lower California. A Commercial and Industrial Survey* (Washington, D. C., 1923), p. 100.

15. Mange, *Garbanzo*, p. 40; Aguilar Camín, *Frontera*, p. 47; Francisco R. Almada, *La Revolución en el Estado de Sonora* (Mexico, 1971), p. 20.

16. Secretaría de Fomento to Gobernador, Mexico, February 6, 1891, 618, AHS; Gobierno del Estado de Sonora, Ley que exonera la Compañía de Irrigación de Sonora y Sinaloa de toda clase de contribuciones del Estado, Hermosillo, November 1, 1892, 618, AHS; Francisco R. Almada, *Diccionario de historia, geografía y biografía sonorenses* (Chihuahua, 1952), pp. 164–165 and 171.

17. Aguilar Camín, *Frontera*, pp. 39 and 55.

18. W. E. Richardson to Gobernador, Hermosillo, November 21, 1908, 2323, AES; Claudio Dabdoub, "Panorama del sur de Sonora en los siglos XIX y principios del XX en sus aspectos económicos y social," Instituto de Investigaciones Históricas, *Primer simposio de historia de Sonora: Memoria* (Hermosillo, 1976), pp. 257–261; Antonio G. Rivera, *La Revolución en Sonora* (Hermosillo, 1969), p. 19; Aguilar Camín, *Frontera*, p. 35; Daniel Cosío Villegas, *El Porfiriato. La vida económica*, Daniel Cosío Villegas, ed., *Historia moderna de México*, 9 vols. (Mexico, 1955–1973), VII, No. 2, 1112.

19. Dabdoub, *Economía*, pp. 207–208; David M. Pletcher, "The Development of Railroads in Sonora," *Interamerican Economic Affairs*, I (March, 1948), p. 31; Department of Commerce, *West Coast*, p. 102.

20. Healy-Genda, ed., *Directorio comercial del Estado de Sonora* (Hermosillo, 1920).

21. United States Department of Commerce and Labor, Bureau of Manufactures, *Commercial Relations of the United States with Foreign Countries* (Washington, D. C., 1911), p. 541.

22. Charles S. Aiken, "The Land of Tomorrow," *Sunset Magazine*, XXII (June 1909), p. 578.

23. *Ibid*.

24. Aguilar Camín, *Frontera*, p. 57.

25. Luis E. Torres to Olegario Molina, Tórin, July 6, 1910, 2532, AES; Secretaría de Fomento to Gobernador, Mexico, September 1, 1910, 2532, AES.

26. Gobernador to Secretario de Fomento, Hermosillo, September 13, 1910, 2543, AES.

27. *Ibid*; Gobernador to Secretario de Fomento, Hermosillo, October 31, 1910, 2532, AES.

28. For example, Lorenzo Torres; Secretaría de Fomento to Gobernador, Mexico, April 30, 1910, 2532, AES.

29. Secretaría de Fomento to Gobernador, Mexico, January 20, 1911, 2656, AES; requests for "Aprovechamientos del agua del río Yaqui," Hermosillo, August 16, 1910, 2532, AES.

30. "En defensa del Estado," *Orientación*, January 15, 1920, cited in Amado Chaverri Matamoros and Clodoveo Valenzuela, *Sonora contra Carranza* (Mexico, 1921), p. 16; Dabdoub, *Panorama*, p. 264.

31. For example: Secretario de Estado to Prefecto, Hermosillo, November [no date] 1907, 2376, AES.

32. "Lo que pasa en el río mayo," *El Distrito de Alamos*, August 7, 1910.

33. Conrado Pérez to Vice Gobernador, Hermosillo, October 11, 1897, 740, AHS; Noticia de los lugares poblados de la municipalidad de Alamos, Alamos, November 7, 1905, 2244, AES.

34. Aguilar Camín, *Frontera*, p. 20.

35. Almada, *Diccionario*, p. 503; Mange, *Garbanzo*, p. 55.

36. Presidente Municipal to Secretario de Estado, Navojoa, August 28, 1906, 2245, AES; Aguilar Camín, *Frontera*, p. 21; Mange, *Garbanzo*, p. 54.

37. Prefecto to Secretario de Estado, Alamos, June 17, 1909, 2475, AES; Aguilar Camín, *Frontera*, p. 19.

38. Pedro H. Zurbarán to Congreso del Estado, Hermosillo, November 18, 1898, 787, AHS.

39. Dabdoub, *Economia*, p. 211.

40. *Ibid.*

41. *Ibid.*, pp. 212–213.

42. *Ibid.*, p. 212; Linda B. Hall, *Alvaro Obregón, Power and Revolution in Mexico, 1911–1920* (College Station, Texas, 1981), p. 13; Roger Dunbier, *The Sonoran Desert. Its Geography, Economy and People* (Tucson, 1968), p. 258.

43. Dabdoub, *Economía*, pp. 211–212.

44. Mange, *Garbanzo*, p. 39.

45. Aguilar Camín, *Frontera*, p. 32.

46. Mange, *Garbanzo*, pp. 50, 56; Gallareta Partida, *Aguas*, p. 396.

47. Ulloa, *Sonora*, pp. 162–164.

48. Department of Commerce, *West Coast*, p. 132.

49. Mange, *Garbanzo*, pp. 52–53.

50. *El Distrito de Alamos*, August 7, 1910.

51. Prefecto to Secretario de Estado, Alamos, October 18, 1909, 2594, AES.

52. Prefecto to Secretario de Estado, Alamos, August 9, 1909, 2471, AES.

53. *Ibid.*

54. Prefecto to Secretario de Estado, Guaymas, August 24, 1909, 2471, AES.

55. Cynthia Radding de Murrieta, "Hipótesis entorno al desarrollo de la sociedad sonorense del siglo XIX," Instituto de Investigaciones Históricas, V *simposio de historia de Sonora: Memoria* (Hermosillo, 1980), pp. 132–133.

56. Aguilar Camín, *Frontera*, p. 33.

57. Zavala, *Perfiles*, p. 76.

58. Gerardo Cornejo, *La sierra y el viento* (Hermosillo, 1982), p. 138.

59. Emigio A. Quirós, R. E. Miranda, and others to Gobernador, Cócorit, March 28, 1891, 627, AHS.

60. Manuel Balbás, *Recuerdos del Yaqui: principales episodios durante la campaña de 1899 a 1901* (Mexico, 1927), p. 9.

61. Presidente Municipal to Luis E. Torres, Cócorit, January 20, 1908, 2308, AES.

62. Gerente to Gobernador, Esperanza, March 18, 1909, 2440, AES; Secretario de Estado to Prefecto, Hermosillo, March 23, 1909, 2440, AES.

63. Alberto Cubillas to Luis E. Torres, Hermosillo, March 22, 1909, 2440, AES.

64. F. A. Salido, Prefecto, to Secretario de Estado, Navojoa, October 19, 1907, 2301, AES; Antonio Oviedo to Tesorero General, Navojoa, November 4, 1907, 2303, AES.

65. Aguilar Camín, *Frontera*, p. 27.
66. Pedro S. Salazar to Presidente Municipal, Alamos, October 7, 1906, 2243, AES.
67. Antonio Morales, Tesorero Municipal, Padrón de los causantes de derechos municipales, Navojoa, October 23, 1907, 2303, AES; Oficial Mayor, Secretaría de Fomento, to Gobernador, Mexico, October 5, 1909, 2525, AES; Aguilar Camín, *Frontera*, p. 21.
68. Presidente Municipal to Secretario de Estado, Navojoa, August 28, 1906, 2246, AES.
69. Aguilar Camín, *Frontera*, p. 37.
70. Presidente Municipal to Secretario de Estado, Navojoa, January 28, 1910, 2542, AES; Alberto Cubillas to Secretario de la Diputación Permanente, Hermosillo, February 2, 1910, 183, AHS.
71. Aguilar Camín, *Frontera*, pp. 34–35 and 37.
72. F. A. Salido, Prefecto, to Secretario de Estado, Navojoa, January 20, 1907, 2301, AES.
73. Flavio A. Bórquez, Benjamín Hill, and others to Gobernador, Navojoa, August 14, 1908, 2646, AES.
74. Secretario de Estado to Prefecto, Hermosillo, October 27, 1908, 2646, AES.
75. Almada, *Diccionario*, pp. 116 and 118.
76. Aguilar Camín, *Frontera*, p. 35.
77. Presidente Municipal to Secretario de Estado, Alamos, June 8, 1906, 2245, AES; Ulloa, *Sonora*, p. 142.
78. Alfredo Breceda, *México revolucionario, 1913–1917*, 2 vols. (Madrid and Mexico, 1920 and 1941), II, 8.
79. Pedro S. Salazar, Prefecto Interino, to Secretario de Estado, Alamos, October 10, 1906, 2087, AES; Almada, *Diccionario*, p. 701; Aguilar Camín, *Frontera*, p. 224; Djed Bórquez, *Obregón. Apuntes biográficos* (Mexico, 1929), p. 11.
80. Enriqueta de Parodi, *Sonora, hombres y paisajes* (Mexico, 1941), p. 73; Pedro J. Almada, *Con mi cobija al hombre* (Mexico, 1936), pp. 15, 140 and 150.
81. Alberto Cubillas to Prefecto, Francisco A. Salido, Hermosillo, June 9, 1910, 2645, AES.
82. Presidente Municipal to Gobernador Cubillas, Navojoa, June 26, 1910, 2542, AES; Luis M. Barrón to Gobernador Cubillas, Navojoa, June 27, 1910, 2542, AES.

CHAPTER 11

1. Héctor Aguilar Camín, *Saldos de la Revolución; cultura y política de México, 1910–1980* (Mexico, 1982), p. 23.
2. Roberto Guzmán Esparza, *Memorias de don Adolfo de la Huerta, según su propio dictado* (Mexico, 1957), p. 14.
3. Consuelo Boyd, "Twenty Years to Nogales: The Building of the Guaymas-Nogales Railroad," *The Journal of Arizona History*, XXII (Autumn, 1981), p. 298.
4. A. F. Garrison, Vice Consul, "Annual Report," September 30, 1872, Guaymas, CD, III–IV.
5. Ramón Corral, *Obras históricas. Reseña histórica del Estado de Sonora, 1856–*

1877. Biografía de José María Leyva Cajeme. Las razas indígenas de Sonora (Hermosillo, 1959), pp. 202–203.

6. Eduardo W. Villa, *Compendio de historia del Estado de Sonora* (Mexico, 1937), p. 74.

7. Departamento de la Estadística Nacional, *Sonora, Sinaloa y Nayarit, estudio estadístico económico social, elaborado por el Departamento de Estadística Nacional. Año 1927* (Mexico, 1928), p. 70.

8. Evelyn Hu-DeHart, *Missionaries, Miners and Indians. Spanish Contact with the Yaqui Nation of Northwestern New Spain, 1633–1820* (Tucson, 1981), p. 40.

9. Prefecto to Secretario de Estado, Ures, January 27, 1910, 2471, AES.

10. Roger Dunbier, *The Sonoran Desert. Its Geography, Economy and People* (Tucson, 1968), pp. 151 and 371.

11. Antonio G. Rivera, *La Revolución en Sonora* (Hermosillo, 1969), p. 144.

12. Esteban Baca Calderón, *Juicio sobre la guerra del Yaqui y génesis de la huelga de Cananea. 1° de junio de 1906* (Mexico, 1956), pp. 17 and 29. Rodolfo F. Acuña, *Sonoran Strongman; Ignacio Pesqueira and His Times* (Tucson, 1974), p. 4.

13. Alfonso Iberri, *El viejo Guaymas* (Mexico, 1952), p. 28.

14. Prefecto to Secretario de Estado, Altar, April 26, 1890, 615, AHS.

15. Carl Lumholtz, *El México Desconocido. Cinco años de exploración entre las tribus de la Sierra Madre Occidental; en la tierra caliente de Tepic y Jalisco y entre los Tarascos de Michacoán*, trans. Balbino Dávalos, 2 vols. (Mexico, 1945), II, 458.

16. Moisés González Navarro, *La colonización en México* (Mexico, 1960), p. 102.

17. Calderón, *Juicio*, p. 19.

18. Francisco P. Troncoso, *Las guerras con las tribus Yaqui y Mayo*, 2 vols. (Hermosillo, 1982), I, 91.

19. González Navarro, *Colonización*, p. 103.

20. Editores, *La Opinión*, to Prefecto, Alamos, March 12, 1885, 552, AHS.

21. Jesús Luna, *La carrera pública de Ramón Corral* (Mexico, 1975), p. 48.

22. Isaac Martínez to Secretario de Estado, Estación Pesqueira, November 11, 1888, 575, AHS.

23. Federico García y Alva, *México y su progreso; álbum-directorio del Estado de Sonora* (Hermosillo, 1905–1907), p. 12.

24. Claudio Dabdoub, *Historia de El Valle del Yaqui* (Mexico, 1964), p. 151.

25. Horacio Sobarzo, *Episodios históricos* (Mexico, 1981), p. 143; Dabdoub, *Historia*, pp. 114–115.

26. Sobarzo, *Episodios*, p. 138.

27. *Ibid.*, pp. 139–142.

28. Ramón Corral, Vice Gobernador, Informe, May 15, 1889, 603, AHS; Manuel R. Uruchurtu, *Apuntes biográficos del señor D. Ramón Corral; desde su nacimiento hasta encargarse del gobierno del distrito federal (1854 a 1900)* (Mexico, 1910), p. 137.

29. Sobarzo, *Episodios*, p. 139; García y Alva, *Progreso*, p. 10; Dabdoub, *Historia*, pp. 141–142.

30. Dabdoub, *Historia*, p. 115.

31. Dunbier, *Sonoran*, p. 102; Hu-Dehart, *Missionaries*, p. 10.

32. Evelyn Hu-DeHart, *Yaqui Resistance and Survival. The Struggle for Land and Autonomy, 1821–1910* (Madison, 1984), pp. 12–13.

33. Corral, *Obras*, p. 195; Troncoso, *Yaqui*, 1: 43.

34. Hu-DeHart, *Yaqui Resistance*, pp. 14–16; Stuart F. Voss, *On the Periphery of Nineteenth-Century Mexico. Sonora and Sinaloa, 1810–1877* (Tucson, 1982), p. 50; Acuña, *Pesqueira*, p. 3.

35. Hu-DeHart, *Yaqui Resistance*, pp. 24–32.

36. *Ibid.*, pp. 34–35 and 55–57.

37. Informe del General Reyes, cited in Troncoso, *Yaqui*, I, 102.

38. Corral, *Obras*, p. 204.

39. Hu-DeHart, *Yaqui Resistance*, pp. 136–143; Pedro N. Ulloa, *El Estado de Sonora y situación económica al aproximarse el primer centenario de la independencia nacional* (Hermosillo, 1910), pp. 29–30.

40. Corral, *Obras*, pp. 195–196.

41. Ramón Corral, Secretario de Estado, to Prefecto, Hermosillo, April 23, 1883, 597, AHS; *La Constitución*, November 23, 1883.

42. Dunbier, *Sonoran*, p. 127.

43. Corral, *Obras*, pp. 248–249; Lumholtz, *México desconocido*, I, 11; Troncoso, *Yaqui*, I, 32.

44. Corral, *Obras*, pp. 254 and 256; Ramón Corral to Gobernador, Hermosillo, November 29, 1880, cited in Troncoso, *Yaqui*, I, 108.

45. Gobernador Ramón Corral to Diputados Secretarios del Congreso Estatal, Hermosillo, June 12, 1888, 588, AHS.

46. Balvanero Robles, Prefecto, to Secretario de Estado, Altar, September 14, 1895, 668, AHS.

47. Corral, *Obras*, pp. 257–259; Villa, *Compendio*, pp. 37–38.

48. Ramón Corral to Gobernador, Hermosillo, November 29, 1880, cited in Troncosco, *Yaqui*, I, 108.

49. Villa, *Compendio*, p. 61.

50. Jesús Estrella to Ramón Corral, La Noria, March 28, 1883, 550, AHS.

51. Corral, *Obras*, pp. 244–245.

52. Dunbier, *Sonoran*, p. 140.

53. Hu-Dehart, *Missionaries*, p. 56.

54. Acuña, *Pesqueira*, pp. 2 and 7–8.

55. Corral, *Obras*, pp. 213 and 246–247.

56. *Ibid.*, pp. 84, and 214–244; *La Constitución*, November 23, 1883, Guillermo Carbó to Gobernador, Primera Zona Militar, April 2, 1883, 550, AHS; Miguel López, Presidente Municipal, to Prefecto, Batuc, March 31, 1883, 550, AHS.

57. Troncoso, *Yaqui*, I, 117.

58. Cornelius C. Smith, *Emilio Kosterlitzky. Eagle of Sonora and the Southwest Border* (Glendale, California, 1970), p. 69; Cuauhtémoc L. Terán, *Jesús García. Héroe de Nacozari* (Hermosillo, 1891), pp. 13–15; Francisco R. Almada, *La Revolución en el Estado de Sonora* (Mexico, 1971), p. 21.

59. Corral, *Obras*, p. 201; Claudio Dabdoub, "José María Leyva (Cajeme), caudillo yaqui de leyenda," Instituto de Investigaciones Históricas, *III simposio de historia de Sonora; Memoria*, 2 vols. (Hermosillo, 1978), II, 404; Torres, cited in Troncoso, *Yaqui*, I, 23.

60. John Kenneth Turner, *Barbarous Mexico* (Chicago, 1910), p. 38.

61. Rafael Izábal, *Memoria de la administración pública del Estado de Sonora durante el periodo constitucional de 1903 a 1907* (Hermosillo, 1907), p. 155.

62. Cyntha Radding de Murrieta, "El espacio sonorense y la periodización de las historias municipales," Instituto de Investigaciones Históricas, *IX simposio de historia de Sonora. Memoria* (Hermosillo, 1984), p. 78; Hu-DeHart, *Missionaries*, p. 4.

63. A. F. Garrison, Vice Consul, "Annual Report," September 30, 1872, Guaymas, CD, III–IV.

64. Luis E. Torres to Gobernador, Tórin, November 27, 1899, Referencia 24-1, AHS; Miguel F. Hermoso to Gobernador, La Colorada, November 28, 1899, Referencia 24–1, AHS; Feliciano Monteverde to Gobernador, Minas Prietas, November 28, 1899, Referencia 24–1, AHS; Presidente Municipal to Gobernador, August 29, 1891, 625, AHS.

65. "Yaquis detenidos en Tuape," Hermosillo, March 13, 1904, 2313, AES.

66. Héctor Aguilar Camín, *La frontera nómada: Sonora y la Revolución Mexicana* (Mexico, 1977), pp. 50 and 54–55; Alfredo Breceda, *México revolucionario, 1913–1917*, 2 vols. (Madrid and Mexico, 1920 and 1941), II, 23.

67. Gobernador Carlos R. Ortiz to Secretario del Estado y del Despacho de Guerra y Marina, Hermosillo, October 12, 1881, cited in Troncos, *Yaqui*, I, 113–114.

68. Corral, *Obras*, pp. 199–200.

69. *La Constitución*, July 28, 1885.

70. A. Willard, Consul, "Annual Report," September 30, 1880, Guaymas, CD, V–VI.

71. A. Willard, Consul, to Department of State, Guaymas, October 21, 1889, CD, VIII–IX.

72. "Yaquis Cease Warring," *The San Francisco Examiner*, May 16, 1897.

73. Voss, *Sonora*, p. 179; Dabdoub, *Historia*, p. 113.

74. Corral, *Obras*, p. 207; Troncoso, *Yaqui*, 1: 49, 51.

75. Gobernador Carlos R. Ortiz to Secretario de Estado y del Despacho de Guerra y Marina, Hermosillo, October 12, 1881, cited in Troncoso, *Yaqui*, I, 114; Ramón Corral to Gobernador, Hermosillo, November 29, 1880, cited in Troncoso, *Yaqui*, 1: 112; Luna, *Corral*, p. 39.

76. Luis E. Torres, J. P. Robles to Secretario de Estado y del Despacho de Guerra y Marina, Hermosillo, May 6, 1881, cited in Troncoso, *Yaqui*, I, 106; Ramón Corral to Diputación Permanente del Congreso del Estado, March 12, 1885, 550, AHS.

77. Gonzáles Navarro, *Colonización*, pp. 12–15; Manuel Balbás, *Recuerdos del Yaqui: principales episodios durante la campaña de 1899 a 1901* (Mexico, 1927), p. 7.

78. Informe del General Reyes, cited in Troncoso, *Yaqui*, I, 104–105.

79. Eberhardt V. Niemeyer, *El General Bernardo Reyes* (Monterrey, Mexico, 1966), p. 28; Dabdoub, *Cajeme*, p. 410.

80. A. Willard, Consul, to J. D. Porter, Guaymas, February 15, 1887, CD, VII.

81. Turner, *Barbarous Mexico*, p. 39.

82. Albert R. Morawetz, Consul, to Robert Bacon, Assistant Secretary of State, Nogales, November 3, 1905, CD, IV.

83. Calderón, *Juicio*, p. 15.

84. May 3, 1906.

85. Secretario de Fomento to Gobernador, Mexico, September 7, 1891, 618, AHS; Presidente Municipal to Secretario de Estado, Guaymas, October 10, 1906, 2249, AES.

86. Fortunato Hernández, *Las razas indígenas de Sonora y la querra del Yaqui* (Mexico, 1902), pp. 134–135; Franciso R. Almada, *Diccionario de historia, geografía y biografía sonorenses* (Chihuahua, 1952), pp. 552–553.

87. Luna, *Corral*, p. 46; Troncoso, *Yaqui*, II, 148; Corral, *Obras*, p. 198.

88. Balbás, *Recuerdos*, pp. 8, 102.

89. Iberri, *Guaymas*, p. 29.

90. April 1, 1890.

91. "How Mexico Fights the Yaqui Rebellion," June 16, 1905.

92. Breceda, *Revolucionario*, I, 48–49.

93. Balbás, *Recuerdos*, pp. 106–107.

94. Albert R. Morawetz, Consul, to Francis B. Loomis, Assistant Secretary of State, Nogales, September 23, 1904, CD, IV; Secretaría de Relaciones Exteriores to Gobernador, Mexico, December 7, 1905, 2138, AES; Birch F. Rhodus, President, to John Hay, New York, January 26, 1905, 2138, AES; Chas. J. Gevry, President, to Consul, Los Angeles, California, September 25, 1905, 2138, AES.

95. H. C. Gerber to Ambassador Clayton Powell, Hermosillo, January 28, 1905, 2138, AES.

96. See *The Bulletin*, San Francisco, July 2, 1905; *San Francisco Examiner*, June 4 and July 23, 1905; *San Francisco Call*, May 21 and June 4, 1905; *San Francisco Examiner*, May 22, 1905.

97. Secretaría de Estado to Gobernador, Hermosillo, July 15, 1905, 2138, AES.

98. Gobernador Ramón Corral to Diputados Secretarios del Congreso del Estado, Hermosillo, June 12, 1888, 588, AHS; Gobernador to Diputados Secretarios del Congreso Estatal, Hermosillo, July 1, 1891, 621, AHS.

99. Ramón Corral, *Memoria de la administración pública del Estado de Sonora presentada a la legislatura del mismo por el gobernador Ramón Corral*, 2 vols. (Guaymas, 1891), II, 225–226; Gobernador to Diputados Secretarios del Congreso del Estado, Hermosillo, November 24, 1894, 662, AHS.

100. Secretario de Estado to V. Ramírez Guerrero, Hermosillo, November 27, 1908, 2410, AES.

101. Turner, *Barbarous Mexico*, p. 44; Informe del General Reyes, cited in Troncoso, *Yaqui*, I, 103; A. Willard, Consul, to W. Hunter, Guaymas, April 3, 1885, CD, V–VI.

102. Troncoso, *Yaqui*, I, 229 and 231.

103. M. Carrillo, General en Jefe, to Secretario de Guerra y Marina, Guaymas, December 20, 1891, cited in Troncoso, *Yaqui*, 2: 15.

104. Troncoso, *Yaqui*, II, 217.

105. "Sonora," *El Fronterizo*, March 18, 1905, 2138, AES.

106. Hernández, *Razas indígenas*, p. 102.

107. Daniel Cosío Villegas, *El Porfiriato. La vida política interior*, Daniel Cosío

Villegas, *Historia moderna de México*, 9 vols. (Mexico, 1955–1973), IX, No. 2, 681.

108. Hu-DeHart, *Yaqui Resistance*, pp. 132 and 147.

109. *Ibid.*, p. 179.

110. *Ibid.*, p. 188.

111. Turner, *Barbarous Mexico*, p. 51; M. Gaxiola to Gobernador Rafael Izábal, Zacatón, November 19, 1905, [no carpetón], AES.

112. Fernando A. Galaz, *Dejaron huella en el Hermosillo de ayer y hoy* (Mexico, 1971), pp. 462–463.

113. Lista de personas a quienes se les han repartido niños yaquis, Hermosillo, 1907, 2193, AES.

114. Corral, *Obras*, p. 150.

115. Dabdoub, *Cajeme*, p. 427.

CHAPTER 12

1. A. Willard, Consul, to W. F. Wharton, Guaymas, August 18, 1889, CD, VIII–IX.

2. Consuelo Boyd, "Twenty Years to Nogales: The Building of the Guaymas-Nogales Railroad," *The Journal of Arizona History*, XXII (Autumn, 1981), p. 297; Robert G. Cleland, *A History of Phelps Dodge, 1834–1950* (New York, 1952), pp. 78–79.

3. Prefecto to Secretario de Estado, Magdalena, September 3, 1885, 586, AHS.

4. Gobernador Ramón Corral to Diputados Secretarios del Congreso Estatal, Hermosillo, June 12, 1888, 588, AHS; Ramón Corral to Diputados Secretarios del Congreso Estatal, Hermosillo, November 14, 1888, 587, AHS.

5. Ramón Corral to Secretario de Hacienda, Hermosillo, November 20, 1889, 610, AHS.

6. Ramón Corral to Secretario de Hacienda, Hermosillo, November 20, 1889, 610, AHS.

7. Ramón Corral to Secretario de Fomento, Hermosillo, March 4, 1887, 575, AHS.

8. A. F. Garrison, Vice Consul, "Annual Report," September 30, 1872, Guaymas, CD, II-IV.

9. J. Alexander Forbes, Consul, "Annual Report," May 1, 1893, Guaymas, CD, VII-IX.

10. Frank W. Roberts, Consul, to Edwin F. Uhl, Nogales, November 14, 1895, CD, II.

11. W. Cromer to A. R. Morawetz, Muncie, Indiana, July 4, 1903, CD, IV.

12. Rafael Izábal to Ramón Corral, Cananea, June 2, 1906, 2184, AES.

13. Presidente Municipal to Secretario de Estado, Nogales, March 26, 1888, 584, AHS.

14. Prefecto to Ramón Corral, Secretario de Estado, Sahuaripa, September 15, 1894, 713, AHS; Frank W. Roberts, Consul, to Edwin Uhl, Assistant Secretary of State, Nogales, November 1, 1894, CD, II; Charles E. Hale, Vice Consul,

to Edwin F. Uhl, Assistant Secretary of State, Guaymas, November 10, 1894, CD, VIII–IX; Ramón Corral to Prefecto, September 27, 1894, 713, AHS; Angel Serrano, Prefecto, to Secretario de Estado, Sahuaripa, September 15, 1894, 713, AHS.

15. Gobernador Ramón Corral to Secretario de Relaciones Exteriores, Hermosillo, March 30, 1898, 756, AHS.

16. Charles E. Hale, Vice Consul, to W. F. Wharton, Guaymas, June 6, 1892, CD, VIII–IX; Charles E. Hale, Vice Consul, to W. F. Wharton, Guaymas, June 19, 1892, CD, XIII–IX.

17. Prefecto to Junta Patriótica de Altar, Altar, September 18, 1888, 602, AHS.

18. Gobernador Ramón Corral to Diputados Secretarios del Congreso del Estado, Hermosillo, May 21, 1887, 575, AHS.

19. A. Willard, Consul, to J. D. Porter, Guaymas, May 5, 1887, CD, VII.

20. Reuben D. George, Vice Consul, to Isaac Gray, United States Minister in Mexico City, Nogales, December 4, 1883, CD, II.

21. Ramón Corral, Secretario de Estado, to M. Mascareñas, Hermosillo, July 26, 1893, 660, AHS; Presidente Municipal to Gobernador Rafael Izabál, Nogales, August 14, 1894, 660, AHS.

22. Ramón Gil Samaniego, Presidente Municipal, to Secretario de Estado, Cucurpe, September 16, 1908.

23. Liborio Vázquez to Secretario de Estado, Agua Prieta, June 2, 1908, 2519, AES.

24. Ramón Corral, Secretario de Estado, to General Angel Martínez, Hermosillo, March 5, 1887, 575, AHS; Lorenzo Chabarin, Prefecto, to Ramón Corral, Altar, February 23, 1887, 575, AHS; Prefecto to Secretario de Estado, Altar, April 13, 1887, 575, AHS; Ramón Corral to Prefecto, Hermosillo, November 14, 1887, 575, AHS.

25. *El Progreso*, October 15, 1892.

26. Diego A. Moreno, Aviso, Santa Ana, April [no date] 1890, 614, AHS.

27. J. B. Storman to Gobernador, Hermosillo, June 16, 1890, 607, AHS.

28. Diego A. Moreno to Gobernador, Santa Ana, June 22, 1890, 614, AHS; Diego A. Moreno to Juez Local, Santa Ana, June 24, 1890, 614, AHS; Diego A. Moreno to Gobernador, Santa Ana, June 26, 1890, 614, AHS.

29. Ramón Corral to J. B. Storman, Hermosillo, June 27, 1890, 614, AHS.

30. Prefecto to Secretario de Estado, Magdalena, September 21, 1900, 1566, AES.

31. Ramón Corral, Secretario de Estado, to Secretario de Fomento, Hermosillo, April 6, 1887, 575, AHS; Noticia de los ingenieros que ejercen en el Estado de Sonora, Hermosillo, July 31, 1894, 662, AHS; Francisco R. Almada, *Diccionario de historia, geografía y biografía sonorenses* (Mexico, 1952), p. 116; Héctor Aguilar Camín, *La frontera nómada: Sonora y la Revolución Mexicana* (Mexico, 1977), p. 109.

32. Eliseo Ramírez Alvarez, "El ingeniero Bonillas delineó el fundo legal de ciudad," *El Imparcial*, August 15, 1983; Ramón Corral, *Memoria de la administración pública del Estado de Sonora presentada a la legislatura del mismo por el gober-*

nador Ramón Corral, 2 vols. (Guaymas, 1891), I, 342; J. F. Darnell, Consul, to David J. Hill, Assistant Secretary of State, Nogales, May 24, 1897, CD, III.

33. Juez de 1ª Instancia to Secretario de Estado, Guaymas, July 21, 1893, 645, AHS; Secretario de Fomento to Gobernador, Mexico, July 4, 1893, 645, AHS.

34. Vicente A. Almada to Ignacio Bonillas, Magdalena, March 10, 1889, 596, AHS; Ignacio Bonillas to Prefecto, Magdalena, March 13, 1889, 596, AHS; Vicente A. Almada, Prefecto, to Ramón Corral, Magdalena, March 13, 1889, 596, AHS; Ramón Corral to Fernando Rodríguez, Hermosillo, March 13, 1889, 596, AHS; Ignacio Bonillas, Presidente Municipal, to Ramón Corral, Magdalena, March 14, 1889, 596, AHS; Ramón Corral to Adolfo Loustannau, Juez de 1ª Instancia, Hermosillo, March 15, 1889, 596, AHS; Ramón Corral to Vicente A. Almada, Hermosillo, March 15, 1889, 596, AHS; Vicente A. Almada, Prefecto, to Secretario de Estado, Magdalena, March 17, 1889, 596, AHS; Ignacio Bonillas to Secretario de Estado, Magdalena, March 22, 1889, 596, AHS; Ramón Corral to Prefecto, Hermosillo, March 27, 1889, 596, AHS.

35. Juez de 1ª Instancia to Secretario de Estado, Alamos, September 3, 1892, 636, AHS.

36. Teodoro O. Paz, *Guaymas de ayer* (Guaymas [1974?]), pp. 5–6.

37. Secretario de Estado to Juez Local, Hermosillo, February 3, 1891, 625, AHS; Miguel Castelan to Secretario de Estado, Nogales, May 18, 1891, 625, AHS.

38. Balvanero E. Robles, Prefecto, to Secretario de Estado, Moctezuma, April 13, 1893, 650, AHS.

39. Ignacio Mariscal to Gobernador, Mexico, Feburary 20, 1906, 2088, AES.

40. B. P. Márquez to Secretario de Estado, Cananea, May 23, 1907, 2215, AES.

41. Albert R. Morawetz, Consul, to Francis B. Loomis, Assistant Secretary of State, Nogales, June 24, 1903, CD, IV.

42. Balvanero E. Robles, Prefecto, to Secretario de Estado, Moctezuma, December 10, 1906, 2185, AES; Comisario de Policía to Secretario de Estado, El Tigre, December 15, 1906, 2185, AES.

43. Balvanero E. Robles, Prefecto, to Secretario de Estado, Moctezuma, February 22, 1906, 2185, AES.

44. A. Willard, Consul, to James D. Porter, Guaymas, December 31, 1885, CD, V-VI.

45. *La Constitución*, November 11, 1883.

46. A. Willard, Consul, to W. Hunter, Guaymas, April 28, 1881, CD, V-VI.

47. Prefecto to Secretario de Estado, San Ignacio, April 15, 1886, 575, AHS; Prefecto to Secretario de Estado, Magdalena, December 23, 1886, 575, AHS; Prefecto to Secretario de Estado, Bacamuchi, March 30, 1887, 575, AHS; Prefecto to Secretario de Estado, Arizpe, April 7, 1887, 575, AHS; Prefecto to Secretario de Estado, Nogales, April 15, 1887, 575, AHS; Ramón Corral to Diputados Secretarios del Congreso del Estado, Hermosillo, May 30, 1887, 575, AHS.

48. Ramón Corral to Prefecto, Hermosillo, June 18, 1895, 713, AHS; Frank

W. Roberts, Consul, to Edwin F. Hale, Assistant Secretary of State, Nogales, July 5, 1895, CD, II.

49. Luis Medina Barón to Gobernador, Fronteras, June 4, 1908, 2414, AES.

50. J. S. Williams to Alberto Cubillas, Nacozari, July 29, 1910, 2644, AES.

51. Luis H. Echevarría to Secretario de Estado, La Morita, August 18, 1892, 627, AHS.

52. Antonio Maza, Vice Consul, to Gobernador, Douglas, October 27, 1905, 2139, AES.

53. E. Arnold, Presidente Municipal, to Luis E. Torres, Naco, April 9, 1908, 2414, AES; Secretario de Estado to Comisario de Policía, Hermosillo, April 9, 1908, 2414, AES.

54. Leonardo Gámez, Prefecto, to Secretario de Estado, Arizpe, March 20, 1888, 585, AHS.

55. Prefecto to Secretario de Estado, Arizpe, January 20, 1890, 614, AHS.

56. Secretario de Estado to Prefecto, Hermosillo, May 7, 1895, 780, AHS.

57. Sóstenes E. Othón, Prefecto, to Secretario de Estado, Arizpe, June 12, 1895, 708, AHS; Sóstenes E. Othón, Prefecto, to Secretario de Estado, Arizpe, July 8, 1895, 708, AES.

58. Sóstenes E. Othón, Prefecto, to Secretario de Estado, Arizpe, April 20, 1895, 713, AHS; Secretario de Estado to Prefecto, April 22, 1895, 713, AHS.

59. Ignacio Elías, Prefecto, to Secretario de Estado, Arizpe, May 2, 1906, 2185, AES.

60. Aniceto C. Campos and others to Gobernador, Fronteras, August 26, 1906, 2087, AES.

61. Ignacio Elías to Presidente Municipal, Arizpe, May 26, 1907, 2201, AES.

62. Epes Randolph to Gobernador, Tucson, August 23, 1908, 2366, AES; Gobernador to Epes Randolph, Hermosillo, August 24, 1908, 2366, AES.

63. Manuel Marcareñas to Luis E. Torres, Nogales, Arizona, October 31, 1908, 2376, AES; Prefecto to Secretario de Estado, Magdalena, October 20, 1908, 2376, AES; McClovio Mimiaga, Juez de 1ª Instancia, Informe, Nogales, December 23, 1908, 2418, AES.

64. Supremo Tribunal de Justicia to Gobernador, Hermosillo, March 15, 1909, 2418, AES.

65. Susan M. Deeds, "La frontera Sonora-Arizona durante la Revolución Mexicana," Instituto de Investigaciones Históricas, *IX simposio de historia de Sonora. Memoria* (Hermosillo, 1984), p. 382.

66. *Ibid.*, p. 378.

67. F. T. Dávila, *Sonora histórico y descriptivo* (Nogales, Arizona, 1894), p. 326.

68. Discurso pronunciado por el primer regidor Francisco L. Castro, Cumuripa, September 16, 1891, 619, AHS.

69. Fernando A. Galaz, *Dejaron huella en el Hermosillo de ayer y hoy* (Hermosillo, 1971), p. 462.

70. Secretario de Estado to Prefecto, Hermosillo, March 23, 1909, 2419, AES; Secretario de Estado to Carlos de Doig Albiar, Hermosillo, June 10, 1910, 2419, AES.

71. Allen T. Bird, *The Land of Nayarit* (Nogales, Arizona, 1904), p. 35.

72. L. W. Mix to Luis E. Torres, Nogales, Arizona, October 30, 1884, 682,

AHS; Ramón Corral, Vice Gobernador, Informe, Hermosillo, May 15, 1889, 603, AHS.

73. *La Bandera Sonorense*, July 27, 1905.

74. G. Macalpin, Presidente del C.O.I.A., to Presidente de la República, Cananea, March 20, 1905, 2298, AES.

75. Gobernador del Estado de Veracruz to Gobernador, Xalapa, December 1, 1906, 2085, AES.

76. Paz, *Guaymas*, pp. 42 and 77; Galaz, *Hermosillo*, p. 630.

CHAPTER 13

1. Harry Magdoff, *Imperialism: From the Colonial Age to the Present* (London and New York, 1978), p. 98.

2. Stuart F. Voss, *On the Periphery of Nineteenth-Century Mexico. Sonora and Sinaloa, 1810–1877* (Tucson, 1982), p. 208.

3. *Ibid.*, pp. 86–91.

4. Gregorio Mora Torres, "Los comerciantes de Guaymas y el desarrollo económico de Sonora, 1825–1910," Instituto de Investigaciones Históricas, *IX simposio de historia de Sonora.* (Hermosillo, 1984), p. 218.

5. Héctor A. Pesqueira, "La etiología del hombre fuerte," Instituto de Investigaciones Históricas, *Primer simposio de historia de Sonora: Memoria* (Hermosillo, 1976), pp. 60–63; Rodolfo F. Acuña, *Sonoran Strongman; Ignacio Pesqueira and His Times* (Tucson, 1974), p. 15.

6. Jesús Luna, *La carrera pública de Ramón Corral* (Mexico, 1975), pp. 11–12.

7. Voss, *Sonora*, p. 298.

8. Francisco R. Almada, *Diccionario de historia, geografía y biografía sonorenses* (Chihuahua, 1952), pp. 538–540; Daniel Cosío Villegas, *El Porfiriato. La vida política interior*, Daniel Cosío Villegas, *Historia moderna de México*, 9 vols. (Mexico, 1955–1073), VIII, No. 1, 605–606.

9. Reseña que el consul de México en Tucson dirige al Secretario de Relaciones, respecto a la situación de Sonora, December 14, 1882, in Francisco P. Troncoso, *Las guerras con las tribus Yaqui y Mayo*, 2 vols. (Hermosillo, 1982), I, 159–160.

10. Secretaría de Estado to Secretario de Relaciones Exteriores, Hermosillo, April 7, 1893, 638, AHS; Francisco R. Almada, *La Revolución en el Estado de Sonora* (Mexico, 1971), p. 13.

11. Beene Delmar Leon, "Sonora in the Age of Ramon Corral, 1875–1900" (Ph.D. thesis, University of Arizona, Tucson, 1972), pp. 69–70.

12. Almada, *Revolución*, pp. 15–16; Hector Aguilar Camin, *La frontera nómada: Sonora y la Revolución Mexicana* (Mexico, 1977), pp. 103–104.

13. Prefecto to Secretario de Estado, Altar, December 3, 1887, 585, AHS.

14. Voss, *Sonora*, p. 209.

15. Prefecto to Secretario de Estado, Hermosillo, July 12, 1884, 616, AHS.

16. Luis G. Dávila to Secretario de Estado, Guaymas, July 12, 1892, 627, AHS.

17. Prefecto to Secretario de Estado, Hermosillo, December 30, 1981, 627,

AHS; Jesús J. Coronado to Presidente Municipal, Arivechi, August 28, 1887, 585, AHS.

18. Prefecto to Secretario de Estado, Altar, October 19, 1892, 628, AHS.

19. Voss, *Sonora*, p. 251.

20. Almada, *Diccionario*, p. 627; Aguilar Camín, *Frontera*, p. 99·

21. Stuart F. Voss, "Towns and Enterprises in Northwestern Mexico—A History of Urban Elites in Sonora and Sinaloa, 1830–1910" (Ph.D. thesis, Harvard University, Cambridge, 1972), p. 341.

22. Angel Almada to Secretario de Estado, Alamos, October 4, 1898, 759, AHS; Secretario de Estado to Presidente Municipal, Hermosillo, October 12, 1898, 759, AHS.

23. A. F. Garrison, Vice Consul, "Annual Report," September 30, 1872, CD, III–IV.

24. Antonio G. Rivera, *La Revolución en Sonora* (Hermosillo, 1969), pp. 15–16; Palemón Zavala, *Perfiles de Sonora* (Hermosillo, 1984), p. 47.

25. A. Willard, Consul, to J. D. Porter, Guaymas, August 15, 1887, CD, VII.

26. J. D. García to Consulate of the United States, Sahuaripa, April 27, 1887, CD, VII.

27. Francisco J. Telles, Prefecto, to Gobernador, Ures, May 11, 1906, 2085, AES.

28. Manuel Castro, Pedro Encinas, and others to Gobernador, Magdalena, [no date] 1896, 711, AHS.

29. Roberto Guzmán Esparza, *Memorias de don Adolfo de la Huerta, según su propio dictado* (Mexico, 1957), p. 14.

30. Eduardo García Robles, Prefecto, to Secretario de Estado, Hermosillo, October [no date] 1892, 628, AHS; *El Progreso*, October 15, 1892; Placido G. Moreno to Luis E. Torres, Pitiquito, October 14, 1892, 628, AHS; Santos O. Lizárraga to Ramón Corral, Pitiquito, October 15, 1892, 628, AHS; Francisco Ortega, Ramón Lizárraga, José Jesús Ortega, D. F. Méndez, and G. Moreno to Ramón Corral, Pitiquito, October 15, 1892, 628, AHS.

31. Secretario de Estado to Prefecto, Hermosillo, August 20, 1906, 2087, AES; F. A. Salido, Prefecto, to Secretario de Estado, Alamos, August 21, 1906, 2087, AES; Secretario de Estado to Miguel F. Duarte, Presidente del Ayuntamiento, Hermosillo, December 19, 1906, 2087, AES.

32. Secretario de Estado to Prefecto, Hermosillo, September 3, 1908, 2473, AES.

33. Tomás Porchas, Miguel Porchas, and others to Gobernador, Sahuaripa, January [no date] 1908, 2263, AES.

34. Prefecto to Secretario de Estado, Ures, January 4, 1887, 575, AHS.

35. Federico Morineau to Dionisio González, Caborca, December 18, 1908, 2532, AES.

36. Manuel Santiago Corbalá Acuña, *Alamos de Sonora* (Mexico, 1977), p. 136.

37. Delmar Leon, *Sonora*, pp. 73–74.

38. Rivera, *Revolución*, p. 16.

39. Francisco J. Telles to Secretario de Estado, Ures, August 18, 1907, 2473, AES.

40. George F. Woodward to Albert R. Morawetz, Moctezuma, July 23, 1904, CD, IV.

41. Secretario de Estado to Jacinto Padilla, Hermosillo, February 14, 1908, 2473, AES.

42. Delmar Leon, *Sonora*, pp. 73–75; Ramón Corral to Diputados Secretarios del Congreso Estatal, Hermosillo, November 26, 1888, 599, AHS.

43. Claudio Dabdoub, "La economía de Sonora en 1907 y su naciente industrialización," Instituto de Investigaciones Históricas, *V simposio de historia de Sonora: Memoria* (Hermosillo, 1980), p. 207.

44. Miguel López to Gobernador, Hermosillo, April 20, 1895, 744, AHS.

45. Jacinto Padilla, Presidente Municipal, to Secretario de Estado, Magdalena, May 25, 1906, 2245, AES.

46. For example: J. A. Rivero, Prefecto, to Secretario de Estado, Guaymas, September 10, 1883, 549, AHS; Prefecto to Secretario de Estado, Altar, August 9, 1884, 849, AHS; Jesús Y. Coronado, Prefecto, to Secretario de Estado, Sahuaripa, July 9, 1892, 626, AHS; Francisco G. Aguilar, Prefecto, to Secretario de Estado, Ures, March 10, 1892, 626, AHS.

47. Almada, *Diccionario*, pp. 89–90.

48. Voss, *Sonora*, p. 208.

49. *Ibid.*, pp. 207–208.

50. Prefecto to Presidentes Municipales, Arizpe, September 29, 1887, 575, AHS.

51. Voss, *Sonora*, p. 198; Voss, *Towns*, p. 494.

52. Aguilar Camín, *Frontera*, p. 100.

53. Nicanor Bidabe and Modesto Mayoral to Gobernador, Nogales, Arizona, October 7, 1910, 2534, AES; E. R. Arnold to Secretario de Estado, Cananea, October 19, 1910, 2534, AES.

54. Almada, *Revolución*, p. 16.

55. Ignacio Bonillas, Prefecto, to Secretario de Estado, Magdalena, February 27, 1892, 627, AHS; E. Campa and others to Gobernador, Río Chico, September 24, 1906, 2190, AES; Visitador de Hacienda, Notas de Minas Prietas, Extraoficialmente, [no date] 1907, 2304, AES.

56. Congreso del Estado to Secretario de Estado, Hermosillo, December 9, 1898, 772, AHS.

57. Prefecto to Gobernador Alberto Cubillas, Sahuaripa, November 9, 1910, 2534, AHS.

58. Rivera, *Revolución*, p. 113.

59. Brígido Caro, Secretario de Estado, to Presidente Municipal, Hermosillo, April 25, 1908, 2311, AES.

60. Secretario de Estado to Prefecto, Hermosillo, October 20, 1897, 759, AHS; Prefecto to Secretario de Estado, Arizpe, October 1, 1888, 596, AHS.

61. Secretario de Estado to Prefecto, August 22, 1906, 2251, AES.

62. Rafael de Zayas Enríquez, *Porfirio Díaz* (New York, 1908), p. 215.

63. Adolfo Balderrama to Secretario de Estado, Magdalena, August 30, 1893, AHS; Manuel Bernal, Presidente de la Mesa Electoral, to Gobernador, Nogales, August 29, 1897, 759, AHS; Cirilo Ramírez to Secretario de Estado, Nogales, September 6, 1897, 759, AHS; J. W. Espinosa and others to Gobernador, Nogales, October 1, 1897, 759, AHS; Aguilar Camín, *Frontera*, p. 109.

64. Secretario de Estado to Prefectos de Distrito, Hermosillo, July 30, 1892, 641, AHS; Secretario de Estado to Prefecto, Hermosillo, August 3, 1893, 619, AHS.

65. Secretario de Estado to Presidente Municipal, Hermosillo, January 10, 1895, 681, AHS.

66. Congreso del Estado to Gobernador, Hermosillo, May 17, 1888, 584, AHS.

67. Secretario de Estado to Presidente del Supremo Tribunal de Justicia del Estado, Hermosillo, September 30, 1908, 2473, AES.

68. Prefecto to Gobernador Alberto Cubillas, August 21, 1909, 2473, AES.

69. Supremo Tribunal de Justicia to Gobernador, Hermosillo, September 5, 1905, 2253, AES; Tesorería General del Estado to Gobernador, Hermosillo, September 6, 1907, 2473, AES.

70. Bruno Méndez to Gobernador, Tórin, May 9, 1891, 619, AHS.

71. Ayuntamiento de Guaymas to Secretario de Estado, Guaymas, August 7, 1892, 626, AHS.

72. Carlos Flores and Emigdio Quirós to Gobernador, Cócorit, April 9, 1892, 627, AHS.

73. Luis E. Torres to Secretario de Estado, Cananea, October 11, 1906, 2087, AES.

CHAPTER 14

1. Eduardo W. Villa, *Compendio de historia del Estado de Sonora* (Mexico, 1937), p. 432.

2. Horacio Sobarzo, "Al lector," Ramón Corral, *Obras históricas del Estado de Sonora, 1856–1877. Biografía de José María Leyva Cajeme. Las razas indígenas de Sonora* (Hermosillo, 1959), p. 18.

3. Daniel Cosío Villegas, *El Porfiriato. La vida política interior,* Daniel Cosío Villegas, *Historia Moderna de México,* 9 vols. (Mexico, 1955–1973), IX, No. 2, 799.

4. Corral, *Obras,* p. 66.

5. Manuel R. Uruchurtu, *Apuntes biográficos del señor D. Ramón Corral: desde su nacimiento hasta encargarse del gobierno del distrito federal (1854 a 1900)* (Mexico, 1910), p. 11; Manuel Santiago Corbalá Acuña, *Alamos de Sonora* (Mexico, 1977), pp. 174–176; Francisco R. Almada, *Diccionario de historia, geografía y biografía sonorenses* (Chihuahua, 1952), pp. 190–194.

6. Jesús Luna, *La carrera pública de Ramón Corral* (Mexico, 1975), p. 10.

7. Cosío Villegas, *Historia,* IX, No. 2, 799.

8. Mrs. Alex Tweedie, *Porfirio Diaz, Seven Times President of Mexico* (London, 1906), p. 379.

9. Enrique Contreras, *Cosas viejas de mi tierra* (Hermosillo, 1965), p. 109; Fernando A. Galaz, *Dejaron huella en el Hermosillo de ayer y hoy* (Hermosillo, 1971), p. 438.

10. Ramón Corral to Juez de 1ª Instancia, Hermosillo, January 7, 1893, 646, AHS.

11. Luna, *Corral*, p. 591; Uruchurtu, *Corral*, p. 133·

12. Contreras, *Mi tierra*, p. 109; Henry Baerlein, *Mexico, The Land of Unrest. Being Chiefly an Account of What Produced the Outbreak in 1910, Together with the Story of the Revolution Down to this Day* (London, 1913), p. 140.

13. Beene Delmar Leon, "Sonora in the Age of Ramon Corral, 1875–1900" (Ph.D. thesis, University of Arizona, Tucson, 1972), pp. 77–78.

14. Alberto Calzadíaz Barrera, *Hechos reales de la Revolución; el General Ignacio L. Pesqueira . . . y surgen Obregón y Calles* (Mexico, 1973), pp. 13–14.

15. Ignacio B. del Castillo, *Biografía de D. Ramón Corral* (Mexico, 1910), p. 41.

16. Sobarzo, *Al lector*, p. 16.

17. Gobernador Ramón Corral to Diputados Secretarios del Congreso del Estado, Hermosillo, June 12, 1888, 588, AHS.

18. Uruchurtu, *Corral*, p. 52.

19. Cosío Villegas, *Historia*, IX, No. 2, 624.

20. Villa, *Compendio*, pp. 422–423; Corbalá Acuña, *Alamos*, pp. 186, 191; Ramón Corral to Diputados Secretarios del Congreso del Estado, Hermosillo, June 12, 1888, 588, AHS.

21. Gobernador Ramón Corral to Diputados Secretarios del Congreso del Estado, Hermosillo, June 12, 1888, 588, AHS.

22. Tweedie, *Diaz*, p. 378.

23. Federico García y Alva, *Album-crónica de las fiestas patrias efectuadas en Sonora en honor del señor vice-presidente de la República Don Ramón Corral y de la señora Amparo V. E. de Corral* (Hermosillo, 1905), no page numbers.

24. Almada, *Diccionario*, pp. 192–193.

25. Delmar Leon, *Sonora*, p. 65.

26. Corbalá Acuña, *Alamos*, p. 177–179; Francisco R. Almada, *La Revolución en el Estado de Sonora* (Mexico, 1971), p. 17.

27. Cosío Villegas, *Historia*, IX, No. 2, 822.

28. *Ibid.*, pp. 822 and 903; Corbalá Acuña, *Alamos*, p. 194.

29. Ignacio B. del Castillo, *Biografía*, p. 34; Corbalá Acuña, *Alamos*, p. 185; Antonio G. Rivera, *La Revolución en Sonora* (Hermosillo, 1969), p. 110; Ramón Corral, Secretario de Estado, to Diputados del Congreso del Estado, Hermosillo, December 5, 1885, 553, AHS.

30. Ramón Corral, Secretario de Estado, to Secretario de Fomento, Hermosillo, March 7, 1887, 575, AHS.

31. Castillo, *Corral*, p. 44; Villa, *Compendio*, p. 419.

32. Héctor Aguilar Camín, *La frontera nómada: Sonora y la Revolución Mexicana* (Mexico, 1977), p. 80.

33. Stuart F. Voss, "Towns and Enterprises in Northwestern Mexico—A History of Urban Elites in Sonora and Sinaloa, 1830–1910" (Ph.D. thesis, Harvard University, Cambridge, 1972), p. 330.

34. Gobernador Ramón Corral to Secretario de 1ª Diputación Permanente del Congreso del Estado, Hermosillo, December 30, 1885, 550, AHS.

35. Villa, *Compendio*, p. 435–436.

36. Luna, *Corral*, pp. 26–27.

37. Conrado Pérez Aranda, Juez de 1ª Instancia, to Gobernador Ramón

304   *Notes to Pages 218–222*

Corral, Alamos, May 4, 1889, 603, AHS; Carlos Ortiz to Presidente de la República, Porfirio Díaz, Mexico, November 21, 1889, 603, AHS.
38. Luis E. Torres to Gobernador Ramón Corral, Ensenada, B. C., April 27, 1889, 603, AHS.
39. Uruchurtu, *Corral*, p. 169–170.
40. *Ibid.*, p. 217.
41. Rivera, *Revolución*, p. 123.
42. Baerlein, *Land of Unrest*, pp. 138 and 140.
43. Uruchurtu, *Corral*, pp. 8–9.
44. Ramón Corral, Gobernador, to Manuel R. Parada, Hermosillo, May 9, 1898, 576, AHS.
45. Ramón Corral, Vice Gobernador, Informe, May 15, 1889, 603, AHS.
46. Ramón Corral, Secretario de Estado, to Prefecto, Hermosillo, May 14, 1887, AHS.
47. Prefecto to Secretario de Estado, Altar, May 19, 1887, 575, AHS.
48. Ramón Corral, Secretario de Estado, to Prefecto, Hermosillo, April 1, 1887, 575, AHS; Prefecto to Secretario de Estado, Guaymas, April 4, 1887, 575, AHS.
49. Ramón Corral, *La cuestión de la harina* (Hermosillo, 1881), pp. 4–30.
50. Ramón Corral to Diputados Secretarios del Congreso del Estado, Hermosillo, November 8, 1889, 598, AHS; Delmar Leon, *Sonora*, p. 46.
51. Rafael Izábal, Gobernador, to Diputados Secretarios del Congreso Estatal, Hermosillo, July 5, 1893, 646, AHS.
52. Corbalá Acuña, *Alamos*, pp. 185–186; Ramón Corral, Secretario de Estado, to Diputados Secretarios del Congreso Estatal, Hermosillo, November 19, 1885, 578, AHS.
53. Secretario de Estado to Prefecto, Hermosillo, July 11, 1893, 646, AHS.
54. Corral, *Obras*, p. 191.
55. Ramón Corral to Gobernador del Estado, Hermosillo, November 29, 1880, in Francisco P. Troncoso, *Las guerras con las tribus Yaqui and Mayo*, 2 vols. (Hermosillo, 1982), I, 110.
56. For a different opinion, see Delmar Leon, *Sonora*, p. 150.
57. Luna, *Corral*, pp. 48–49.
58. Rivera, *Revolución*, p. 107.
59. Ramón Corral to Prefectos, Hermosillo, September 1, 1885, 550, AHS.
60. Ramón Corral to Gobernador Rafael Izábal, Mexico, June 2, 1906, 2184, AES.
61. Ramón Corral to Gobernador Rafael Izábal, Mexico, June 8, 1906, 2184, AES.
62. Luna, *Corral*, p. 164.
63. Ramón Corral to Ignacio L. Almada, Juan Rivas, and Torribio Corbalá, Alamos, May 14, 1888, 596, AHS.
64. Ramón Corral to Quirino Corbalá, Hermosillo, January 26, 1890, 635, AHS; Ramón Corral to Jesús Antonio Almada, Hermosillo, February 1, 1890, 635, AHS; Lauro Quirós to Jesús Antonio Almada, Alamos, January 24, 1890, 635, AHS.

65. Angel Almada to Luis E. Torres, Alamos, September 7, 1907, 2366, AES.

66. Corral, *Obras*, pp. 330–334.

67. García y Alva, *Album-crónica*, no page number.

68. David Hannay, *Diaz* (New York, 1917), p. 292.

69. Tweedie, *Porfirio Diaz*, p. 378.

70. García y Alva, *Album-crónica*, no page number.

71. Ramón Corral to Gobernador Rafael Izábal, Mexico, June 6, 1906, 2184, AES.

72. Ramón Corral to Gobernador Rafael Izábal, Mexico, June 2, 1906, 2184, AES.

73. Ramón Corral to Gobernador Rafael Izábal, Mexico, June 6, 1906, 2184, AES.

74. Ramón Corral, *Memoria de la administración pública del Estado de Sonora presentada a la legislatura del mismo por el gobernador Ramón Corral*, 2 vols. (Guaymas, 1891), I, 341.

75. Ramón Corral to C . . ., Hermosillo, May 25, 1893, 682, AHS.

76. Ramón Corral, Gobernador, to Diputados Secretarios del Congreso Estatal, Hermosillo, June 12, 1888, 588, AHS; Ramón Corral, Vice Gobernador, Informe, Hermosillo, May 15, 1889, 603, AHS.

77. Ramón Corral to Consul Alejandro Willard, Hermosillo, June 15, 1888, 673, AHS.

78. Ramón Corral, Gobernador, to Diputados Secretarios del Congreso del Estado, Hermosillo, September 18, 1889, 599, AHS.

79. Ramón Corral, Gobernador, to Diputados Secretarios de la Legislatura del Estado, Hermosillo, June 22, 1893, 576, AHS.

80. C. H. Ward to Gobernador, Hermosillo, January 29, 1898, 576, AHS.

81. Ramón Corral to Edmund Harvey, Hermosillo, March 26, 1889, 606, AHS.

82. Tweedie, *Diaz*, p. 379.

83. Ramón Corral to Ramón Aragón, Hermosillo, June 15, 1888, 673, AHS.

84. Ramón Corral, Gobernador, to Diputados Secretarios del Congreso Estatal, Hermosillo, June 12, 1888, 588, AHS; Porfirio Díaz to Gobernador Ramón Corral, Mexico, April 16, 1888, 586, AHS.

85. Secretario de Estado to Prefecto, Hermosillo, April 11, 1888, 586, AHS.

86. A. Willard, Consul, to Ramón Corral, Guaymas, April 18, 1889, 596, AHS.

87. Delmar Leon, *Sonora*, p. 78.

88. Cited in Luna, *Corral*, p. 65.

89. Informe, Hermosillo, [no date], 635, AHS.

90. Uruchurtu, *Corral*, pp. 113, 190; Luna, *Corral*, p. 35; Villa, *Compendio*, pp. 436, 443.

91. Uruchurtu, *Corral*, pp. 55, 197; Pedro N. Ulloa, *El Estado de Sonora y situación económica al aproximarse el primer centenario de la independencia nacional* (Hermosillo, 1910), p. 121; Presidente Municipal to Secretario de Estado, Hermosillo, November 9, 1906, 2245, AES; Aguilar Camín, *Frontera*, p. 91; Prefecto to Secretario de Estado, May 16, 1906, 2248, AES; Ley que aprueba un

contrato, Hermosillo, June 30, 1898, 576, AHS; M. M. Martínez to Secretario de Estado, Hermosillo, August 3, 1907, 2218, AES.

92. Luna, *Corral*, p. 34.

93. Rafael Izábal, Gobernador Constitucional del Estado de Sonora a todos . . . ., Hermosillo, August 6, 1895, 671, AHS.

94. Luna, *Corral*, p. 163.

CHAPTER 15

1. Rafael Izábal, Gobernador, to Diputados Secretarios del Congreso del Estado, Hermosillo, July 5, 1893, 640, AHS.

2. Presidente Municipal to Secretario de Estado, Sahuaripa, April 8, 1893, 640, AHS; Prefecto to Secretarios de Estado, Sahuaripa, May 13, 1893, 640, AHS.

3. Rafael Izábal to Eugenio Fuentes, Hermosillo, July 8, 1892, 635, AHS.

4. Angel Bassols Batalla, *México. Formación de regiones económicas* (Mexico, 1979), p. 2215.

5. Rafael de Zayas Enríquez, *Porfirio Díaz* (New York, 1908), p. 257.

6. Alberto Cubillas, *Informe leído por el C. Alberto Cubillas, vice-gobernador constitucional del Estado de Sonora* (Hermosillo, 1909), p. 16.

7. Rafael Izábal, Informe, Hermosillo [1907?], 1244, AES.

8. Secretario de Estado to Prefecto, Hermosillo, December 6, 1910, 2639, AES.

9. S. David y Hnos. and others to Gobernador, Hermosillo, December 7, 1910, 2535, AES.

10. Arturo Morales, Presidente Municipal, to Secretario de Estado, Guaymas, June 5, 1906, 2131, AES; Jesús M. de Fourcade to Gobernador, Guaymas, December 10, 1907, 2336, AES.

11. Prefecto to Secretario de Estado, Arizpe, November 21, 1907, 2258, AES; Ignacio E. Elías to Gobernador, Arizpe, June 2, 1908, 2336, AES.

12. Francisco Chiapa to Secretario de Estado, Moctezuma, January 14, 1908, 2258, AES; Presidente Municipal to Secretario de Estado, Fronteras, February 26, 1907, 2131, AES.

13. Presidente Municipal to Secretario de Estado, Altar, September 19, 1906, 2131, AES.

14. Comisario de Policía to Secretario de Estado, Cócorit, October 17, 1906, 2131, AES.

15. M. Encinas, Prefecto, to Secretario de Estado, Sahuaripa, January 3, 1906, 2104, AES.

16. Report of Louis Hostetter, Consul, Hermosillo, Sonora, in United States Department of Commerce and Labor, Bureau of Manufactures, *Commercial Relations of the United States with Foreign Countries* (Washington, D. C., 1911), p. 539.

17. Rafael Izábal, *Memoria de la administración pública del Estado de Sonora durante el periodo constitucional de 1903 a 1907* (Hermosillo, 1907), p. 166.

18. Zayas Enríquez, *Díaz*, p. 248.

19. *Ibid.*, p. 229.

20. Roberto Guzmán Esparza, *Memorias de don Adolfo de la Huerta, según su propio dictado* (Mexico, 1957), p. 11.

21. Manuel Santiago Corbalá Acuña, *Alamos de Sonora* (Mexico, 1977), p. 199.

22. Alberto Cubillas, Secretario de Estado, to Gobernador Rafael Izábal, Hermosillo, October 20, 1904, 2314, AES.

23. Stuart F. Voss, "Towns and Enterprises in Northwestern Mexico—A History of Urban Elites in Sonora and Sinaloa, 1830–1910" (Ph.D. thesis, Harvard University, Cambridge, 1972), p. 565.

24. Antonio G. Rivera, *La Revolución en Sonora* (Hermosillo, 1969), p. 155.

25. "El Progreso Latino y La Bandera Sonorense," *El Centinela*, May 12, 1906.

26. Prefecto to Gobernador Alberto Cubillas, Ures, July 9, 1909, 2542, AES; Alberto Calzadíaz Barrera, *Hechos reales de la Revolución; el General Ignacio Pesqueira . . . y surgen Obregón y Calles* (Mexico, 1973), pp. 37–38; John Kenneth Turner, *Barbarous Mexico* (Chicago, 1910), p. 194.

27. Palemón Zavala, *Perfiles de Sonora* (Hermosillo, 1984), p. 55.

28. *Ibid.*, p. 47.

29. José Calixto Rangel Contla, *La pequeña burguesía en la sociedad mexicana, 1895–1960* (Mexico, 1972), pp. 191–192.

30. Boleta en que se consigna el numero de personas que en el Estado de Sonora ejercen algunas de las profesiones, Hermosillo, July 25, 1884, 859, AHS.

31. Cuauhtémoc L. Terán, *Jesús García. Héroe de Nacozari* (Hermosillo, 1981), pp. 18–19.

32. Ramón Corral, *Memoria de la administración pública del Estado de Sonora presentada a la legislatura del mismo por el gobernador Ramón Corral*, 2 vols. (Guaymas, 1891), I, 346–347.

33. Juan de Dios Bojórquez, "Champ," *Rodolfo Campodónico, autor de "Club Verde"* (Mexico, 1936), p. 42.

34. *Ibid.*, p. 41.

35. Alfredo Breceda, *México revolucionario, 1913–1917*, 2 vols. (Madrid and Mexico, 1920 and 1941), 1: 32.

36. Esteban Baca Calderón, *Juicio sobre la guerra del Yaqui y génesis de la huelga de Cananea. 1° de junio de 1906* (Mexico, 1956), p. 19.

37. Serafico Robles and others to Gobernador, Hermosillo, November 20, 1907, 2257, AES.

38. Santiago López Alvarado to Secretario de Estado, Guaymas, September 10, 1910, 2639, AES.

39. Presidente Municipal to Secretario de Estado, Bacerac, April 13, 1907, 2132, AES; Comisario de Policía to Secretario de Estado, Tórin, May 17, 1907, AES; 2131, AES.

40. E. R. Arnold to Luis E. Torres, Cananea, October 31, 1907, 2258, AES.

41. Tesorero General del Estado to Gobernador, Hermosillo, November 18, 1907, 2257, AES.

42. Francisco R. Almada, *La Revolución en el Estado de Sonora* (Mexico, 1971), p. 26.

43. Rivera, *Revolución*, p. 128.

44. *Ibid.*, pp. 127, 146 and 158; Enriqueta de Parodi, *Sonora, hombres y paisajes* (Mexico, 1941), p. 62; César Tapia Quijada, *Apuntes sobre la huelga de Cananea* (Hermosillo, 1956), p. 55; Calderón, *Juicio*, p. 10.

45. Rivera, *Revolución*, pp. 140–141.

46. Almada, *Revolución*, pp. 29–30, 132; Rivera, *Revolución*, pp. 114–115; Beene Delmar Leon, "Sonora in the Age of Ramón Corral, 1875–1900" (Ph.D. thesis, University of Arizona, Tucson, 1972), pp. 71–72.

47. Bojórquez, *Champ*, p. 73; Calzadíaz, *Hechos*, p. 34; Prefecto to Secretario de Estado, Guaymas, July 6, 1909, 2542, AES; Francisco I. Madero to Emilio Vázquez Gómez, San Pedro, Coahuila, February 2 and 4, 1910, in Corbalá Acuña, *Alamos*, p. 332.

48. Alberto Cubillas to Juez Isidro Castenedo, Hermosillo, October 13, 1910, 2645, AES.

49. Francisco I. Madero to Emilio Vázquez Gómez, San Pedro, Coahuila, February 4, 1910, in Corbalá Acuña, *Alamos*, p. 328.

50. Isaac Piña to Gobernador Alberto Cubillas, January 4, 1910, 2542, AES; Corbala Acuña, *Alamos*, pp. 326–327.

51. Francisco I. Madero to Emilio Vázquez Gómez, San Pedro, Coahuila, February 2 and 4, in Corbala Acuña, *Alamos*, pp. 331–332; Gobernador to Prefecto, Hermosillo, January 11, 1910, 2542, AES.

52. Francisco I. Madero to Emilio Vázquez Gómez, San Pedro, Coahuila, February 4, 1910, in Corbala Acuña, *Alamos*, p. 328.

53. E. Salido Muñoz, Jesús A. Cruz, Alfonso Goycolea, Antonio A. Goycolea, J. S. Urrea, L. Salido, Rafael Güerena, and Heliodoro Garcés Jiménez Almada to Porfirio Díaz, Alamos, January 9, 1910, 2542, AES.

54. Hector Aquilar Camin, *La frontera nomada; Sonora y la Revolucion Mexicana* (Mexico, 1977), p. 43.

55. Alberto Cubillas, Gobernador, to Prefecto, Hermosillo, January 10, 1910, 2542, AES.

56. *Ibid.*, p. 105; Fernando A. Galaz, *Dejaron huella en el Hermosillo de ayer y hoy* (Hermosillo, 1971), p. 650.

57. Gobernador to Enrique Creel, Gobernador de Chihuahua, Hermosillo, January 13, 1910, 2644, AES.

58. Juan Sánchez Azcona to Gobernador, Mexico, May 21, 1910, 2542, AES.

59. Rivera, *Revolución*, pp. 167 and 173.

60. Francisco R. Almada, *Diccionario de historia, geografía y biografía sonorenses* (Chihuahua, 1952), p. 307.

61. *Ibid.*, p. 644; Breceda, *México revolucionario*, II, 29; Secretario de Comunicaciones y Obras Públicas to Gobernador, Mexico, June 19, 1906, 2129, AES; Presidente Municipal to Secretario de Estado, Guaymas, October 10, 1906, 2249, AES; Arturo Morales to Alberto Cubillas, Guaymas, January 27, 1909, 2473, AES.

62. Almada, *Diccionario*, p. 614; Roberto Guzmán Esparza, *Memorias de don Adolfo de la Huerta, según su propio dictado* (Mexico, 1957), p. 12; Juzgado 2° de 1ª Instancia del Distrito de Hermosillo, Hermosillo, January 1, 1907, 2246, AES.

63. Almada, *Diccionario*, p. 56; Aguilar Camín, *Frontera*, p. 122; Evelyn Hu-DeHart, *Yaqui Resistance and Survival. The Struggle for Land and Autonomy, 1821–1910* (Madison, 1984), p. 172.

64. Jefatura de Hacienda to Gobernador, Guaymas, July 14, 1899, 678, AHS; "Contrato," Hermosillo, August 3, 1899, 779, AHS.

65. Almada, *Diccionario*, p. 692.

66. *Ibid.*, p. 774.

67. *Ibid.*, p. 357; Voss, *Towns*, p. 489; Aguilar Camín, *Frontera*, pp. 44, 85; Alfonso Iberri, *El viejo Guaymas* (Mexico, 1952), p. 157.

68. Aguilar Camín, *Frontera*, pp. 77, 81; Breceda, *México revolucionario*, II, 25.

69. Aguilar Camín, *Frontera*, pp. 63–64.

70. Secretario de Estado to Secretario de Guerra y Marina, Hermosillo, July 13, 1908, 2320, AES; Cuauhtémoc A. Iberri, Presidente Municipal, to Secretario de Estado, Guaymas, August 29, 1906, 2087, AES; Voss, *Towns*, p. 491.

71. Aguilar Camín, *Frontera*, pp. 72, 107.

72. Rivera, *Revolución*, p. 208; Zavala, *Perfiles*, p. 52.

73. Calzadíaz Barrera, *Hechos*, pp. 5, 7, 10–11, 13, 25, 29, 34–35.

74. Guzmán Esparza, *Memorias*, pp. 18–19.

75. Presidente Municipal to Secretario de Estado, Hermosillo, November 9, 1906, 2245, AES.

76. Daniel Cosío Villegas, *El Porfiriato. La vida política interior*, Daniel Cosío Villegas, *Historia moderna de México*, 9 vols. (Mexico, 1955–1973), IX, No. 2, 742.

77. Carlos Richard Macías, "Plutarco Elías Calles: una biografía política. Los primeros años (1877–1911), " Instituto de Investigaciones Históricas, *IX simposio de historia de Sonora. Memoria* (Hermosillo, 1984), p. 364.

78. Ignacio Elías to Secretario de Estado, Arizpe, September 26, 1908, 2430, AES.

79. Macías, *Calles*, p. 367.

BIBLIOGRAPHY

ARCHIVAL SOURCES

Mexico

AHS: Archivo Histórico de Sonora, Hermosillo, Mexico.
AES: Archivo Histórico del Gobierno del Estado de Sonora, Hermosillo, Mexico.
Centro de Estudios de Historia de México, Condumex, Mexico City, Mexico.
Ramón Corral papers.

United States

National Archives, Washington, D. C.
CD: United States Department of State. Dispatches from United States Consuls in Guaymas, Sonora, Mexico, 1832–1896. Vols. 3–9.
CD: United States Department of State. Dispatches from United States Consuls in Nogales, Sonora, Mexico, 1889–1906. Vols. 1–4.

LEGISLATIVE JOURNALS

Diario Oficial, Mexico City
La Constitución, Hermosillo
La Estrella del Occidente, Ures

NEWSPAPERS

Sonora

El Correo de Sonora, Guaymas
El Centenario, Cananea
El Centinela, Hermosillo
El Distrito de Alamos
El Imparcial, Guaymas
El Noticioso, Guaymas
El Progreso, Altar

El Sol, Hermosillo
El Trancazo, Huatabampo
La Bandera Sonorense, Ures

Mexico

El Imparcial, Mexico City
La Patria, Mexico City

United States

Arizona Daily Star, Tucson, Arizona
Daily Dispatch, Douglas, Arizona
El Fronterizo, Tucson, Arizona
El Independiente, Nogales, Airzona
San Francisco Bulletin, San Francisco, California
San Francisco Call, San Francisco, California
San Francisco Examiner, San Francisco, California
St. Louis Daily Globe Democrat, St. Louis, Missouri
The Arizona Republic, Phoenix, Arizona
The Daily News, Nogales, Arizona
The Oasis, Nogales, Arizona

BOOKS AND PAMPHLETS

Primary Sources

Almada, Bartolomé Eligio. *Almada of Alamos. The Diary of Don Bartolome.* Translated and with a narrative by Carlota Miles. Tucson, 1962.
Almada, Pedro J. *Con mi cobija al hombre.* Mexico, 1936.
———. *Mis memorias de revolucionario.* Mexico, 1938.
Balbás, Manuel. *Recuerdos del Yaqui: principales episodios durante la campaña de 1899 a 1901.* Mexico, 1927.
Barroso, Filiberto Vásquez. *Informe. El 16 de septiembre de 1902, al terminar el periodo administrativo del primer ayuntamiento de Cananea, Sonora.* Hermosillo, 1902.
Bird, Allen T. *The Land of Nayarit.* Nogales, Arizona, 1904.
Breceda, Alfredo. *México revolucionario, 1913–1917.* 2 vols. Madrid and Mexico, 1920 and 1941.
Calderón, Esteban Baca. *Juicio sobre la guerra del Yaqui y génesis de la huelga de Cananea. 1° de junio de 1906.* Mexico, 1956.
Cámara Agrícola Nacional del Estado de Sonora. *Estatutos.* Hermosillo, 1910.
Colegio de México. *Estadísticas económicas del Porfiriato. Comercio exterior de México, 1877–1911.* Mexico, 1960.
Compañía del Ferrocarril de Nacozari. *Tarifa. Carga por distancia.* Mexico, 1902.
Corral, Ramón. *Cuentas de la construcción del cementerio nuevo de Hermosillo.* Hermosillo, 1892.

————. *La cuestión de la harina*. Hermosillo, 1881.

————. *Memoria de la administración pública del Estado de Sonora presentada a la legislatura del mismo por el gobernador Ramón Corral.* 2 vols. Guaymas, 1891.

————. *Obras históricas. Reseña histórica del Estado de Sonora, 1856–1877. Biografía de José María Leyva Cajeme. Las razas indígenas de Sonora.* Hermosillo, 1959.

Cubillas, Alberto. *Informe leído por el C. Alberto Cubillas, vice-gobernador constitucional del Estado de Sonora.* Hermosillo, 1909.

Dávila, F. T. *Sonora histórico y descriptivo.* Nogales, Arizona, 1894.

Departamento de la Estadística Nacional. *Sonora, Sinaloa y Nayarit. Estudio estadístico económico social, elaborado por el Departamento de Estadística Nacional. Año 1927.* Mexico, 1928

Dirección General de Estadística. *Importación y exportación.* Mexico, 1907.

Foster, Harry L. *A Gringo in Mañana Land.* New York, 1924.

Galaz, Fernando A. *Dejaron huella en el Hermosillo de ayer y hoy.* Hermosillo, 1971.

Gamboa, Federico, ed. *Diario de Federico Gamboa; selección, prólogo y notas de José Emilio Pacheco.* Mexico, 1977.

García y Alva, Federico. *México y su progreso; album–directorio del Estado de Sonora.* Hermosillo, 1905–1907.

————. *Album-crónica de las fiestas patrias efectuadas en Sonora en honor del señor vice-presidente de la República Don Ramón Corral y de la Señora Amparo V. E. de Corral.* Hermosillo, 1905.

Guzmán Esparza, Roberto. *Memorias de don Adolfo de la Huerta, según su propio dictado.* Mexico, 1957.

Healy-Genda, ed. *Directorio comercial del Estado de Sonora.* Hermosillo, 1920.

Hernández, Fortunato. *Las razas indígenas de Sonora y la guerra del Yaqui.* Mexico, 1902.

Ingersoll, Ralph McA. *In and Under Mexico.* New York and London, 1924.

Izábal, Rafael. *Memoria de la administración pública del Estado de Sonora durante el periodo constitucional de 1903 a 1907.* Hermosillo, 1907.

Johnson, Carlos H. *Asunto "San Marcial." Protesta que el Ciudadano Americano Don Carlos H. Johnson presenta ante el Supremo Masgisterio de la Nación contra procedimientos atentatorios del Gobierno del Estado de Sonora.* Hermosillo, 1902.

Lumholtz, Carl. *El México desconocido. Cinco años de exploración entre las tribus de la Sierra Madre Occidental; en la tierra caliente de Tepic y Jalisco y entre los Tarasco de Michoacán.* Translated by Balbino Dávalos. Mexico, 1945.

Ministerio de Fomento. *Dirección General de Estadística. Censo General de la República Mexicana.* Mexico, 1897.

Molina, Olegario. *Memoria, presentada al Congreso de la Unión, de Fomento, Colonización e Industria de la República Mexicana.* Mexico, 1910.

Secretaría de Comunicaciones y Obras Publicas. *Reseña histórica y estadística de los ferrocarriles de jurisdicción federal, desde 1° de enero al 30 de junio de 1897.* Mexico, 1897.

————. *Movimiento general que han tenido los terrenos pertenecientes a la Federación en el semestre transcurrido, del 1° de julio al 31 de diciembre de 1896.* Mexico, 1897.

————. *Movimiento general que han tenido los terrenos pertenecientes a la Federación en el semestre transcurrido del 1° de enero al 30 de junio de 1897.* Mexico, 1897.

————. *Movimiento general que han tenido los terrenos pertenecientes a la Federación, en el semestre transcurrido del 1° de julio al 31 de diciembre de 1897.* Mexico, 1898.

Secretaría de Estado y del Despacho de Hacienda y Crédito Publico. *Ley de Ingresos y Presupuestos de Egresos del Erario Federal, el 1° de julio de 1894 y termina el 30 de junio de 1895.* Mexico, 1894.

Secretaría de Fomento, Colonización e Industria. *Cuadros relativos al movimiento general que han tenido los terrenos baldíos pertenecientes a la federación, en el semestre transcurido del 1° de enero al 30 de junio del presente año.* Mexico, 1898.

Secretaría de Obras Públicas. *Ferrocarriles de México. Reseña histórica—reglamentos (siglo XIX).* Mexico, 1976.

Siqueiras, David Alfaro. *Me llamaban el coronelazo (Memorias).* Mexico, 1977.

State of Sonora. *Resolutions Passed by the Convention of Cattlemen of Sonora to Combat the Microbe Producing Texas Fever. Relative Dispositions Enacted by the State Government.* Hermosillo, 1909.

Troncoso, Francisco P. *Las guerras con las tribus Yaqui y Mayo.* 2 vols. Hermosillo, 1982.

Turner, John Kenneth. *Barbarous Mexico.* Chicago, 1910.

Tweedie, Mrs. Alex. *Porfirio Diaz, Seven Times President of Mexico.* London, 1906.

Ulloa, Pedro N. *El Estado de Sonora y situación económica al aproximarse el primer centenario de la independencia nacional.* Hermosillo, 1910.

United States Department of Commerce, Bureau of Foreign and Domestic Commerce. *Mexican West Coast and Lower California. A Commercial and Industrial Survey.* Washington, D. C., 1923.

United States Department of Commerce and Labor, Bureau of Manufactures. *Commercial Relations of the United States with Foreign Countries.* Washington, D. C., 1903.

United States Department of State, Bureau of Foreign Commerce. *Commercial Relations of the United States with Foreign Countries.* Washington, D. C., 1911.

Uruchurtu, Manuel R. *Apuntes biográficos del senor D. Ramón Corral: desde su nacimiento hasta encargarse del gobierno del Distrito Federal (1854 a 1900).* Mexico, 1910.

Vásquez Barroso, Filiberto. Informe. El 16 de septiembre de 1902, al terminar el periodo administrativo del primer ayuntamiento de Cananea, Sonora. Hermosillo, 1902.

Velasco, Luis A. *Geografía y estadística de la República Mexicana.* Mexico, 1893.

Zamora, Agustín A. *La cohetera, mi barrio.* Hermosillo, 1982.

Zavala, Palemón. *Perfiles de Sonora.* Hermosillo, 1984.

Zayas Enríquez, Rafael de. *Los Estados Unidos Mexicanos. Sus progresos en veinte años, 1877–1897.* New York, 1897.

————. *Porfirio Díaz.* New York, 1908.

Secondary Sources

Acuña, Rodolfo F. *Sonoran Strongman; Ignacio Pesqueira and His Times.* Tucson, 1974.

Aguilar Camín, Héctor, *La frontera nómada: Sonora y la Revolución Mexicana.* Mexico, 1977.

————. *Saldos de la Revolución: cultura y política de México, 1910–1980.* Mexico, 1982.

Almada, Francisco R. *Diccionario de historia, geografía y biografía sonorenses.* Chihuahua, 1952.

————. *La Revolución en el Estado de Sonora.* Mexico, 1971.

Amin, Samir. *Unequal Development; An Essay on the Social Formations of Peripheral Capitalism.* London and New York, 1976.

Bancroft, Hubert H. *History of the North Mexican States and Texas.* San Francisco, 1889.

————. *Recursos y desarrollo de México.* San Francisco, 1892.

Baerlein, Henry. *Mexico, The Land of Unrest. Being Chiefly an Account of What Produced the Outbreak in 1910, Together with the Story of the Revolution down to this Day.* London, 1913.

Bassols Batalla, Angel. *México. Formación de regiones económicas.* Mexico, 1979.

Bernstein, Marvin D. *The Mexican Mining Industry, 1890–1950. A Study of the Interaction of Politics, Economics and Technology.* Yellow Springs, 1965.

Bird, Allen T. *The Land of Nayarit.* Nogales, Arizona, 1904.

Bojórquez, Juan de Dios. *"Champ," Rodolfo Campódonico, autor de "Club Verde."* Mexico, 1936.

————. *El héroe de Nacozari.* Havana, Cuba. 1926.

————. *Forjadores de la Revolución Mexicana.* Mexico, 1960.

Borquez, Djed (Pseudonym for Juan de Dios Bojórquez). *Calles.* Mexico, 1923.

————. *Monzón; semblanza de un revolucionario.* Mexico, 1942.

————. *Obregón. Apuntes biográficos.* Mexico, 1929.

Calvo Berber, Laureano. *Nociones de historia de Sonora.* Mexico, 1958.

Calzadíaz Barrera, Alberto. *Hechos reales de la Revolución; el General Ignacio L. Pesqueira . . . y surgen Obregón y Calles.* Mexico, 1973.

Cardoso, Fernando Henrique, and Faletto, Enzo. *Dependency and Development in Latin America.* Translated by Marjory Mattingly Urquidi. Berkeley, Los Angeles and London, 1979.

Castillo, Ignacio B. del. *Biografía de D. Ramón Corral.* Mexico, 1910.

Chaverri Matamoros, Amado and Valenzuela, Clodoveo. *Sonora contra Carranza.* Mexico, 1921.

Cleland, Robert Glass. *A History of Phelps Dodge, 1834–1950.* New York, 1952.

Coatsworth, John H. *El impacto económico de los ferrocarriles. El Porfiriato.* 2 vols. Mexico, 1976.

Contreras, Enrique. *Cosas viejas de mi tierra.* Hermosillo, 1965.

Corbalá Acuña, Manuel Santiago. *Alamos de Sonora.* Mexico, 1977.

Cornejo, Gerardo. *La sierra y el viento.* Hermosillo, 1982.

Cosío Villegas, Daniel. *El Porfiriato. La vida económica,* Daniel Cosío Villegas. ed. *Historia moderna de México.* 9 vols. Mexico, 1955–1973. VII, 1 and 2.

————. *El Porfiriato. La vida política interior.* Daniel Cosío Villegas. ed. *Historia moderna de México.* 9 vols. Mexico, 1955–1973. VIII.

————. *El Porfiriato. La vida política interior.* Daniel Cosío Villegas. ed. *Historia moderna de México.* 9 vols. Mexico, 1955–1973. IX.

Cota Meza, Ramón. *Centenario de Santa Rosalía.* La Paz, Baja California, 1983.

Dabdoub, Carlos. *México. Estudio socio-económico (1521–1976).* Mexico, 1977.

Dabdoub, Claudio. *Historia de El Valle del Yaqui.* Mexico, 1964.

Dedera, Don, and Robles, Bob. *Goodbye Garcia Adios.* Flagstaff, Arizona, 1976.

Dunbier, Roger. *The Sonoran Desert. Its Geography, Economy and People.* Tucson, 1968.

Echeverría, A. G., ed. *Campaña nacionalista; por la patria y por la raza.* Hermosillo, 1965.

González Navarro, Moisés. *La colonización en México.* Mexico, 1960.

Hall, Linda B. *Alvaro Obregon, Power and Revolution in Mexico, 1911–1920.* College Station, Texas, 1981.

Hannay, David. *Diaz.* New York, 1917.

Hobson, J. A. *Imperialism.* New York and London, 1902.

Hornaday, William T. *Camp-Fires on Desert and Lava.* New York, 1921.

Hu-DeHart, Evelyn. *Missionaries, Miners and Indians. Spanish Contact with the Yaqui Nation of Northwestern New Spain, 1633–1820.* Tucson, 1981.

———. *Yaqui Resistance and Survival. The Struggle for Land and Autonomy, 1821–1910.* Madison, 1984.

Iberri, Alfonso. *El viejo Guaymas.* Mexico, 1952.

Instituto de Investigaciones Históricas. *Primer simposio de historia de Sonora: Memoria.* Hermosillo, 1976.

———. *Segundo Simposio de Historia de Sonora: Memoria.* Hermosillo, 1977.

———. *III Simposio de historia de Sonora: Memoria.* 2 vols. Hermosillo, 1978.

———. *V Simposio de historia de Sonora: Memoria.* Hermosillo, 1980.

———. *VII Simposio de historia de Sonora: Memoria.* Hermosillo, 1981.

———. *IX Simposio de historia de Sonora: Memoria.* Hermosillo, 1984.

Lenin, V. I. "Imperialism: The Highest Stage of Capitalism." International Publishers. ed. *Lenin. Selected Works.* New York, 1971.

León de la Barra, Eduardo. *Los de arriba.* Mexico, 1979.

López, E. Y. *Bibliografía de Sonora.* 2 vols. Hermosillo, 1960 and 1974.

Luna, Jesús. *La carrera pública de Ramón Corral.* Mexico, 1975.

Magdoff, Harry. *Imperialism: From the Colonial Age to the Present.* London and New York, 1978.

Medina Hoyos, Francisco. *Cananea, cuna de la Revolución Mexicana.* Mexico, 1956.

Medina Ruiz, Fernando. *Calles. Un destino melancólico.* Mexico, 1960.

Molina Molina, Flavio. *Historia de Hermosillo antiguo.* Hermosillo, 1983.

Niemeyer, Eberhardt V. *El General Bernardo Reyes.* Monterrey, Mexico, 1966.

Parodi, Enriqueta de. *Sonora, hombres y paisajes.* Mexico, 1941.

Paz, Teodoro O. *Guaymas de ayer.* Guaymas, [1974?].

Rangel Contla, José Calixto. *La pequeña burguesía en la sociedad mexicana, 1895–1960.* Mexico, 1972.

Ready, Alma, ed. *Nogales, Arizona 1880–1980.* Nogales, Arizona 1980.

Rivera, Antonio G. *La revolución en Sonora.* Hermosillo, 1969.

Rivera, Gustavo. *Breve historia de la educación en Sonora e historia de la escuela normal del Estado.* Hermosillo, 1975.

Ruiz, Ramón Eduardo. *The Great Rebellion; Mexico, 1905–1925.* London and New York, 1980.

San Domingo, Manuel. *Historia de Agua Prieta, Sonora.* Agua Prieta, Sonora, 1951.

Smith, Cornelius C. *Emilio Kosterlitzky. Eagle of Sonora and the Southwest Border.* Glendale, California, 1970.

Sobarzo, Horacio. *Episodios históricos.* Mexico, 1981.

Spicer, Edward H. *The Yaquis: A Cultural History.* Tucson, 1980.

Szymanski, Albert. *The Logic of Imperialism.* New York, 1981.

Tapia Quijada, César. *Apuntes sobre la huelga de Cananea.* Hermosillo, 1956.

Taracena, Angel. *Porfirio Díaz.* Mexico, 1960.

Terán, Cuauhtémoc L. *Jesús García. Héroe de Nacozari.* Hermosillo, 1981.

Trueba, Alfonso. *El padre Kino; misionero itinerante y ecuestre.* Mexico, 1955.

Ulloa, Berta. *Historia de la Revolución Mexicana. Periodo 1914–1917. La encrucijada de 1915.* Mexico, 1979.

———. *Historia de la Revolución Mexicana, 1914–1917. La Constitución de 1917.* Mexico, 1983.

Valadés, José C. *El Porfirismo. Historia de un regimen. El crecimiento.* 2 vols. Mexico, 1948.

Vaughan, Mary K. *The State, Education, and Social Classes in Mexico, 1880–1928.* DeKalb, 1982.

Villa, Eduardo W. *Compendio de historia del Estado de Sonora.* Hermosillo, Mexico, 1937.

———. *Galería de sonorenses ilustres.* Sonora, 1948.

Voss, Stuart F. *On the Periphery of Nineteenth-Century Mexico. Sonora and Sinaloa, 1810–1877.* Tucson, 1982.

ARTICLES

Aiken, Charles S. "The Land of Tomorrow." *Sunset Magazine.* XXII, June, 1909.

Boyd, Consuelo. "Twenty Years to Nogales: The Building of the Guaymas-Nogales Railroad." *The Journal of Arizona History.* XXII, Autumn, 1981.

Brooks, Sidney. "The Coming Copper Famine." *North American Review.* XXVII, April, 1918.

Dumke, Glen S. "Douglas, Border Town." *Pacific Historical Review.* XVIII, August, 1948.

Emmons, S. F. "The Cananea Mining District of Sonora, Mexico." *Economic Geology.* V, June, 1910.

Hardy, Osgood. "El Ferrocarril Sud-Pacifico." *Pacific Historical Review.* XX, August, 1951.

Hobsbaum, E. J. "The Crisis of the Seventeenth Century." Asten, Trevor. ed. *Crisis in Europe, 1560–1660.* New York, 1967.

Krutz, Gordon V. "Chinese Labor, Economic Development and Social Reaction." *Ethnohistory.* XVIII.

Mange, Joaquín. "Historia del negocio del garbanzo." Montaño, Raul E. and Gaxiola, Octavio P. eds. *Album del Mayo y del Yaqui; directorio comercial, 1933.* Navojoa, Sonora, 1932.

Nelson, Daniel. "Fifth Column at Cananea. A Stockholder Circumvents Colonel W. C. Greene." *The Journal of Arizona History.* XX, Spring, 1979.

Pletcher, David M. "The Development of Railroads in Sonora." *Interamerican Economic Affairs.* I, March, 1948.

Ramírez Alvarez, Eliseo. "El Ingeniero Bonillas delineó el fundo legal de la ciudad. *El Imparcial.* August 15, 1983.

Torrance, Minnie M. "La Profesora McClure." *The Journal of Arizona History.* XX, Spring, 1979.

Wallace, Mildred Y. "I Remember Chung." *The Journal of Arizona History.* XX, Spring, 1979.

UNPUBLISHED MANUSCRIPTS

Delman Leon, Beene. "Sonora in the Age of Ramón Corral, 1875–1900." Ph.D. thesis, University of Arizona, Tucson, 1972.

Flores García, Silvia Raquel. "La importancia del ferrocarril en la fundición de Nogales, 1880–1884." Instituto Nacional de Antropologia e Historia. Hermosillo, 1983.

Kroeber, Clifton B. "Map, Land and Water; Mexico's Farmlands Irrigation Policies, 1885–1911." Occidental College. Los Angeles, 1983.

Medina Hoyos, Francisco. "Cananea. Cuna de la Revolución y génesis del sindicalismo mexicano." Archivo Histórico de Sonora. Hermosillo, 1956.

Officer, James E.; Elías Chomina, Armando; and Pellat Sotomayor, Carmen. "Los hijos de Pancho: la familia Elías, guerreros sonorenses." University of Arizona. Tucson, 1982.

Radding de Murrieta, Cynthia. "El espacio sonorense y la periodización de las historias municipales." Instituto Nacional de Antropología e Historia. Hermosillo, 1982.

Ready, Alma, and Suárez Barnett, Alberto. "William Barnett, Gringo Rancher of La Arizona, Sonora." Pimería Alta Historical Museum. Nogales, Arizona, 1982.

Suárez Barnett, Alberto. "Los presupuestos de egresos del gobierno del Estado, 1863–1910." Nogales, Sonora, 1983.

Uribe García, Jesús Félix. "Monografía sobre la historia de las comunicaciones en Sonora, segunda mitad del siglo XIX, las diligencias." Instituto Nacional de Antropología e Historia. Hermosillo, 1981.

Voss, Stuart F. "Towns and Enterprises in Northwestern Mexico—A History of Urban Elites in Sonora and Sinaloa, 1830–1910." Ph.D. thesis, Harvard University, Cambridge, 1972.

INDEX

ABOUT THE AUTHOR

Ramón Eduardo Ruiz, the son of Mexican parents, has been writing about Mexico since 1951. A professor of Latin American history at the University of California (San Diego), he is the author of more than a dozen books, nearly all on Mexican history. *The Great Rebellion: Mexico, 1905–1924* won the prize for best book of 1981 of the Pacific Coast Council on Latin American Studies, and "Book World" of the *Washington Post* picked his *Cuba: The Making of a Revolution* as one of the best history books of 1968.